The Cambridge Companion to Joseph Conrad offers a wide-ranging introduction to the fiction of one of the most influential novelists of the twentieth century. Through a series of essays by leading Conrad scholars aimed at both students and the general reader, the volume stimulates an informed appreciation of Conrad's work based on an understanding of his cultural and historical situations and fictional techniques. A chronology and overview of Conrad's life precede chapters that explore significant issues in his major writings and deal in depth with individual works. These are followed by discussions of the special nature of Conrad's narrative techniques, his complex relationships with late-Victorian imperialism and with literary Modernism, and his influence on other writers and artists. Each essay provides guidance to further reading, and a concluding chapter surveys the body of Conrad criticism.

THE CAMBRIDGE
COMPANION TO
JOSEPH
CONRAD

For Bruce who was there at the beginning, with respect, admiration & friendship.

London
July 1996

Cambridge Companions to Literature

The Cambridge Companion to Old English Literature
edited by Malcolm Godden and Michael Lapidge

The Cambridge Companion to Dante
edited by Rachel Jacoff

The Cambridge Chaucer Companion
edited by Piero Boitani and Jill Mann

The Cambridge Companion to English Medieval Theatre
edited by Richard Beadle

The Cambridge Companion to Shakespeare Studies
edited by Stanley Wells

The Cambridge Companion to English Renaissance Drama
edited by A. R. Braunmuller and Michael Hattaway

The Cambridge Companion to English Poetry, Donne to Marvell
edited by Thomas N. Corns

The Cambridge Companion to Milton
edited by Dennis Danielson

The Cambridge Companion to British Romanticism
edited by Stuart Curran

The Cambridge Companion to James Joyce
edited by Derek Attridge

The Cambridge Companion to Ibsen
edited by James McFarlane

The Cambridge Companion to Brecht
edited by Peter Thomson and Glendyr Sacks

The Cambridge Companion to Beckett
edited by John Pilling

The Cambridge Companion to T. S. Eliot
edited by A. David Moody

The Cambridge Companion to Renaissance Humanism
edited by Jill Kraye

The Cambridge Companion to Faulkner
edited by Philip M. Weinstein

The Cambridge Companion to Thoreau
edited by Joel Myerson

The Cambridge Companion to Edith Wharton
edited by Millicent Bell

The Cambridge Companion to Realism and Naturalism
edited by Donald Pizer

The Cambridge Companion to Twain
edited by Forrest G. Robinson

The Cambridge Companion to Whitman
edited by Ezra Greenspan

The Cambridge Companion to Hemingway
edited by Scott Donaldson

The Cambridge Companion to Joseph Conrad
edited by J. H. Stape

Portrait of Joseph Conrad by Ellen Heath (1898). By permission of Leeds City Art Galleries

THE CAMBRIDGE
COMPANION TO
JOSEPH
CONRAD

EDITED BY
J. H. STAPE

Japan Women's University, Tokyo

CAMBRIDGE
UNIVERSITY PRESS

Published by the Press Syndicate of the University of Cambridge
The Pitt Building, Trumpington Street, Cambridge CB2 1RP
40 West 20th Street, New York, NY 10011–4211, USA
10 Stamford Road, Oakleigh, Melbourne 3166, Australia

© Cambridge University Press 1996

First published 1996

Printed in Great Britain at the University Press, Cambridge

A catalogue record for this book is available from the British Library

Library of Congress cataloguing in publication data applied for

ISBN 0 521 44391 1 hardback
ISBN 0 521 48484 7 paperback

CE

CONTENTS

CONTENTS

NOTES ON CONTRIBUTORS

JACQUES BERTHOUD is Professor of English at York University. The author of *Joseph Conrad: The Major Phase* (Cambridge University Press, 1978), he has edited *The Nigger of the 'Narcissus'*, *Almayer's Folly*, and *Chance* for Oxford's World's Classics and *The Shadow-Line* for Penguin Books.

KEITH CARABINE is Senior Lecturer in English at the University of Kent at Canterbury. Editor of *Nostromo* for Oxford's World's Classics, he is co-editing *Under Western Eyes* in the Cambridge Edition of Conrad. The author of numerous articles on Conrad, he has also edited *Joseph Conrad: Critical Assessments* (Helm Information, 1992).

GAIL FRASER is Instructor in English at Douglas College, New Westminster, British Columbia. The author of *Interweaving Patterns in the Works of Joseph Conrad* (UMI Research Press, 1988), she has written several articles on Conrad and is currently writing a study of women in Conrad's fiction.

KENNETH GRAHAM is Professor of English at the University of Neuchâtel. He has written *English Criticism of the Novel 1865–1900* (Oxford University Press, 1965), *Henry James: The Drama of Fulfilment* (Oxford University Press, 1975), *Indirections of the Novel: James, Conrad, and Forster* (Cambridge University Press, 1988), and *Henry James: A Literary Life* (Macmillan, 1995).

ROBERT HAMPSON is Lecturer in English at Royal Holloway and New Bedford College, University of London. The author of *Joseph Conrad: Betrayal and Identity* (Macmillan, 1992), he has co-edited *Lord Jim* and has edited *Victory*, *Heart of Darkness*, and a number of Kipling's works for Penguin Books. He is the former editor of *The Conradian*.

ELOISE KNAPP HAY is Professor of English at the University of California at Santa Barbara. She has published *The Political Novels of Joseph Conrad*

(University of Chicago Press, 1963) and *T. S. Eliot's Negative Way* (Harvard University Press, 1982) as well as numerous articles on James, Proust, Kipling, and Forster. She is currently completing *Hawthorne/ Tocqueville:: Dickens/ Burke.*

OWEN KNOWLES is Senior Lecturer in English at the University of Hull. The author of *Joseph Conrad: A Chronology* (Macmillan, 1990) and *An Annotated Critical Bibliography of Joseph Conrad* (Harvester Wheatsheaf, 1992), he is the former editor and current reviews editor of *The Conradian.*

JAKOB LOTHE is Professor of Comparative Literature at the University of Oslo. He has written a number of articles on modern literature and is the author of *Conrad's Narrative Method* (Oxford University Press, 1989) and the editor of *Conrad in Scandinavia* (Columbia University Press, 1995).

GENE M. MOORE is Lecturer in English at the University of Amsterdam. The author of *Proust and Musil: The Novel as Research Instrument* (Garland Publishing, 1985), he has edited *Conrad's Cities: Essays for Hans van Marle* (Rodopi, 1992). He is co-editing *Suspense* in the Cambridge Edition of Conrad and is editing *Conrad on Film* (forthcoming, Cambridge University Press).

J. H. STAPE is Professor of English at Japan Women's University, Tokyo. Co-editor of *An Outcast of the Islands* and *The Rover* for Oxford's World's Classics, he has edited Virginia Woolf's *Night and Day* (Blackwell, 1994). His publications include *Angus Wilson: A Bibliography, 1947–87* (Mansell, 1988), *An E. M. Forster Chronology* (Macmillan, 1993), and volumes on Forster (1993) and Woolf (1995) in Macmillan's 'Interviews and Recollections' series.

CEDRIC WATTS is Professor of English at the University of Sussex. Among his many books on Conrad are *Joseph Conrad's Letters to R. B. Cunninghame Graham* (Cambridge University Press, 1969), *A Preface to Conrad* (Longman, 1982; revised 1993), and *Joseph Conrad: A Literary Life* (Macmillan, 1989). He has edited a number of Conrad's works for Penguin Books, Oxford's World's Classics, and Everyman, and has written on Shakespeare and Thomas Hardy.

ANDREA WHITE is Lecturer in English at California State University at Northridge. She is the author of *Joseph Conrad and the Adventure Tradition: Constructing and Deconstructing the Imperial Subject* (Cambridge University Press, 1993).

PREFACE

Like the work of other major writers, that of Joseph Conrad has occasioned a large critical industry devoted to its interpretation and appreciation. And since Conrad is read both in translation and in the original throughout the world, this body of criticism spans linguistic and cultural boundaries to include commentaries not only, as might be expected, in French, Italian, and Polish but even, for instance, in Japanese and Swahili.

Conrad's almost universal presence on school reading-lists and in university courses as well as at the corner bookshop testifies to the fundamental centrality of his writing to modern literature and the modern experience. In English alone the books, articles, and notes published about his life and work amount to several thousand items, and even the guides directing the student or the interested general reader to this mass of material now total some thousand pages.

While it does not and cannot make Conrad's writings easier, the present volume of a dozen essays aims at increasing their accessibility. It opens with an overview of Conrad's life and then proceeds to engaged readings of the major fiction. These chapters, devoted to individual works or to groups of texts, develop formal and thematic concerns with an eye on a range of ideological issues. This essential contextualization should help readers appreciate an author whose work is sometimes regarded as dauntingly complex and whose imaginative world and cultural framework may at moments seem remote from their own. The chapters that follow explore some of the larger questions raised by Conrad's writings as a whole. They focus on the special nature of his narrative techniques, on the current debates about his relationship to imperialism and to literary Modernism, and on the varied influence his work has exerted on other writers. Lastly, a guide to further reading provides information about Conrad scholarship and the body of standard Conrad criticism.

The emphasis of this volume falls on informed appreciation based on an understanding of Conrad's cultural contexts and fictional techniques. Conrad's own life, the object of considerable interest and comment, is discussed since it illuminates a number of the preoccupations of his fiction. These concerns are particularly contemporary in their nature and scope, and include, for instance, the complex interrelationships between an individual and his or her social and economic milieu, ethnicity and multi-cultural identity, linguistic confrontation and alienation, and the interactions between empire and colony.

The contributors to this volume live and teach in a number of countries and are actively engaged in the on-going process of discovering and re-discovering Conrad through a variety of perspectives. They bring to bear diverse scholarly and critical traditions – American, British, and Continental. The volume takes advantage of the rich heritage of Conrad studies that has evolved from the 1940s, and, more particularly, takes note of the critical movements and debates of the past two decades.

The task of preparing this volume has been greatly eased by the generous advice of Dr Owen Knowles, Hans van Marle, Dr Gene M. Moore, and, at Cambridge University Press, Josie Dixon and Kevin Taylor.

J. H. STAPE

1857	Józef Teodor Konrad Korzeniowski, only child of poet, dramatist, translator, and political activist, Apollo Korzeniowski and Ewelina (or Ewa), née Bobrowska, born on 3 December in or near Berdichev in the Ukraine.
1861	Apollo Korzeniowski arrested and imprisoned in Warsaw for anti-Russian conspiracy.
1862	The Korzeniowskis are exiled to Vologda, northern Russia.
1865	Death of Ewa Korzeniowska.
1868	Apollo Korzeniowski and his son move to Lwów.
1869	Death of Apollo Korzeniowski in Cracow. Maternal uncle, Tadeusz Bobrowski, becomes young Korzeniowski's guardian. Privately tutored because of ill health, also occasionally attends schools during the next few years.
1873	Visits Austria, Germany, Switzerland, and northern Italy with his tutor Adam Pulman.
1874	Leaves Poland for Marseilles to become a trainee seaman in the French Merchant Service. Works for shippers and bankers Delestang et Fils.
1874–7	Passenger and apprentice in the *Mont-Blanc* and 'steward' in the *Saint-Antoine* (to the Caribbean).
1878	Shoots himself in the chest in Marseilles after accumulating gambling debts but escapes serious injury. Joins the steamship *Mavis*, his first British ship. Serves as ordinary seaman in the *Skimmer of the Sea* (English coastal waters).
1878–80	Ordinary seaman in the *Duke of Sutherland* (to Australia) and in the steamship *Europa* (Mediterranean).
1880	Passes examination for second mate. Third mate in the *Loch Etive* (to Australia).
1881–4	Second mate in the *Palestine*, *Riversdale*, and *Narcissus* (to South-East Asia and India).

1884	Passes examination for first mate.
1885–6	Second mate in the *Tilkhurst* (to Singapore and Calcutta).
1886	Becomes a British subject. Passes examination for master's certificate.
1886–7	Second mate in the *Falconhurst*. First mate in the *Highland Forest* (to Java). Injured on board, is hospitalized in Singapore.
1887–8	First mate in the steamship *Vidar* (from Singapore to various Netherlands East Indies ports).
1888	Master of the *Otago*, joined in Bangkok, sails to Australia and Mauritius.
1889	Resigns from the *Otago*. Settles briefly in London and begins *Almayer's Folly*.
1890	Friendship with marriage relation and writer Marguerite Poradowska. In the Congo Free State for the Société pour le Commerce du Haut-Congo as second in command and, temporarily, captain of the river steamer *Roi des Belges*.
1891	Manages the warehouse of Barr, Moering in London.
1891–3	First mate in the passenger clipper *Torrens* (to Australia). Meets John Galsworthy, among her passengers. Visits Bobrowski in the Ukraine.
1894	*Almayer's Folly* accepted for publication. Meets Edward Garnett, publisher's reader, and Jessie George, a typist, whom he later marries. Signs on as second mate in the *Adowa* but sails only to France and back. End of his sea career.
1895	*Almayer's Folly* published under the pen name 'Joseph Conrad'.
1896	*An Outcast of the Islands* published. Marries Jessie George (24 March) and honeymoons in Brittany. Begins *The Rescuer*. Settles in Stanford-le-Hope, Essex. Becomes acquainted with H. G. Wells and initiates a correspondence with Henry James.
1897	Begins friendships with writer and political figure R. B. Cunninghame Graham and with Stephen Crane. *The Nigger of the 'Narcissus'* published.
1898	Son Borys born. *Tales of Unrest* published ('Karain', 'The Idiots', 'An Outpost of Progress', 'The Return', 'The Lagoon'). Collaborates with Ford Madox Hueffer (later Ford) and takes over from him lease of The Pent, Postling, Kent.
1899	'Heart of Darkness' serialized.
1899–1900	*Lord Jim* serialized
1900	In Belgium with Ford. J. B. Pinker becomes Conrad's agent. *Lord Jim* published in book form.

1901	*The Inheritors* (collaboration with Ford) published.
1902	*Youth: A Narrative; and Two Other Stories* published ('Youth', 'Heart of Darkness', 'The End of the Tether').
1903	*Typhoon, and Other Stories* ('Typhoon', 'Amy Foster', 'Falk', 'To-morrow') and *Romance* (collaboration with Ford) published.
1904	*Nostromo* serialized and published in book form. Jessie Conrad injures her knees, remaining partially disabled for life.
1905	Sojourn on Capri. *One Day More*, dramatization of 'To-morrow', staged in London.
1906	Sojourn in Montpellier. Son John born. *The Mirror of the Sea* published. *The Secret Agent* serialized in US.
1907	Sojourn in Montpellier and in Geneva. *The Secret Agent* published in book form. Moves to Someries, Luton Hoo, Bedfordshire.
1908	*A Set of Six* published ('Gaspar Ruiz', 'The Informer', 'The Brute', 'An Anarchist', 'The Duel', 'Il Conde').
1909	Moves to Aldington, Kent. Breaks with Ford.
1910	Completes *Under Western Eyes* and suffers a nervous breakdown. Moves to Capel House, Orlestone, Kent.
1910–11	*Under Western Eyes* serialized and published in book form.
1912	*Some Reminiscences* (later *A Personal Record*) and *'Twixt Land and Sea* published ('A Smile of Fortune', 'The Secret Sharer', 'Freya of the Seven Isles'). *Chance* serialized in New York.
1914	*Chance* published in book form. First financial success. Visits Poland in summer with family. Trapped for some weeks by the outbreak of war, returns to England via Austria and Italy.
1915	*Within the Tides* ('The Planter of Malata', 'The Partner', 'The Inn of the Two Witches', 'Because of the Dollars') and *Victory* published.
1917	*The Shadow-Line* published.
1919	Moves to Spring Grove, near Wye, Kent. Basil Macdonald Hastings's dramatization of *Victory* staged in London. Moves to Oswalds, Bishopsbourne, near Canterbury. *The Arrow of Gold* published. Begins 'Author's Notes' for Doubleday and Heinemann Collected Editions.
1920	*The Rescue*, begun in 1898, published.
1921	Visits Corsica, doing research for *The Rover* and *Suspense*. *Notes on Life and Letters* published. Collected Editions begin publication.

1922	Dramatization of *The Secret Agent* staged in London.
1923	Visits the United States to a rapturous reception. *The Rover* serialized in US and published in book form.
1924	Declines a knighthood. Dies of a heart attack at Oswalds on 3 August, aged 66. Buried in Roman Catholic section of Canterbury cemetery. *The Nature of a Crime* (collaboration with Ford) published in book form.
1925	*Tales of Hearsay* ('The Warrior's Soul', 'Prince Roman', 'The Tale', 'The Black Mate') and *Suspense* published.
1926	*Last Essays*, edited by Richard Curle, published.
1928	*The Sisters* (fragment) published.

ABBREVIATIONS

Citations to Conrad's writings are to Dent's Collected Edition. Where a volume in this edition has been reprinted by Oxford University Press in its World's Classics series it is cited by the title assigned to it in that series. Full publication details of works referred to are given in the Works Cited section at the end of each chapter.

AF	*Almayer's Folly*
AG	*The Arrow of Gold*
Ch	*Chance*
HD	*'Heart of Darkness' and Other Tales*
In	*The Inheritors*
LE	*Last Essays*
LJ	*Lord Jim*
MS	*The Mirror of the Sea*
NLL	*Notes on Life and Letters*
NN	*The Nigger of the 'Narcissus'*
No	*Nostromo*
OI	*An Outcast of the Islands*
PR	*A Personal Record*
Re	*The Rescue*
Ro	*The Rover*
SA	*The Secret Agent*
SL	*The Shadow-Line*
SS	*A Set of Six*
Su	*Suspense*
TH	*Tales of Hearsay*
TLS	*'Twixt Land and Sea*
TOT	*'Typhoon' and Other Tales*
TU	*Tales of Unrest*
UWE	*Under Western Eyes*

Vi	*Victory*
WT	*Within the Tides*
YOS	*Youth: A Narrative; and Two Other Stories*

Letters *The Collected Letters of Joseph Conrad.* Ed. Frederick R. Karl and Laurence Davies. Cambridge: Cambridge University Press, 1983–.

In quotations, spaced points (. . .) indicate an ellipsis by the writer, while unspaced points (...) occur in the work being cited.

1

OWEN KNOWLES

Conrad's life

Conrad's earliest sense of himself, as a six-year-old child in 1863, was typically multiple, as 'Pole, Catholic, Gentleman' (Baines, *Joseph Conrad: A Critical Biography*, p. 14). In 1874, he was an adolescent thought by some to be 'betraying' his country in his desire to escape Poland for a freer life as a seaman in France. By 1878 he had joined the British Merchant Service, though still officially a Russian subject and unable to speak English. Nicknamed 'Polish Joe' by other crew members, he was about to discover sustaining social and corporate ideals under the Red Ensign. By 1904, nine years after publishing his first novel, he produced the most radically experimental English novel of the early Modernist period, the monumental *Nostromo*. At his death in Canterbury in August 1924 he was already a legend in his own lifetime.

Surprised though the Polish-born 'Joseph Conrad' may have been to become a published English author in 1895 at the age of thirty-seven, it should come as no surprise, given the extraordinarily varied and cosmopolitan influences at work on him, that he should turn out to be the novelist of paradox and riddle. The logic connecting the various diverse phases of his life often appeared so mysterious to Conrad himself that he would repeatedly speak and write about it in terms of a dream-like 'affair'.

Such a life-history, particularly in its early stages, presents a teasing challenge to many of the conventions of biographical method.[1] Like his fictional Lord Jim, Conrad as subject can disappear from view for long periods, with the result that many of the critical moments in his early life – his childhood illnesses, youthful suicide attempt, and affairs of the heart – retain a high degree of mystery. When the subject does make an appearance, he can often be glimpsed only through layers of hearsay, reticence, reminiscence, and accompanying myth. In mocking the biographer's desire for clarity of outline and developing chronology, Conrad's life has often seemed to demand creative rescue-work akin to the freely novelistic methods of evocation he used in his own autobiographical volumes, *The Mirror of the*

Sea and *A Personal Record*. In these works, the truly authentic portrayal of a life-history calls for the dissolution of all boundaries between novel and biography in order 'to make you see the subject in his scenery' and thereby produce an impressionist rendering of 'such affairs as are our human lives' (Ford, *Joseph Conrad: A Personal Remembrance*, p. 6). The conventional biographer may frown upon such renderings by Conrad or of 'Conrad' by others as unofficial and unreliable, but in Conrad's case they sometimes provide the only available access to him.[2] Two such characteristic glimpses from intimate sharers in the 'affair' of Conrad's life may serve to introduce his highly distinctive linguistic, cultural, and literary position.

The first glimpse, from Conrad's wife Jessie, bears upon their unusual marriage and honeymoon in 1895 and her sense of embarking on a strange 'joint adventure' with a solitary Pole sixteen years her senior who, she felt, 'had hardly known anything of a mother's care, and had no sort of experience of any sort of home life' (*Joseph Conrad as I Knew Him*, p. 25). Their honeymoon in Brittany involved for Conrad a return to a country and language that instantly seems to have brought out his most animated social side. The English language, on the other hand, was at this time a private and domestic one shared between Conrad and his wife, since she could speak no French and needed her husband to translate everything, causing the Bretons to regard them both as '*les Anglais*'. But it turns out that Jessie Conrad was doubly estranged by language when her new husband fell ill:

> For a whole long week the fever ran high, and for most of the time Conrad was delirious. To see him lying in the white canopied bed, dark-faced, with gleaming teeth and shining eyes, was sufficiently alarming, but to hear him muttering to himself in a strange tongue (he must have been speaking Polish), to be unable to penetrate the clouded mind or catch one intelligible word, was for a young inexperienced girl truly awful.
>
> (*Joseph Conrad as I Knew Him*, p. 35)

This thumbnail sketch brings the man and the writer close in several ways. It anticipates a subject that Conrad would treat in 'Amy Foster', a short story about the hostile reception afforded a Polish castaway in a Kentish village and turning upon a tragic linguistic misunderstanding between him and his English wife. It also prefigures what for Jessie Conrad would become a common experience: the persistent conjunction in her husband's writing career of illness and artistic creation. More importantly, English-speaking readers may find in Jessie Conrad's description of this 'joint adventure' a resonant prefiguration of what it means to encounter the writer of *Almayer's Folly* – of whom an early English reviewer wrote that 'he gives you the idea of muttering the story to himself' (Sherry, ed., *Conrad: The Critical Heritage*, p. 58), of 'Heart of Darkness', with its evocation of spiralling delirium, and of *Under Western Eyes*, whose Russian setting and themes of betrayal evoke a host of ancestral Polish voices. As with Jessie Conrad, the reader's larger 'adventure' also involves attuning an ear to a writer curiously suspended between linguistic and cultural traditions, now 'one of us' in his closeness to day-time English voices, now unusually mobile in his ability to cross boundaries, but at key moments challenging the very basis of what is seemingly clear and penetrable.

A second glimpse, this time from Ford Madox Ford, recalls Ford's early transactions with Conrad as a collaborator:

> His voice was then unusually low, rather intimate and caressing. He began by speaking slowly but later on he spoke very fast. His accent was precisely, rather dusky, the accent of dark rather than fair races. He impressed the writer at first as a pure Marseilles Frenchman: he spoke English with great fluency and distinction, with correctitude in his syntax, his words absolutely exact as to meaning, but his accentuation so faulty that he was at times difficult to understand ... He gesticulated with his hands and shoulders when he wished to be emphatic, but when he forgot himself in the excitement of talking he gesticulated with his whole body, throwing himself about in his chair, moving his chair nearer to yours. Finally he would spring up, go to a distance, and walk backwards and forwards across the end of the room.
>
> (*Joseph Conrad: A Personal Remembrance*, pp. 34–5)

Stressing the qualities of the hypersensitive or 'neurasthenic' personality noted by many others, Ford's observations provide further interesting clues as to why Conrad, as man and writer, is invariably thought to be 'elusive' and 'protean'. In the first place, this picture suggests why the traditional image of Conrad, partly fostered by himself, as *homo duplex* or of Anglo-Polish origin will no longer serve. Polish, English, *and* French influences upon him made up a genuinely tri-lingual and tri-cultural identity. Nor, secondly, do the snapshots offered by Jessie Conrad and Ford suggest that Conrad, as man or writer, enjoyed any easy trans-cultural rites of passage. As their reminiscences show, he could be taken for many things – an English country gentleman, a French dandy, a 'dusky' Slav, even on occasion for an 'Oriental' in his inscrutability. According to his wife, their effect was to make her husband characteristically feel 'a foreigner in England' like the central character in 'Amy Foster' (*Joseph Conrad as I Knew Him*, p. 124).

The whole tenor of Conrad's life as Polish émigré and seaman seems to have encouraged in him habits of mind associated with what has later come to be identified as the hybrid 'marginal man' who, living 'in two worlds, in both of which he is a stranger', needs self-consciously to fashion an identity from a medley of competing demands and allegiances. Studies of the émigré or expatriate as marginal man present him from several aspects. On the one hand, he is likely to be an individual whose feelings of unmoored strangeness or alienation within his adopted country can result in 'spiritual instability, intensified self-consciousness, restlessness and malaise' (Levine, *The Flight from Ambiguity*, p. 75). At one extreme, this syndrome includes a susceptibility to charges of betrayal, since to admit loyalty to multiple allegiances may in itself bear the appearance of disloyalty to any one of them. At another extreme, the émigré's insecurity within his adopted country may encourage a propensity towards outward 'correctitude', to use Ford's term, in relation to host-traditions, as tended to happen to a degree with Conrad. But the marginal man's relative sense of cultures and cultural identity may also lead to a richly composite individual, who, by his very ability to cross boundaries, enjoys the best of several worlds. A related freedom enjoyed by the expatriate in the country of his or her adoption stems from the off-centre position allowed by the unusual combination of nearness and distance in relation to host-traditions. In other words, the expatriate may have the special advantages of someone belonging-yet-not-belonging, of the kind described by Conrad to a fellow Polish émigré: 'Both at sea and on land my point of view is English, from which the conclusion should not be drawn that I have become an Englishman. That is not the case. Homo duplex has in my case more than one meaning. You will understand me' (*Letters*, III, p. 89). In literary terms, all of these things tend to mean that while Conrad occupies a marginal position in relation to the traditions of 'national' British literature, he is not thereby rendered traditionless. On the contrary, as a Pole, he insisted upon the largeness and historical depth of his Western legacy, and as a writer, his work implicitly announces a kinship with wider and freer European traditions, most especially with the literary heritage of France.[3]

I

To add substance to this blueprint, we need to follow, at least in broad outline, the pattern of 'standing jumps' into which Conrad's early life falls.[4] English novelist he did become, but he was born on 3 December 1857 in or near Berdichev in a Ukrainian province of Poland that had long been under Tsarist rule. Critics often speak of the impact of unhappy early years upon such writers as the Brontës and Dickens, but compared with theirs, Conrad's first traumatic years seem darker by several shades. Indeed, looking back on those years, he had good grounds for regarding them as the first of his metaphorical 'standing jumps', in this case into the toils of a tragic national history that turned upon 'Oppression, not merely political, but affecting social relations, family life, the deepest affections of human nature, and the very fount of natural emotions' (*NLL*, p. 130). The only child of Apollo Korzeniowski, a writer, translator, and Polish patriot of some national importance, and Ewa (née Bobrowska), Józef Teodor Konrad Korzeniowski (Nałęcz coat-of-arms) was given a name of complex ancestral significance. Both parents were members of the landowning gentry or *szlachta* class and devout Catholics, though from families of very different political traditions and commitments. The Korzeniowskis actively espoused soldierly and chivalric virtues, upholding a tradition of patriotic insurrection against the beast of 'Muscovy' in the name of national independence and democratic reforms, and as a result their family lands had been confiscated by the authorities. Conrad's father's political affiliations were with the revolutionary 'Reds', and his spiritual home with the Messianic myths of national suffering and deliverance forged by an earlier generation of Polish Romantic writers. The name 'Konrad' links Apollo's son to the doomed but heroic freedom-fighter of Adam Mickiewicz's dramatic poem *Konrad Wallenrod* (1828). It identifies its bearer simultaneously with the lost historical causes of suffering Poland and the binding values of courage, honour, and readiness for patriotic self-sacrifice.

Just what the Korzeniowski inheritance might hold would be evident to Conrad through his very early experience of membership in a family whose destiny was in the hands of an oppressive autocratic machine. Isolated exile, the ever-present threat of sickness and death, the absence of a secure home, and tragedy both familial and national following upon the failure of the 1863 insurrection were virtually the first of Conrad's life-sensations. When he was only three, his parents were arrested on charges of clandestine revolutionary activity and banished by the Russian authorities to a bleak internment in the Russian town of Vologda, their son being allowed to go with them. Her health undermined by the harsh conditions of exile, Conrad's mother died when he was eight, and for the next four years the young boy was sequestered with an ever gloomier father until the latter's death when Conrad was twelve. Through his father, Conrad made contact with extremes of Messianic political fervour but also, after the failure of the 1863 insurrection, with their effect upon an individual whose life was given over to monastic withdrawal, fixed obsessions, and a mourning for great lost causes and dear ones. As Conrad later saw him, he was 'A man of great sensibilities; of exalted and dreamy temperament; with a terrible gift of irony and of gloomy disposition; withal of strong religious feeling degenerating after the loss of his wife into mysticism touched with despair' (*Letters*, II, p. 247). Some elements of these early years – hardly to be described as a recognizable 'childhood' – irresistably bring to mind the bleak personal and political *données* of the later writer's fiction, with its various intuitions of life as a solitary ordeal and 'a choice of nightmares' (*HD*, p. 228) as well as its recurrent studies of refined idealism being corrupted and transformed into fixed idea.

Difficult though Conrad's early years were, they at least unfolded within a distinctly cosmopolitan literary and linguistic atmosphere that seems to have encouraged him to dabble in writing, master French, and, above all, to become 'a great reader' (*PR*, p. 70). Partly through his father's work as a translator, he had easy access to several national literatures – Polish naturally (particularly Słowacki and Mickiewicz), but also English (Shakespeare, Marryat, Dickens, as well as the literature of exploration, including Burton and Stanley), French (de Vigny, Garneray, and Hugo), Spanish (Cervantes), and American (Fenimore Cooper). Little is known about the early formal education Conrad may have received when he and his father were allowed to return to Austrian Poland, though the boy's illnesses – migraine, nervous ailments, and epileptic symptoms – probably explain why it was irregular and placed in the hands of several tutors. What he presumably also missed (and here we meet another example of the individual standing on the sidelines) were those processes of socialization that inevitably accompany full-time institutional schooling.

Being orphaned at the age of twelve brought a further sense of transplantation, when Conrad was placed under the guardianship of his maternal uncle Tadeusz Bobrowski, whose practical, conservative approach to life stood in marked contrast to the revolutionary fervour of Conrad's father. In Bobrowski's view, his family traditionally affirmed the tenets of enlightened conservatism associated with the 'Whites', trusting to 'realistic' political adjustment and conciliation as means to eventual Polish autonomy. Thinking himself no less patriotic than Apollo, Bobrowski asserted the need 'to make a sober assessment of our position, to abandon our traditional dreams, to draw up a programme of national aims for many years to come, and above all, to work hard, to persevere, and to observe a strict social discipline' (Najder, ed., *Conrad under Familial Eyes*, p. 36). Here was Conrad's first major exercise in forging an identity from irreconcilable opposites: was he the inheritor of an enlightened conservative ethic of honourable 'work' or, as his uncle tended to present it, a young man susceptible to the dangerously unbalanced romantic excesses of the Korzeniowskis? Judging from the evidence of Conrad's later life – which Bobrowski oversaw from a distance until his death in 1894 – the answer was never to be clear-cut and indeed probably contributed to Conrad's awareness of himself as *homo duplex*, suspended between revolutionary and conservative, chivalric and egalitarian, romantic and pragmatic traditions.

But, according to the later Conrad, one decision at the time does mark a decisive rejection, his turning away from his family's religious traditions: 'I always, from the age of fourteen, disliked the Christian religion, its doctrines, ceremonies and festivals' (*Letters*, II, p. 468).[5]

In 1872, there is a sudden intimation of one of the most far-reaching changes in Conrad's life, an 'adventure' perhaps fostered by his early reading, but, as Ian Watt suggests, one with roots in an irresistible compulsion 'to bid a resounding farewell to everything he knew in a homeland which was heavy with memories of irreparable national and personal loss' (*Conrad in the Nineteenth Century*, p. 5). Between the ages of fifteen and seventeen Conrad astonished his guardian by repeatedly expressing a desire to go to sea, a strange calling to someone living in a mainly inland country and one apparently viewed by many of his relatives as either foolishly quixotic or a scandalous 'betrayal of patriotic duties' (Najder, ed., *Conrad under Familial Eyes*, p. 141). The youth persisted, and in 1874 travelled on a Russian passport to Marseilles to become a seaman. While the charge of betrayal would return to plague Conrad, and figures in later psychobiographical readings of his fiction as a form of expiatory 'confession', he left Poland for a very good practical reason.[6] As the son of a political prisoner, he was faced with a possible twenty-five years conscription in the Russian army. Again, unprecedented though Conrad's departure for France may have seemed both to his family and himself, it is also important to place it within the wider context of nineteenth-century emigration from Poland. During the early part of the century, Paris had become a well-established centre for expatriate Polish writing, but, more significantly, between 1870 and 1914, two and a half million Poles emigrated to the New World, while half a million settled in Western Europe.

What Conrad discovered in 1874, with great relish it seems, was a bustling, cosmopolitan city full of social, cultural, and bohemian excitements, where 'the puppy opened his eyes' and 'life' began (*Letters*, III, p. 240). As a crucially formative stage in his rites of passage towards adulthood, his four-year stay in Marseilles must have represented a memorably romantic and myth-like initiation, but also one bringing chastening disappointments. If much of what the 'puppy' was doing during this period remains unknown, it is because the main source of information about these years is *The Arrow of Gold*, a late novel in which autobiography mingles intriguingly with fiction and myth. It depicts a youthful hero involved in gun-running for the Spanish Carlist cause and who, as the result of a love affair, is wounded in a duel. Some of the events depicted in the novel must, however, be re-assessed in the light of what Tadeusz Bobrowski appears to have found when in 1878 he was called to attend to his 'wounded' nephew

in Marseilles. Bobrowski's more prosaic account suggests that after difficulties concerning Conrad's status in French ships, financial setbacks over a
proposed smuggling expedition, and indiscreet gambling in Monte Carlo,
the errant young man returned to Marseilles virtually penniless and shot
himself in the chest: 'he is not a bad boy, only one who is extremely
sensitive, conceited, reserved, and in addition excitable. In short I found in
him all the defects of the Nałęcz family' (Najder, ed., *Conrad's Polish
Background*, p. 177). Shadowy and contradictory though much of the
evidence from this time is, it seems to indicate that Conrad's suicide attempt
was essentially a desperate plea for help rather than a serious attempt to
take his life.

The year 1878 marks yet another sharp change in direction, since it
signals the moment when, unable any longer to serve in French ships,
Conrad made his first contact with the British Merchant Service and would
soon come to seek an identity and vocation in its traditions. If sea-life
quickly lost its romance (Conrad was, after all, as a seaman connected with
another lost cause, the disappearing world of sailing ships) and later
brought him into conflict with some of his employers and captains, it also
introduced him – through the British Merchant Service – to social traditions
that he could increasingly associate with the idea of home. It provided a
surrogate family of 'brothers' whose corporate life turned upon values of
fidelity and solidarity, a hierarchical society, and a code of time-honoured
traditions and working truths symbolized by the Red Ensign. Conrad's
subsequent passage into English life, not perhaps such a drastic move as his
earlier departure for France but still a momentous event, has too full a
history to recount in detail. His later autobiographies tend to glamorize and
mythologize his entry into English life as a case of instant 'adoption' by the
country and its language as of a fellow-spirit. The real truth is that his
passage was slow and uncertain: first through the acquisition of the language, followed by his marine examinations, release from Russian nationality, and naturalization in 1886 at the age of twenty-nine. However, we
cannot but confront the startling fact that until the age of twenty-one
Conrad seems not to have known English – and go on to acknowledge the
minor miracle that within fifteen years, and while still a seaman, he was
beginning a narrative in English that would accompany him around the
world for the next five years and turn out to be his first published novel.

A crucial turning point in his later sea-career was a traumatic visit to the
Belgian Congo in 1890 where, undergoing a physical and mental breakdown that would leave him with an enduring legacy of ill health, he seems
to have been awakened to the possibility of a new life ashore. When he
finally took up permanent residence on dry land in 1894, he ended a sea-

career spanning twenty years that had taken him to the then-remote corners of the world, including the Caribbean, the Far East, Africa, and Australia.[7] The rich potential in his experiences for imaginative fiction would later prompt Henry James to exclaim, 'No one has *known* – for intellectual use – the things you know' (Jean-Aubry, ed., *Twenty Letters to Joseph Conrad*, p. 12). Conrad's first novel, *Almayer's Folly*, appeared in print in 1895, when he was at a relatively late age for a writer – thirty-seven. In the following year he married Jessie George and settled in rural Essex near the Thames. The next thirty years would see the emergence and development of the astonishingly prolific and arduous career of the writer identified by the pen name 'Joseph Conrad'.

If the strange materials of this life have naturally attracted the psycho-analytic critic, they also suggest the blueprint of what one biographer calls 'our representative modern man and artist' (Karl, *Joseph Conrad: The Three Lives*, p. xiv). But in some ways Conrad's example is a strange and resonant variation on a type, built as his life was upon the imputation of betrayal, linguistic dislocation, shifting cosmopolitan influences, and the consequent search for supporting social and intellectual traditions. Additionally, though in hindsight, Conrad's life may resemble the Joycean undertaking of fleeing the nets of family, religion, and country to embrace a freer vocation of art-in-exile, its developing patterns are, in Conrad's case, more irregular and problematic. Divided between two careers, one turning upon the fixed standards of maritime practice and the other upon the potentially anarchic regions of imaginative writing, Conrad's adult life develops with no such vocational certitude. Furthermore in his case, the embrace of a writing career would involve a flight beyond his native tongue to the third of his languages.

II

Conrad's literary career is commonly divided into three periods: a short early period of largely Malay fiction ending in 1896; the major phase extending from 1897 to 1911; and a more diverse body of later fiction that many critics divide into two phases – a period of transitional writing extending from 1911 to 1917, and a decline encompassing his last years from 1918 to his death in 1924.[8] The short period commonly called Conrad's 'apprenticeship' might more aptly be described as the first act of settlement by an already mature individual and precociously gifted writer within a literary culture largely strange to him. If this settlement was initially tentative in the sense that until 1898 Conrad hovered between a writing career and a return to sea, it also offered many favourable omens that the movement from ship's deck to writing-desk would be permanent.

As a beginning writer Conrad was especially fortunate in his early literary friends and contacts, who collectively formed the first of the many unofficial support groups that Conrad tended to need. Among this group, Edward Garnett, a critic, publisher's reader, and nurturer of literary talent, was a key influence. As a reader of manuscripts for the firm of T. Fisher Unwin, he was instrumental in seeing Conrad's first novel into print, and until about 1900 remained at hand as a sympathetic mentor, 'creative' reader of Conrad's work-in-progress, and regular reviewer of his published work. John Galsworthy, himself to become a Nobel Prize winning writer, and Edward Sanderson, a schoolmaster Conrad met in the *Torrens*, also came to Conrad's support at this crucial time. Other contacts in 1897 with the American writers Henry James and Stephen Crane, and the Scottish socialist and writer R. B. Cunninghame Graham provided Conrad not only with the promise of friendship but – just as important for the beginning writer – a sense of supporting literary and intellectual kinship.

Another propitious sign was that critical reviews of Conrad's first two novels, *Almayer's Folly* and *An Outcast of the Islands*, were generally as favourable as any beginning writer could hope for. He found literary champions in two of the leading authors of the day, H. G. Wells and Arnold Bennett, and had some grounds for thinking of himself as a favoured child of the critics.[9] Outwardly the Far Eastern settings of his early work fitted the taste for exotic fiction created by Robert Louis Stevenson and Rudyard Kipling and prompted many reviewers to place Conrad with those writers. More flatteringly, other early critics chose to stress the measure of his difference from English fiction of the day and invoked a range of French authors – Hugo, Loti, and Zola among others. Such a reception must have left Conrad with the feeling that he could simultaneously find a commercial niche as an English writer without compromising his increasingly serious artistic ambitions.

By late 1896, however, several ominous signs indicated that this honeymoon period was ending. Embroiled in a long, despairing struggle to write 'The Rescuer', a novel that he would soon abandon, Conrad noted apprehensively: 'Gone are alas! those fine days of "Alm: Folly" when I wrote with the serene audacity of an unsophisticated fool. I am getting more sophisticated from day to day. And more uncertain!' (*Letters*, I, p. 319). This anticipation of future ordeals went hand in hand with a further chastening recognition: in the competitive world of the late-Victorian book-market good critical reviews did not necessarily guarantee commercial success.

III

The Nigger of the 'Narcissus' (1897), with its famous prefatorial statement of artistic faith, represents an important landmark at the beginning of Conrad's major phase. The work is especially interesting in showing an author who, in attempting to seek a wider readership, was inevitably led to negotiate with his own very rich and diverse traditions, present in the completed story in a strangely mingled state of flux. Under the influence of Garnett, to whom *The Nigger* was dedicated, Conrad decided to embrace sea fiction for the first time as a promisingly commercial 'English' subject matter. The story's English elements are, however, in themselves of uncertain quality. Through his depiction of the sea and the family of seamen aboard the *Narcissus* Conrad implicitly affirms some of the deepest spiritual ties that had brought him to England. By contrast, the tale's more studied English features can be brittle and awkwardly second-hand, as is the case with Conrad's early exercise in demotic English for the Cockney Donkin or in his emulation of the popular sea story's sentimental patriotism. Moreover, as a work destined to appear in the *New Review*, *The Nigger*'s version of social and political England was almost certainly influenced by Conrad's attempt to strike the right chord with its editor, the militant Tory W. E. Henley, and emulate the journal's masculine, anti-sentimental, and oligarchic position.

As an experiment in methods of descriptive rendering, *The Nigger* thrives on variety and fullness of detail. At some of its most typical moments its cultivated Englishness is only one strand in a more strangely complex interweaving of literary inheritances and cultural traces. For example, a sprinkling of Polonisms – as when Wait says at one point to Donkin, 'Don't be familiar ... We haven't kept pigs together' (*NN*, p. 23) – indicates a writer whose original linguistic roots lie elsewhere. But an altogether more powerful influence can be detected in the tale's underlying affiliation with French literary styles. Numerous borrowings in the text provide interesting evidence of Conrad's closeness to the French writers he admired and show something of his habit of 'Englishing' French originals.[10] Other styles in *The Nigger* suggest a fascinated attraction for what a French writer would term *la belle page*, the 'beautiful' page, that in Conrad's hands reproduces in English the ornate rhetoric, heavily imaged style, and flowing rhythms of French neo-Romantic prose. Thus, *The Nigger* can stand as a wonderfully revealing example of Conrad's 'in between' position as a writer: in this case, at a point at the beginning of his major period when he is freshly defining his position in relation to an English readership.

The years from 1898 to 1902, a crucially formative stage in Conrad's difficult maturity, constitute a phase when outwardly his life would seem to have been domesticated and socialized. He became a family man with the birth of his first son in 1898, when the Conrads also moved to a somewhat more permanent home at Pent Farm, near Hythe in Kent. The year 1898 marks the beginning of Conrad's ten-year friendship with Ford Madox Ford, grandson of the Pre-Raphaelite painter Ford Madox Brown, with whom he also arranged to collaborate and who would by 1905 seem like 'a sort of life-long habit' (*Letters*, III, p. 287). By 1898 he also found a new patron and father-figure in William Blackwood, grandson of the founder of the famous publishing company and its literary journal, *Blackwood's*, who acted as his main publisher throughout this four-year period. His position in relation to the commercial world of publishing was formalized in a new way in 1900 when he signed up with the literary agent J. B. Pinker, thus beginning a twenty-year association that would require Pinker to play many parts – friend, generous banker, father-figure, and general factotum.

Yet in reality this period represents Conrad's first painful initiation into the many severe difficulties that would afflict his career during the next ten years or so. An air of dispirited agitation pervades the main body of his letters of this time, remarkable for its growing sense of the writer's vocation as combining the tribulations of a Faustian pact and the unending ordeal of Sisyphus who moves his burden upward only to find that once he reaches the top he must begin again. As a 'personal record' very different from his own reticent autobiographical reminiscences of that name, these letters provide unique insights into the convulsions of the Conradian creative process and the writer's attempt to cope with recalcitrant materials, threatening depression, and erratic temperamental imperatives. One source of perpetual frustration was rooted in Conrad's sense of unmoored isolation and estrangement from the literary and linguistic traditions that supported the native-born English writer. A related sense of crisis stemmed from writer's block and 'a terror of the inkwell' (*Letters*, III, p. 53) or from what he felt to be his proneness to un-businesslike dreaming. And, finally, the creative ordeal embraced a series of real or psychosomatic illnesses that on completing a novel left him close to physical and mental breakdown.

The outward manifestation of such a compositional process was what Conrad would come to call the 'runaway' novel – that is, a work originally conceived as a short story that, batch by batch of manuscript, slowly expanded, complicated, and accreted until it far exceeded its anticipated scope and over-ran deadlines. It is probably impossible to judge how far the final shape of such a novel was determined by the internal demands of the subject itself and how far by the temperamental imperatives brought into play by the act of composition. But it remains true that such compositional agonies would prolong the gestation of most of Conrad's full-length novels up to and including *Under Western Eyes*. Indeed, there are strong grounds for concluding that such compositional stops and starts were, in Conrad's case, not so much an interruption of creative rhythms as conditions that came to be strangely essential to them. In other words, from a whole range of seemingly negative obstacles Conrad generated, however painfully, a productive and energizing momentum.

The major fruits of the years from 1898–1902 – what Conrad would come to call his 'Blackwood's' period – represent another important stage in his struggle to negotiate with his English cultural identity and audience. These years are linked with the emergence of his famous narrator Marlow, who would determine the experimental nature of his three turn-of-the-century works, 'Youth', 'Heart of Darkness', and *Lord Jim*. While Marlow's evolution is too complicated to pursue here, it is nevertheless useful to indicate some of the ways in which he satisfies Conrad's preference for ambiguous borderlines.[11] If Marlow partly grows out of his creator's need to find an English identity and voice, it may also be true, as John Galsworthy long ago remarked, that 'though English in name', Marlow is 'not so in nature' ('Reminiscences of Conrad', p. 78). Galsworthy may have had in mind the way in which Marlow, though dramatized as a decent English sea-captain from the 'ranks', has an inordinate habit of being ambushed, challenged, and finally suspended between finely shaded alternatives. Another set of borderlines emerges through the teasing narrative possibilities associated with Marlow's address to his audience. He brings with him the framed oral tale, a narrative convention popular in *Blackwood's* stories of the time. In Conrad's hands, this frame, with its English narrator and audience, may initially promise detachment and security, but these both soon prove to be illusory. The frame can be complicated by Marlow's difficulties in making meanings for a 'decent' English audience or rendered less secure by the invasion of the nightmarishly alien. Likewise, the oral features of the yarn do not forbid the use of more recognizably 'written' styles: indeed, purposeful juxtapositions between the two become a staple of the Marlow stories. These and other Marlovian engagements with problems of where and how to establish borders surely indicate on Conrad's part both a new ambition to build his own off-centre position into his fiction and a growingly sophisticated sense of how a concept of 'Englishness' can be used to complicate the contract between writer and English reader. Figuratively speaking, it proves to be a contract with much fine print and several hidden codicils.

The year 1902 began with Conrad's feeling an enormous expansion of literary power: 'I am *modern*, and I would rather recall Wagner the

musician and Rodin the Sculptor who both had to starve a little in their day
... They too have arrived. They had to suffer for being "new". And I too
hope to find my place in the rear of my betters. But still – my place' (*Letters*,
II, p. 418). The novels to follow, *Nostromo*, *The Secret Agent*, and *Under
Western Eyes*, all have an air of dangerous audacity in their subjects and
experimental techniques. One marked change in these Edwardian works is
that Conrad's solitaries do not now have the possible protection afforded by
ship-board life. They are, so to speak, taken onto dry land, into societies
that are shifting, unfriendly, and subject to all the vagaries of recognizably
modern political machinery. During the 1890s the significant term
Weltpolitik (literally, 'world politics') had come into being. Initially coined
to describe German foreign policy, it later signified more generally the overt
drive for imperial power among the advanced industrialized nations and the
consequent growth of aggressive nationalism. Unlike most of the domestic
British fiction of the time, Conrad's work seems uniquely at home in
exploring the despoiling effect upon individual lives of violent and aggressive *Weltpolitik*. In these works, moreover, Marlow vanishes as a narrative
agent, and with him largely disappears whatever reassurance might come
from having a central human quester and individual who attempts to speak
as 'our' representative. He is replaced in a novel like *Nostromo* or *The
Secret Agent* by manifold human centres, multiple isolated consciousnesses,
and an omniscient authorial voice that can sometimes seem to be as cold
and impersonal as the world upon which it comments. Accordingly, this
body of fiction seems altogether more bleak and radical in viewing the
relationship between the self and the world in terms of fundamental contradiction and ironic paradox. If these novels can be said to have a single
generic trait, it borders on that of the tragic farce.

The connection Conrad made between literary newness and suffering
was, from 1902 onwards, painfully affirmed in his ordeals of composition
and his runaway debts. After finishing *Nostromo*, he was unsure about
what kind of 'trick' he had achieved with the novel, an intended short story
that had protracted itself over two years and whose composition prompted
him, in numerous agonized letters, to draw upon the image of the writer as
a blindfolded tightrope walker: one false step and everything was lost.
Under Western Eyes, planned in 1907 to take a mere six weeks to
complete, extended over two painful years as Conrad responded to the
promptings of a subject that had 'long haunted' him (*Letters*, IV, p. 14).
Underlying many of these difficulties was an added problem created by his
changed position in relation to his publishers. On severing his link with
Blackwood, Conrad lost an invaluable form of personal support and
patronage. As a result, he was forced to enter the marketplace of the

burgeoning Edwardian publishing industry, with its fixed contracts, hard deadlines, and pressure for saleable copy. He was ill fitted to survive in such a market, committed as he was to a form of experimental novel whose gestation involved an enormous expenditure of energy, time, and living costs. One of his solutions to the problem of spiralling debts was to rely upon the enormous good will of his agent and borrow heavily on the strength of his future payments and royalties. Pinker's patience in the face of his client's mounting debts was remarkable, but it could not be as boundless as Conrad sometimes seems to have demanded. With yet more financial burdens placed upon him in 1904, Conrad was increasingly driven to bifurcate his writing life between serious projects and more marketable copy in an effort to buy himself time. For example, the whole of 1905, following the publication of *Nostromo* and preceding the composition of *The Secret Agent*, was given over to the quick production of short stories and saleable journalistic material. More commonly, Conrad can be found from 1904 onwards to resemble the Indian juggler who must keep several balls in the air at the same time. Thus, at one period during the writing of *Nostromo*, he would compose the novel during the day-time, and in the evening dictate reminiscences to Ford and cobble together a one-act play out of an earlier story.

These mounting and converging pressures over a whole decade partially help to explain why *Under Western Eyes* is a novel associated with breakdown – not only Conrad's own on its completion in 1909, but the breakdown of his relationships with two of his closest support-figures, Pinker and Ford. The main disruptive pressures, however, undoubtedly derived from the power of the novel's subject to attack and 'haunt' Conrad during its painfully prolonged composition. Its central character, Razumov, an isolated Russian student, illegitimate, and orphaned at a very early age, lives and works in a relentlessly autocratic Russia that he identifies as his sole parent and from which he expects to gain the only rewards he can anticipate in life. His existence is transformed into crisis by the sudden appearance of Haldin, a fellow student but a revolutionary. Razumov informs on him to the authorities, and his further ordeal takes place among a community of Russian émigrés, including the dead Haldin's sister, Natalia, in Geneva, the setting for Razumov's conscience-stricken exile, double life, and quest for expiation.

Even this bare summary may suggest how the novel's subject would inevitably engage the deepest sensitivities of a writer of Polish origin whose early life unfolded against a background of Messianic and revolutionary traditions (represented in the novel by Haldin), who in later life repeatedly faced the imputed charge of betrayal (echoed and refracted in Razumov's ordeal), and who had become the 'respectable' English writer (perhaps mockingly represented in the narrator, an English language teacher). The challenge offered to Conrad by his subject did not simply involve a localized clash of sympathies, but an invitation to explore some of the deepest tensions within his Polish inheritance as well as his constituted identity as *homo duplex*.[12] As Conrad's preface to the novel indicates, the decision to deal with things Russian entailed a further challenge to his inherited convictions in demanding from him a greater detachment than he had ever been called upon to make. Yet the claim to detachment would always be tested by another powerful 'haunting' felt in the novel's agitated dialogue with – and attempted repudiation of – the Russian writer, Feodor Dostoevsky, and the world of his *Crime and Punishment*.

The act of unburdening a subject that 'must come out' (*Letters*, IV, p. 14) was attended by two severe external disruptions. A ten-year friendship with Ford floundered in 1908, partly through Conrad's disapproval of the distress caused by Ford's chaotic private life, but also through growing professional differences. Simultaneously, Conrad's relations with Pinker were moving towards breaking point. All of the agent's attempts to provide Conrad with deadlines, thereby linking payments to fixed amounts of copy, had failed during the composition of *Under Western Eyes*. In December 1909, when Conrad's debts to Pinker amounted to £2,700 (today the equivalent of at least £100,000), the agent's patience finally snapped and prompted the ultimatum that he could advance no more money unless *Under Western Eyes* were finished within a fortnight. Initially threatening to throw the manuscript into the fire, an infuriated Conrad was probably stung into driving on towards its completion, and upon delivering the manuscript in London, had an explosive row with Pinker that led to a two-year estrangement. Immediately upon returning home, Conrad collapsed with a severe physical and mental breakdown that confined him to his bed for three months. Jessie Conrad described her ailing husband as follows: 'Gout everywhere, throat, tongue, head … Poor boy, he lives the novel, rambles all the time and insists the Dr and I are trying to put him into an asylum'.[13]

IV

'I feel as if I had somehow smashed myself', Conrad wrote in 1911 (*Letters*, IV, p. 407), anticipating a new but recurrent strain in his letters of the next two or three years: that he is past his best, tired with the uphill struggle of the writer's life, and has written himself out. By unforeseen coincidence, Conrad anticipates the main thrust of the 'achievement-and-decline' view of his career held by a number of later critics and biographers. According to this view, argued most forcefully in Thomas C. Moser's study of 1957, Conrad's major works belong to the years 1897–1911, after which his writing suffers from a debilitating enervation and exhaustion, first undergoing a sharp decline through its creator's disabling involvement with the 'uncongenial subject' of love and sexually charged relations, and then suffering from a progressively simplified 'affirmation' that culminates in the exhausted weariness of the last novels.

Much recent criticism has challenged this view, both by questioning the sometimes reductive psychoanalytic assumptions underpinning it and by pointing to ways in which Conrad's later fiction may demand altered critical perspectives. Welcome though this debate is, the full evidence needs to include, not only the internal testimony provided by the novels, but also a consideration of the larger valedictory patterns at work in Conrad's final years. Three important changes in Conrad's life during 1910–14 suggest that this period constituted a crucial watershed.

First, there is the evidence provided by Conrad's own painfully acute sense of physical and creative fatigue after 1910. His letters of the time repeatedly complain of a depletion manifested inwardly by constant 'nervous exasperation' with himself (*Letters*, IV, p. 487) and outwardly by long fallow periods caused by illness or depression alternating with spells of wearily dogged composition. His moving confession to Bertrand Russell in 1913 included the wish to 'live on the surface & write differently' and a feeling that 'he was weary of writing & felt he had done enough, but had to go on & say it again' (Clark, *The Life of Bertrand Russell*, p. 212). The connection here between creative weariness and the compulsion to 'say it again' may explain the recurrent sense of retrospective return underlying much of Conrad's post-1909 writing. A tendency to repeat past formulae – as if in an effort to recapture earlier achievements – is certainly evident in the resuscitation of Marlow in *Chance* in 1914 as well as the return to Eastern subjects and romance conventions in most of the stories making up *'Twixt Land and Sea* and *Within the Tides*. After the First World War, this impulse to re-visit earlier territory, intensified by what resembles a retrospective 'homing' flight to the romance of his early days as material for fiction, became even more pronounced. As if to ensure that his career had no loose ends, he revived unfinished projects of a much earlier time in the form of *The Rescue* and *Suspense*, and revisited *Victory* and *The Secret Agent* to adapt them for the stage.

Secondly, Conrad's breakdown in 1910 roughly coincides with a time when an older circle of friends had disappeared to be gradually replaced by a group of younger admirers, some of whom would also become his first critics – Stephen Reynolds, André Gide, Bertrand Russell, Richard Curle, Jean-Aubry, and Hugh Walpole. Their support had a positive effect in consolidating Conrad's reputation, but it came with an undiluted hero-worship that quickly helped to inspire the legend of Conrad the 'wonderful' Great Man. Some evidence suggests that a tired Conrad was ready to enjoy the acting out of such a legend that, by 1914, made his visit to Poland something of a triumphal homecoming by a famous native son and internationally renowned writer.

The third important change was Conrad's movement towards financial security and, it can be argued, a more relaxed sense of what 'the public' wanted from him. *Chance* had turned out to be a popular and commercial success. The terms in which he conceived of this novel – 'It's the sort of stuff that *may* have a chance with the public. All of it about a girl and with a steady run of references to women in general all along'[14] – as well as the changes he made to give it a happy ending are of a kind that coincided with the spirit of the high-powered publicity campaign being mounted by *The New York Herald*, which serialized the story, and his publisher F. N. Doubleday, who had bought the American rights and would carefully orchestrate an American publicity tour for Conrad in 1923.

During the First World War, in which he produced only one major work, *The Shadow-Line*, a lonely Conrad was caught in the toils of a drab and uncreative 'sick-apathy' (Jean-Aubry, ed., *Joseph Conrad: Life and Letters*, II, p. 163). This was punctured by anxiety about his son Borys, who was on active service, and by his own inability to do more for the war effort than write a few propaganda pieces. All of these things combined to make Conrad feel that the broken Europe of the war years mirrored the terms of his own nightmarish disintegration. In May 1917, he described himself to Edward Garnett in these terms: 'I am like you my dear fellow; broken up – and broken in two – disconnected. Impossible to start myself going, impossible to concentrate to any good purpose. Is it the war perhaps? Or the end of Conrad, simply?' (Garnett, ed., *Letters from Joseph Conrad*, p. 198). This sense of ending and cataclysm was intensified, according to his wife, by the fact 'that the war brought back even more vividly than ever his tragic early life to his recollection, and ... that for a long time before his death he felt the call of his native land' (*Joseph Conrad as I Knew Him*, p. 16). But elsewhere the sense of creative disablement is extended to include the impact of war upon all endeavours in literary art: 'It seems almost criminal levity to talk at this time of books, stories, publication. This war attends my uneasy pillow like a nightmare. I feel oppressed even in my sleep and the moment of waking brings no relief' (Jean-Aubry, ed., *Joseph Conrad: Life and Letters*, II, p. 168).

These war-time sentiments form part of the wider context for the achieve-ment-and-decline debate. Conrad's sad lament echoes representatively at the time, shared by other members of an older generation of writers with strong roots in the nineteenth century, who endured the war from a position of helpless inactivity and felt it to be a comprehensive defeat of the liberal conscience. Henry James also speaks with Conrad, and for their generation:

> The war has used up words; they have been weakened; they have deteriorated like motor-car tyres; they have during the last six months been, like millions of other things, more overstrained and knocked about and voided of the happy semblance than in all the long ages before and we are now confronted with a depreciation of all our terms, or, otherwise speaking, a loss of expression, through increase of limpness, that may well make us wonder what ghosts will be left to walk. ('Henry James first interview', p. 4)

James died in 1916 and thus did not survive as a 'ghost'. Conrad, outliving James by several years, felt increasingly 'overstrained and knocked about' as his literary generation was about to make way for a group of younger writers – Eliot, Joyce, Pound, and Woolf – whose work would represent a new phase of post-war Modernism.

The last ten years of Conrad's career also display a developing pattern of what Michael Millgate, in his study of literary career closure, has called 'testamentary acts' or the end-games of writers who, aware of approaching death, make 'conscious and unconscious attempts to impose upon posterity versions of their works and selves specifically reflective of the aesthetic perceptions, moral discriminations, and creative choices they have arrived at late in life – however profoundly these may differ from those which prevailed earlier in their careers' (*Testamentary Acts*, p. 4). Although Conrad did not make a will until 1922, by 1918 he was already – according to Jean-Aubry – 'haunted by the idea of his approaching end and wanted to set himself straight with the future' (*The Sea Dreamer*, p. 274). Under such circumstances, creative work – most of it now being dictated – may have taken second place behind important acts of valediction and settlement with the future. For example, these years find the writer very obviously fashion-ing himself for posterity, allowing himself to be interviewed, painted, sculpted, and, as on his visit to America in 1923, lured into public reading and speech-making. In yet other ways, he seems also to have willingly participated in the growing Conrad industry, either through his involvement in selling manuscripts, signing copies of his works, and agreeing to the production of limited-edition pamphlets for the collectors' market, or in active dialogue with a growing number of appreciative critics.

Another time-consuming activity of these years was the preparation of a fittingly prepared canon of his works for future readers through the publication of a collected edition. As early as 1913 F. N. Doubleday had broached the possibility of such an edition, and quickly secured Conrad's agreement for an American-based edition to be co-published in England by Heinemann. The whole project involved Conrad in following the process undertaken by Henry James in preparing the famous 'New York Edition' of his novels and stories. Conrad revised earlier texts, brought together scattered occasional writings from the past, wrote an 'Author's Note' for each volume, prepared publicity, and carefully meditated the physical appearance of the editions. Ironically, at a time in his later life when Conrad as a writer was predisposed to revive some of the exotic qualities of his earlier fiction, he had instructed Doubleday:

> I want the edition to be perfectly distinctive and to bear no specialized symbols or marks. I am something else, and perhaps something more, than a writer of the sea – or even of the tropics. I am not even generally exotic, tho' at first the critics were rather inclined to class me under one of these heads. But this is no longer the case. I am acknowledged to be something, if not bigger, then, at any rate, as something larger.[15]

Almost simultaneously, Conrad could see his whole career being re-played through the French translation of his works under the editorship of André Gide, another collection in which he took an involved interest. In much of all this there is a sense in which Conrad is a willing spectator upon the formation of his own museum, even exercising a curatorial function in the choice of exhibits. Honorary degrees and a knighthood were offered and turned down, but Conrad hoped for the still more glittering award of a Nobel Prize. One of the final acts of his life was a testamentary one – sorting out and negotiating with Ford the collaborative properties of earlier days. Soon after, on 3 August 1924, the years of strain and ill health took their toll and Conrad died of a heart attack at the age of sixty-six.

If we alter the emphasis of the previous questions posed of Conrad's later years and ask why it was that, despite ill-health and the numerous obstacles of old age, he persisted with the literary life until death, several possible responses suggest themselves. For one thing, Conrad was in later life a heavily contracted author working to fulfil his publishing contracts; for another, he wished to provide financial security for his wife and sons. More importantly, it is possible to see his later years as fundamentally consonant with his early beginnings as a writer. Like Joyce and Yeats, his view of the artist invariably borrows Promethean imagery in order to suggest the heroic endeavour involved in both wrestling with the gods in the name of artistic creation and in fashioning a lifetime's work as an epic monument for posterity. As early as 1896 Conrad spoke of his desire for unattainable 'perfection' in art and continued: 'I would blaze like a bonfire and shall consume myself to give the feeble glimmer of a penny dip – if even so much' (*Letters*, I, p. 319). Such wry self-deprecation is characteristically Conradian. But it should not disguise the note of heroic ambition and what it implies of great daring, self-sacrifice, and absolute single-mindedness. As Zdzisław Najder aptly points out (*Joseph Conrad: A Chronicle*, p. 492), the lines from Spenser's *The Faerie Queene* used as an epigraph for *The Rover* and inscribed on Conrad's tombstone – 'Sleep after toyle, port after stormie seas/Ease after warre, death after life, does greatly please' – have one kind of aptness if their original Spenserian context is ignored. In Spenser's poem, however, these words are spoken by Giant Despayre, who is unavailingly soliciting the Red Crosse Knight to commit suicide. This context, with its implication of courageous resistance under pressure *usque ad finem*, seems an eminently appropriate one for Joseph Conrad.

NOTES

1 Karl's 'Three problematical areas in Conrad biography' presents a stimulating discussion of the challenges posed by Conrad's life (or lives) to the Conrad biographer and conventional biographical method. For guidance on the numerous biographies of Conrad, see 'Further reading' at the end of this volume.

2 Ray, ed., *Joseph Conrad: Interviews and Recollections*, offers an attractive collection of impressions and reminiscences of Conrad at various stages of his life by family, friends, and fellow writers.

3 The question of Conrad's Continental affiliations has naturally attracted a good deal of critical attention. Watt's *Conrad in the Nineteenth Century* surveys the possible European literary and philosophic influences at work in Conrad's early fiction. Among the best of the more specialized studies are Hervouet, *The French Face of Joseph Conrad*; Busza, 'Conrad's Polish literary background'; and Berman, 'Introduction to Conrad and the Russians'.

4 The term 'standing jump' figures in Conrad's description of his departure from Poland: 'I verily believe mine was the only case of a boy of my nationality and antecedents taking a, so to speak, standing jump out of his racial surroundings and associations' (*PR*, p. 121).

5 See Lester, *Conrad's Religion*, for a comprehensive account of Conrad's religious background as well as the part played by Western and Eastern religions in his fiction.

6 Morf's pioneer study of 1930, *The Polish Heritage of Joseph Conrad*, offers the first psychoanalytic pursuit of Conrad's 'alien complex', postulating that Conrad's life unfolded in the shadow of his distant past by virtue of his persistent guilt-complex at having betrayed the Polish national cause. He explores all of Conrad's novels as 'confessionals', efforts by symbolic indirection to justify or expiate his 'betrayal'. Morf's core idea has commended itself to some later

critics, including Bernard C. Meyer, though Meyer moves well beyond Morf in applying psychoanalytic methods to Conrad's life and fiction.

7 See Allen, *The Sea Years of Joseph Conrad*, for a comprehensive, though not always reliable, account of Conrad's maritime career. Sherry's *Conrad's Eastern World* and *Conrad's Western World* suggest how Conrad made imaginative use of his sea experiences in his fiction.

8 See Watts, *Joseph Conrad: A Literary Life*, for a study of the formation and development of Conrad's career as an author.

9 Sherry, ed., *Conrad: The Critical Heritage*, provides a wide selection of contemporary reviews and essays, along with a detailed survey of the growth of Conrad's reputation during his lifetime.

10 See Kirschner, *Conrad: The Psychologist as Artist*, pp. 200–5. Kirschner was the first critic to recognize Conrad's many borrowings in *The Nigger* from Maupassant.

11 Watt's chapters on Marlow in *Conrad in the Nineteenth Century* (see especially pp. 200–14, 223–41, and 310–38) provide a good starting point for a consideration of the narrator's evolution and functions. See Vidan, 'Conrad in his *Blackwood's* context', for an inquiry into the relationship between the Marlow narratives and the general 'horizon of expectation' associated with *Blackwood's* readers of the 1890s.

12 See Carabine in ch. 7 of this volume for a discussion of the effect of competing voices and interpretive models upon the form of *Under Western Eyes*.

13 Letter from Jessie Conrad to Alice Rothenstein, 6 February 1910, Houghton Library, Harvard University.

14 Letter to J. B. Pinker, 6 April 1913, Berg Collection, New York Public Library.

15 Letter to John Quinn, 19 May 1916, Manuscripts Division, New York Public Library.

WORKS CITED

Allen, Jerry. *The Sea Years of Joseph Conrad*. Garden City, NY: Doubleday, 1965; London: Methuen, 1967

Baines, Jocelyn. *Joseph Conrad: A Critical Biography*. London: Weidenfeld & Nicolson: New York: McGraw-Hill, 1960. Reprinted Penguin Books, 1971

Berman, Jeffrey. 'Introduction to Conrad and the Russians'. *Conradiana* 12.1 (1980), 3–12

Busza, Andrzej. 'Conrad's Polish literary background and some illustrations of Polish literature on his work'. *Antemurale* 10 (1966), 109–255

Clark, Ronald W. *The Life of Bertrand Russell*. London: Cape and Weidenfeld & Nicolson, 1975

Conrad, Jessie. *Joseph Conrad as I Knew Him*. London: Heinemann; Garden City, NY: Doubleday, 1926

Conrad, Joseph. 'The Crime of Partition'. *Notes on Life and Letters*. 1921. London: Dent, 1970, pp. 115–33

    The Nigger of the 'Narcissus'. 1897. Ed. Jacques Berthoud. Oxford: Oxford University Press, 1984

'Heart of Darkness' and Other Tales. Ed. Cedric Watts. Oxford: Oxford University Press, 1990

'The Mirror of the Sea' and 'A Personal Record'. 1906 and 1912. Ed. Zdzisław Najder. Oxford University Press, 1988

Ford, Ford Madox. *Joseph Conrad: A Personal Remembrance*. London: Duckworth; Boston: Little, Brown, 1924

Galsworthy, John. 'Reminiscences of Conrad'. In *Castles in Spain and Other Screeds*. London: Heinemann; New York: Scribner's, 1928, pp. 74–95

Garnett, Edward, ed. *Letters from Joseph Conrad, 1895–1924*. London: Nonesuch; Indianapolis: Bobbs-Merrill, 1928

Hervouet, Yves. *The French Face of Joseph Conrad*. Cambridge: Cambridge University Press, 1990

James, Henry. 'Henry James's first interview'. *New York Times Magazine*, 21 March 1915, pp. 3–4

Jean-Aubry, G. *The Sea Dreamer: A Definitive Biography of Joseph Conrad*. Tr. Helen Sebba. London: Allen & Unwin, 1957

Jean-Aubry, ed. *Twenty Letters to Joseph Conrad*. London: Curwen, 1926

Joseph Conrad: Life and Letters. 2 vols. London: Heinemann; Garden City, NY: Doubleday, Page, 1927

Karl, Frederick R. *Joseph Conrad: The Three Lives—A Biography*. New York: Farrar, Straus, and Giroux; London: Faber & Faber, 1979

'Three problematical areas in Conrad biography'. In *Conrad Revisited: Essays for the Eighties*. Ed. Ross C. Murfin. University: Alabama University Press, 1985, pp. 13–30

Kirschner, Paul. *Conrad: The Psychologist as Artist*. Edinburgh: Oliver & Boyd, 1968

Lester, John. *Conrad's Religion*. London: Macmillan, 1988

Levine, Donald M. *The Flight from Ambiguity: Essays on Social and Cultural Theory*. Chicago: University of Chicago Press, 1985

Meyer, Bernard C. *Joseph Conrad: A Psychoanalytical Biography*. Princeton, NJ: Princeton University Press, 1967

Millgate, Michael. *Testamentary Acts: Browning, Tennyson, James, Hardy*. Oxford: Clarendon, 1992

Morf, Gustav. *The Polish Heritage of Joseph Conrad*. London: Sampson Low, Marston, 1930; New York: Richard R. Smith, 1931

Moser, Thomas C. *Joseph Conrad: Achievement and Decline*. Cambridge, MA: Harvard University Press, 1957. Reprinted Hamden, CT: Archon Books 1966

Najder, Zdzisław. *Joseph Conrad: A Chronicle*. Tr. Halina Carroll-Najder. New Brunswick, NJ: Rutgers University Press; Cambridge: Cambridge University Press, 1983

Najder, Zdzisław, ed. *Conrad's Polish Background: Letters to and from Polish Friends*. Tr. Halina Carroll. London: Oxford University Press, 1964

Conrad under Familial Eyes. Tr. Halina Carroll-Najder. Cambridge: Cambridge University Press, 1983

Ray, Martin, ed. *Joseph Conrad: Interviews and Recollections*. London: Macmillan, 1990

Sherry, Norman. *Conrad's Eastern World*. Cambridge: Cambridge University Press, 1966

Conrad's Western World. Cambridge: Cambridge University Press, 1971

Sherry, Norman, ed. *Conrad: The Critical Heritage*. London: Routledge & Kegan Paul, 1973

Vidan, Ivo. 'Conrad in his *Blackwood's* context: an essay in applied reception theory'. In *The Ugo Mursia Memorial Lectures, University of Pisa, September 7th–11th 1983*. Ed. Mario Curreli. Milan: Mursia International, 1988, pp. 399–422

Watt, Ian. *Conrad in the Nineteenth Century*. Berkeley: University of California Press, 1979; London: Chatto & Windus, 1980

Watts, Cedric. *Joseph Conrad: A Literary Life*. London: Macmillan, 1989

2

GAIL FRASER

The short fiction

I

Although his fascination with 'the novel' as a form of art has been well documented by Ford Madox Ford and others, Conrad seldom used the term to refer to his own longer works. In their subtitles, he described six of his novels as 'tales' and one as a 'story', thus emphasizing the older and larger category of narrative fiction. In his letters also, he preferred not to distinguish between short fiction and novels, referring to both forms as 'stories'.[1] This blurring of generic boundaries reflects the organic evolution of many of his works. For example, *Nostromo*, which he was still calling a 'story' after writing 560 manuscript pages, actually began as a short story before it became a 'long short story', and then a 'long story' or 'novel'. Indeed, any overview of Conrad's creative process would reveal an essentially Darwinian approach to writing fiction in that his art forms are continually being modified by the pressures of their 'environment'. Perhaps for this reason, he often exploited comparisons with elemental or natural forces to describe his working methods: 'I am letting myself go with the *Nigger*. He grows and grows', 'The Typhoon is still blowing', 'Verloc' – a little earlier called 'this beast' – 'is extending', 'Razumov will grow into a short book before I am done with him', and so on (*Letters*, I, p. 312; II, p. 307; III, p. 318; IV, p. 76). Of all Conrad's stories and novels, only 'The Lagoon', an early work of some 6,000 words, conforms to guidelines on length set in advance of composition.[2]

Few writers beginning a project would claim to have a completely detailed or accurate idea of how their work will turn out; nevertheless, Conrad's case invites special attention. To appreciate the full extent of his creative elasticity, we need only compare it to the practice and personality of Henry James, who shared many of his artistic concerns and who, like him, challenged late-Victorian techniques in both short fiction and the novel. To begin with, James's relationship with the marketplace was based on clear, often precise, understandings. Once he had decided on ideas for his stories, he was not adverse to negotiating contracts that specified their page lengths, and when asked to contribute a work he was skilled in tailoring material to fit even the shortest form (5–6,000 words).[3] Conrad seldom agreed to write to measure in this way. In the serial market, *Blackwood's Edinburgh Magazine* published his short and long fiction with a famous disregard for the demands of time and space.[4] The lengths of stories he promised to complete for his volumes were flexible (within limits), and he often had no contract and no specific periodical in mind when he began a project. Conceding that his indifference to various editors' requests for a word or page count was to his 'disadvantage', he nevertheless insisted that he could not do otherwise (*Letters*, IV, pp. 353–4). Apparently, the same conditions that stimulated James's imagination and ingenuity were antagonistic to Conrad's.

When we look at the record of their works-in-progress, the difference between the two writers becomes even more striking. In contrast to Conrad, who began all of his long fictions (with two significant exceptions) as short stories, James allowed only one of his 'tales' – *The Spoils of Poynton* – to evolve into a novel. The distinction between these two types of creative energy is most dramatically illustrated by James's experience with *The Bostonians*. Although he originally conceived the work as 'shortish' (taking up six serial instalments), James explained even before he began to write that the subjects of *The Bostonians* and *The Princess Casamassima* were 'big & important; & the treatment will be equally so'.[5] In fact, at the time he made this statement he had already renegotiated his contract, asking for an extension in order to earn 'enough ready money to carry me through the time it will take me to complete my novel'.[6] Invariably, Conrad's approach to a new project was more modest and open-ended. In the fictions that were to engage him most seriously, he planned nothing more detailed than a 'sketch' before he began to write, and once embarked on a work – *The Secret Agent*, for example – he might initially anticipate little more than 8,000 words.[7] In most cases, he had advanced into the second half of either a long short story or one of his novels before deciding that 'it must be worked out' in the shape it had organically assumed. But even works he later described as 'fake' or 'magazine-ish', such as 'Gaspar Ruiz' and 'Freya of the Seven Isles', grew well beyond their original boundaries.

This pattern has led some critics to suggest that Conrad found the short form difficult or uncongenial.[8] Perhaps the most famous examples of his reluctance to conclude (*Lord Jim* and *Under Western Eyes* come to mind) have obscured a significant fact about the *beginnings* of his fiction. The only two works that he began as novels rather than short stories or 'sketches' proved to be the most difficult of all to complete.[9] One – 'The Sisters' – remains a fragment; the other – *The Rescue* – refused to take shape for twenty-three years, although he wrote the whole of Part I before laying it aside and made several later attempts to continue the narrative. These two failures of will and imagination suggest that the shorter form tended to concentrate his ideas in a way that was essential to the making of his art.

Conrad's description of his creative impasse with *The Rescue* seems to support this conclusion. Before he abandoned the novel in August 1896, he wrote that the story's plot would not emerge from 'the chaos' of his 'sensations', and that he could not invent an 'illuminating episode that would set in a clear light the persons and feelings' (*Letters*, I, pp. 288, 296). As usual, Conrad is far more revealing about artistic problems in his day-to-day accounts of work-in-progress than in the 'Author's Notes' he wrote towards the end of his career. His comments about *The Rescue* hint at the necessity of the 'illuminating episode' in generating a search for meaning and providing a structure for his impressions. (We might also note that his description of 'episode' anticipates the epiphanic form taken by some of his best-known short fiction; for example, 'Youth' and 'Heart of Darkness'.) When he constructed his novels, Conrad began with an episode, situation, or 'moral pivot', and multiplied its implications as he developed his narrative line. Thus a dramatic focus in *An Outcast of the Islands*, the work he completed with such notable success before his struggles with 'The Sisters' and *The Rescue*, is Willems's 'sudden descent', his 'enslavement' by Aïssa as he disappears into the jungle at the end of Part I. This scene, whose action is twice deferred for ironic effect, is reworked in a tragic mode in the climax; it is also the 'situation' Conrad had in mind when he still thought of *Outcast* as a short story.[10] Many writers of long novels – Dickens and Edith Wharton are examples of how wide the range can be – have shaped their work by charting the overall development of different plot lines, characters, and motifs. Conrad seems to have achieved his best work, regardless of length, by allowing the single episode to open up thematic and formal possibilities as he wrote. And it may well be that such artistic risk-taking demanded modest beginnings.

There may also be more than one reason why Conrad found the short form so appealing when he first thought of an idea for a story. It had been successfully exploited by writers like Maupassant, Flaubert, and Turgenev, whose craftsmanship he carefully studied and admired. Perhaps for this reason, almost from the beginning of his career as an author Conrad avoided the temptation to describe short fiction as a lesser art. Before his first volume of short stories appeared, he wrote to T. Fisher Unwin, his English publisher at the time, that the current 'slump' in the market was illogical, because 'the intrinsic value of a work can have nothing to do' with its length (*Letters*, II, p. 49). In this respect he was – again – unlike Henry James, whose fondness for the *nouvelle* is well known but who emphasizes the limitations of the short story when describing the challenge of writing within a form 'that, at the best, would give little' (Preface to 'The Author of Beltraffio', p. 233).

In his turn, Conrad pointed to the aesthetic opportunities offered by the short form because of its ability to 'show forth' the characteristic elements of a writer's style: 'It takes a small-scale narrative (short story) to show the master's hand' (*Letters*, I, p. 124). The context of this intriguing statement helps to determine its meaning, which might otherwise be taken more simply, if sceptically, to mean that short fiction is superior to the novel. Conrad was writing to Marguerite Poradowska – his confidante and 'chère Maître' – about her most recent work, a series of short sketches. In the same letter he describes her style in somewhat personal terms, as 'full of charming touches – of discriminating observations, of things taken from life'. If style indeed reflects the writer's view of her world, as Conrad implies, his reference to 'the master's hand' could indicate that Poradowska's short 'scenes' gave him a clearer, more direct sense of her artistic individuality than her novels, and that this effect is characteristic of the genre.[11]

When we look at his own writing from this perspective, we can see that some of the earlier short fictions served as testing grounds for the very techniques that make his work recognizably 'Conradian'. In 'An Outpost of Progress', for example, he exploited grotesque images and sudden shifts in perspective to create an ironic style that sets him apart from Flaubert and Maupassant. Almost simultaneously, in 'The Lagoon', he experimented with a more searching and ambiguous version of the 'teller and listener' narrative method favoured by Turgenev in his shorter works. The intense concentration of discrete aspects of Conrad's style in each of these stories is suggested in a study of his use of adjectives, which concludes that 'An Outpost of Progress' and 'The Lagoon' are 'so different that they might almost have been written by different writers' (Lucas, 'Conrad's adjectival eccentricity', p. 134). In Conrad's case at least, the ability of the shorter form to 'show forth' a certain element of the artist's style and personality is evident throughout his career. 'Amy Foster', a story about a Carpathian peasant's experience of cultural alienation after he is cast away on the Kentish coast, gives us a more clearly focused view of Conrad (or an aspect of Conrad) than does a wide-ranging, more complex work like *Nostromo* or *The Secret Agent*. Another case in point, 'The Secret Sharer', reflects the writer's acknowledged sense of himself as *homo duplex* with a more sustained emphasis than we find in his novels.

The shorter forms of Conrad's fiction have yet another significance in the larger pattern of his writings, for they are part of an important alternating rhythm. Some of his letters record that subjects for short stories were always 'reposing at the back of [his] head', and that he liked to describe them to friends, agents, and prospective publishers when he was already fully extended with work on a long novel (*Letters*, IV, p. 473). He also confessed to a sense of emotional release when he turned from the longer work to take up an idea for short fiction: 'Typhoon' would be 'a fresh start' after the 'nightmare' of finishing *Lord Jim* (*Letters*, II, pp. 289, 293), and writing 'The Secret Sharer' in the midst of *Under Western Eyes* gave him confidence (*Letters*, IV, p. 296). 'The Planter of Malata', begun 'on a sudden impulse' when he was writing *Victory*, would let him 'go back to the novel with a better heart'.[12] Although the shorter works almost invariably turned out to be less 'easy' than he anticipated, Conrad's inclination to find a 'short turn' for his material was often strongest when he had just completed a novel, was in the latter stages of writing one, or was unable to make headway, as with *The Rescue* and *Chance*. This creative cross-rhythm is one of the forces that may have shaped Conrad's shorter fiction; others were, as we shall see, more public and demonstrable.[13]

II

In contrast to almost all Victorian and late-Victorian fiction writers, who began their careers by publishing short stories, poems, or journalistic pieces in periodicals, Conrad's first two works were novels, and neither *Almayer's Folly* nor *An Outcast of the Islands* was serialized. His real education in the literary marketplace began in the summer of 1896, with his attempts to place three short stories: 'The Idiots,' 'An Outpost of Progress,' and 'The Lagoon'. Relying on Edward Garnett for advice and emotional support, he contemplated his new venture, 'The Idiots', ironically: 'I *would not* have it published unless You see and pass it as fit for the twilight of a popular magazine' (*Letters*, I, p. 284). As his experience with 'publishers and other horrors' grew during the next few months, he found that it was sometimes possible to reconcile conflicting interests: *The Cornhill* was 'not a bad mag. to appear in' (*Letters*, I, p. 286), and it also paid handsomely. Just as often, however, he had to compromise. *The Savoy*'s reputation for political conservatism did not appeal to him, but he wrote to Unwin that 'there is no particular gratification in being accepted *here* rather than *there*. – If the "Savoy" thing asks for my work – why not give it to them? I understand they pay tolerably well' (*Letters*, I, p. 293). Still again, the periodical edited by W. E. Henley was so prestigious that he (almost) expressed lack of interest in payment: 'I will take any offer (not absurdly low) they may make because I do wish to appear in the *New Review*' (*Letters*, I, p. 319). By November 1897, when he had given up trying to serialize 'The Return', Conrad already had a good sense of the opportunities to be gained and lost in the magazine market, and two or three months later was using his connections to help Stephen Crane.

As this apprentice period suggests, the contradictions involved in Conrad's attitude towards serialization are nowhere more evident than in the marketing and publishing of his short fiction. One of the most pressing considerations, given his ever-increasing debts, was the need for money. Since the late 1880s, when British magazines had begun to pay well for short fiction, the sale of a story could be important to a writer's survival – and Conrad's case was often desperate. In effect, not only would relief be immediate (if temporary), it would be large in proportion to time spent at the desk. Written in less than three weeks in July 1896, 'An Outpost of Progress' earned £50 – as much as Conrad had received for the copyright to *An Outcast of the Islands*, which had taken a year to complete. Even when he began to serialize the longer works, magazine payment for the stories was comparatively higher: for 'Karain', for example, £40 (one instalment); for *Lord Jim*, £300 (fourteen instalments). Moreover, after hiring J. B. Pinker, a literary agent, to market his work, Conrad's ability to earn 'immediate bread and butter' by writing short fiction increased. On receipt of the 'Typhoon' manuscript – the first piece he handled for Conrad – Pinker advanced £100 on the serial rights: a practice he continued with all works to follow. (Its destabilizing effect on Conrad's already disordered affairs is indicated by the fact that *Pall Mall Magazine* paid only £75 for the story.) When we consider the full extent of Conrad's indebtedness – £2,250 by the spring of 1910 – and realize that the same story could be sold to an American magazine for an equal return, we can better appreciate the temptation to compromise his art.[14]

One area of compromise, which was particularly damaging to works of short fiction, was largely unavoidable. When Conrad learned that 'An Outpost of Progress', his first story to be published, would be printed in two instalments, he objected that its division would damage the cumulative effect of his ironic method: 'I told the unspeakable idiots that the thing halved would be as innefective [*sic*] as a dead scorpion. There will be a part without the sting – and the part with the sting – and being separated they will be both harmless and disgusting' (*Letters*, I, p. 320). In this and later stories like 'Amy Foster' and 'The Secret Sharer', serial division into two or three parts destroyed the reader's sense of uninterrupted communion with the author and his work – a feature that helps to distinguish the genre. In this respect, Conrad would have agreed with most critics writing about short fiction today, who argue that the experience of reading a shorter work is different from that of reading a novel because of the way memory functions in relation to quantity and duration (Friedman, 'Recent short story theories', p. 25). Because we can remember more of the details in short fiction, each carries more weight than in a novel and repays the reader's most concentrated attention: 'as to me I depend upon the reader *looking back* upon my story as a whole', Conrad wrote (*Letters*, II, p. 441). In protesting against a practice so widespread as to include carefully edited magazines like *Cosmopolis* and *Blackwood's* as well as those he characterized as 'inept' – *Harper's*, for example – Conrad was in fact arguing for the integrity of the modern short story as an art form. Wherever possible, he sought to minimize the damage by suggesting where breaks should be, but inevitably, the printing of his work in weekly or monthly instalments hampered the reader's ability to connect motifs and images central to a story's meaning.

Conrad's failure to sell 'The Return' points to another limitation of magazine as opposed to book publication: the editorial concern to satisfy middle-class tastes. To be sure, 'The Return' is uneven, but its multi-layered irony and forceful images put it on a much higher level than the standard magazine fiction of the time. The difficulty for *Chapman's Magazine*, not to mention the other periodicals both Conrad and Unwin canvassed unsuccessfully, was its subject: the fierce emotions and sexual discord beneath the surface of a 'typical' middle-class marriage. Indeed, Conrad's treatment of the woman's frustration is so explicit that he asked Edward Garnett for his wife's opinion of the manuscript, but as far as we know, it was never given. 'Falk', was never serialized – its hero confesses to cannibalism – and two more stories, 'The Idiots' and 'Freya of the Seven Isles', were refused at least once, apparently because they made too little concession to market formulae: an inoffensive subject, simplicity of style or treatment, and a happy ending. Of course, magazine editors were not always hostile to provocative themes and experimental techniques in short fiction, as witness the publication of 'An Outpost of Progress' and 'Heart of Darkness'. But quality in itself was not a reliable indicator as to the favourable reception of Conrad's work. Pinker's relative slowness in placing 'Amy Foster', one of his very finest stories, was most probably due to its tragic climax and unflinching scepticism.

Complicating the issue of 'popularity' were Conrad's artistic motives for wanting to learn 'what pleases the general public' (*Letters*, IV, p. 102), and his recognition that magazines – regardless of their quality – reached and influenced many different types of readers. This last fact was signally important to his view of the writer's role as he described it in the Preface to *The Nigger of the 'Narcissus'*, which stressed the ability to appeal across social and professional boundaries to 'the solidarity in dreams ... which binds together all humanity' (p. xl). In his most considered statements – such as the famous defence of his art written to a magazine editor in 1902 – he gives the common reader the same inherent value as, say, H. G. Wells or Bernard Shaw:

> my talent ... appeals to such widely different personalities as W. H. [*sic*] Henley and Bernard Shaw – H. G. Wells and professor Yrgö Hirn of the Finland University – to Maurice Greiffenhagen a painter and to the skipper of a Persian Gulf steamer who wrote to the papers of my 'Typhoon' – to the Ed of PMM [*Pall Mall Magazine*] to a charming old lady in Winchester.
>
> (Letters, II, p. 416)

As his reference to 'Typhoon' suggests, Conrad was well aware of the strategic position held by short fiction in bridging the gap between the studio or study and the outside world.

At the turn of the century, historians tell us, the market for short stories was 'enormous, and apparently insatiable'. More specifically, this market lay almost entirely in the periodical press rather than collections in book form (Orel, *The Victorian Short Story*, pp. 186–91). Moreover, in their magazine versions, short fiction enjoyed a built-in advantage over the serialized novel, because several short pieces could target a larger range of audiences in the same period of time. An astonishing number and variety of periodicals were soliciting stories at the time Conrad was writing them; from 'literary' journals, to 'family' magazines, to, for example, the *Gentleman's Journal*, which asked him for 'a *man's story*' (*Letters*, IV, p. 298). Partly in response to a climate so favourable to short fiction, he decided to sell 'Typhoon', 'Falk', and 'Amy Foster' away from *Blackwood's*, which had published 'Karain' and 'Youth' and had serialized *Lord Jim*, telling Pinker that he wished 'to reach another public than *Maga's*' (*Letters*, II, p. 321). The apparent failure of this strategy affected him strongly: writing to David Meldrum, *Blackwood's* London advisor, a year later, he complained about the 'delay in placing the three stories', adding that it had 'dispirited me for a time in a most ridiculous and lamentable manner – for after all I *do* know fairly well what I am doing and the unwillingness of editors to publish the stuff does not affect its value' (*Letters*, II, p. 368). Thus we see that Conrad's short fiction played a double role at a transitional point in his career. On the one hand, it helped him push beyond the familiar world of *Blackwood's* audience; on the other, it provided clear evidence of the gap between artistic endeavour and the marketplace.

To what extent, then, did the various pressures of the serial market shape Conrad's work? Let us first remember that he began most of his stories without being under contract to a magazine. Only in the pieces actually commissioned by *Blackwood's* – 'Youth', 'Heart of Darkness', and 'The End of the Tether' – can we speculate with any confidence about the influence of a particular audience or editor. But because the nature of his relationship with *Blackwood's* yielded, in 'Youth', an ideological agenda that contrasts markedly with some of his other stories, it deserves close attention.

By publishing short fiction in *Blackwood's*, Conrad was taking the first important step in building a public. Sales of his first two novels had been disappointing, and although *Cosmopolis*, *The Cornhill*, and the *New Review*, which had serialized his previous fiction, were well thought of, *Blackwood's* had a larger circulation in Britain as well as overseas. To Conrad, who in 1897 was beginning to put down deeper roots in England, this extended family of readers was greatly appealing: 'There isn't a single club and messroom and man-of-war in the British Seas and Dominions', he wrote later, 'which hasn't its copy of Maga – not to speak of all the Scots in all parts of the world' (*Letters*, IV, p. 506). Narrating from Marlow's point of view in 'Youth' – that is, as a typically British seaman who has experienced his own 'voyage out' – Conrad could explore his readers' cultural traits and values by indirection, and as an insider. (In contrast, the narrator who introduces Marlow opens the story from an outsider's perspective, by drawing our attention too pointedly to the national myth: 'This could have occurred nowhere but in England, where men and sea interpenetrate'.) Although Conrad took pains in the book version to emphasize Britain's *difference* from other European countries rather than her superiority, Marlow's elaboration of the national character in the magazine version has a clear ideological intention: to endorse the traditionalist values celebrated by *Blackwood's* since the early 1800s, and thus to involve his readers in the ongoing debate about England's perceived weakening of spirit, body, and will. In this respect, 'Youth' aspires to the role assumed much more crudely by Ford some years later in *The English Review*, when he inveighed against those who 'proclaim all day long that we are growing effeminate ... open to invasion, lacking in patriotism ... our hardihood all gone, our manhood degenerate' (Editorial, p. 359).

The story's most dramatic episode is also the occasion for Marlow's strongest appeal to patriotic feeling. When the *Judea*'s cargo of coal catches fire and explodes, her crew of 'Liverpool hard cases' responds with impressive discipline and will: 'But they all worked', Marlow says. 'That crew of Liverpool hard cases had in them the right stuff. *It's my experience they always have*. It is the sea that gives it – '.[15] The italicized sentence, which asserts that 'the right stuff' will never diminish, is one of many similar additions made after the manuscript stage and before serial publication. These include the keyword 'everlasting' in Marlow's praise of the national spirit.[16] In his first draft Conrad had already transformed the cosmopolitan crew that sailed with him in 1892 into gritty English sailors that 'to an onlooker' seemed no more than 'a lot of profane scallywags without a redeeming point' (*HD*, p. 118). Revising his work, he continued to keep one eye on the reports of 'degeneration' that were appearing almost daily in the periodical press. In this way, he could claim with his *Blackwood's* audience a solidarity that drew upon the deepest reserves of patriotic feeling.

When we look at the fiction Conrad wrote before and after 'Youth', we find a more ambiguous and ironic treatment of this subject.[17] In 'Heart of Darkness', which *Blackwood's* published from February to April 1899, he even used the same narrative method pioneered in 'Youth' to question the value of so-called British traits like 'efficiency'. But a more striking contrast to the influence of *Blackwood's* readers on the serial version of 'Youth' is Conrad's sceptical portrayal of patriotic sentiment in 'Typhoon'. In that story, the justly famous episode of the Siamese flag introduces the theme, for MacWhirr's failure to understand Jukes's nationalistic indignation leads to an ironic view of the younger man. Conrad shows us Jukes's conventionally egoistic interpretation of the transfer from British to Siamese colours as 'a personal affront', and points to the disjunction between his words – 'Dash me if I can stand it: I'll throw up the billet' – and actions (*TOT*, pp. 9–10). As the narrative continues, he emphasizes the first mate's irrational fear of the coolies during and after the typhoon, and his equally xenophobic insistence that the Siamese flag must expose the ship to acts of violence and revenge. Conrad's rejection of patriotic rhetoric in 'Typhoon' illustrates the limited influence of serial readers on the ideology of his fiction as a whole. To any significant degree, it begins and ends with 'Youth'.

The pressures of serial publication on the form and style of Conrad's short fiction become most evident after Pinker's failure to place 'Falk' and 'Amy Foster' as quickly as he had hoped. Written after 'Amy Foster' and as a companion-piece to it, 'To-morrow' conforms much more readily to the standard pattern of magazine fiction. Although the story emphatically lacks a happy ending, Conrad achieves his 'short turn' by stressing the plot's implacably ironic 'twist of fate' and limiting the development of his characters so that Captain Hagberd, Bessie, and Harry, the long-lost son, bear a strong resemblance to popular stereotypes. Not quite two months after 'To-morrow' was finished, Pinker placed it with *Pall Mall Magazine*: its publication in August 1902 marks the beginning of a period in which

Conrad's shorter fiction became less experimental in form and subject, and seemed more deliberately conceived with 'the needs of a magazine' in mind (*Letters*, II, p. 373). Unlike 'The Lagoon' and 'Karain', in which he frames an adventure narrative with sceptical or ambiguous points of view, stories such as 'Gaspar Ruiz' (1905), 'An Anarchist' (1905), 'The Informer' (1906), and 'The Brute' (1906) are essentially anecdotal. Indeed, most readers find 'The Black Mate' (1908) and 'The Inn of the Two Witches' (1912) formulaic.

This development reflects a shift in Conrad's attitude towards the genre. Whereas earlier in his career he had reviewed his achievement in 'Karain' with a critical eye, finding 'something magazine'ish about it' (*Letters*, II, p. 57), he now strove, in the main, to produce short fiction that would appeal to the public's tastes rather than attempting to change them. One should not conclude, however, that he applied completely different artistic standards to all of his less serious fiction. When Garnett suggested that 'a happy ending' might make 'Freya of the Seven Isles' more acceptable to the editors of *Century Magazine*, Conrad's response was unequivocal: 'As to faking a "sunny" ending to my story I would see all the American Magazines and all the american Editors damned in heaps before lifting my pen for that task' (*Letters*, IV, p. 469). Revising his next work of fiction, the long novel *Chance*, Conrad decided to write a 'nicer' ending for the serial version; the new coda, in which Marlow acts as matchmaker for Flora and Powell, aimed at satisfying readers of *The New York Herald* without violating the plot's romantic structure. By refusing to alter 'Freya', a tragic story of separation and defeat, he was insisting on its imaginative integrity while acknowledging, at the same time, its slight material and simplified treatment. 'I've tried', he wrote to Garnett, 'to do a magazine-ish thing with some decency' (*Letters*, IV, p. 464).

III

When one begins to describe the nature of Conrad's overall achievement in short fiction, one soon discovers that his most forceful and suggestive works focus on the same concerns that inform his major novels. Thus 'Heart of Darkness' is like *Lord Jim*, parts of *Nostromo*, and other longer works in its emphasis on isolation from one's kind as a test of moral identity. In the same way, 'Typhoon' shows us the alienating power of a great wind and Captain MacWhirr's 'loneliness of command' in the face of cosmic and human chaos. Both 'Amy Foster' and 'The Secret Sharer' describe the community's rejection of an outsider, while affirming (at least in 'The Secret Sharer') individual attempts to seek out the common ground. In these stories, moreover, Conrad continues the work of Maupassant, Flaubert, and other European writers by challenging some of the genre's most cherished conventions, such as the positing of a consistently reliable story-teller who 'has counsel to give' (Benjamin, 'The storyteller', p. 85). Thus 'Heart of Darkness', 'Typhoon', 'Amy Foster', and 'The Secret Sharer' comprise a small but thematically significant and formally innovative body of work. Before he wrote these stories, however, Conrad had already demonstrated both his mastery of the shorter form and his radical efforts to renew it.

'All the bitterness of those days, all my puzzled wonder as to the meaning of all I saw – all my indignation at masquerading philanthropy – have been with me again, while I wrote ... I have divested myself of everything but pity – and some scorn' (*Letters*, I, p. 294). Readers of 'An Outpost of Progress' will find that Conrad's irony yields more scorn than pity; never-theless, it is the disruptive shifts from a critical distance to a more direct engagement that make this story so distinctively modern. Thus Kayerts, the ineffectual chief of an isolated trading-post, is viewed with sardonic detach-ment until he begins to fight with Carlier, his equally incompetent 'second in charge', over a few lumps of sugar. Suddenly, Conrad takes us inside the chief's mind as he recognizes that 'the position was without issue – that death and life had in a moment become equally difficult and terrible' (*HD*, p. 29). Like Kayerts, we must 'decode' important events from seemingly unconnected sense impressions: the shooting of Carlier – 'a loud explosion' and then 'a roar of red fire, thick smoke' (p. 30) – and the steamer's arrival – 'there was a fog, and somebody had whistled in the fog' (p. 32).[18] In the same way, Conrad uses grotesque images, like the Company steamer as a shrieking animal and the corpse of Kayerts as a dangling puppet, to dislodge us from safe positions of ironic detachment.

Given the expansionist views of many British readers in 1897, this story's content is as provocative as its technique. To be sure, the account of Carlier's former career as a cavalry officer in 'an army guaranteed from harm by several European Powers' refers specifically to Belgium, but Conrad's real target is European colonization as a whole. His title exploits one of the most familiar phrases in imperialist rhetoric; his two main char-acters, a bureaucrat and a soldier, represent the very foundations of Euro-pean social order; his references to 'the two pioneers of trade and progress' and 'those who ... bring light, and faith, and commerce to the dark places of the earth' parody contemporary journalese and mock Europe's 'civilizing mission'. Another important tenet of imperialist ideology, social Darwinism, is satirized in the scene in which a group of native traders visits the station. Conrad contrasts Kayerts and Carlier to the natives, who are 'perfect of limb' and stately of movement; even more pointedly, the white men use terms like 'the funny brute', 'Fine animals', and 'that herd' to describe the 'proceedings' from the heights of their verandah (pp. 9–10). The climactic order of such scenes, which reinforces the impression of Kayerts and Carlier as helpless victims of ideas and practices originating 'at home' in Europe, demonstrates Conrad's skill in handling an extended time period within the scope of a ten thousand word story. In 'The Idiots', written two months previously, he had made a rather heavy-handed first attempt, and it was five years before he succeeded again, with an impressive concentration, juxtapositioning, and selection of material, in 'Amy Foster'.

A more typical form of Conrad's best work in the genre is found in 'Youth', a story somewhat longer than 'An Outpost', which focuses on a single episode or event. Underrated by most critics, 'Youth' has a fast-moving and uncluttered narrative line, vivid immediacy and concreteness of impression, and a comic irony that (for the most part) undercuts the narrator's tendency to become sentimental about his past. The story reworks Conrad's real-life voyage between 1881 and 1883 as second mate in the *Palestine*. Although 'Youth' is not, as its author would sometimes insist, a strictly autobiographical work, the *Judea*'s initially slow progress from London to the Tyne and the delay in loading her, the storm that almost sinks her in the Channel, the months-long wait in Falmouth for repairs before she could set out again for Bangkok, the smouldering fire in her hold followed by the coal-gas explosion and ensuing conflagration, and her crew's approach to an Eastern shore in open boats are all verifiable parts of what he called 'a record of experience'. Perhaps for this reason, one might take all the more notice of the changes he made to his raw material, such as the invented collision with a steamer in Newcastle harbour (which adds to the *Judea*'s trials) and the altered composition of the ship's crew. Also significant is the romantic heightening of the land-fall: after the *Palestine* sank the crew rowed for about fourteen hours only, and landed at Muntok, which Conrad later remembered as 'a damned hole without any beach and without any glamour'.[19]

'There are those voyages', says Marlow at the beginning of his narrative, 'that seem ordered for the illustration of life, that might stand for a symbol of existence' (*HD*, pp. 93–4). Like 'Heart of Darkness', 'Typhoon', and 'The Secret Sharer', 'Youth' develops the implications of a single event, shaping it into an intensely metaphoric statement. Thus the differences between Conrad's and Marlow's voyages are significant because they help to 'illustrate' the absurdities and contradictions inherent in all human endeavour, the transformative yet transient power of youth, and the supreme value of collaborative labour and national solidarity. But the freshness and appeal of these themes is due to Conrad's bold experiments with impressionistic techniques. The use of Marlow as narrator opposes the spontaneous egoism of twenty to the wry wisdom of forty-two in a way that relativizes romantic illusions. The dual perspective also allows Conrad to distance himself from the text, to explore moral issues with flexibility, and to involve his readers through a surrogate audience – those four listeners grouped around the mahogany table. In their originality and Modernist verve, these strategies point the way to 'Heart of Darkness' and *Lord Jim*, but they also reward the readers of this fine early story.

With 'Typhoon', written some two and a half years later, Conrad continued to break new ground. Although a 'storm-piece' like *The Nigger of the 'Narcissus'*, this story is concerned with the manifold ways in which the steamer's ordeal differs from that of a sailing ship. The division of crew members into 'sailors and firemen', the patently unromantic labours of such as Hackett and Beale, the increased isolation of the captain – Conrad portrays these historical changes in a manner that combines vivid particulars with symbolic heightening. As to fresh techniques or approaches, his own commentary is somewhat misleading: 'This is my first attempt at treating a subject jocularly so to speak' (*Letters*, II, p. 304). It is certainly true that Captain MacWhirr's lack of imagination and stolidity of manner are portrayed comically, especially in his exchanges with Mr Jukes, the ship's first mate. As we have seen in the episode of the Siamese flag, however, much of this humour rebounds on Jukes and carries a greater burden of criticism. Particularly in the matter of the coolies, Jukes's imagination and high emotions lead to an increasing lack of judgement, charity, and genuine insight. Of course this type of ironic reversal does not signal a new direction in Conrad's work. Rather, two of the chief stylistic innovations in this story involve the author's handling of chronology and the shift away from a stable moral perspective in the coda.

Perhaps the most celebrated ellipsis in modern short fiction occurs between chapters V and VI of 'Typhoon', when Conrad passes over the climactic fury of the storm with an understatement:

> Before the renewed wrath of winds swooped on his ship, Captain MacWhirr was moved to declare, in a tone of vexation, as it were: 'I wouldn't like to lose her'.
>
> He was spared that annoyance.
>
> VI
>
> On a bright sunshiny day, with a breeze chasing her smoke far ahead, the *Nan-Shan* came into Fu-chau. (*TOT*, pp. 90–1)

This leap forward in time goes well beyond Maupassant's dictum that fiction presents an '*illusion* of reality' through 'selectivity' and 'orchestrated events' ('The Novel', p. 27). A post-modernist in this respect at least, Conrad draws attention to the art of 'yarning' (associated with Jukes) and challenges the reader's imagination to fill the gap. The impact of the ellipsis is all the greater because it follows immediately upon a very different type of narrative chronology. In his graphic presentation of the storm and its twenty-minute period of calm, Conrad makes the time of the story and the time of the narrative as equal as possible.[20] The result is to immerse readers in the 'real' ordeal and to emphasize the importance of 'direct' experience as a source of integrity and wisdom.

'Typhoon' does not explore this theme without some degree of scepticism. In the coda, the story-teller's moral authority dissolves and we see the various failures of MacWhirr, Jukes, and Rout to communicate in writing what they have learned. In the central action of the story, however, MacWhirr's simple practicality and humane instincts take on mythic significance. The image of his single voice penetrating 'the enormous discord of noises, as if sent out from some remote spot of peace beyond the black wastes of the gale' (p. 44) suggests the persistence of these virtues in a twentieth-century context of 'alienation' and apocalyptic philosophy.

Like 'Typhoon', 'Amy Foster' and 'The Secret Sharer' show us how Conrad's best short fiction tends to emphasize mythic or universal paradigms of experience. To be sure, in 'Amy Foster' Yanko Goorall's plight is also movingly concrete and individualized. Beginning with an account of the voyage by train and ship from a village in the Carpathian mountains and focusing on his experience as an unwelcome newcomer to Colebrook, Conrad renders many sights and sounds from Yanko's pious, childlike point of view and even reproduces the young man's speech patterns. Accordingly, common aspects of English village life are defamiliarized so that we share the foreigner's sense of cultural dislocation.[21] Yanko notices the 'bare poverty of the churches among so much wealth' and wonders 'why they were kept shut up on week-days' (*TOT*, p. 229); he describes the villagers' faces as 'closed' and 'mute', like 'faces of people from the other world – dead people –' (p. 227). Nor is Yanko's the only perspective rendered in such concrete and impressionistic terms. Portraying Colebrook's view of Yanko, Conrad uses regional language, colloquialisms, and the exact tones of the community's disapproval: '*They* wouldn't in their dinner hour lie flat on their backs on the grass to stare at the sky' (p. 230). Thus the differences between Yanko and the villagers are richly particularized while at the same time Conrad stresses their universality.

Although one of the sources for 'Amy Foster' is a local anecdote about a shipwrecked crew member of a German vessel, the plight of the foreigner in a tightly-knit community who is persecuted because of his strangeness is a recurrent theme in English and Continental literature. In this respect the story is linked to several well-known novels, including Victor Hugo's *Les Travailleurs de la mer* (1866) and H. G. Wells's *The Invisible Man* (1898). In the shorter fiction, the archetype of the outsider/castaway is thrown into relief, partly through the use of Dr Kennedy as narrator and partly because Conrad conflates the scene of Yanko's death with that of his arrival on the Kentish shore. At the beginning of his narrative Kennedy points to Yanko's place in the long tradition of the castaway, detailed in 'relations of ship-wrecks in the olden time':

> Often the castaways were only saved from drowning to die miserably from starvation on a barren coast; others suffered violent death or else slavery, passing through years of precarious existence with people to whom their strangeness was an object of suspicion, dislike or fear.   (*TOT*, p. 211)

Some of the key events in Yanko's experience are starkly reminiscent of Kennedy's account: he suffers a form of slavery under Mr Swaffer, he never gains more than a 'precarious footing' in the community, and he survives near-drowning and starvation on one night of 'storm and expo-sure' only to die 'sick – helpless – thirsty' on another (pp. 232, 239). His stoning by village boys and his dependence on Amy's gifts of bread and water heighten the ritualized aspect of his ordeal and further emphasize the story's sombre theme, that the fear and ignorance at the heart of group prejudice are ageless and irreducible. After the story appeared in print, Conrad feared that he had tried to 'make too much' of a 'simple' idea (*Letters*, II, pp. 391–2), but it is the combination of archetypal patterning and concretely realized multiple points of view that gives 'Amy Foster' its power to move and engage the reader.

In 'The Secret Sharer', the plight of the outsider is more ambiguously treated. Part of the story's fascination is its reluctance to endorse in a straightforward way the young captain's decision to shelter Leggatt and help him evade 'the law of the land'. In this respect 'The Secret Sharer' dramatizes a familiar Conradian paradox, for the captain's immediate sympathy for the outlaw conflicts with his need to achieve solidarity with his officers and crew. His division of loyalties is represented as an intensely problematic division of self: 'I was not wholly alone with my command; for there was that stranger in my cabin. Or rather, I was not completely and wholly with her. Part of me was absent' (*TOT*, p. 277). Conrad opposes the L-shaped cabin, which symbolizes the captain's 'secret partnership' with Leggatt, to the ship's deck and the 'established routine' of the community he ostensibly leads. In the story's dramatic ending, however, these contradictory stresses are resolved, and even before the Koh-ring crisis, the captain confesses that he is 'less torn in two' when he is with his 'double' (p. 275). Earlier still, before Leggatt's mysterious arrival, he admits that he is both a stranger to the ship and a stranger to himself. To integrate himself into the ship's community as commander, the captain must first demonstrate solidarity with Leggatt, the outsider and his 'other self'.

In posing this dilemma of dual responsibility, Conrad adds an important dimension to the *Doppelgänger* tradition, which conventionally treats the protagonist's 'double' as a side of the self that has been hidden or repressed. 'The Secret Sharer' is like other fictions of this type because it explores Leggatt's role as counterpart of the captain's outward, public identity: to deny his existence (as in a lie to Captain Archbold) would amount to self-mutilation. In effect, though, it is the captain's moral feelings for Leggatt as another individual – a fellow officer – that set this story apart from works like Stevenson's *Dr Jekyll and Mr Hyde* or Dostoevsky's 'The Double'.

Conrad's allusions to the Cain and Abel story in Genesis, and his direct reference to the passage in which the Lord sets his mark upon Cain, gives the captain's act of fellowship a parabolic resonance. The contrasts between Leggatt and Cain are as important as the parallels. Unlike Cain, Leggatt kills an 'Abel' who is threatening the safety of the community; unlike Cain as well, Leggatt goes into the wilderness without 'the brand of the curse ... to stay a slaying hand' (p. 294). At the same time, the captain's instinct to protect Leggatt does not merely constitute an affirmative response to the question 'Am I my brother's keeper?' Rather, it involves his discovery of an authentic self – in the sense used by psychologists who give primary significance to the interdependence of public and private roles – by recognizing his responsibility for another human being.

These three achievements, as well as 'Heart of Darkness' and his earlier stories, demonstrate Conrad's strong impulse to experiment with both style and content within the shorter form. Such is not always the case with writers who concentrate on both short fiction and novel genres. Often, as with Faulkner, they use their stories to work through the ideas that are developed more fully and more innovatively in their longer fictions. Even after the publication of 'To-morrow', when Conrad's short fiction became less complex in theme and less bold in technique, there were significant changes of direction in 'Il Conde', 'The Secret Sharer', and 'The Duel'. In at least one other sense of the term, then, the body of Conrad's shorter works bears witness to his 'Darwinian' approach to the writing of fiction.

NOTES

1 Critics have yet to decide what distinguishes a 'long short story' or 'novella' – a term Conrad never used – from a 'novel', if the work in question exceeds 35 or 40,000 words. In the class of short fiction, I include works that both Conrad and his publishers treated as 'stories' rather than 'novels' when they were printed in book form. For example, although 'The End of the Tether' is longer than *The Shadow-Line*, it was published in a volume of stories, whereas *The Shadow-Line* appeared separately as a novel. For alternative ways of handling this problem, see Graver, *Conrad's Short Fiction*, pp. viii–ix, and Hynes, 'The art of telling', pp. xi–xii.

2 On 3 June 1896, *The Cornhill Magazine* had solicited a short story of from 6,000 to 8,000 words. Their letter is reproduced in Graver, *Conrad's Short Fiction*, pp. 17–18.

3 See Memorandum of Agreement dated 13 April 1883 between Henry James and James R. Osgood & Co. Reproduced in Anesko, *'Friction with the Market'*, pp. 83–4. Anesko also provides useful extracts from James's unpublished letters.

4 On 8 September 1898, William Blackwood wrote to Conrad, 'I have always looked upon the writing of fiction as something not to be bounded altogether by time or space', Blackburn, ed., *Joseph Conrad: Letters to William Blackwood and David S. Meldrum*, pp. 28–9. Blackwood's generosity with regard to the ever-lengthening serialization of *Lord Jim* is well known, but his willingness to give Conrad a free hand at the very beginning of a project is equally remarkable (see *Ibid.*, pp. 35–6, and 57).

5 Letter to William James, 20 May 1884, James Papers, Houghton Library, Harvard University. Quoted in Anesko, *'Friction with the Market'*, p. 85. Although *The Bostonians* is universally regarded as an example of James's failure to control his material, he seems to have been aware almost from its inception that his work might extend.

6 Letter to James R. Osgood, 29 January 1884, James Papers, Duke University. Quoted in Anesko, *'Friction with the Market'*, p. 86.

7 When Conrad sent the first pages of manuscript to J. B. Pinker, he estimated that the story would be 'not very much' longer than 'The Brute', which is 8,200 words (*Letters*, III, p. 317).

8 Ford claimed that Conrad 'never wrote a true short story' (*Joseph Conrad: A Personal Remembrance*, p. 218). For a recent and less dogmatic commentary, see Higdon and Sheard, ' "The end is the devil" '.

9 *Almayer's Folly* is in some respects a special case. Conrad took five years to write his first novel, during which he was also employed in the Congo and at sea. We do not know if the work began as a short story.

10 Some time between mid-August and late October 1894, Conrad had developed a 'sketch' that focused on a single event (*Letters*, I, p. 185).

11 On the other hand, Said interprets the phrase to mean that 'evolution, order, and mastery could be enacted' within a more disciplined form (*Joseph Conrad and the Fiction of Autobiography*, p. 27).

12 Letter to J. B. Pinker, Friday [November] 1913, Berg Collection, New York Public Library.

13 The formal and thematic links between 'Heart of Darkness' and *Lord Jim*, and

'The Secret Sharer' and *Under Western Eyes* point to yet another way in which Conrad's short and long fictions are interrelated. See Fraser, *Interweaving Patterns in the Works of Joseph Conrad*, ch. 5 and 6.

14 For an account of Conrad's finances, see Watts, *Joseph Conrad: A Literary Life*, and Carabine, Review of *Joseph Conrad: A Literary Life*. Both contrast the size of the payments Conrad received for stories to the wages of his maid and secretary. The £75 paid for 'Typhoon' was not, in fact, large compared with the £125 that *The Strand* paid H. G. Wells in the same year for a story of much lesser quality (Wilson, ed., *Arnold Bennett and H. G. Wells*, p. 59).

15 *Blackwood's Edinburgh Magazine*, September 1989, p. 323 (emphasis added).

16 These changes to Conrad's text have been established by comparing the serial version with the manuscript, entitled 'A Voyage' (Everett Needham Case Library, Colgate University).

17 On the contradictions inherent in the ending of *The Nigger of the 'Narcissus'*, see Berthoud, Introduction, pp. xii–xiii.

18 The term was coined by Ian Watt. See his *Conrad and the Nineteenth Century*, pp. 176–7.

19 Letter of 24 April 1922. Quoted in Najder, *Joseph Conrad: A Chronicle*, p. 77.

20 Conrad's intensely scenic presentation gives the impression of equivalence because its 'speed' is 'steady'. See Genette, *Narrative Discourse*, p. 87.

21 In revising the story, Conrad focused on heightening Yanko's impressions and opposing them to the point of view of the villagers. See Fraser, 'Conrad's revisions to Amy Foster'.

WORKS CITED

Anesko, Michael. *'Friction with the Market': Henry James and the Profession of Authorship*. New York: Oxford University Press, 1986

Benjamin, Walter. 'The storyteller'. *Illuminations*. 1955. Ed. Hannah Arendt. New York: Schocken Books, 1968, pp. 83–109

Berthoud, Jacques. Introduction. *The Nigger of the 'Narcissus'*. Ed. Jacques Berthoud. Oxford: Oxford University Press, 1984, pp. vii–xxvi

Blackburn, William, ed. *Joseph Conrad: Letters to William Blackwood and David S. Meldrum*. Durham, NC: Duke University Press, 1958

Carabine, Keith. Review of *Joseph Conrad: A Literary Life* by Cedric Watts. *The Conradian* 16.2 (1992), 85–91

Conrad, Joseph. *'Heart of Darkness' and Other Tales*. Ed. Cedric Watts. Oxford: Oxford University Press, 1990

The Nigger of the 'Narcissus'. 1897. Ed. Jacques Berthoud. Oxford: Oxford University Press, 1984

'Typhoon' and Other Tales. Ed. Cedric Watts. Oxford: Oxford University Press, 1986

Ford, Ford Madox. Editorial. *The English Review* 1 (1909), 356–60

Joseph Conrad: A Personal Remembrance. 1924. New York: Octagon, 1965

Fraser, Gail. 'Conrad's revisions to "Amy Foster"'. *Conradiana* 20.3 (1988), 181–93

Interweaving Patterns in the Works of Joseph Conrad. Ann Arbor: UMI Research Press, 1988

Friedman, Norman. 'Recent short story theories: problems in definition'. In *Short Story Theory at a Crossroads*. Ed. Susan Lohafer and Jo Ellyn Clarey. Baton Rouge: Louisiana State University Press, 1989, pp. 13–31

Genette, Gérard. *Narrative Discourse: An Essay in Method*. Tr. Jane E. Levin. Ithaca: Cornell University Press, 1980

Graver, Lawrence. *Conrad's Short Fiction*. Berkeley: University of California Press, 1969

Higdon, David Leon and Robert F. Sheard. ' "The end is the devil": the conclusions to Conrad's *Under Western Eyes*'. *Studies in the Novel* 19 (1987), 187–96

Hynes, Samuel. 'The art of telling: an introduction to Conrad's tales'. *The Complete Short Fiction of Joseph Conrad*. Ed. Samuel Hynes. London: Pickering; Hopewell, NJ: Ecco Press, 1992, III, pp. xi–xiii

James, Henry. Preface to 'The Author of Beltraffio'. In *The Art of the Novel*. Ed. Leon Edel. New York: Scribner's, 1934, pp. 232–40

Lucas, Michael. 'Conrad's adjectival eccentricity'. *Style* 25 (1991), 130–9

Maupassant, Guy de. 'The Novel'. *Pierre and Jean*. 1888. Tr. Leonard Tancock. Harmondsworth: Penguin Books, 1979, pp. 21–35

Najder, Zdzisław. *Joseph Conrad: A Chronicle*. Tr. Halina Carroll-Najder. New Brunswick, NJ: Rutgers University Press; Cambridge: Cambridge University Press, 1983

Orel, Harold. *The Victorian Short Story: Development and Triumph of a Literary Genre*. Cambridge: Cambridge University Press, 1986

Said, Edward W. *Joseph Conrad and the Fiction of Autobiography*. Cambridge, MA: Harvard University Press, 1966

Watt, Ian. *Conrad in the Nineteenth Century*. Berkeley: University of California Press, 1979; London: Chatto & Windus, 1980

Watts, Cedric. *Joseph Conrad: A Literary Life*. London: Macmillan, 1989

Wilson, Harris, ed. *Arnold Bennett and H. G. Wells*. Urbana: University of Illinois Press, 1960

3

CEDRIC WATTS

'Heart of Darkness'

Conrad's 'Heart of Darkness' is a rich, vivid, layered, paradoxical, and problematic novella or long tale; a mixture of oblique autobiography, traveller's yarn, adventure story, psychological odyssey, political satire, symbolic prose-poem, black comedy, spiritual melodrama, and sceptical meditation. It has proved to be 'ahead of its time': an exceptionally proleptic text. First published in 1899 as a serial in *Blackwood's Edinburgh Magazine*, it became extensively influential during subsequent decades, and reached a zenith of critical acclaim in the period 1950–75. During the final quarter of the twentieth century, however, while its influence became even more pervasive, the tale was vigorously assailed on political grounds by various feminist critics and by some left-wing and Third World commentators.[1] In this essay, I discuss the novella's changing fortunes in 'the whirligig of time' (Feste's phrase from *Twelfth Night*) and argue that even now it retains some capacity to criticize its critics.

I

The phrase 'ahead of its times' first needs defence. What put it *ahead* of them was that it was intelligently *of* them: Conrad addressed issues of the day with such alert adroitness and ambiguity that he anticipated many twentieth-century preoccupations.

In some obvious respects, 'Heart of Darkness' belongs to the late nineteenth century. This is a tale of travel, of adventurous exploration, of an 'outpost of progress'. It draws on the kind of material made popular by Rider Haggard, Rudyard Kipling, R. L. Stevenson, and numerous lesser writers: appropriate fiction for the heyday of imperialism. It is a story of a journey into 'darkest Africa', a region given publicity not only by the explorations of H. M. Stanley but also by the Berlin Conference of 1885, which had recognized the existence of the 'Congo Free State' as the personal possession of King Leopold II of Belgium. It was an era of intense international rivalry for colonial possessions. There was widespread interest in the political, moral, and psychological challenges afforded to Europeans by African colonization. The tale dealt with atavism and decadence, at a time when these topics had been given currency by Zola and the 'Naturalists', by Cesare Lombroso (the criminologist) and Max Nordau (author of *Degeneration*), and by the controversies over the Aesthetic Movement. Nordau, for instance, claimed that civilization was being corrupted by the influence of people who were morally degenerate; and his account of the 'highly-gifted degenerate', the charismatic yet depraved genius, may have influenced Conrad's depiction of Kurtz. A larger matter still was that the popularization of Darwin's theory of evolution had raised widespread anxieties about human nature, its origins, and its future. Finally, the popularization of Lord Kelvin's Second Law of Thermodynamics, the law of entropy, had suggested that eventually, as the sun cooled in the heavens, life would become utterly extinct on this planet, which would be doomed to ultimate darkness. In his tale, Conrad addressed or alluded to all these issues.[2] Characteristically, he had combined popular elements with highly sophisticated analysis. The popular elements included topical allusions, an adventurous narrative, and a range of exotic material. The treatment was challengingly versatile and oblique.

In 'Heart of Darkness', a story is told by a British gentleman to other British gentlemen. The convention of 'the tale within the tale' was familiar and, at that time, particularly appropriate. Among writers of the era whose works Conrad appreciated, it was used by Turgenev, Maupassant, James, Kipling, Crane, Cunninghame Graham, and Wells. This convention was not only a reflection of the social customs of an age of gentlemen's clubs and semi-formal social gatherings at which travellers would meet to compare notes and exchange yarns about foreign experiences. It also emphasized the interplay of personal and social experience, perhaps dramatizing relativism of perception, limitations of knowledge, or conflicts between private and public codes. From its very title onwards ('Heart of Darkness' invokes contradictory notions), the tale is full of paradoxes. And the 1890s were a decade in which paradoxes, whether small or large, abounded in literature. They occurred not merely in the quotable epigrams of Oscar Wilde but in the large-scale paradoxes in the works of, for instance, Samuel Butler, Edward Carpenter, George Bernard Shaw, Thomas Hardy, and Wilde again (in his essay 'The Soul of Man under Socialism', for example). Here ideological contradiction gained rhetorical compression. Previously, Baudelaire had declared that nature provided 'forests of symbols',[3] and, in an era when symbolism in prose and verse commanded fresh interest, Conrad was able to voice his paradoxes not only through explicit statement but also through ambiguous images and many-faceted symbols. The narrative of 'Heart of Darkness' offers, for example, the following paradoxes:

> Civilization can be barbaric. It is both a hypocritical veneer and a valuable achievement to be vigilantly guarded.
>
> Society saves us from corruption, yet society is corrupt.
>
> Imperialism may be redeemed by 'an idea at the back of it', but imperialism, irredeemably, is 'robbery with violence'.
>
> Brotherhood transcends racial differences, but 'we live, as we dream – alone'.
>
> The truth should be communicated, but women should be denied it. Communication of the essential is impossible.
>
> Morality is a sham. Without it, human beings become sham humans.
>
> Awareness is better than unawareness. We may become aware that it is better to be unaware, and we may even learn that ignorance is bliss.
>
> A person who sells his soul does at least have a soul to sell, and may gain a significance denied to the mediocre.

Repeatedly, images prove paradoxical. The customary associations of white and black, of light and dark, are variously exploited and subverted. The city is 'sepulchral'; London is associated with 'brooding gloom'; and the very title of the tale refers not only to the heart of 'darkest Africa' but also to Kurtz's corruption, to benighted London, and to innumerable kinds of darkness and obscurity, physical, moral, and ontological.

Few prominent features of 'Heart of Darkness' could not be traced back through the nineteenth century into the distant past. Its satiric treatment of imperialism had precedents in Swift's *Gulliver's Travels* (1726), in Voltaire's *Candide* (1759), and in Byron's *Don Juan* (1819–24). The charismatic Kurtz, brilliant yet depraved, corrupted yet fascinating, descends from the 'hero-villains' of Gothic fiction, the most notable of these being Emily Brontë's Heathcliff (who, like Ann Radcliffe's Montoni, is in turn a literary descendant of Milton's Satan, regarded by the Romantics as a sublime rebel). Furthermore, the tale's imagery suggests, Kurtz is a modern Faust, who has sold his soul for power and gratification; so perhaps Charlie Marlow owes a debt to Christopher Marlowe.[4] Even that oblique narrative convention that was so popular in the 1890s can be related to the poetic convention of the dramatic monologue, exploited by Browning and Tennyson, and to the sophisticated employment of multiple narrators in Brontë's

Wuthering Heights. And the method could be traced via Coleridge's 'Rime of the Ancyent Marinere' back to Chaucer's *Canterbury Tales* and ultimately to the inset narratives of the Homeric epics. Marlow's nightmarish journey is explicitly likened to Dante's imaginary journey in *The Inferno*; and the allusions to ancient Rome help to recall *The Aeneid*, particularly Book VI, in which Aeneas, the legendary imperialist, travels through the underworld.[5]

Of course, the novella also has a diversity of sources in Conrad's personal experience. His scepticism about 'the imperial mission' can be related to the facts that he was born into a Poland which (having been partitioned by Austria, Prussia, and Russia) had vanished from the map of Europe, and that his parents were redoubtable patriots who were exiled by the Russian authorities as punishment for their conspiratorial patriotism. Partly as a result of his parents' political struggle against Russian oppression, both of them died when Conrad was still a boy. Hence his keen sense of the price in human terms exacted by political idealism, and, indeed, by idealism of various kinds. Hence, too, his marked sense of isolation. The contrast between the romanticism of his father, Apollo Korzeniowski, and the astutely sceptical advice of his uncle and guardian, Tadeusz Bobrowski, helped to develop his sense of paradox and ethical conflict.[6] Then Conrad's many years at sea nurtured a respect for the ethical implications of seamanship – for an ethic of work and duty. This is an ethic that Marlow finds sustaining and of which the tale's marine boiler-maker is a modest examplar, and it is made incongruously tangible in that manual of seamanship, by 'Tower, Towson – some such name', found in the heart of the jungle.

'Heart of Darkness' was prompted mainly by Conrad's own journey into the Congo in 1890. During this journey, he noted evidence of atrocities, exploitation, inefficiency, and hypocrisy, and it fully convinced him of the disparity between imperialism's rhetoric and the harsh reality of 'the vilest scramble for loot that ever disfigured the history of human conscience' (*LE*, p. 17).[7] That experience provided a basis for the knowledgeable indignation of 'Heart of Darkness'. Certainly, however, the combination of that indignation and a visionary-symbolic intention results in satiric exaggeration: the inefficiency and incompetence displayed in the tale are so widespread as to make it seem unlikely that the imperialists in Africa could ever establish viable railways, road systems, or towns. Similarly, as Norman Sherry has shown, the real-life counterpart to Kurtz, Georges Antoine Klein, was a counterpart only in the fact that he was an ailing trader in the Congo who had to be transported back downstream on Conrad's vessel and who died on the voyage. There is no evidence at all that he shared Kurtz's brilliance and depravity.[8]

Other, more intimate, personal factors also provided materials for the tale. Conrad was a lively raconteur who used to swap yarns with G. F. W. Hope, W. B. Keen, and C. H. Mears on Hope's yawl, the *Nellie*, anchored in the Thames. Hence, the setting and manner of the tale's opening. Hope was a company director, like the host in the tale; Keen an accountant; Mears a solicitor. Conrad went to Brussels to gain employment with the Belgian company that organized trade in the Congo; Marlow travels to the 'sepulchral city', identifiably Brussels, for his interview. Conrad, like Marlow, gained the interview through the influence exerted by an aunt (though in Conrad's case the person he addressed as 'Aunt' – Marguerite Poradowska – was the wife of a distant cousin). Madame Poradowska was in mourning when Conrad called on her after his journey to the Congo, for her husband had recently died; and, since Conrad was emotionally attracted to her, she evidently provided a model for the bereaved Intended, for whom Marlow feels incipient love.[9] If Marlow has various features in common with Conrad, the depiction of Kurtz was probably inflected by the author's sense of similarity between Kurtz's plight and that of the dedicated creative writer. In a passage of the autobiographical work *A Personal Record* that offers reflections on his own aims as an author, Conrad says:

> In that interior world where his thought and his emotions go seeking for the experience of imagined adventures, there are no policemen, no law, no pressure of circumstance or dread of opinion to keep him within bounds. Who then is going to say Nay to his temptations if not his conscience?   (p. xviii)

If, therefore, the tale can be so clearly related to Conrad's own prior experience, to various concerns of the 1890s, and to a diversity of long literary traditions, what makes it proleptic? How did it come to be 'ahead of its times'? The answer lies in the combination of intrinsic and extrinsic factors. The intrinsic factors include: its satiric verve and sceptical boldness; its suggestive density and ambiguity – the layered narrations, ironic meanings, symbolic suggestions; its radical paradoxicality; and its designed opacities. The extrinsic factors include the following. The burgeoning of what became known as cultural Modernism, and the consequent readiness of numerous critics to appreciate and commend the features they recognized as Modernist.[10] The related development of critical procedures that were particularly responsive to ambiguity, irony, and symbolic multiplicity within a work. The increase of scepticism concerning religion, history, civilization, and human nature; though complicated by some religious nostalgia, by surviving modes of faith, and by some humanistic hopes. The general development of antipathy to imperialism: an antipathy that, for many readers, the text seemed to echo (though in course of time other readers disputed this). 'Heart of Darkness' was abundantly suggestive and remarkable quotable. Repeatedly it seemed, prophetically, to sum up areas of experience that gained new prominence in the light of historical events in the twentieth century. If offered a concise iconography of modern corruption and disorder. The tale became an anthology of epitomes.

The First World War showed how men could be engulfed, diminished, and destroyed by man-made organizations and technology. Conrad seemed to have anticipated this in his depiction of the ways in which men in Africa served, and died for, a remorseless organization. He portrays men dwarfed by the system that dominates them and by an alien environment. Hitlerism and the Holocaust seemed to have been anticipated in the depiction of Kurtz's charismatic depravity: Kurtz, potentially ' a splendid leader of an extreme party', celebrated for his intoxicating eloquence, is the persuasive genius whose grandiose ambitions are reduced to the exclamation 'Exterminate all the brutes!'[11] During the century, there was increasing recognition of a vast disparity between the (often religious or idealistic) propaganda of imperialism and its harshly exploitative realities. This too served to vindicate much of the tale, which declared: 'The conquest of the earth ... mostly means the taking it away from those who have a different complexion or slightly flatter noses than ourselves' (HD, p. 140). That 'Heart of Darkness' even seemed to have offered a critical commentary on the Vietnam War was recognized by Francis Ford Coppola's spectacular film, Apocalypse Now (1979), which simultaneously generated the film Heart of Darkness, a record of the making of Apocalypse Now that was a testament to Kurtzian corruption and decadence in real life. Later, Nicolas Roeg directed another version for the cinema. It seemed that the sombre, sceptical aspects of the tale had been amply vindicated by the follies and brutalities of twentieth-century history.

In 1902, Edward Garnett, Conrad's friend and sometime literary mentor, wrote: ' "Heart of Darkness" in the subtlety of its criticism of life is the high-water mark of the author's talent' (Sherry, ed., Conrad: The Critical Heritage, p. 133). By 1974, C. B Cox could confidently declare: 'This masterpiece has become one of those amazing modern fictions, such as Thomas Mann's Death in Venice or Kafka's The Trial, which throw light on the whole nature of twentieth-century art, its problems and achievements' (Introduction, p. vii). Repeatedly, the tale seemed to have heralded twentieth-century cultural preoccupations. Sigmund Freud's emphasis on the divided self, on the striving, lustful, anarchic id seeking gratification despite the countervailing pressure of the ego or super-ego, had been anticipated in the depiction of Kurtz's ferocious fulfilments in the Congo. C. G. Jung, in turn, seemed almost to be recalling Kurtz and the tale's imagery of light and darkness when he emphasized that the 'visionary mode of artistic creation' is

> a strange something that derives its existence from the hinterland of man's mind – that suggests the abyss of time separating us from pre-human ages, or evokes a super-human world of contrasting light and darkness. It is a primordial experience which surpasses man's understanding, and to which he is therefore in danger of succumbing.
>
> (*Modern Man in Search of a Soul*, p. 180)

The interest of Freud and Jung (and later of Northrop Frye, Joseph Campbell, and Claude Lévi-Strauss) in the importance of myth was shared by numerous Modernist writers, and here again Conrad seemed to have anticipated them. In 1923, T. S. Eliot praised James Joyce for developing in *Ulysses* the 'mythic method', whereby references to ancient myths could coordinate works which addressed 'the immense panorama of futility and anarchy which is contemporary history' ('*Ulysses*, order and myth', p. 483). But that readiness to stage ironic contrasts between the mythic past and the materialistic present, a readiness so marked in Eliot's *The Waste Land* itself, was already a feature of 'Heart of Darkness', which, while describing present-day confusion, invoked memories of the Faust myth, *The Divine Comedy*, and *The Aeneid*. Indeed, Eliot acknowledged a debt to Conrad: the original epigraph of *The Waste Land* was a passage from 'Heart of Darkness' that concludes with Kurtz's words, 'The horror! The horror!', and the descriptions of the Thames in 'The Fire Sermon' draw details from the opening of Conrad's tale.[12] More importantly, 'Heart of Darkness' had suggested the appalling paradox that whereas the majority of men who lead secular lives are heading for a death which is extinction, Kurtz has at least the significance granted by the intensity of his evil. If he has sold his soul, at least he had a soul to sell. And this paradox, too, Eliot developed in *The Waste Land* and in his critical essays: '[D]amnation itself is an immediate form of salvation – of salvation from the ennui of modern life, because it at last gives some significance to living ... The worst that can be said of most of our malefactors ... is that they are not men enough to be damned' (*Selected Essays*, pp. 427, 429). Graham Greene exploited the same paradox in *Brighton Rock* (1938), and Greene often acknowledged his debt to Conrad. In the film *The Third Man* (1949), written by Greene and directed by Carol Reed, the villain, Harry Lime, has a Kurtzian charisma, and one of his henchmen is called 'Baron Kurtz'. Lime was played by Orson Welles, who had himself attempted to make a film of 'Heart of Darkness'. In 1899, in its vividly graphic techniques, particularly the rapid montage, the overlapping images, and the symbolic use of colour and *chiaroscuro*,

'Heart of Darkness' had been adventurously cinematic at a time when film – rudimentary then – was not.

Familiar characteristics of Modernist texts are the sense of absurdity or meaninglessness, of human isolation, and of the problematic nature of communication. Eliot, Kafka, Woolf, and Beckett are among the writers who grappled with these matters, all of which had been sharply depicted in 'Heart of Darkness'. The sense of the defilement of the natural environment by man's technology, another powerful feature of the narrative, was later to be addressed by Eliot, Lawrence, Greene, and numerous subsequent writers. Kurtz's words 'The horror! The horror!' were eventually repeated by Colonel Kurtz, played by a mumbling Marlon Brando, in *Apocalypse Now*; but before repeating them, he quoted a few lines from Eliot's poem, 'The Hollow Men'. This made a neat cultural irony, since 'The Hollow Men' takes as its epigraph 'Mistah Kurtz – he dead' and develops the Conradian theme of the absurdity of secular existence.

The tale's cultural echoes extend through time and across continents. Kurtz is a literary father of Thompson, the demoralized imperial idealist in the acclaimed novel of Kenya in the 1960s, *A Grain of Wheat* (1967) by Ngugi Wa Thiong'o. Kurtz's report for 'The Society for the Suppression of Savage Customs' has its counterpart in Thompson's essay, 'Prospero in Africa'. Kurtz concludes: 'Exterminate all the brutes!'; Thompson reflects: 'Eliminate the vermin' (pp. 48–50, 117). A radically different novel, Robert Stone's *Dog Soldiers* (1975), a prize-winning thriller depicting drug-driven corruption and brutality in the United States, took as its apt epigraph the following lines from Conrad's tale:

> 'I've seen the devil of violence, and the devil of greed, and the devil of hot desire; but, by all the stars! these were strong, lusty, red-eyed devils, that swayed and drove men – men, I tell you. But as I stood on this hillside, I foresaw that in the blinding sunshine of that land I would become acquainted with a flabby, pretending, weak-eyed devil of a rapacious and pitiless folly.'
>
> (p. 155)[13]

II

By the 1970s, 'Heart of Darkness' had accumulated extensive critical acclaim and been widely disseminated as a 'set text' in colleges and universities. It was now 'canonical'. Even if it had flaws (perhaps 'adjectival insistence'),[14] its strengths far exceeded its weaknesses. Its cultural influence was clearly pervasive. This novella served as a reference-point, an anthology of scenes and passages that in various ways epitomized twentieth-century problems and particularly twentieth-century modes of exploitation, corruption, and decadence. Yet, as Feste says in *Twelfth Night*, 'the whirligig of time brings in his revenges', and in the 1970s radical critical attacks on 'Heart of Darkness' developed. For Terry Eagleton, a Marxist, Conrad's art was an art of ideological contradiction resulting in stalemate:

> Conrad neither believes in the cultural superiority of the colonialist nations, nor rejects colonialism outright. The 'message' of *Heart of Darkness* is that Western civilisation is at base as barbarous as African society – a viewpoint which disturbs imperialist assumptions to the precise degree that it reinforces them.   (*Criticism and Ideology*, p. 135)

But already a far more damaging political attack had been made. In a 1975 lecture, the distinguished Nigerian novelist, Chinua Achebe, declared that Conrad was 'a bloody racist' ('An image of Africa', p. 788). Achebe asserted that 'Heart of Darkness' depicts Africa as 'a place of negations ... in comparison with which Europe's own state of spiritual grace will be manifest' (p. 783). The Africans are dehumanized and degraded, seen as grotesques or as a howling mob. They are denied speech, or are granted speech only to condemn themselves out of their own mouths. We see 'Africa as setting and backdrop which eliminates the African as human factor. Africa as a metaphysical battlefield devoid of all recognizable humanity, into which the wandering European enters at his peril' (p. 788). The result, he says, is 'an offensive and totally deplorable book' that promotes racial intolerance and is therefore to be condemned.

Achebe's lecture had a powerful impact, and its text was repeatedly reprinted and widely discussed. 'Heart of Darkness', which had seemed to be bold and astute in its attacks on imperialism, was now revealed as a work that, in the opinion of a leading African writer, was actually pro-imperialist in its endorsement of racial prejudice. The next onslaught came from feminist critics and had a similar basis. While Achebe had seen the Africans as marginalized and demeaningly stereotyped, various feminist critics felt that the tale similarly belittled women. Nina Pelikan Straus, Bette London, Johanna M. Smith, and Elaine Showalter were among those who claimed that 'Heart of Darkness' was not only imperialist but also 'sexist'. Straus declared that male critics had repeatedly become accomplices of Marlow, who 'brings truth to men by virtue of his bringing falsehood to women' ('The exclusion of the Intended', p. 130). Kurtz's Intended, denied a name, is also denied access to truth so as to maintain the dominative brotherhood of males:

> The woman reader ... is in the position to insist that Marlow's cowardice consists of his inability to face the dangerous self that is the form of his own

masculinist vulnerability: his own complicity in the racist, sexist, imperialist, and finally libidinally satisfying he has shared with Kurtz.   (p. 135)

Smith, similarly, alleged that the tale 'reveals the collusion of imperialism and patriarchy: Marlow's narrative aims to "colonize" and "pacify" both savage darkness and women' ('Too beautiful altogether', p. 180).

In short, a text that had once appeared to be 'ahead of its times', a nineteenth-century tale that anticipated twentieth-century cultural developments and epitomized twentieth-century concerns, now seemed to be dated – outstripped by recent advances. A text that had so often been praised for its political radicalism now looked politically reactionary. The problems raised by the controversy over the merits of 'Heart of Darkness' were now problems not merely about the reading of details but also about the very basis of evaluation of literary texts, about the relationship between literary appreciation and moral/political judgement.

III

If we re-read 'Heart of Darkness' in the light of Achebe's comments, various disturbing features soon gain prominence. For example, although the Europeans manifest various kinds of corruption and turpitude, the Faustian theme associates supernatural evil with the African wilderness. The dying Kurtz crawls ashore towards some ritual ceremony, and Marlow tries to head him off:

> 'I tried to break the spell – the heavy, mute spell of the wilderness – that seemed to draw him to its pitiless breast by the awakening of forgotten and brutal instincts, by the memory of gratified and monstrous passions. This alone, I was convinced, had driven him out to the edge of the forest, to the bush, towards the gleam of fires, the throb of drums, the drone of weird incantations; this alone had beguiled his unlawful soul beyond the bounds of permitted aspirations'.   (p. 234)

And within the wilderness:

> 'A black figure stood up, strode on long black legs, waving long black arms, across the glow. It had horns – antelope horns, I think – on its head. Some sorcerer, some witch-man, no doubt: it looked fiend-like enough'.   (p. 233)

In religious matters, Marlow seems usually a sceptic. Certainly there is an atheistic implication in his remark that life is 'that mysterious arrangement of merciless logic for a futile purpose'. Yet, where Kurtz's depravity is concerned, Marlow seems willing to endorse a belief in supernatural evil – and that evil is specifically associated with the people of the African jungle. A sceptical reader today might conclude that we are being offered not only a mystification of corruption, but also a racist mystification. One problem here, however, is that the observations quoted are Marlow's, and they thus lack the authority that would be granted by an 'omniscient narrator'. Achebe says that Conrad 'neglects to hint however subtly or tentatively at an alternative frame of reference ... Marlow seems to me to enjoy Conrad's complete confidence' (p. 787). Against this, however, one might object that Conrad has deliberately opted for doubly oblique narration. Marlow's tale, which is interrupted by dissenting comments by his hearers, is being reported to us by an anonymous character. Marlow himself has explicitly drawn attention to the difficulty of seeing truly and reporting correctly, and he is known for his 'inconclusive' narratives. His tone when describing Kurtz's last hours is more insistently rhetorical and less observantly acute than at other times. The general effect of the oblique procedures may be to make us think: 'Marlow can probably be trusted most of the time, but we need to keep up our guard. He isn't fully reliable'. Indeed, Conrad took greater pains than did most users of the oblique narrative convention to preserve the possibility of critical distance between the reader and the fictional narrator.

Nevertheless, Achebe forcefully exposed the text's temporality. A number of features, including Marlow's casual use of the term 'nigger', clearly reveal the tale's Victorian provenance. Its defenders now ran the risk of using a suspect logic. When Marlow said things of which they approved, they might give Conrad credit; when he said things that embarrassed them, they might cite the oblique convention, blame Marlow, and exonerate Conrad. Clearly, such logic could be neatly reversed by their opponents.

Achebe's telling attack was fierce and sweeping, and deliberately polemical, and he later moderated its ferocity.[15] Other Third World writers, including Ngugi Wa Thiong'o, Wilson Harris, Frances B. Singh, and C. P. Sarvan, argued that while Conrad was certainly ambivalent on racial matters, 'Heart of Darkness' was progressive in its satiric accounts of the colonialists. Singh noted that though 'Heart of Darkness' was vulnerable in several respects, including the association of Africans with supernatural evil, the story should remain in 'the canon of works indicting colonialism'. Sarvan concluded: 'Conrad was not entirely immune to the infection of the beliefs and attitudes of his age, but he was ahead of most in trying to break free'.[16] To be fair to 'Heart of Darkness', as to any literary text, we need to take account of its date. As Sarvan indicates, relative to the standards prevailing in the 1890s, the heyday of Victorian imperialism, 'Heart of Darkness' was indeed progressive in its criticism of imperialist activities in Africa, and, implicitly, of imperialist activities generally. Conrad was writing at a time when most British people, including many socialists, would have regarded imperialism as an admirable enterprise. He was also helping the cause of Africans in the Congo by drawing attention to their ill-treatment. In practice, the tale contributed to the international protest campaign that strove to curb Belgian excesses there. E. D. Morel, leader of the Congo Reform Association, stated that 'Heart of Darkness' was 'the most powerful thing ever written on the subject'. Conrad sent encouraging letters to his acquaintance (and Morel's collaborator in the campaign), Roger Casement, who in 1904 published a parliamentary report documenting atrocities committed by Belgian administrators.[17] Achebe says that 'Heart of Darkness' marginalizes the Africans, but Marlow gives them prominence when he describes, with telling vividness, the plight of the chain-gang and of the exploited workers dying in the grove. What the other Europeans choose to ignore, Marlow observes with sardonic indignation. Relegation, which is criticized, is a theme of the narrative.

That the tale appeared in 1899 offers some defence against feminists' attacks, too, though it is defence and not vindication. Marlow's patronizing views of women, which might well have been quite widely shared by men of that time, are problematized by the text in ways that yield ironies that feminist critics could exploit. Marlow, who says that women are 'out of touch with truth ... in a world of their own' (p. 148), depends on his aunt for a job, and therefore her world is also his. Furthermore, Marlow's lie to the Intended – the cause of so much critical debate – is presented in a debate-provoking way. Marlow registers confusion ('It seemed ... that the heavens would fall'; 'The heavens do not fall for such a trifle'), and he had previously said 'I hate, detest, and can't bear a lie', so his own words expose a double standard by which women are (a) culpably ignorant of truth, and (b) in need of falsehood supplied by males. In any case, characteristically 'virile' activities of men – colonial warfare and the conquest of the 'wilderness' – have been depicted by Marlow as virtually deranged in their destructive futility.

A larger question is raised by these political criticisms of 'Heart of Darkness'. A standard procedure, illustrated by Achebe and Straus, is to judge the tale according to whether its inferred political outlook tallies with that of the critic: to the extent that the critic's views are reflected, the tale is commended; to the extent that they are not, the tale is condemned. This procedure is familiar but odd. It assumes the general validity of the critic's outlook; but different people have different outlooks. Moreover, the critic's outlook may not remain constant, but may be modified by experience, including encounters with literary works. In this respect, 'Heart of Darkness' seems to ambush its adversaries. Marlow has been changed by his experience of Africa, and is still being changed. One of the subtlest features of the text is the dramatization of his uncertainties, of his tentativeness, of his groping for affirmations that his own narrative subsequently questions. Through Marlow, this liminal and protean novella renders the process of teaching and learning, and of negotiating alternative viewpoints. To take an obvious example: he offers conflicting interpretations of Kurtz's cry, 'The horror! The horror!'. Perhaps they refer to Kurtz's corruption, perhaps to the horror of a senseless universe. But there may be another meaning: no final resolution is offered. Marlow addresses a group of friends on a vessel. They may not share his views; and, indeed, they voice dissent – 'Try to be civil'; 'Absurd'. A commentator who declares Conrad 'racist' or 'sexist' may be imposing on Conrad readily available stereotypes, but, at its best, the tale questions the process of imposing stereotypes. Such phrases as 'weaning those ignorant millions', 'enemies, criminals, workers ... rebels', 'unsound method' or 'leader of an extreme party' are invested with sardonic irony. In addition, a political commentator on the text may seem imperialistic in seeking to incorporate literary terrain within the territory of his or her own personal value-system. If we abolished all those past texts that, to our fallible understandings, failed to endorse present values or prejudices, few works would survive. A literary work may have a diversity of political implications and consequences, but it is not a political manifesto. It is an imaginative work that offers a voluntary and hypothetical experience. Its linguistic texture may be progressive when its readily paraphrasable content may not. All its implications remain within the invisible quotation marks of the fictional. In other works, the same author could, of course, deploy quite different materials with contrasting implications. In 'Heart of Darkness', Marlow says that women are out of touch with truth; but in *Chance*, he says that women see 'the whole truth', whereas men live in a 'fool's paradise' (p. 144). Meanwhile, in 1910, Conrad signed a formal letter to the Prime Minister, Herbert Asquith, advocating votes for women (*Letters*, IV, p. 327).[18] Awareness of Conrad's complexity may entail recognition of a currently widespread critical habit: the reductive falsification of the past in an attempt to vindicate the political gestures of the present. 'Heart of Darkness' reminds us that this habit resembles an earlier one: the adoption of a demeaning attitude to colonized people in the attempt to vindicate the exploitative actions of the colonizer. The 'pilgrims' in the tale have fathered some of the pundits of today.

We read fiction for pleasures of diverse kinds; and Conrad earned his living as an entertainer, not as a writer of religious or political tracts. The pleasures generated by 'Heart of Darkness' have many sources. They lie in part in its evocative vividness, its modes of suspense, its originality, and its power to provoke thought. Paraphrase is a necessary critical tool, but paraphrase is never an equivalent of the original, whose vitality lies in its combination of particular and general, of rational and emotional. A political scansion of the work is not the only mode of scansion, nor is it necessarily the most illuminating. Literary criticism has an identity distinct from political advocacy, just as creative writing is distinct from political non-fiction. As the text moves through time, the changing historical and cultural circumstances will variously increase and reduce its cogency. Texts may thus apparently die for a period and then regain their vitality. Shakespeare's *King Lear* vanished from the stage for about 150 years, and audiences seeing *King Lear* in the eighteenth century saw Nahum Tate's play not Shakespeare's. May Sinclair's fine novel, *Life and Death of Harriett Frean* (1922), was neglected for decades until Virago Press republished it. The reputation of 'Heart of Darkness' is now a matter of controversy, and its standing may decline; but its complexity guarantees that it will prove fruitful to many readers for a long time yet.

As we have seen, the very ambiguity of that title, 'Heart of Darkness' (originally 'The Heart of Darkness'), heralded that complexity. The titular phrase then evoked the interior of 'darkest Africa'; but it also portended the corruption of Kurtz, and the tale begins with visual reminders of ways in which London, centre of the empire 'on which the sun never sets', can itself be a heart of darkness – palled in 'brooding gloom'. So, from the outset, the narrative probes, questions, and subverts familiar contrasts between the far and the near, between the 'savage' and the 'civilized', between the tropical and the urban. Repeatedly, the tale's descriptions gain vividness by Conrad's use of delayed decoding, a technique whereby effect precedes cause.[19] He presents first the impact of an event, and only after a delay does he offer its explanation. This is exemplified by the descriptions of, for example, the chaos at the Outer Station, eventually explained as railway-building, or of the exploited Africans in the chain-gang, who 'were called criminals'. The technique lends graphic vividness and psychological realism to the process of perception, but it also emphasizes an ironic disparity, or possible disparity, between the events that occur and their conventional interpretation. Delayed decoding is used in numerous ways: in the treatment of small details, of large events, and even of plot sequences within the tale. Sometimes the irony lies in the fact that the interpretation is tardy, or inadequate, or constitutes a reductive falsification. And here lies a warning for commentators on 'Heart of Darkness'. One of the features that made it outstanding among texts of the 1890s was its recognition of the disparities between the realities of experience and the inadequacies of conventional interpretations of it. The tale repeatedly implies an irreducible excess that eludes summary. It may thus warn commentators that they, confined to the limited discourse of rational non-fictional prose, are likely to be outdistanced by the multiple resources of the fictional text. The anonymous narrator speaks with romantic eloquence of all the great men who have sailed forth on the Thames, but Marlow interjects 'And this also ... has been one of the dark places of the earth', and proceeds to remind him that Britain would once have seemed as savage a wilderness to Roman colonizers as Africa now seems to Europeans. This is a rebuke to empire-builders and to believers in the durability of civilization; it invokes a humiliating chronological perspective; and it may jolt the reader into circumspection.

Reflections on this passage might induce caution in any commentator who initially fails to relate 'Heart of Darkness' fairly to the time of its writing, or who assumes the superiority of a present-day viewpoint that is itself a product of the times: 'We live in the flicker'. As 'Heart of Darkness' repeatedly implies, a value judgement cannot, in logic, be deduced from a statement of fact. The narrative is partly about the struggle to maintain a humane morality when that morality no longer seems to bear guaranteed validity. In this respect, 'Heart of Darkness' remains cogent and may teach circumspection to its critics. The tale has sombre implications, and so has the story of its reception over the years, but the eloquence, virtuosity, and intensity with which 'Heart of Darkness' addressed its era were exemplary, and seem likely to ensure its longevity.

NOTES

1 This novella's critical fortunes may be traced in Sherry, ed., *Conrad: The Critical Heritage*, Harkness, ed., *Conrad's 'Heart of Darkness' and the Critics*, Murfin, ed., *Joseph Conrad: 'Heart of Darkness': A Case Study in Contemporary Criticism*, Bloom, ed., *Joseph Conrad's 'Heart of Darkness'*, Carabine, ed., *Joseph Conrad: Critical Assessments*, Kimbrough's Norton volumes of 1963, 1971, and 1988, and Burden, *'Heart of Darkness': An Introduction to the Variety of Criticism*. Fothergill's *Heart of Darkness* provides a useful introductory summary.

2 Documents concerning the history of the 'Congo Free State' and Conrad's journey in that region are reprinted in *Heart of Darkness*, Kimbrough, ed., *Joseph Conrad's 'Heart of Darkness'*, pp. 78–192. For the cultural background, see Watt, *Conrad in the Nineteenth Century*. On Nordau and Kelvin, see Watts, *Conrad's 'Heart of Darkness': A Critical and Contextual Discussion*, pp. 132–4, 14–15. (Nordau had written to Conrad to congratulate him on *The Nigger of the 'Narcissus'*.)

3 Baudelaire, 'Correspondances', *Les Fleurs du mal*, pp. 17–18.

4 See Watts, *The Deceptive Text*, pp. 74–82.

5 See Evans, 'Conrad's underworld', and Feder 'Marlow's descent into hell'.

6 On the Polish background, see Najder, *Joseph Conrad: A Chronicle*, pp. 2–53 *et passim*.

7 See 'The Congo Diary' in Kimbrough, ed., *Joseph Conrad's 'Heart of Darkness'*, pp. 159–66.

8 Ch. 1–12 of Sherry's *Conrad's Western World* deal with the fictional transformation of factual materials concerning Africa. Klein is discussed on pp. 72–8.

9 Conrad said that there was 'a mere shadow of love interest just in the last pages' (*Letters*, II, pp. 145–6).

10 On Conrad's relation to Modernism, see Graham, ch. 11 of this volume, and Watt, *Conrad in the Nineteenth Century*, pp. 32–3 *et passim*.

11 This link was recognized in George Steiner's novel, *The Portage to San Cristobal of A. H.* (1981), in which the Kurtzian role is taken by an aged but still eloquent Adolf Hitler, discovered in the depths of the jungle.

12 See Eliot, *The Waste Lane*, pp. 3, 125.

13 The version in Stone (p. vii) has minor misquotations.

14 'So we have an adjectival and worse than supererogatory insistence on "unspeakable rites", "unspeakable secrets", "monstrous passions", "inconceivable mystery", and so on … Conrad … is intent on making a virtue out of not knowing what he means', Leavis, *The Great Tradition*, pp. 198–9.

15 For example, the revised version in Kimbrough, ed., *Joseph Conrad's 'Heart of Darkness'*, pp. 251–62, deletes a passage linking Conrad to 'men in Nazi Germany who lent their talent to the service of virulent racism', and concedes that 'Heart of Darkness' has 'memorably good passages and moments'. The phrase 'a bloody racist' became 'a thoroughgoing racist'. Carabine, ed., *Joseph Conrad: Critical Assessments*, II, also prints the revised version although erroneously identifying it as the 1977 text.

16 Sarvan in Kimbrough, ed., *Joseph Conrad's 'Heart of Darkness'* p. 285. Ngugi Wa Thiong'o is cited on p. 285; articles by Harris and Singh are reprinted, pp. 262–80. Carabine, ed., *Joseph Conrad: Critical Assessments*, II, pp. 405–80, also offers a range of responses to Achebe.

17 On Morel, see Hawkins, 'Conrad's critique of imperialism', p. 293. On Casement, see *Letters*, III, pp. 87, 95–7, 101–3.

18 See also Davies, 'Conrad, *Chance*, and women readers'.

19 On delayed decoding, see Watt, *Conrad in the Nineteenth Century*, pp. 175–9, 270–1, 357, and Watts, *The Deceptive Text*, pp. 43–6, and *A Preface to Conrad*, pp. 114–17.

WORKS CITED

Achebe, Chinua. 'An image of Africa: racism in Conrad's "Heart of Darkness"'. *Massachusetts Review* 17.4 (1977), 782–94. Reprinted (revised) in Kimbrough, ed., *Joseph Conrad's 'Heart of Darkness'*, pp. 251–62

Baudelaire, Charles. *Les Fleurs du mal*. 1857. Paris: Aux quais de Paris, 1957

Bloom, Harold, ed. *Joseph Conrad's 'Heart of Darkness'*. New York: Chelsea House, 1987

Burden, Robert. *'Heart of Darkness': An Introduction to the Variety of Criticism*. London: Macmillan, 1991

Carabine, Keith, ed. *Joseph Conrad: Critical Assessments*. 4 vols. Robertsbridge: Helm Information, 1992

Conrad, Joseph. *Chance*. 1914. Ed. Martin Ray. Oxford: Oxford University Press, 1988

'Heart of Darkness' and Other Tales. Ed. Cedric Watts. Oxford: Oxford University Press, 1990

'A Familiar Preface'. *'The Mirror of the Sea' and 'A Personal Record'*. 1906 and 1912. Ed. Zdzisław Najder. Oxford: Oxford University Press, 1988, pp. xi–xxi

'Geography and some explorers'. 1924. *Last Essays*. Ed. Richard Curle. London: Dent, 1926. Reprinted 1955, pp. 1–22

Cox, C. B. Introduction. *Youth: A Narrative/Heart of Darkness/The End of the Tether*. London: Dent; Vermont: Tuttle, 1974

Davies, Laurence. 'Conrad, *Chance*, and women readers'. *The Conradian* 17.1 (1993), 75–88

Eagleton, Terry. *Criticism and Ideology: A Study in Marxist Literary Theory*. London: Verso, 1976

Eliot, T. S. *The Waste Land: A Facsimile and Transcript of the Original Drafts including the Annotations of Ezra Pound*. Ed. Valerie Eliot. London: Faber & Faber, 1971

Selected Essays. London: Faber & Faber, 1951

'*Ulysses*, order and myth'. *The Dial* 75 (1923), 480–3

Evans, Robert O. 'Conrad's underworld'. *Modern Fiction Studies* 2.2 (1956), 56–92

Feder, Lillian. 'Marlow's descent into hell'. *Nineteenth Century Fiction* 9.4 (1955), 280–92

Fothergill, Anthony. *Heart of Darkness*. Milton Keynes: Open University Press, 1989

Harkness, Bruce, ed. *Conrad's 'Heart of Darkness' and the Critics*. Belmont, CA: Wadsworth, 1960

Harris, Wilson. 'The frontier on which "Heart of Darkness" stands'. *Research on African Literatures* 12 (1981), 86–92. Reprinted Kimbrough, ed., *Joseph Conrad's 'Heart of Darkness'*, pp. 262–8

Hawkins, Hunt. 'Conrad's critique of imperialism'. *PMLA* 94 (1979), 286–99

Jung, C. B. *Modern Man in Search of a Soul*. London: Routledge & Kegan Paul, 1933. Reprinted 1966

Kimbrough, Robert, ed. *Joseph Conrad's 'Heart of Darkness'*. 3rd edn. New York: Norton, 1988

Leavis, F. R. *The Great Tradition: George Eliot, Henry James, Joseph Conrad*. London: Chatto & Windus; New York: G. W. Stewart, 1948. Reprinted Harmondsworth: Penguin Books, 1962

London, Bette. *The Appropriated Voice: Narrative Authority in Conrad, Forster, and Woolf*. Ann Arbor: University of Michigan Press, 1990

Murfin, Ross C., ed. *Joseph Conrad: 'Heart of Darkness': A Case Study in Contemporary Criticism*. New York: Bedford Books of St Martin's Press, 1989

Najder, Zdzisław. *Joseph Conrad: A Chronicle*. Tr. Halina Carroll-Najder. New Brunswick, NJ: Rutgers University Press; Cambridge: Cambridge University Press, 1983

Sarvan, C. P. 'Racism and the 'Heart of Darkness'. *International Fiction Review* 7 (1980), 6–10. Reprinted Kimbrough, ed., *Joseph Conrad's 'Heart of Darkness'*, pp. 280–5

Sherry, Norman. *Conrad's Western World*. Cambridge: Cambridge University Press, 1971

Sherry, Norman, ed. *Conrad: The Critical Heritage*. London: Routledge & Kegan Paul, 1973

Showalter, Elaine. *Sexual Anarchy*. London: Bloomsbury, 1991

Smith, Johanna M. ' "Too beautiful altogether': patriarchal ideology in "Heart of Darkness" '. In *Joseph Conrad: 'Heart of Darkness': A Case Study in Contemporary Criticism*. Ed. Ross C. Murfin. New York: Bedford Books of St Martin's Press, 1989, pp. 179–95

Steiner, George. *The Portage to San Cristobal of A. H.* London: Faber & Faber, 1981

Stone, Robert. *Dog Soldiers*. London: Secker & Warburg, 1975. Reprinted London: Pan Books, 1988

Straus, Nina Pelikan. 'The exclusion of the Intended from secret sharing in Conrad's "Heart of Darkness" '. *Novel* 20.2 (1987), 123–37

Thiong'o, Ngugi Wa. *A Grain of Wheat*. London: Heinemann, 1967. Reset 1975

Watt, Ian. *Conrad in the Nineteenth Century*. Berkeley: University of California Press, 1979; London: Chatto & Windus, 1980

Watts, Cedric. *Conrad's 'Heart of Darkness': A Critical and Contextual Discussion*. Milan: Mursia, 1977

The Deceptive Text: An Introduction to Covert Plots. Brighton: Harvester; Totowa, NJ: Barnes & Noble, 1984

A Preface to Conrad. 2nd edn. London: Longman, 1993

4

J. H. STAPE

Lord Jim

I

Any reading of *Lord Jim* that aspires to be comprehensive must come to terms with the novel's title-character. To borrow Emerson's words, he incarnates the 'plain old Adam, the simple genuine self against the whole world', a notoriously unequal struggle with a foreordained outcome. Conrad's earlier Malay novels, the 'Lingard Trilogy' of *Almayer's Folly*, *An Outcast of the Islands*, and the unfinished 'The Rescuer', similarly focus on individuals living in exile from their culture and blindly in pursuit of an unhappy fate.[1] But while the early novels describe the failure of unsympathetic protagonists (and Lingard, too, in his naïveté and braggadocio is distanced from the reader), *Lord Jim* is famously ambiguous. A technical *tour de force*, it painstakingly dissects and then reassembles the activities and consciousness of a young man, who in his failings and virtues appears to be 'one of us'. Because of a multiplicity of virtuoso narrative techniques that sometimes alienate the reader, Jim, however, is both at the novel's centre and on its periphery. He is thus always present either as a massively constructed figure in the foreground, in the manner of the memorable characters of Dickens or George Eliot, or as a hovering evoked presence in the background.

The reason for this centrality lies partly in Conrad's desire to extend generic conventions. Conrad's third full-length novel, *Lord Jim* is his most sustained attempt to write a *Bildungsroman*, the novel of education tracing a youthful protagonist's confrontation with and painful initiation into the moral and social demands of adulthood. Conrad's interest in the form is apparent in *An Outcast of the Islands*, 'Youth', and 'Heart of Darkness'. Much later, *The Shadow-Line*, whose plot more typically moves from initial crisis to resolution and social integration, extends some of the formal challenges Conrad set for himself in the writing of *Lord Jim*. As Bakhtin has suggested, the *Bildungsroman* concentrates on 'the image of *man in the process of becoming*' ('The *Bildungsroman*', p. 19). In contrast, Jerome Hamilton Buckley in his study of the form emphasizes its concern with social relationships through which the hero moves to come to terms with 'the conflict of generations, provinciality, the larger society ... ordeal by love, the search for a vocation and a working philosophy' (*Season of Youth*, p. 18). This kind of novel has, in fact, a double focus, on the protagonist's outer world, his pre-existing social context, and his developing inner world, which is shaped by various trials and experiences.

The form demands an acute sense of social nuance as well as the ability to convey with extreme subtlety the fleeting movements of thought and feeling. While this genre has a long tradition in English – aspects of it are to be found in Fielding, for instance – Conrad's immediate models are almost certainly French. Stendhal's *Le Rouge et le noir* (1831) and Flaubert's *L'Éducation sentimentale* (1869) importantly influence the portrayal of Jim. The youthful protagonists of these novels are, however, basically unsympathetic, and differ crucially from Jim in the scope of their ambitions, which are sometimes trivial or even contemptible. Corrosive narrative ironies further distance them from the reader, whereas in *Lord Jim* ironic detachment is balanced by compassionate identification.

Conrad alters the traditional *Bildungsroman*'s formal structure in a number of ways. He grafts on to it features of adventure fantasy characteristic of Robert Louis Stevenson, including an exotic tropical setting and a sensational incursion by bloodthirsty pirates. More importantly, the novel's essentially tragic vision, pervasive reliance on intricate and multi-layered symbols, and various narrative strategies subvert the fundamentally realist texture of this kind of fiction. And, lastly, its philosophical interest – the question, as Stein formulates it, of 'how to be' – so complicates the novel that the positive movement towards restored social harmony characteristic of the novel of education becomes impossible.

Like all of Conrad's major works, *Lord Jim* is influenced by, and transforms widely scattered sources from various literary and cultural traditions. Conrad's wide-ranging reading in the classics and in French, English, and Polish literature, his experience at sea and in the Far East, his reliance on real-life situations and persons, whether heard of or known at first-hand, enrich the literary legacy that he borrows from and alters.[2] The novel is, moreover, deeply personal, with roots in Conrad's past. It obliquely depicts the situation of the orphaned child and expatriate adolescent, the victim of tragic national and family circumstances, and it expresses some of the insecurities and anxieties Conrad felt throughout his precarious adult life. It also draws on his experience as a self-elected creative artist giving shape to an interior vision in a foreign land and language. (In some senses, Conrad was, like his protagonist, a heroic exile in search of a social identity from an audience that could only partially understand him.[3]) In its recourse to numerous and widely scattered public sources – newspapers, books, port gossip – the novel may also lay claim to 'communal authorship' (Henricksen, *Nomadic Voices*, p. 85). Given its diverse origins, mixed literary paternity, generic heterogeneity, and highly complicated rhetorical and thematic ambitions, *Lord Jim* is, not surprisingly, a self-reflexive text, at moments almost obsessively concerned with the mechanics of its telling and the procedures that generate and shape its thematics.

The first full-length work of Conrad's artistic maturity, the novel was serialized in fourteen monthly instalments during the years 1899–1900 in the staid and establishment *Blackwood's Edinburgh Magazine*. Its immediate origins lie in a fragment entitled 'Tuan Jim: A Sketch', which Conrad first thought of as a short story for serial publication.[4] Its green seeds can, however, be discerned in 'The Lagoon', a story written during 1896 in the interstices of Conrad's work on 'The Rescuer'. 'The Lagoon' is set in the same Malay world as that work, which would be completed only twenty years later, and as *Lord Jim*, the novel he had yet to foresee. Like them, the story focuses on an exile, who is initiated into moral complexity in his confrontation with conflicting rights. Acting out of self-interest, he betrays a basic trust, and like all such betrayals in Conrad's fiction this inevitably culminates in self-betrayal. Like *Lord Jim*, 'The Lagoon' ends in an ambiguous act of self-destruction.

Conrad revealingly described the history of the story's writing in terms of obsession and illness: 'The short story like a fell disease got me under – and *The Rescuer* has to wait' (*Letters*, I, p. 298). Putting aside a longer work for a more urgent and concentrated creative variation is a recurrent pattern in Conrad's writing career, just as works first conceived as stories tended to get away from him and grow into full-length novels.[5] *Lord Jim* itself was originally thought of as a short story centred upon the pilgrim ship episode, which is based on an historical event – the abandonment of the *Jeddah* by her English crew in August 1880, a maritime scandal much commented on in the London and colonial press.

Conrad had no fully worked out plan for the novel before beginning it, and even when it was far advanced he was characteristically predicting a conclusion long before he neared it. The book increased inexorably beyond his original word-estimates to his worried publisher, and in its 'Author's Note' he admits that he had not envisioned its final length. The absence of a plan may have engendered some of the brilliant improvisatory techniques that define the novel's Modernism including the shift from an omniscient third-person to an involved first-person narrator in chapter 5. While the third-person narrative method briefly and evocatively presents essential background information about Jim's early years, the alteration in technique has a number of wide-ranging thematic and formal consequences. In the first instance, the shift to a first-person narrator enacts the novel's central rhetorical dilemma in complicating and destabilizing an initial security that in its detachment and serenity offers too Olympian a perspective. It also appears that third-person narration quickly proved uncongenial and finally even inimical to the story – in fact, stories – Conrad discovered he wanted to tell.

In shifting to a dramatized narrator who witnesses and participates in the action, the theme of solidarity – the individual's necessary dependence on and commitment to a group – gains considerable depth in the interplay between Jim's experiences and Marlow's telling. This represents yet another formal variation on the *Bildungsroman*, which sometimes features a surrogate father-figure for the hero who typically quarrels with or otherwise distances himself from his actual father. Conrad, however, complicates this pattern by developing a double plot in which both the youthful quester and his experienced mentor undergo change. Henry James's 'The Turn of the Screw', which Conrad read in the autumn of 1898 (*Letters*, II, p. 111), might possibly account for some of the novel's formal strategies. But in any case, the early conception of the story and the manner of its telling appear to have given way to pressures that Bakhtin has identified as essentially novelistic. The basic and rather simple short story material succumbed to centrifugal forces – stylistic polyphony, chronological insecurity, and ideological indeterminacy – that are characteristic of the novel as a generic hybrid with origins in the drama, biography, and the historical chronicle.

II

Widely considered a key work, even 'a supreme exemplar' (Raval, 'Narrative authority in *Lord Jim*', p. 91) of literary Modernism, *Lord Jim* unflinchingly challenges late nineteenth-century modes of perception and literary representation. Its final title – *Lord Jim, A Tale* – moves in contradictory directions, conflating the aristocratic with the intimate and the familiar, and the uniquely individual and 'real' with the collective and fictive. (Conrad also considered as sub-titles 'A Sketch' and 'A Romance', phrases that likewise emphasize generic identity.) Well reviewed on its publication in book form in October 1900, the novel, despite the sophisticated demands it makes – especially on a first reading – has retained its place as one of Conrad's most widely enjoyed and studied books. It has remained so for the brilliance of its technical innovations as well as for its sheer story-telling power. As Cedric Watts has aptly summarized, *Lord Jim* holds a secure place as 'one of Conrad's greatest novels and, therefore, as one of the world's literary masterpieces' (Introduction, p. 19).

One of the main fascinations and pleasures of *Lord Jim* resides in exploring the interrelationships between its array of narrative techniques – the use of a highly individualized frame narrator, chronological dislocations, impressionistic devices, ironic juxtapositions, thematic appositions, and delayed decoding, to name but the most obvious – and the intricate moral, philosophical, political, and ideological cruxes that these complex strategies introduce and elaborate. *Lord Jim* demands at least one re-reading to determine the basic facts of its relatively simple plot and requires multiple re-readings to come to terms with its issues. The extensive body of criticism from a wide variety of approaches attests to its richness as a self-interrogating philosophical work.[6]

In structuring his novel so as to require repeated readings, Conrad subverts the traditional posture of the mid- and late-Victorian novelist. In the novels of Thackeray or Trollope the omniscient narrator and 'dear reader' collude to unravel a number of interwoven plots that work towards a predictable conclusion. In contrast, in *Lord Jim* Conrad eschews the traditional English novel's sub-plotting (so demonstrating a significant formal debt to Continental, especially French, fiction) and makes a number of complicated demands that deliberately, almost aggressively, seek to unsettle the reader. In the end, these technical manoeuvres place the reader in a position of fundamental relativism and puzzled incertitude about the meanings unfolded by Marlow's compulsive telling of Jim's tale. Far from being mere 'playfulness' of the kind deconstructionist readings might privilege, Conrad's insistent refusal to ground the text by continuously undermining narrative authority purposefully encourages a nostalgic, almost wistful, longing for a once-present centre. At moments, then, the reader pines for a narrator whose stability might provide a perspective from whence he can point towards answers to the complex questions that Marlow raises.

Drawn partly from the cultural and linguistic dislocations of Conrad's youth, this instability fundamentally informs his philosophic outlook and affects the shape and interests of his writings.[7] On the other hand, the novel's rhetoric appears at times to search for, or even posit a core of more than simply situational values, harking back to those 'few very simple ideas ... as old as the hills', notably, fidelity, which Conrad in his autobiographical reflections espouses as his own (*PR*, p. xix). This contrary tendency has persuaded some readers to search for, and insist upon, resolutions and to claim that a truth or truths, even if merely tentative, emerge from the novel's intense inquiry into the bases of conduct. Critics have thus located in one or another of the commentators on Jim's actions a privileged guide to interpreting his experience and, by extension, to *the* meaning of the novel. Stein or the French Lieutenant have often been viewed as especially reliable interpreters although the imagery surrounding them importantly qualifies, and possibly finally undercuts the validity of their significant but partial pronouncements.[8]

The loss of fixed standards that the novel registers is articulated in a series of rhetorical ploys and in its hauntingly elegiac tone. These act in concert to lament innocence lost – Jim's (though his may in the end ironically remain intact) as well as that of late-Victorian Britain itself. Nourished on a panoply of comforting 'certitudes' about its existential and political position in the world, nineteenth-century Britain, in common with the empires of any age, voiced only occasional doubts about its influence and values. Like Conrad's earlier fiction, this novel persistently queries these, particularly the imperialist endeavour to which so many formidable energies and resources had been committed.[9]

The loss of certitude established by duplicitous narrative strategies destabilizes the reader and announces a major preoccupation: the question of interpreting what appears to occur in the world of observable 'fact', the world that Marlow at the outset of the *Patna* Inquiry appears to hold in contempt. The enlargement, one might say explosion, of Conrad's initial conception of his story necessitated and gave rise, however, to a densely tangled and a 'richly, even extravagantly textured' narrative method (Berthoud, *Joseph Conrad: The Major Phase*, p. 64) that exhaustively probes the nature of the observing self and the means by which it recounts the observable. The multiplicity of witnesses, the metaphor of inquiry, the dislocated chronology, the increasingly fragmented and uncertain sources of information (particularly in the last third of the novel) as well as the explicitly averred distrust of all verbalization collectively emphasize the impossibility of arriving at conclusions. In working through these techniques, *Lord Jim* portends the fiction that Conrad would write over the next ten years of his life, the period that constitutes his major creative phase.

Among these narrative strategies, the frame narrative, a time-honoured device that Conrad had already used in 'Youth', 'Heart of Darkness', and some of his early stories, is singularly appropriate to the telling of Jim's latent tale. This subliminal narrative focuses on the intermingled motivations, fears, and irrationality that hedge his inner life. Conrad's recourse to a frame lends a depth and tonal variety to his material that it would otherwise lack. Moreover, it integrally supports the formal elegiac romance, the recollection and judgement in retrospect of one man by another.[10]

(F. Scott Fitzgerald's *The Great Gatsby*, a novel obviously much indebted both to 'Heart of Darkness' and *Lord Jim*, is another instance of this genre.) The contours and tensions of the *senex-puer* (old man/young man) relationship are central to the form with its opposition of youthful ardour and sagacious distance and the counterpointing of the voices of innocence and experience. Another function of the frame is the dramatization of the contrast between a man from the ranks with his fixed standard of conduct and the man whose 'soft spot' (*LJ*, p. 13) unfixes such ardent belief.

The use of Marlow, who had appeared in 'Youth' and 'Heart of Darkness', and the alternation between Jim's bright-eyed naïveté and optimism with his older, more experienced, and, at the novel's opening, apparently more certain point of view, not only solves compositional and structural problems but richly complicates and expands the novel's themes. Marlow the yarning sailor offers an additional advantage in reducing conventional dialogue, a weak point for Conrad whose grasp of conversational idiom remained problematic throughout his career. More importantly, the mediation of Jim through another voice tends to underscore or at least provide the illusion of balance. It offers a means of judgement that is at once slightly removed but, because it is intimate and individual, inevitably committed and partial. Lastly, the method results in a gain in immediacy, since Marlow's 'you' embraces not only the circle of listeners he addresses (after chapter 36 this is reduced to an anonymous 'privileged man') but obviously includes and forcefully engages the reader. The frame narrative thus forces the reader's active complicity in deciphering Jim's story.

III

Poised at the close of an increasingly sceptical century, *Lord Jim* exposes a series of cultural illusions of which Jim is the heir, symbol, and victim. An ambiguously 'simple' personality, his motives, emotions, and instincts appear uncomplicated, but prove doggedly intractable to his own and Marlow's sustained exertions to present and understand them. The novel's epigraph (absent from its serial version) taken from the German Romantic poet Novalis importantly sets the mood of self-inquisition: 'It is certain any conviction gains infinitely the moment another soul will believe in it' (p. 1). Emphasizing an inherently social concept of the self, the epigraph also asserts the self's ineluctable fragility and insecurity and establishes that its autonomy and individuality are fictions sustained by the community. Even before the novel opens Conrad thus sets individual identity in a precarious social frame.

This undermining of cherished notions of autonomy continues with a full-scale questioning of the concept of the heroic self by a dismantling of its exterior posturing and its inner basis in the imagination. As has been widely recognized, the strategically placed training-ship episode that follows the introductory information about Jim's later inglorious career as a water-clerk foreshadows his abandonment of the *Patna* and his later habitual retreat eastwards before the accusation, or even the fear of accusation, of dereliction of duty. The episode cruelly dissects Jim's naïve desire for 'heroic' stature and mocks his stereotypically youthful vapourings. He has yet to possess the carefully honed and automatic practical responses required for outward success or inner achievement, what the French Lieutenant prosaically qualifies as 'habit – habit – necessity ... the eye of others' (p. 147). Such an attitude requires an effacement of self before the work at hand. Jim, by contrast, denies his failure in the training-ship by a characteristic and imaginative optimism, projecting a vision of himself that lacks any basis in reality and that, in fact, finds the conditions of the world itself inadequate. The episode is a key to Jim's psychology, which Conrad borrows, in part, from Flaubert's *Madame Bovary* (1857) and less obviously but just as pervasively from Stendhal's Julien Sorel, the hyper-romantic anti-hero of *Le Rouge et le noir*. Conrad takes pains to emphasize that while Jim's situation is 'individual' it is the embarrassingly universal condition of youth. Marlow's repeated characterization of Jim as 'one of us', whatever its implication of class membership, professional identity, and national allegiance, encompasses the doom of youthful ambitions that must eventually fade before maturity's unavoidable compromises and defeats.

Two thematic appositions, one preceding and the other following the training-ship episode, frame Jim's idealistic self-image. Jim's parson father, who possesses 'a certain knowledge of the Unknowable' (p. 5), a 'knowledge' obviously ironized by the rhetoric describing it, takes refuge in a belief that has never been tried. He has consequently denied himself the chance of any achievement. More adventurous, the Malay pilgrims undertaking their arduous journey to Mecca are similarly prompted by an unquestioning fidelity to 'the call of an idea' (p. 14). Jim's failure and values are, then, positioned between two traditional systems of belief that motivate the behaviour of their adherents. In thus situating this episode Conrad emphasizes Jim's egotistic 'belief' in himself and the profoundly cultural moorings of his heroic desire. Jim's conception of the hero as a solitary individual braving the elements and overcoming his fears to sacrifice himself for the benefit of others is, however, upheld by his society. Adumbrated here, the point is fully demonstrated later in Jim's mythification by the inhabitants of Patusan, who believe him to be greater and wiser than themselves, lacking their disabling weaknesses. While this plays upon a familiar imperialist trope – an awed native population's deification of a European – its psychological dimensions are characteristic of mythifying projects that possess little explicitly political content. Moreover, Conrad's main target is the innately contradictory functioning of the imagination. On the one hand, an indispensable source for conceptions beyond actual or perceived boundaries, it is, on the other, a mechanism that is capable of, even fundamentally oriented to, the engendering of mere illusion. The later Stein and Patusan chapters elaborate and qualify these ideas with considerable nuance.

Two juxtaposed scenes further amplify Conrad's views about the nature of the imagination: Marlow's visit to the *Patna*'s chief engineer in hospital and the Malay helmsman's appearance at the *Patna* Inquiry. A superb example of 'impressionist immediacy' (Watt, *Conrad in the Nineteenth Century*, p. 274), Marlow's visit to the hospital is an extended and ultimately futile attempt to make sense of the *Patna* affair from the inside. Rather than finding an explanation, Marlow confronts an imagination completely broken down, incapable of distinguishing between or separating off reality from illusion. The chief engineer's ravings, the result of acute alcohol poisoning, none the less have, as the attendant surgeon says in words that playfully recall Hamlet's madness, 'some sort of method' (p. 54).[11] In the first instance, the hallucinations articulate the chief engineer's guilt about abandoning the passengers in his charge, but his tormented and pathetic cries for 'Help' also dramatize his fear of being engulfed, 'drowned' as it were, by madness. (Conrad may also be slyly glancing here at the Romantic visionary, the victim of absinthe or opium.) The very incoherence of the chief engineer's actions and words voice a naked terror of complete mental extinction, and far from being not 'material' (p. 55), as Marlow ironically and possibly somewhat impercipiently dismisses it, the testimony born out of these 'jim-jams' (p. 55) – an outrageous pun on Jim's 'jam' – bears suggestively on the reader's understanding of Jim's moral and psychological experience. Lastly, the scene serves to introduce the moral issues that the *Patna* Inquiry, which however blunt and inadequate, is convened to take up.

While the scene is clearly linked to exploring the nature of the imagination, it may also be seen as significantly contributing to the novel's unending inquisition into its own methods. The chief engineer's condition represents an obvious extreme: the imagination appears in its negative capacity as a destructive and devouring rather than as a creative and interpreting force. His condition thus directly addresses a peril that Jim confronts, albeit somewhat less intensely, and also self-reflexively comments on the situation of the artist engaged in mediating between his fictions and the world about him. It explicitly reminds the reader that however imperfect and arbitrary language may be as a medium for conveying basic conditions of existence – let alone its more enigmatic ones – it none the less emphatically remains, even when lacking obvious sense, a gesture towards significant if possibly intrinsically inexpressible meaning. Finally, the scene cautions against narcissistic obsession with narrative process: the imagination risks inward collapse and resultant stasis. Drunk on itself the more it gazes on its workings, a text is threatened by a kind of linguistic and narrative vertigo occasioned by the sheer variety of possible choice.

A further cautionary perspective on Jim's imaginative capacity – in fact, on the functioning of the imagination itself – is provided by the evidence presented during the second day of the *Patna* Inquiry. Like the chief engineer's testimony, the Malay helmsman's, delivered as a trance-like invocation of former ships and affirming 'secret reasons' for the officers' desertion of their post, complicates the reader's response to Jim. At the moment of the officers' abandonment of the *Patna*, the helmsman reveals that he 'thought nothing' (p. 98). This failure of imagination is no less radically disabling in its ultimate consequences, were such a condition to be widely shared, as the chief engineer's. Preserved by a strict, absolutely automatic, adherence to the code of seamanship and to the unthinking, performance of the immediate task, the helmsman is simply unable to conceive of an alternate ordering of his activities. In this presumed reliability for the task at hand, however, lies a comforting strength and a no less obvious limitation. As Chester, who is clearly one of the novel's 'beetles', cynically exhorts, the ordinary, plodding, unheroic apprehension and acceptance of 'things exactly as they are' (p. 161) is undoubtedly necessary for continuing existence.[12] (A characteristically Conradian irony is that this self-styled realist advances his argument while attempting to convince Marlow of a bizarrely whimsical plan to place Jim on a waterless guano island.) Such an acceptance, whether motivated by foolishness or by cynicism, incompletely prepares one for the vicissitudes and challenges of life. Tony Tanner's view that the Malay helmsman figures among Conrad's 'elect' or 'blessed' (p. 31) because in his lack of an imagination he is faithfully devoted to his work is a misreading. Unlike Singleton in *The Nigger of the 'Narcissus'*, who at first sight might appear to be a possible parallel, the Malay helmsman is presented with little rhetorical heightening and hence lacks the dignity bestowed on Singleton's conscientious, sacrificial labour. Moreover, as Conrad establishes here and through Captain Whalley of 'The End of the Tether', a lack of imagination is as fatal as the possession of one constantly caught up with its own processes.

This argument is more fully developed in the positioning of Captain Brierly's suicide at a significant juncture in the telling of Jim's story. Brierly's is another case of extreme, seemingly impersonal, identification with the established code of seamanship, an emptying out of the private self in order to preserve the community. This identification, however, lies at the opposite pole from that of the *Patna*'s helmsman for it is informed by an imaginative capacity that eventually undoes itself. Entirely dependent upon the code for his self-conception, Brierly collapses inwards on belatedly realizing what the code obdurately consists of and requires – a ruthless sacrifice of, rather than, an investment of self. The thematic apposition of the two scenes leaves little doubt about the text's persuasion. While, on the one hand, the life-impulse is inevitably self-directed and narcissistic, it requires an external foothold to provide balance and social identity. Brierly's identification with Jim appears to convince him of his inability to sustain the fiction of a merely public persona. Such are the insights that Marlow gleans in retrospect from his discussion about Jim with Brierly, but in the end the motives for Brierly's suicide are fundamentally resistant to explanation. Old Jones's 'Why?' (p. 64), reverberates, unanswerable and naïve because such questions cannot, in one sense, be asked. Their seriousness and futility are underlined by comic pathos as the mournful howls of Rover, Brierly's dog, punctuate the scene. Ironically, the dog would have been faithful until death had its master not prevented it from jumping overboard with him, and Rover's purely instinctive impulse, an unthinking fidelity, must be constrained in order for him to survive.

Pitilessly, and with some grim and possibly sardonic humour, the scene thus exposes humanity's remoteness from instinct. Jim, a simple man, confronts this as a crisis, although his jump, as a wholly natural impulse, appears to be an instinctive gesture to save his life. But it is also, metaphorically and psychologically, a shrinking from chaos and dissolution. At the same time, it flies in the face of ingrained societal pressures to forego his own life in service to others. The end of the novel ironically inverts these terms when Jim foregoes the equally natural impulse to 'save' himself, a plea that Jewel touchingly makes to him, in order to comply with impersonal societal norms of rectitude and justice and to settle his score with what he finally sees as his fate. Doramin in taking his revenge is purposefully described as an elemental force, an 'ox under a yoke' making 'choking, inhuman sounds' (p. 415). He represents the basic urge of a society to protect itself at all costs. Jim in dying for an abstract and ideal version of himself repudiates this instinct, preferring dignity to mere survival.

IV

Self-assured at the outset and consciously playing the role of the experienced mentor observing at a distance and with dispassion the younger quester's fumbling, Marlow undergoes some destabilizing of his ego and beliefs the more closely he observes Jim. In this respect *Lord Jim* is a *Bildungsroman* with two heroes. The crisis Marlow experiences is similar to but considerably less radical than the one that the Marlow of 'Heart of Darkness' experiences in bearing witness to Kurtz, for as in that novella it involves the preservation of saving illusions. In addition to its allegiance to the novel of education, *Lord Jim* thus opens out to include anxieties that the later twentieth century would term the mid-life crisis, a period of reorientation brought on by a realization of mortality. Marlow's befriending of Jim, an emotional commitment that includes identification and sympathy, precipitates a reappraisal of his basic principles and commitments. He seeks out Stein partly as a practical solution to Jim's difficulties, but does so partly for help with the philosophical problems that his friendship for Jim has awakened him to. If Jim needs Marlow's immediate help, Marlow finds that he depends upon Jim to confirm his own sense of selfhood.

The characterization of the novel as the 'great poem of friendship in the Conrad canon' (Batchelor, *The Life of Joseph Conrad*, p. 61) accurately captures the intensity Conrad brings to his exploration of this subject, embracing not only Marlow's affectionate concern for him but also Jim's cross-cultural and reciprocal friendship with Dain Waris as well as Marlow's friendship for Stein. Sympathy and the tangled skeins of relationship and identity between equals, however, lessen and finally disable Marlow's ability to judge and lead him as well to the more humane insight, beyond mere legalism, that 'Nobody, nobody is good enough' (p. 319). The more closely he observes, the less capable is he of maintaining a perspective on his constantly altering subject, and in beginning to sympathize, Marlow ceases to investigate. His changing stance itself becomes a secondary theme in the Patusan section which, while dramatizing Jim's ambiguous achievement and troubling end, contrapuntally details Marlow's growing emotional and moral uncertainty about the bases of his own life. As Jim becomes less isolated, assumes a social identity and role, and extends his feeling self through his love of Jewel, Marlow's doubts accumulate and thicken. Unhindered by these earlier, he had readily leapt to conclusions about Jim's conduct in the *Patna* affair, but in the face of Jim's seemingly simpler actions and choices in Patusan he falters, his faith in 'fixed standards' undermined by deepened experience.

The moral issues in the Patusan section are made to appear deliberately more clear cut than those of the *Patna* section. This is especially so should one leave to one side (as Conrad largely does although a number of the novel's more recent critics do not) the benevolent paternalism underlying Jim's successful endeavours to impose government upon a lawless community unceasingly engaged its own undoing. This community is in fact less specifically Malayan or South-East Asian in its tensions and constitution – its political pettinesses, fundamental rapacity, and tendency to self-destruction – than, as in Balzac's sweeping panorama of French society, simply and emblematically human. Patusan's universality is underlined by its mixed ethnic composition. Jim arrives to a political situation composed of complex alliances and intrigues in which Sherif Ali, an Arab, is a contending power in the backwater that Doramin's Bugis had earlier invaded, and in so doing Islamized the native Dyak population. Ali is abetted in his stratagems by a shopkeeper from the Chinese community, a member of yet another group of 'outsiders'. While Conrad's focus is on English and Dutch colonial ambitions in the region, these new 'outsiders' can lay no special claims to imperialism, a point likewise made in the strife between the mixed ethnic societies of his earlier Malay novels. Like Patusan itself, then, the excessively intricate political and moral situations explored in *Lord Jim* belie superficial appearances.

The Patusan episodes are developed in obvious counterpoint to the *Patna* affair, and while they have often been found to be wanting in depth and subtlety, their greater structural simplicity and pervasive romance elements contribute to the full development of the novel's enquiry. Jim's existential isolation in the *Patna* affair – 'His saved life was over for want of ground under his feet, for want of sights for his eyes, for want of voices in his ears' (p. 115) – contrasts sharply with his rootedness in Patusan. In discovering love and friendship he consequently finds responsibility. (Conrad returns to this idea in *Under Western Eyes* in which Razumov's betrayal of Haldin occurs because of his remoteness from human attachment. The novel's Geneva sections, which see him forging links outside himself, particularly in his love for Natalia, delineate the development of his conscience and the discovery of a moral nature.) Loyalty and fidelity, keywords frequently sounded in Conrad's writing, find their basis in emotional commitment whereby the presence of a necessary Other sustains one's own 'conviction'. It is hardly surprising that even 'duty', a word that connotes cold necessity and forbearance before the task at hand, finds its ultimate fulfilment, according to the first narrator of Jim's story, in romantic terms: in the 'perfect love of the work' (p. 10).

The second part of *Lord Jim* is, however, far from being a simple tale of romantic love and heroic adventure in an exotic setting. The standard folkloric and mythic motifs that give Jim the stature of an archetypal solar hero, the 'love story' itself, the biblical echoes (especially of the death of Christ), of tragedy, hagiography, and elegy, and the characteristics of the novel of education and of ordeal – all prior, inherited forms – pointedly serve to emphasize Jim's typicality as a fated hero cut from the pages of fiction and emerging from the tales of folklore. These authoritative forms enable a contextualization of Jim and, to some extent, balance the almost over-exuberant originality of narrative device of the *Patna* chapters. Conrad's reliance on these forms even at the expense of some dramatic slackening is thus thematically productive. The Patusan section deepens and expands earlier ideas, and rather than being awkwardly broken-backed, as F. R. Leavis and some later critics have argued, *Lord Jim* works towards and achieves a tightly intermeshed thematic coherence precisely through its formal hybridism.

This generic diversity also encourages a variety of readings of Jim's highly ambiguous death. The division between the profound subjectivity of romantic inclination, the apprehension of the external world as far as possible in one's own terms, the way of Cervantes's Don Quixote, and the pragmatic necessity of dealing with it 'exactly as it is', the way of Sancho Panza, presents an age-old dilemma that the novel's closing action makes acute. Jim's death, which pointedly dramatizes the struggle between objectivity and subjectivism, offers a notoriously difficult interpretive crux and raises a number of questions about narrative closure. Ian Watt asserts that Jim, unique among the protagonists of twentieth-century literature, 'dies for his honour' (*Conrad in the Nineteenth Century*, p. 356). Benita Parry likewise speaks of Jim's death as a 'triumph' and a 'victory' (*Conrad and Imperialism*, pp. 95, 98). On the other hand, Tony Tanner argues that Jim's death is 'an easy way out', an 'escape' from life's complications (*Conrad: 'Lord Jim'*, p. 55). Jacques Berthoud subtly suggests that it possesses multiple meanings, being one thing for Jim himself, who, like a figure in French tragedy, pursues an inflexible code to its logical and merciless extreme, and another for Marlow, who interprets it as the crowning 'ambiguity of a tormented career' (*Joseph Conrad: The Major Phase*, p. 93). Recent critics have tended to emphasize the social implications and consequences of Jim's death. From this perspective, he dies 'essentially in disgrace' (Conroy, 'Colonial self-fashioning in Conrad', p. 35), egotistically abandoning Jewel and leaving behind him renewed political chaos in Patusan, the final consequence of a blundering imperialist adventurism however well intentioned.

In common with numerous Modernist works, aspects of *Lord Jim* tend to work towards a deliberate inconclusiveness of meaning that frustrates while it simultaneously stimulates a search for resolution. Marlow's persistent interrogation of motives and the metaphor of inquiry itself have by the novel's conclusion educated the reader into epistemological scepticism, a doubting of the adequacy of any means of apprehension and analysis. This encourages an open verdict in the face of absent, or in the presence of conflicting and unreliable, evidence. Conrad's closing rhetorical strategies none the less have a contrary pull: the final pages express an overwhelming poignancy, an almost unbearable sense of loss for Jim, who has been needed – by Marlow, by Jewel, and by the society in which he has attained prestige and a position of influence. It is here that Conrad most notably departs from the pattern of the nineteenth-century *Bildungsroman* whose hero after his initial social maladjustment in the end accepts the world's terms. At the conclusion of *Lord Jim*, however, it is not the protagonist who is chastened, becoming smaller in his identification with a conforming group, but the world itself that has shrunk. (The setting sun and blood red sky at Jim's death are mythic gestures accompanying the death of the hero.) The tone of lamentation and the heightened, even lush, rhetoric of Marlow's grief further indicate that Jim's passing is not that of a mere individual but, in part, the death of a belief held by the community at large. The mood of sombre finality occasioned by Stein's weary drift towards death in the novel's concluding sentence also implies that Jim's death entails a larger loss.

It is not entirely surprising, then, that, despite Conrad's avowed religious scepticism, some readers have argued for a specifically Christian context for this novel with its underlying structure of sacrifice, atonement, and redemption, reinforced by the biblical echoes surrounding Jim's death. But to limit the novel in this way is to neglect its essential tendency towards paradox. It strenuously attempts open-endedness in respect to Marlow's and our own judgement of Jim. The frequent repetition of the words 'enigma' and 'mystery', the imagery of clouds, mist, fog, dream, and insubstantiality, as well as Marlow's insistence on his inability to see clearly and his own too quick classification of Jim in the earlier sections warn the reader against a leap to judgement. On the other hand, Jim has undoubtedly been 'true' to the deepest impulses of his personality and to the uneasy contradictions that constitute his nature. For all romantics, as Stein's famous butterfly image indicates, this includes a yearning for transcendence, a desire to evade compromise and contingency, and it is thus a longing for the release that can be found only in death. One of Conrad's final ironies is that Jim finds this most intensely personal of desires within the social arena: he voluntarily appears before Doramin, who as leader of his people represents the merciless impartiality of law. In thus presenting himself, Jim, as Stein perceives when he emphatically counters Jewel's accusation of his falsity, is 'Not false!' but 'True! true! true!' (p. 350). In a world hemmed in by social constraint, the achievement of inner truth – the code words 'honour' or 'self-knowledge' are traditional but only partial ways of describing this – comes, as some readers have objected, at a high social price. Inherently, possibly vehemently, anti-social, it contains an element of a heroic and conceivably noble protest against the community's incessant demand for conformity. Thus, in Jim's willing death one hears a distant echo of the denunciation that Ibsen's Hedda Gabler in her suicide hurls at an uncomprehending world in doing expressly what, in Judge Brack's richly resonant words, 'one doesn't do'. And in it too are elements of the artist's uncompromising commitment to an individual vision that has its own imperatives, whether or not these receive society's sanction. For the romantic, the world is always less than it should or than it might be, and Jim's tragic flaw begins and ends in his having an imagination at all. Readings of the novel inevitably part and will no doubt continue to do so at precisely this point, dividing according to whether the reader gives pre-eminence to the individual – on the self 'against the whole world' – or upon a social vision that urges the priority of communal rights and obligations, on Jim's being, in Marlow's multi-faceted and often repeated phrase, 'one of us'.

NOTES

1 'The Rescuer', begun in 1898, was eventually completed and published in 1920 as *The Rescue*. The earlier version is at issue here.

2 On Conrad's historical sources and reading, see Sherry, *Conrad's Eastern World*, pp. 41–170. Van Marle and Lefranc, 'Ashore and afloat', offer corrections regarding the novel's setting, and Stape, 'Gaining conviction', proposes an additional literary source.

3 'Amy Foster', written in May-June 1901, less than a year after Conrad had finished *Lord Jim*, centrally takes up questions about identity and cultural displacement.

4 See Gordan, *Joseph Conrad: The Making of a Novelist*, for a study of the manuscript. Hay, 'Lord Jim: from sketch to novel', discusses the differences between the novel's *ur-* and final versions and speculates that Conrad may have begun *Lord Jim* as early as 1896.

5 See Fraser, *Interweaving Patterns in the Works of Joseph Conrad*, on the interrelationships between Conrad's short fiction and novels.

6 A basic list of responses to *Lord Jim* since 1960 includes Batchelor, *Lord Jim*; Murfin, *'Lord Jim': After the Truth*; Tanner, *Conrad: 'Lord Jim'*; Verleun, *Patna and Patusan Perspectives*; Watt, *Conrad in the Nineteenth Century*, pp. 254–356, and the essays in Bloom, ed., *Joseph Conrad's 'Lord Jim'*, and in Moser, ed., *Lord Jim*. For a brief survey of the novel's critical fortunes, see Batchelor, *Lord Jim*, pp. 187–212, and for reviews, see Sherry, ed., *Conrad: The Critical Heritage*, pp. 111–27.

7 See Wollaeger, *Joseph Conrad and the Fictions of Skepticism*, for an extended discussion of this topic.
8 Both readings underplay contradictory textual pulls: the French Lieutenant is undermined by his mechanical gestures and physical rigidity whereas the play of light imagery in the famous Stein scene of ch. 20 argues a fundamental ambiguity.
9 See White's discussion of Conrad and imperialism in ch. 10 of this volume.
10 See Bruffee, *Elegiac Romance*, ch. 3 and 4 for a discussion of 'Heart of Darkness' and *Lord Jim* in this context. Watt, *Conrad in the Nineteenth Century*, pp. 331–8, offers an especially nuanced reading of the Marlow–Jim friendship, and Lange, 'The eyes have it', and McCracken, ' "A hard and absolute condition of existence" ', analyze masculine identity and homosociality.
11 The Hamlet–Jim parallel is also explicitly evoked by Stein's question 'how to be'? (*LJ*, p. 214). A number of critics follow up Shakespearean parallels and influences; see, for instance, Batchelor, *Lord Jim*; Gillon, *Conrad and Shakespeare*; Hay, '*Lord Jim* and le *Hamletisme*'; and Schultheiss, 'Lord Hamlet and Lord Jim'.
12 See Tanner, *Conrad: 'Lord Jim'*, for an extended reading of the novel's butterfly and beetle metaphors.

WORKS CITED

Bakhtin, M. M. *The Dialogic Imagination: Four Essays*. Ed. Michael Holquist. Tr. Caryl Emerson and Michael Holquist. Austin: University of Texas Press, 1981
  'The *Bildungsroman* and its significance in the history of realism (Toward a historical typology of the novel)'. In *Speech Genres and Other Late Essays*. Ed. Caryl Emerson and Michael Holquist. Tr. Vern W. McGee. Austin: University of Texas Press, 1986, pp. 10–59
Batchelor, John. *The Life of Joseph Conrad: A Critical Biography*. Oxford: Blackwell, 1994
  Lord Jim. London: Unwin Hyman, 1988
Berthoud, Jacques. *Joseph Conrad: The Major Phase*. Cambridge: Cambridge University Press, 1978
Bloom, Harold, ed. *Joseph Conrad's 'Lord Jim'*. New York: Chelsea House, 1987
Bruffee, Kenneth A. *Elegiac Romance: Cultural Change and Loss of the Hero in Modern Fiction*. Ithaca: Cornell University Press, 1983
Buckley, Jerome Hamilton. *Season of Youth: The Bildungsroman from Dickens to Golding*. Cambridge, MA: Harvard University Press, 1974
Conrad, Joseph. 'A Familiar Preface'. *'The Mirror of the Sea' and 'A Personal Record'*. 1906 and 1912. Ed. Zdzisław Najder. Oxford: Oxford University Press, 1988, pp. xi–xxi
  Lord Jim, A Tale. 1900. Ed. John Batchelor. Oxford: Oxford University Press, 1983
Conroy, Mark. 'Colonial self-fashioning in Conrad: writing and remembrance in *Lord Jim*'. *L'Epoque Conradienne* 19 (1993), 25–36
Fraser, Gail. *Interweaving Patterns in the Works of Joseph Conrad*. Ann Arbor: UMI Research Press, 1988

Gillon, Adam. 'Conrad and Shakespeare' and Other Essays. New York: Astra Books, 1976

Gordan, John Dozier. Joseph Conrad: The Making of a Novelist. Cambridge, MA: Harvard University Press, 1940

Hay, Eloise Knapp. 'Lord Jim: from sketch to novel'. Comparative Literature 12 (1960), 289–309. Reprinted (revised) in Moser, ed. Lord Jim, pp. 418–37

'Lord Jim and le Hamletisme'. L'Epoque Conradienne 16 (1990), 9–27

Henricksen, Bruce. Nomadic Voices: Conrad and the Subject of Narrative. Urbana: University of Illinois Press, 1992

Lange, Robert J. G. 'The eyes have it: homoeroticism in Lord Jim'. West Virginia Philological Papers 38 (1992), 59–68

Leavis, F. R. The Great Tradition: George Eliot, Henry James, Joseph Conrad. London: Chatto & Windus; New York: G. W. Stewart, 1948

McCracken, Scott. '"A hard and absolute condition of existence": reading masculinity in Lord Jim'. The Conradian 17.2 (1993), 17–38

Marle, Hans van and Pierre Lefranc. 'Ashore and afloat: new perspectives on topography and geography in Lord Jim'. Conradiana 20 (1988), 109–35

Moser, Thomas C., ed. Lord Jim: An Authoritative Text, Backgrounds, Sources. New York: Norton, 1968

Murfin, Ross C. 'Lord Jim': After the Truth. New York: Twayne, 1992

Parry, Benita. Conrad and Imperialism: Ideological Boundaries and Visionary Frontiers. London: Macmillan; Topsfield, MA: Salem Academy/Merrimack Publishing, 1984

Raval, Suresh. 'Narrative authority in Lord Jim: Conrad's art of failure'. ELH 48 (1981), 387–410. Reprinted in Bloom, ed., Joseph Conrad's 'Lord Jim', pp. 77–98

Schultheiss, Thomas. 'Lord Hamlet and Lord Jim'. Polish Review 11 (1966), 103–33

Sherry, Norman. Conrad's Eastern World. Cambridge: Cambridge University Press, 1966

Sherry, Norman, ed. Conrad: The Critical Heritage. London: Routledge & Kegan Paul, 1973

Stape, J. H. '"Gaining conviction": Conradian borrowing and the Patna episode in Lord Jim'. Conradiana 25 (1993), 222–34

Tanner, Tony. Conrad: 'Lord Jim'. London: Arnold; New York: Barron's Educational Series, 1963

Verleun, Jan. Patna and Patusan Perspectives: A Study of the Function of Minor Characters in 'Lord Jim'. Groningen: Bouma's Boekhuis, 1979

Watt, Ian. Conrad in the Nineteenth Century. Berkeley: University of California Press, 1979; London: Chatto & Windus, 1980

Watts, Cedric. Introduction. Lord Jim. Ed. Cedric Watts and Robert Hampson. Harmondsworth: Penguin Books, 1986, pp. 11–30

Wollaeger, Mark A. Joseph Conrad and the Fictions of Skepticism. Stanford: Stanford University Press, 1991

5

ELOISE KNAPP HAY

Nostromo

In 1907, Conrad wrote to his literary agent, J. B. Pinker, that 'the public mind runs on questions of war and peace and labour'. He adds that he plans 'to treat those subjects ... from a modern point of view' (*Letters*, III, pp. 439–40). These matters had become his subject already, however, when he wrote *Nostromo* four years earlier, and they continued to preoccupy him for the rest of his life. Labour relations had figured largely in his fiction even earlier, since 1897 when *The Nigger of the 'Narcissus'* and other sea stories presented sea-captains like Allistoun, and Marlow in Africa, managing their sometimes mutinous subaltern officers and crews. *Nostromo* is the first to introduce the other, equally 'modern', topic of 'war and peace', which for Conrad turns out to mean revolution and its consequences in a post-colonial world.

Readers for generations have related *Nostromo* to Leo Tolstoy's *War and Peace* (1869). The Russian novel may not have been a deliberate model, yet similarities abound: the vast compass of history the two novels re-enact, the celebration of a nation's repulse of an invading army, and the multiple plots and family histories that centre on the making of marriages and the reasons for their success or failure. In *Nostromo*, the families are the Goulds, the Decouds, the Avellanos – all of whom as 'Creoles': that is, South American natives of European descent – and a fourth family, the Italian Violas, who count Nostromo as their 'son'. *Nostromo* is also, again like Tolstoy's novel, a narrative structured by a war of ideas, especially the idea of historical determinism versus individual freedom. But whereas history is determined by individual wills in *War and Peace*, the autonomy of the actors in *Nostromo* is overshadowed by a force in history over which they have little control, the power of silver. By contrast with Tolstoy's, Conrad's novel is especially 'modern' in that its perspective on history is ironic and bleak rather than heroic and triumphal. We can well ask, indeed, if *Nostromo* is the first case of Conrad's writing *against* the Russian novels he despised, as he would do again in the anti-Dostoevskian *Under Western Eyes*. That he was being subjected to, and made to compete with, the growing craze for

Russian fiction in England at just this time, may have been all the more galling because the chief English translator of that fiction was Constance Garnett, the wife of his friend Edward.

As John Halverson and Ian Watt have shown, following hints in the 'Author's Note', Conrad's sense of having a story to tell was sparked by the tale of a clever Italian sailor who stole a lighter loaded with silver off the coast of South America ('The Original Nostromo', pp. 49–52). Though Claudine Lesage has convincingly demonstrated that Conrad used his memories of ports near Marseilles for the setting of *Nostromo*, his many reasons for setting the tale in Latin America appear in letters to Cunninghame Graham as far back as 1898. Then and later, Conrad had written to his part-Spanish, mainly-Scottish friend – who had extensively explored the continent – fuming against the rising imperialism of the United States in the Philippines and the Caribbean (*Letters*, II, p. 60; III, p. 102). Various histories and biographies of Garibaldi furnished Conrad with much of the novel's material on Europeans in Latin America, while Cunninghame Graham supplied him with documents on the history and people of the countries, and Conrad haunted the London Library for his materials.[1] *Nostromo* was the first novel he wrote from very slight personal experience, the first in which his insatiable reading was his mainstay.

With *Nostromo*, Conrad thus turned from his seaman's memories of the Malay Archipelago and Africa to writing about the Western hemisphere, where he had been for many weeks when he was seventeen and eighteen, making three voyages to Caribbean ports and Venezuela in 1875 and 1876. Wars for independence had liberated most of these areas from Spain, and post-independence revolutions were breaking out while Conrad was there. He later claimed more than once to have assisted a Corsican shipmate (Dominic Cervoni, one model for Nostromo) in carrying guns for the rebel cause in Colombia (van Marle, 'Lawful and lawless', pp. 92–111). Childhood associations with Latin America sharpened his interest, since, as a boy of five, he had been introduced to the dramatic history and tragic exploitation of that continent in a gift book entitled *Les Anges de la terre, personifiés par leurs vertus et leurs belles actions* [The Angels of the Earth, Personified by their Virtues and Great Deeds]. The book includes among lesser known men and women the lives of Columbus and the Dominican friar Bartolomé de Las Casas (1474–1566), who transcribed the *diario* of Columbus and spent years writing back to Spain from Latin America, protesting the Spaniards' treatment of the Indians. Conrad remembered the 'soul' of Las Casas while writing *Nostromo* (*Letters*, III, p. 102).

Many readers, including Terry Eagleton, Edward Said, and Fredric Jameson, have singled out the theme of imperialism as the main focus of

Nostromo. Yet imperialism is far less an issue than the drama of conflicting revolutionary ideologies, initiated and fed from within the imaginary republic of Costaguana. While M. C. Bradbrook's classic study of Conrad pointed out that 'revolution and counter-revolution ... are the centre of the book' (*Joseph Conrad: England's Polish Genius*, p. 45), recent critics have evidently taken their sights less from the novel itself than from the Marxism that has mushroomed in academic circles since the 1960s. Imperialism, 'the conquest of the earth' by various means, was indeed Conrad's explicit theme in 'Heart of Darkness'. But writing about *Nostromo*, Edward Said sees what he calls the 'paternalistic arrogance of imperialism' as both the novel's subject and also as Conrad's point of view in it ('Through gringo eyes', p. 70). Said concentrates on 'the imperialist project' – in the singular – which he says *Nostromo* 'both criticize[s] and reproduces', thus targeting Conrad too with the poisoned arrow. Arguing that Conrad focuses on the whites in Costaguana and fails to allow for meaningful 'indigenous' activity, Said takes the line that Chinua Achebe made famous in his 1975 critique of 'Heart of Darkness'. Like Achebe, he charges that when 'there is something indigenous to be described', Conrad makes it 'unutterably corrupt, degenerate, irredeemable' ('An image of Africa', p. 72).

If one strictly defines 'indigenous', this can only refer to the novel's Indians, whose lives are seen as poor, burdened, exploited, and fairly quiescent, as was historically the case in their region. But Conrad's Indians are in no way corrupt or degenerate. A number of his mestizos fit this description; however, among them there are also a number of admirable men and women, such as the heroic Hernandez, Don Pépé, and the families of the mine workers he oversees. The only 'imperialists' to whom recent critics can refer are the obnoxious American financier, Holroyd, and the British railway manager, Sir John, who both have openly imperialist designs on the country. Still, these two men are distant threats, not central figures. They are, to my reading, chiefly significant as showing how tragically embroiled with foreign interests the principal characters, Charles Gould and his wife, become, despite their original hopes of setting Costaguana on an independent, prosperous, and democratic course. Gould is insistently presented as a native Costaguanero, his family having been rooted in the region for generations. He has no ties or interests in other countries, though like his forefathers he chooses an English woman, raised in Italy, for his wife. As the novel's chief actor, he is as much a revolutionary as the mestizo Montero brothers. His object in reopening the Gould family's silver mine is to revolutionize a long history of brutal regimes in his homeland by using his inherited silver mine and his abilities as a mining engineer to create prosperity and the conditions for good government.

The novel's other two main characters, also white, are the equally native (though 'Frenchified') Decoud and the titular Italian seaman, Nostromo, who – like the Goulds – are innocent of 'imperialist' designs. The most dangerous empire-builder, Holroyd, makes no effort to control the Gould mine during the novel, but Gould and his wife are doomed and alone as the narrative ends, while predators outside the vulnerable 'treasure house' of Sulaco, including Holroyd, are poised to strike. In so far as the revolutions in the novel are motivated either by greed – as with the Montero brothers – or by faith resting on material interests – as with the Goulds – they cannot produce the just peace that the people long for.

Conrad begins *Nostromo* with an old folktale, kept alive by the poor in Costaguana, a story of 'two wandering sailors – Americanos, perhaps, but gringos of some sort', who persuaded 'a gambling, good-for-nothing' Indian to help them find a cursed treasure lying in a desolate ravine (*No*, p. 4). When it is found, the 'impious' white men, fall under the spell of the treasure and are fated to keep watch over it forever. The poor Indian, whose wife has some masses said for him, is 'probably permitted to die ... a Christian would have renounced and been released' (p. 5). The superstition provides an allegorical framework for the obsession with the silver that gradually takes possession of the novel's two central gringos, Gould and Nostromo.[2]

As Conrad's novel develops, Gould and his new wife, Emilia, challenging the ban his father has laid against reviving the mine, claim Gould's inherited treasure for use in ending the wearisome chain of revolutions, counter-revolutions, and terrifying interludes that have reigned in the land since the Spanish conquerors were ousted some three or four generations earlier. It will turn out that Gould's generously conceived revolution can only add to the calamitous chain, bringing the likely outcome, at the end of the novel, of yet another revolution to come in the name of 'the people' and more than one imperialist invasion, as ruthless as the Spaniards' ever was.

Many of Conrad's best works from 1903 on would further probe the meanings of revolution in the age of revolutions, which Conrad dated from the eighteenth century in France. These works include his essay 'Autocracy and War', written not long after *Nostromo*, the four stories in *A Set of Six*, *The Secret Agent*, and *Under Western Eyes*. Taken together with *The Rescue*, *The Rover*, and *Suspense*, these major works on 'war and peace and labour' show how closely Conrad's historical vision resembles the later view of Hannah Arendt, who said in 1963 that 'war and revolution still constitute [our world's] two central political issues. They have outlived all their ideological justifications' – 'such as ... capitalism and imperialism, socialism and communism, which ... have lost contact with the major realities of our world'. According to Arendt, 'no cause is left but the most ancient of all, the cause of freedom versus tyranny' (*On Revolution*, p. 1). She could have been reading from Conrad's books.

Nostromo, the first in this coherent group of narratives, becomes a valuable intertext for all that follow. Conrad seems to assume that the revolutions he focuses on in later works, ending with *The Rover* and *Suspense*, will be read with *Nostromo* in mind. Without the Western history provided there, one loses an important thread while trying, for instance, to interpret his protest in the 'Author's Note' to *A Personal Record* against being called 'the son of a Revolutionist'. Conrad says, 'No epithet could be more inapplicable to a man with such a strong sense of responsibility in the region of ideas and action' as his father's. He also denies that the word 'revolutionary' can apply to the Polish uprisings of 1831 and 1863, which he terms 'purely revolts against foreign domination'. 'The Russians themselves called them "rebellions"', he recalls, adding that his father was no revolutionary 'in the sense of working for the subversion of any [legitimate] social or political scheme' (*PR*, pp. vii–viii).

Does this mean that Conrad despised all revolutionaries? Many have seen in his work a fascinated ambivalence towards revolution, including a repressed desire to condemn his father's engagement in what they interpret as the 'revolution' of 1863, and a disastrous one. Still others, including myself, have argued that Conrad was single-mindedly clear in distinguishing a violent revolution to overthrow the legitimate government of a country, such as that governing Poland before 1792, from rebellions to drive out an invader, like the Russians in Poland after 1792. In *Nostromo*, legitimacy is not an issue, however. For 'Costaguana', Conrad's imaginary country somewhere on the western coast of South America, any question of legitimacy has been obliterated long before the novel opens and probably never existed in the Western history available to Conrad.

The reader is assumed to possess a considerable amount of historical information: from 1492 on, constant waves of Spanish and other European colonizers voyaged to the New World to settle and be overthrown in a series of revolutions, fomented often by Europeans, in which the rallying cry was mostly, 'Get rid of the foreigners!' Just who the 'foreigners' are is a pervasive irony in *Nostromo*, since nearly everyone who has had a voice in any government since the first colonizers decamped is descended from Europeans, or derives his ideas mainly from Europe, and can thus be called foreign.

The long view is characteristic in *Nostromo*. Conrad names his republic 'Costaguana' no doubt because it recalls not only the Spanish for 'coast' but also the first name for the land, given by the natives to Columbus when he reached 'the Indies'. The 'Indians call it "Guanahani"', Columbus wrote back to Spain (Greenblatt, *Marvelous Possessions*, p. 52). Though many have seen '*guana*' as alluding only to *guano*, the bird excrement used for making explosives, which Conrad had used symbolically – and aptly – in *Lord Jim*, the word *guana*, referring to a yellow-flowered coastal tree, would seem more appropriate to the fragrant seaboard described in *Nostromo*. It would also seem more acceptable to the country's inhabitants, especially since Conrad wanted the name to have an aboriginal association.

The novel virtually sanctions South American revolutions fought against the Spanish invaders, most clearly those led by Garibaldi, which are reflected in Giorgio Viola's dimming idealism. Viola looks back to 'the old, humanitarian revolutions' (*No*, p. xliv), as Conrad described them later in his 'Author's Note' (1919), implicitly contrasting Garibaldi's wars for liberation with the recent, enslaving Bolshevik Revolution. Though the 'old Garibaldino' Viola's revolution is recalled at length early in the novel, the originating revolution of the main action is Gould's. His programme is emphatically not 'imperialistic', meaning controlled by 'foreigners' – as the infamous Pedrito Montero would have us believe, anticipating the views of Parry, Said, and Jameson. Gould is not 'British', as these critics say, but as Conrad says, an 'American' (p. 83), a third-generation Costaguanero. In reopening the silver mine and depending initially, as he must, on the odious Holroyd as well as the shadowy Sir John, Gould risks allowing the mine to fall under foreign control. It never does in the novel, however, so a share in the profits of the enterprise – which brings prosperity to the country – is all that these actual 'foreigners' can gain. Holroyd's intention of following his investment with a crusade to revolutionize all Latin America with 'the purer form of Christianity' (p. 80) is certainly a kind of cultural imperialism. But in the course of the novel it exists only as a possibility, never an actuality. His seasoned business associates 'mutter darkly and knowingly' that 'the Holroyd connection meant by-and-by to get hold of the whole Republic of Costaguana, lock, stock, and barrel. But in fact ... He was not running a great enterprise there ... He was running a man!' (p. 81).

Holroyd's name makes one think of 'holy rood'. It is also a near anagram for Henry Cabot Lodge, the United States senator who zealously supported cultural and economic expansion into Latin America as well as acquisition of the Philippines and Cuba, winning great popular sympathy when he was backed by Presidents McKinley and Roosevelt – while Conrad was writing the novel. But Holroyd and Sir John are minor characters, and one of Holroyd's uglier statements is his threat to Gould that he will 'drop him in time' if the mine falls into hostile hands. This suits Gould perfectly, since with such an agreement 'the mine preserved its identity ... and it remained dependent on himself alone' (p. 82).

Our attention is thus drawn not to new kinds of imperialism but to the

Realpolitik Gould must deal in if his generous ideal is to be realized. He gradually comes to see that, although he never sells out to Holroyd or any other foreigner, his own fixation on the silver has been contagious in Costaguana, creating an obsession with the mine-based economy as noxious to the people as an invasion from abroad would be. Gould's utopian early vision proves prophetic in ways he does not foresee when he hopefully says that if only 'the material interests once get a firm footing', they will create the beneficial conditions required for their security: 'That's how your money-making is justified here in the face of lawlessness and disorder. It is justified because the security which it demands must be shared with an oppressed people. A better justice will come afterwards' (p. 84). The all-seeing narrator adds that Gould 'was prepared to stoop for his weapons' but that he 'was competent because he had no illusions' (p. 85). The assessment should warn us not to put complete faith in Decoud, who believes to the contrary that Gould lives 'on illusions' (p. 239). The authorial voice by contrast momentarily offers a realist's benediction on Gould's revolutionary intentions, which the unmercenary Emilia even finds splendid, at first.

Hope and enterprise in this anti-Tolstoyan epic will nevertheless end in tragedy – all the more because the Goulds' valiant endeavours can only turn their love for each other and the people depending on them to dust and corruption. Dr Monygham, the novel's moral conscience, eventually sums up the failure of Gould's ostensibly successful undertaking: Material interests have their own law and justice, founded on expediency. It is inhuman, without the rectitude and force 'that can be found only in moral principle'. Monygham foresees that soon the Gould Concession will 'weigh as heavily upon the people as the barbarism, cruelty, and misrule' of former years (p. 511). Thus, late in the novel, we are directed to look for the 'moral principle' that might have undergirded Gould's enterprise, a principle that would have spared the people of Costaguana, including the Goulds, from their bondage to the mine.

This is easy to miss, especially if we read the novel as suggesting that all would have been well if only the 'material interests' had been controlled entirely by native workers. Whether controlled by 'foreigners' or by others, it is the loss of faith in any power beyond material wealth that dooms a nation. 'Silver is the pivot of moral and material events' in the novel, as Conrad said (Jean-Aubry, ed., *Joseph Conrad: Life and Letters*, II, p. 296).

Gould's *ideas* are English in their utilitarian principles, though he is explicitly an 'Americano', and his control is not loosened in the end. Or rather, and it comes to the same thing, the mine's control over him is eventually complete. He is affectionately, and of course ironically, known as 'el Rey', successor to the (relatively speaking) good Don Carlos IV of Spain. When Emilia Gould refers to her husband's homeland – 'your country' – it is always Costaguana (p. 86). The narrator's description of Gould's Uncle Harry fits Gould himself: 'He was of the country, and he loved it, but he remained essentially an Englishman *in his ideas* ... He simply stood up for social order out of pure love for rational liberty and from his hate of oppression' (p. 64; emphasis added). These are the ideas that prompt his determination to revolutionize Costaguana.

The other central revolution, to which Gould's immediately gives rise, that of the Monterists, is also nativist and also coloured by European ideas, though instigated by born Costaguaneros. This uprising inspires the novel's most brilliant chapters: Decoud's attempt to save the mine's silver, taking a lighter-load of it by night into the Golfo Placido with Nostromo's help; the collision of the lighter with one of the insurrectionist ships; the burying of the silver on an island, to be recovered, or rather stolen, later by Nostromo; the despair of Decoud, leading to his suicide; and the hoodwinking of the Monterists by Dr Monygham, convincing them – while he himself thinks the silver is lost – that they may yet find it somewhere in the gulf, thus winning time for Gould's supporters to recapture Sulaco. One suspects that, unlike Gould's, the Marxist and other nascent revolutions brewing at the end of the novel, heralded by 'secret societies' and the pale blond photographer, are to be controlled by foreigners and by foreign theories. By then Teresa Viola's dying words apply to many besides herself: 'Their revolutions, their revolutions ... Look, Gian' Battista, it has killed me at last ... this one has killed me', meaning the Monterists' (p. 253).

Many readings of *Nostromo*, and critics like Cedric Watts, persuade one of another revolution adumbrated at the end of the novel that has been overlooked. The novel is structured on five ideologies of revolution: Gould's, Giorgio Viola's, the Monterists', the Marxist's, and a psychological revolution that occurs within Nostromo himself, which calls for more attention than it has received. The novel's much discussed and often confusing time shifts serve to juxtapose these past, present, and future movements to form a composite pattern, almost a modernist collage if one concentrates, as one must, on what is happening to ideas rather than to individuals. Returned to chronological order, the five revolutions help account for the jarring dislocations and hollowness that have been found in the narrative by critics from Leavis to Said and Jameson.[3] Such effects are unoffensive, however, when we focus attention on the mental changes in Nostromo himself and, through him, on the one hopeful revolution still in process when the novel ends. This psychological revolution, justifying Nostromo's place as titular hero, transforms him from a mere instrument of

the mining interests to a self-activating 'man of the People ... a power –
within the People', who (the 'Author's Note' tells us) becomes at last 'the
enigmatical patron of the new revolutionary agitation' (pp. xliv–xlvi). The
inner changes that free him from the material interests, and free others
through him, can ultimately bring about the clear sky mentioned in the
novel's epigraph – 'So foul a sky clears not without a storm'. This clearing,
of course, like the coming storm before it, will appear after the novel's end
and is left to the reader to imagine.

Initially in the novel's main plot, Gould's revolution and the mine it
depends on create a tiny empire within an empire – *'Imperium in Imperio'*
(p. 135), an empire on the model of the Roman *civitas* – that is, developed
by citizens of the country for themselves rather than controlled by foreign
invaders. The ironic link with Italian history was evidently part of Conrad's
first plan for the novel, for as late as May 1903, when he was at least five
months into its writing, he told Cunninghame Graham, 'I am placing it in a
Republic I call Costaguana. It is however concerned mostly with Italians'
(*Letters*, III, p. 34).

There were strong reasons for setting his first novel on revolution in the
Western hemisphere. Foremost perhaps was his view that the discovery and
development of the New World, even before the existence of the United
States, had set the stage for the first political revolutions in Europe. Conrad
alludes to this in 'Geography and some explorers' (1924) when he writes
that 'the discovery of America was the occasion of the greatest outburst of
reckless cruelty and greed known to history' (*LE*, p. 3). After Columbus, he
says, most explorers 'were prompted by an acquisitive spirit, the idea of
lucre in some form, the desire of trade or the desire of loot, disguised in
more or less fine words' (p. 10). Pursuit of this new and global voracity
paved the way later in history for the 'opening' of Africa, which Conrad in
this essay calls 'the vilest scramble for loot that ever disfigured the history of
human conscience' (p. 17).

Nostromo is thus set in the primal scene where, according to Conrad,
'history' began to be most 'disfigured'. As in *Under Western Eyes*, where
Razumov dreams of beginning to write a history for Russia, history is
something that can be *figured*, well or ill. Conrad speaks of both history and
the 'human conscience' as capable of being shaped and consciously directed.
If the silver of the mine in *Nostromo* represents 'the arch-beginning' of an
era, as Said agrees (*Beginnings*, p. 117), we learn from Hannah Arendt's
On Revolution that the beginning and instigator of *all revolutions*, properly
speaking, was also the discovery of the New World and its wealth (p. 15).

This is no overstatement. Arendt makes clear that the Western hemisphere made possible for the first time the utopian idea of a society that

could be rid of poverty. Not that political convulsions had not occurred earlier. Aristotle understood the economic motivations prompting the violent 'overthrow of government by the rich and the establishment of an oligarchy ... [and later] the overthrow of government by the poor and establishment of a democracy' (Arendt, *On Revolution*, p. 14). But no writer, Arendt contends, till after Columbus doubted that poverty was 'inherent in the human condition'. As she explains further, the utopian idea that 'life on earth might be blessed with abundance instead of being cursed by scarcity ... was American in origin; it grew directly out of the American colonial experience' and initiated the age of revolutions in the modern sense: The 'stage was set when first Locke – probably under the influence of the prosperous conditions of the colonies in the New World – and then Adam Smith held that labor and toil, far from being the appanage of poverty ... were, on the contrary, the source of all wealth' (*On Revolution*, p. 15). The 'labour theory of value' was soon both in the minds of Ricardo and Marx.

Charles Gould comes naturally by his revolutionary plan, as the son of 'ancestral Goulds' in South America: 'liberators, explorers, coffee planters, merchants, revolutionists' (p. 48). His own formula for political change matches Arendt's description of all true revolutions – 'inextricably bound up with the notion that the course of history suddenly begins anew ... [that] a story never known or told before, is about to unfold' (*On Revolution*, p. 21). Gould attempts, and nearly manages to accomplish in one lifetime, the centuries-long revolutions from feudalism to liberal capitalism and thence to the establishment of the dreamed-of peaceable kingdom. That Gould begins by depending on financiers like Holroyd may introduce imperialist powers into Costaguana, but Holroyd speaks for many foreign capitalists when he declares he will 'stay' only as long as Gould keeps order and control. The financier promises to disappear if another revolution occurs, in which case, of course, Sir John's railway would also be appropriated. Holroyd and Sir John wish to see the continent transformed under their influence – Protestant and North American in Holroyd's case, technological and British in Sir John's – while reaping the profits thereof.

Gould will politically back only the native and moderate Blancos. The greatest threat to this capitalist's peace, never mind justice, which he thinks will come 'later', is the revolution of General Montero's military regime. This menace inspires Sulaco's declaration of independence from the volatile mainland, a plan masterminded by Decoud, culminating in a separate government growing from Gould's original movement.

Hunt Hawkins clarifies Gould's reliance on a 'national bourgeoisie' and discusses the Monterist revolution as evidence of Conrad's thorough understanding of violent movements in Latin America as well as Africa. Citing extensively from the political philosopher and psychiatrist Frantz Fanon, Hawkins notes that the failure of Gould's 'national bourgeoisie' opens the door to a coup by the army, which has enflamed 'popular resentment against the constitutional government due to its alliance with foreign money interests and its inability to improve living conditions ... The army's own attitude towards the West is schizophrenic', Fanon makes clear. On the one hand, it is nationalistic, disliking foreign interference and therefore repudiating foreign loans. On the other hand, it craves the capital and hardware only the [foreigners] can provide'. Usually the money interests, like Gould with his silver, succeed in buying off the army, which then slides into corruption, relying more and more on brute force. The dictator eventually dies or becomes disfunctional, is then replaced by another dictator or, 'at the insistence of [First World] nations, by the "national bourgeoisie" which is supposed to "clean up the economy"'. Hawkins observes how neatly this description fits the Monterist revolution, inspired by Gould's.

But, significantly, it is the third revolution treated in the novel. The ideology of revolution held by Giorgio Viola is given first place in Conrad's plot, as distinct from the chronology of events. With Viola's history in chapters 3 and 4, we are given the first deeply examined point of view, following the vivid description of the coastal scene and a brief overview of events to come. (As prelude to Viola's story, Conrad presents the endpoint of the novel in the absurdly cheerful hindsight of Captain Mitchell, who remembers all the novel's violent events as past, undifferentiated, and unidentified revolutions between which the band played in the park.) Though Jameson calls 'the story of old Viola ... strictly superfluous' (*The Political Unconscious*, p. 273), the early presentation of Viola's beliefs is, to the contrary, crucial to understanding the Goulds' and later the Monteros' mentalities.

Viola's story, being the first serious scrutiny of a revolutionary's mind, is also necessary in recalling the great South American revolutions already fought for freedom from Spain between 1820 and 1865. These first revolutions, unlike Gould's, were fought without dependence on 'material interests'. Viola came from Italy with his hero, the fisherman Garibaldi, 'for the cause of freedom in America', to aid such natives as the 'negro company' who 'died heroically' at the siege of Montevideo (p. 30).

Men like Garibaldi and Viola thus took arms only for ideas, never for material gain. Now an old man, disheartened by Garibaldi's failure in Italy to liberate the poor from oppression by 'kings and ministers', Viola recovers some hope of finding Emilia Gould, and apparently also her husband, living by the ideals he has fought for. Hannah Arendt traces such revolutionary concerns as those of Viola and Emilia Gould to the French Revolution, during which the oppressed multitude, which had been 'hidden in darkness and shame', for the first time emerged into the public realm (p. 41). Pointedly, during Emilia Gould's two-month journey through the country, while her husband hunts up labourers for the mine, she is spurred into continuous action by the land's poverty made visible. We are told that she, with her education in Italy and years spent studying the peasants there, quickly becomes herself 'a Costaguanera' (p. 89). Her 'revolutionary time', like Viola's formerly, is inspired by 'self-forgetfulness ... devotion to a vast humanitarian idea' and 'a sort of austere contempt for all personal advantage' (pp. 31, 46).

We need to remember the intellectual kinship between Garibaldi's revolutions and Emilia Gould's conception of her husband's revolution, which she had believed would bring 'law, good faith, order' and a security that would be 'shared with an oppressed people' in Costaguana (p. 84). She is exhilarated, dedicated like Garibaldi to a new beginning in the social structure as she works for the social transformation of Sulaco. Journeying into the 'interior unaffected by the slight European veneer of the coast towns', she sees the 'people, suffering and mute, waiting for the future in a pathetic immobility of patience' (p. 88). That future is what she with her husband came to Costaguana to ensure, and later – even when disheartened, like Giorgio, with their revolution's blasted hopes – she still works so that, as she puts it, the present will 'contain the care of the past and of the future in every passing moment' (p. 521). She does not warrant the charge that Irving Howe's fine old study of Conrad brought against *Nostromo*, that she merely represents Conrad's 'apolitical' retreat 'to the resources of private affection' (*Politics and the Novel*, p. 23).

Mrs Gould's vision is the undimmed, principled aspect of Gould's original plan, and she repeatedly takes political action. She backs Decoud, who trusts her alone, in effecting Sulaco's secession from a corrupt nation. She is the first to recognize the worth of the outcast Hernandez, who is then brought to the aid of Gould's counter-revolution and later made Minister of War. And, finally, by inspiring Dr Monygham's activities, she works the last wonders that save the new republic. Conrad's original epigraph for *Nostromo*, as indicated in proofs, gave a kind of centrality to Mrs Gould, and also to Antonia Avellanos and the Viola sisters Linda and Giselle, all of them passionate women whose love can save neither the men they love nor (in the case of Emilia and Antonia) the admirable causes these women devote themselves to. The epigraph, from Scott's *The Lay of the Last Minstrel*, was to be ironically, 'Love rules the court, the camp, the grove' (Canto III, stanza 2).[4] What remains in the novel without irony is the view, well put in 1939 by E. M. Forster, that only when 'private decencies can be transmitted to public affairs' will democracy win its third cheer ('What I Believe', p. 18).

Howe followed Max Weber in fearing with some justice that the modern reformist passions of the last century could be withdrawing from public into private spheres of individualism and the family, as Conrad and Forster may appear to do. Said's reading of Mrs Gould's story is similar to Howe's saying that although 'only Mrs. Gould knows Sulaco for what it is', her act of refusing to hear where the lost silver is buried 'is nugatory by the standards of modern politics' (*Beginnings*, pp. 108–9). Surely, though, 'the standards of modern politics' are just what the novel sets out to repudiate, and possibly Mrs Gould's greatest impact should be on the reader, made to see her the way Nostromo sees her, as the only one qualified to release the hold of the silver's evil influence. If she were to accept the confession of Nostromo – now justly, if incongruously, called by his proper surname, Fidanza – on the silver's whereabouts, she would be honour-bound to inform others.[5] The superstitious Capataz clearly expects her to do so, thus freeing himself from the burden of guilt, for he credits the folktale's wisdom, that 'a Christian would have renounced and been released' (p. 5). He does not bind her to secrecy as confession to a priest would do, for he follows Viola in despising priests. But she refuses to learn where the silver is buried, since knowledge of its existence would discredit Gould as well as the thief. The hoped for revolution came to depend on the safety of the 'incorruptible' silver (p. 300), and Gould's victory rested on Monygham's ruse that the silver had been sunk. By disposing of the silver in effect, Emilia Gould once again takes upon herself a public responsibility. She also once again provides a model for action that is based on 'care of the past and of the future' in the present moment, an essential concern in Conrad's political programme.

The novel's design is constructed with utmost care. None of the late scenes, beginning with Fidanza's attempted confession and ending with Linda Viola's agonized cry when she hears of his death, is dispensable, as some readers have held. These crucial events help to focus on the fifth and last revolution – that occurring in the mind of Nostromo. His interior transformation foreshadows that ultimate clearing of the sky proposed in the epigraph. The dying Fidanza is thrown back on his own resources by Mrs Gould's refusal, but he immediately finds a more effective way of renouncing the silver, as his consciousness of playing out the remembered pattern of the folktale impels him to do (pp. 255, 258–60, 263–4).

The Capataz de Cargadores has been joining secret societies, and as he lies dying, shot in error by Viola, who is not wrong to think he kills a robber, Fidanza is confronted by the Marxist photographer, representing yet another potential revolution, the fourth in sequence after Viola's, Gould's, and the Monteros', which came to the fore while this 'man of the people' was slowly amassing his fortune. But Gian' Battista Fidanza has been changing ever since his deathly venture to save the silver and is no longer willing to serve other men's commands. He has remembered Teresa Viola's dying insult, that he sold himself for nothing to the exploiting *hombres finos*, and he has taken possession of the cursed treasure as his due. He is no longer called 'Nostromo' – 'our man', a mere possession of the 'material interests' – except by the obtuse Captain Mitchell. When the Marxist photographer grills him for information about capitalist conspiracies, the Marxist remembers Fidanza's charge that Monygham is 'the worst despiser of all the poor – of the people' (p. 518), based on the doctor's apparent betrayal of Hirsch and on his related willingness to sacrifice Fidanza himself for Mrs Gould's safety. The Marxist thus wishes to blacklist the doctor, the one man among the *hombres finos* who has no revolutionary ideology whatsoever and is certainly no capitalist 'enemy of the people', as the Marxist styles him (p. 563). This novel of ideas hangs finally on Fidanza's response in one last politically charged scene.

Up to now, we have assumed that Fidanza too has lacked an ideology, except for his self-absorbed individualism and instinctive association with 'the people', that is, with the unprivileged many in both hemispheres. In the hospital scene towards the end, he becomes a changed man in the face of death, however, and we see that he makes common cause with Emilia Gould in an ideology of revolution that has been gathering force since the early chapters focusing on Giorgio Viola. The Marxist offers him a chance to deliver the silver over to the powerful revolution mounting against the capitalists, who have used him, the Capataz, as a mere object, playing with his life as a trifle. The full force of his response depends on alterations in his consciousness that remain inarticulate.

We recall the sudden leap he made from being an unthinking 'animal' to recognizing the full value of his own labour. After rescuing the silver and swimming ashore, 'waking as a ... wild beast', he had discovered 'the man' in himself (p. 412). The narrator's metaphor here had already connected such an awakening-to-manhood with the influence of Mrs Gould, who had been 'able to appreciate the great worth of the people' and to see 'the man under the silent, sad-eyed beast of burden' (p. 89). In his rebirth from the sea, Fidanza had embodied that coming-to-consciousness in a labour leader who realizes what his employers have failed to see: their dependence on workers like him for their prosperity, instead of his dependence on them. The Capataz emerged from the sea to begin his mental journey from being an 'object man' – Frantz Fanon's term – to becoming his own man, the indispensable transition without which true revolution is impossible (*Toward the African Revolution*, p. 35).

Now, helped by Mrs Gould, the Capataz makes another leap in his mental revolution, judging and acting, as she has just done effectually, to repudiate any revolution that ties its expectations to economic returns. Refusing to become a pawn in yet another conspiracy, Fidanza makes silence his sign of resistance. In this he stands parallel to the now silent Gould, who is also aware of having become a slave to the silver.[6] In the 'Author's Note', Conrad says, the Capataz is 'freed at last from the toils of ... wealth', and we may logically conclude that his final act of defiance, casting a 'glance of enigmatic and mocking scorn' at the Marxist, has liberated him in an earthly sense before death does the rest.[7]

Of course this might prove only that Gian' Battista, a name that means 'the precursor' to readers of the Bible, has achieved a revolution merely in his own thinking. When Conrad, however, names him 'patron of the new revolutionary agitation' in the 'Author's Note' (p. xlvi), it seems right to call this the novel's fifth – and most important – revolution, an inevitable outgrowth of his witnessing the old 'abstract' humanitarian revolutions for independence, embodied in Viola's memory, then the liberal capitalist revolution of the Goulds, which inspired the so-called 'democratic' revolution of the Monterists that failed, and penultimately the beginning of the international Marxist revolution. Support in reading Fidanza's last act as one of solidarity with another, non-Marxist, revolution can be found in many of Conrad's statements elsewhere, for example in 'Autocracy and War', *Under Western Eyes*, and *The Rover*.

Old Peyrol in *The Rover* is a 'man of the people' like Fidanza, and likewise has great contempt for the political movements swaying the revolutionary world around him. Like Fidanza too, old Peyrol moves from a stand of political indifference to die with a gesture of defiance, which is both a personal and a political act of conviction.[8] Similarly the clearest voice on revolutions in *Under Western Eyes* seems to be that of Nathalia Haldin, who sharply criticizes the English, and presumably the 'Glorious Revolution' of 1688, on grounds that even many English historians find accurate. She says the English 'hate' revolution and are a nation 'which has made a bargain with fate ... so much liberty for so much hard cash' (p. 134). This is precisely the bargain that Charles Gould makes in *Nostromo*. Though Natalia Haldin appears absurdly utopian to her unimaginative English professor, her political ideas curiously echo Conrad's own in 'Autocracy and War'.

Here, blaming the violence of modern wars on nations that rely for their well-being on commercial success and action of aggressive kinds, Conrad writes, sounding much like Natalia Haldin: 'The ultimate triumph of concord and justice remains', he says, 'as yet inconceivable' because the jungle has not yet been cleared for its building (pp. 84, 107); 'The true peace of the world . . . will be built on less perishable foundations than those of material interests' (p. 107). In this essay he urges that political action must be based on 'the constructive instinct of the people', 'a collective conscience', and an as yet to be achieved moral 'principle' (pp. 91, 111) – like Dr Monygham's prescription.

Fredric Jameson, going far beyond Irving Howe but in the same direction, finds that in *Nostromo* and all of Conrad's novels, his political vision substitutes romance and dream for the real concerns of life –namely how we earn our livelihood. Even in Conrad's idealization of shipboard life (which one would think has something to do with earning one's bread), Jameson finds Conrad escaping into a fantasy world, divorced from material reality (e.g., pp. 213–14). Behind his immoderate attacks on Conrad, very similar to Said's, Jameson seems, however, to posit a utopia of his own, a Marxist utopia where physically satisfied lives flourish without illusions concerning non-physical needs. This seems to be as much a fantasy world as any that Conrad constructs, certainly in the very substantial world of *Nostromo*.

In this novel, we follow the growth of the title hero's mind, from seeing himself as merely a reflection in the eyes of others to an identity, and as an acute Fanon said, 'the liberation of the individual does not follow national liberation. An authentic national liberation exists only to the precise degree to which the individual has irreversibly begun his own liberation' (*Toward the African Revolution*, p. 103).

Profound political thinkers have long held these views. Consider, for instance, a letter from John Adams to Thomas Jefferson, written in 1815. Adams asks Jefferson: 'What do We Mean by the Revolution? The War? That was no part of the Revolution. It was only an Effect and Conse-quence of it. The Revolution was in the Minds of the People, and this was effected from 1760–1775 in the course of fifteen Years, before a drop of blood was drawn' (*The Adams-Jefferson Letters*, II, p. 455). *Nostromo* takes its title, Conrad makes clear, from the way its hero represents 'the People' in both the New World and the Old. The novel's most unfinished, most continuous, revolution seems prophetically to be that of 'our man' – the reader's man in the end – transformed from one who had gratefully cherished the name 'Nostromo' (in its English mispronunciation) to one who rejects all outside domination, including that of the corruptingly incorruptible silver.

NOTES

1   Sherry, *Conrad's Western World*, pp. 147–201, and Watt, *Joseph Conrad: 'Nostromo'*, pp. 19–51, are especially helpful in describing Conrad's main sources.

2   Wallace S. Watson found that Conrad borrowed a good deal for *Nostromo*, including the treasure-hunting motif and the anecdote that introduces it, from Victor Hugo's *Les Travailleurs de la mer*, set in Guernsey and the English Channel. The passages I use are cited extensively in Hervouet's *The French Face of Joseph Conrad*.

3   See, for instance, Leavis, *The Great Tradition*, pp. 173–226; Said, *The World, the Text, and the Critic*, pp. 95–6, 101; and Jameson, *The Political Unconscious*, p. 278.

4   I am grateful to J. H. Stape for calling this epigraph to my attention.

5   McLauchlan, *Conrad: 'Nostromo'*, pp. 8–9, neatly summarizes the significance of the name Conrad selected for the novel's title.

6   For other aspects of speech and silence in *Nostromo*, see Fogel, 'Silver and silence', pp. 103–25. I would add that the inflated rhetoric that he associates with imperial expansion is more particularly associated with the naive liberalism of Don José Avellanos and the revolutionary verbiage of Pedrito Montero.

7   In treating Nostromo's last exchange with the Marxist photographer, I follow the Modern Library edition, which is closer to the 1904 manuscript in the Rosenbach Museum than is the Dent edition republished in the World's Classics series. This late edition, like all those published from 1918 on, has Fidanza respond to the Marxist with only silence and 'a glance of enigmatic and profound inquiry' (p. 563). The change suggests that Fidanza is pondering his relation to the Marxist rather than rejecting his revolution outright. While the earlier ending seems more consistent with Fidanza's transformation from being the tool of others to becoming his own man, the later ending stresses the indeterminate position he holds in dying – consistent with Archbishop Corbelàn's warning to Gould that the people will eventually, in one way or another, revolt against the inequalities created by the wealth of his mine.

8   Hay, 'Conrad's Last Epigraph and *The Faerie Queene*' argues that Conrad deliberately used the words of Giant Despayre in his epigraph to *The Rover* to cast light on Peyrol's suicidal contest with a pursuing English warship at the novel's end. To recall Forster's phrase, the old rover's act is at once a 'private decency', saving Arlette's lover, and a 'public affair', expressing Peyrol's loyalty to France and his contempt for the Revolution, which makes his virtual suicide triply understandable.

WORKS CITED

Achebe, Chinua. 'An image of Africa: racism in Conrad's "Heart of Darkness"'. *Massachusetts Review* 17.4 (1977), 782–94. Reprinted *Hopes and Impediments: Selected Essays, 1967–87*. London: Heinemann, 1988; New York: Doubleday, 1989, pp. 1–13

Adams, John. *The Adams-Jefferson Letters*. 2 vols. Ed. Lester J. Cappon. Chapel Hill: University of North Carolina Press, 1959

Arendt, Hannah. *On Revolution*. New York: Viking, 1963

Bradbrook, M. C. *Joseph Conrad: England's Polish Genius*. Cambridge: Cambridge University Press; New York: Macmillan, 1941. Reprinted New York: Russell & Russell, 1965

Carabine, Keith. Introduction. *Nostromo*. Ed. Keith Carabine. Oxford: Oxford University Press, 1984

Conrad, Joseph. 'Autocracy and War'. 1905. *Notes on Life and Letters*. 1921. London: Dent, 1970, pp. 83–114

  'Geography and some explorers'. 1924. *Last Essays*. Ed. Richard Curle. London: Dent, 1926, pp. 1–21. Reprinted 1955

  'The Mirror of the Sea' and 'A Personal Record'. 1906 and 1912. Ed. Zdzisław Najder. Oxford: Oxford University Press, 1988

  Nostromo. 1904. Ed. Keith Carabine. Oxford: Oxford University Press, 1984

  Nostromo. 1904. New York: Random House, 1951

Eagleton, Terry. *Criticism and Ideology: A Study in Marxist Literary Theory*. London: Verso Press, 1976

Fanon, Frantz. *Toward the African Revolution*. Tr. Haakon Chevalier. New York: Monthly Review Press, 1967

Fogel, Aaron. 'Silver and silence: dependent currencies in *Nostromo*'. In *Joseph Conrad's Nostromo*. Ed. Harold Bloom. New York: Chelsea House, 1987, pp. 205–27

Forster, E. M. 'What I Believe'. 1939. *Two Cheers for Democracy*. Ed. Oliver Stallybrass. London: Arnold, 1972, pp. 65–73

Greenblatt, Stephen. *Marvelous Possessions: The Wonder of the New World*. Chicago: Chicago University Press, 1991

Halverson, John and Ian Watt. 'The original Nostromo: Conrad's source'. *Review of English Studies*, ns 10 (1959), 49–52

Hawkins, Hunt. '*Nostromo* and neo-colonialism', Joseph Conrad Society of America Session, Modern Language Association Convention, San Francisco, December 1991

Hay, Eloise. 'Conrad's last epigraph and *The Faerie Queene*: a reassessment of *The Rover*'. *Conradiana* 2.3 (1970), 9–15

Hervouet, Yves. *The French Face of Joseph Conrad*. Cambridge: Cambridge University Press, 1991

Howe, Irving. *Politics and the Novel*. New York: Meridian Books, 1957

Jameson, Fredric. *The Political Unconscious: Narrative as a Symbolic Act*. Ithaca: Cornell University Press, 1981

Jean-Aubry, G., ed. *Joseph Conrad: Life and Letters*. 2 vols. London: Heinemann; Garden City, NY: Doubleday, Page, 1927

Leavis, F. R. *The Great Tradition: George Eliot, Henry James, Joseph Conrad*. London: Chatto & Windus; New York: G. W. Stewart, 1948

Lesage, Claudine. *La Maison de Thérèse – Joseph Conrad: les années françaises, 1874–1878*. Sterne: Presses de l'UFR Clerc – Université de Picardie, 1993

McLauchlan, Juliet. *Conrad: 'Nostromo'*. London: Arnold, 1969

Marle, Hans van. 'Lawful and lawless: young Korzeniowski's adventures in the Caribbean'. *L'Epoque Conradienne* 17 (1991), 91–113

Najder, Zdzisław, ed. *Conrad under Familial Eyes*. Tr. Halina Carroll-Najder. Cambridge: Cambridge University Press, 1983

Parry, Benita. *Conrad and Imperialism: Ideological Boundaries and Visionary Frontiers*. London: Macmillan; Topsfield, MA: Salem Academy/Merrimack Publishing, 1984

Said, Edward. *Beginnings: Intention and Method*. New York: Basic Books, 1975
Culture and Imperialism. New York: Knopf, 1993
'Through gringo eyes: with Conrad in Latin America'. *Harper's Magazine*, April 1988, 70–2
The World, the Text, and the Critic. Cambridge, MA: Harvard University Press, 1983

Sherry, Norman. *Conrad's Western World*. Cambridge: Cambridge University Press, 1971

Watson, Wallace. 'Joseph Conrad's debts to the French'. PhD thesis, Indiana University, 1966

Watt, Ian. *Joseph Conrad: 'Nostromo'*. Cambridge: Cambridge University Press, 1988

Watts, Cedric. *Joseph Conrad: 'Nostromo'*. London: Penguin Critical Studies, 1990

6

JACQUES BERTHOUD

The Secret Agent

'All the damned professors are radicals at heart.'
The Secret Agent, ch. 2

I

For Conrad the publication of what is now regarded as his consummate achievement in the art of fiction turned out to be a strangely uneasy event. Despite the usual family illnesses and financial problems, the first draft had been written in the remarkably short time of nine months, February to October 1906, and without the usual outcries of compositional anguish. But as he reached the stage of serialization, October 1906 to January 1907, and then of revision for book-publication, when he added 28,000 words to the original draft during May to July 1907, he suddenly seemed to lose confidence – though less perhaps in the novel itself than in the thought of the reception that awaited it.[1]

Our main evidence for this is his correspondence, which whenever it touches on the work-in-progress acquires a strangely defensive note. On 12 September 1906, he wrote to John Galsworthy, to whom he had sent part of the manuscript: 'In such a tale one is likely to be misunderstood. After all you must not take it too seriously. The whole thing is superficial and is but *a tale*' (*Letters*, III, p. 354). This is a very uncharacteristic plea for a shallow reading, and the elaborate reason he offers for it scarcely improves matters:

> I had no idea to consider Anarchism politically – or to treat it seriously in its philosophical aspect: [but] as a general manifestation of human nature in its discontent and imbecility. The general reflections ... come in by the way and are not applicable to particular instances – Russian or Latin ... As to attacking anarchism as a form of humanitarian enthusiasm or intellectual despair or social atheism that – if it were worth doing – would be the work of a more vigorous hand and for a mind more robust, and perhaps more honest than mine. (*Letters*, III, pp. 354–5)

This amounts to saying that anarchism is a wholly incidental element, and that what the novel does is to present individuals, who happen to be anarchists but who could equally have been Fenians or Mormons, in order to criticize them as moral beings, and not as agents of national interests, or representatives of a counter-politics, or embodiments of an ideology. But as an account of Conrad's private intentions, this must be less than candid, for although he consistently repudiated literary and theoretical programmes, he equally denounced the kind of fiction that failed to admit or accept its author's real convictions. Moreover, as a description of the text we have, it is certainly erroneous, for *The Secret Agent* plainly contains versions of national mentalities, such as the Russian (Mr Vladimir), the American (the Professor), and the British (Winnie Verloc, the Assistant Commissioner), and indeed instances of 'humanitarian enthusiasm' (Michaelis), 'social atheism' (the Professor), and even 'intellectual despair' (the drift of the narrator's 'general reflections').

Even after Methuen's publication of the book on 10 September 1907, Conrad remained evasive. On 7 October, he wrote to his socialist friend R. B. Cunninghame Graham to express relief that Graham had liked the scenes at Chesham Square and at Westminster; yet he instantly reverted to the self-defensive note: 'I don't think that I've been satirizing the revolutionary world. All these people are not revolutionaries—they are shams' (*Letters*, III, p. 491). But this is precisely what has become one of the standard objections to the novel. To quote Irving Howe's classic version: 'gradually to deprive characters of their pretensions or illusions' is not the same thing as 'to deny them the mildest claim to dignity and redemption'; to do *that* is to commit an artistic crime against them.[2] Conrad exempts the Professor from caricature: 'I did not intend to make him despicable. He is incorruptible at any rate ... At the worst he is a megalomaniac of an extreme type. And every extremist is respectable' (*Letters*, III, p. 491). Yet even here Conrad manages to convert the political into the psychological, and reduce intentions into causes: in this view the Professor is genuinely mad, not genuinely wrong. Indeed, the whole letter is riven by an inconsistency. On the one hand, Conrad justifies the satire on the Establishment in terms of how things are: thus he tells Graham that Vladimir is based on the real-life General Seliwertsov ('whom Padlewski shot ... in the nineties'); and he thanks Graham, as a former Member of Parliament, for confirming the veracity of his presentation of Sir Ethelred, the Secretary of State, modeled on the great Liberal minister Sir William Harcourt. Yet on the other hand, the moment the London anarchists come into sight this criterion disappears – even though it would have been extremely easy for Conrad to invoke the louche and even fraudulent frequenters of the anarchist Soho clubs of the eighties and nineties – and all satirical intent is disavowed.

The embarassment betrayed in these letters has been explained by Conrad's fear of offending the left-wing susceptibilities of his two correspondents. But political disagreement did not usually inhibit him. He found no difficulty, for example, in questioning Cunninghame Graham's confidence in the transcendental merits of universal education or of democratic 'fraternity' (*Letters*, II, pp. 157–61). His unease about the reception of *The Secret Agent* is more than diplomatic. In any case, it extended well beyond his friends, and in doing so took other, if related, forms. Conrad had always been economical in his disclosure of the extent of his real-life sources; with *The Secret Agent* he became positively parsimonious. He could not deny, of course, that its main plot had been prompted by the only anarchist outrage to have occurred in Victorian England – the apparently accidental explosion of a bomb near the Greenwich Observatory on 15 February 1894, which killed the man who was carrying it, one Martial Bourdin, brother-in-law of one H. B. Samuels, a desultory anarchist pamphleteer. Thus he admitted to his publisher, Algernon Methuen, in early November 1906, that his new novel was 'based on the inside knowledge of a certain event in the history of active anarchism', though he could not prevent himself from adding, predictably, that it has 'no social or philosophical intention' (*Letters*, III, pp. 370–1). But these minimal revelations, or the exiguous identifications provided by the 'Author's Note' of 1920, were designed not to satisfy, but to disarm, curiosity. How determined he was, in fact, to cover his tracks is shown in his response, less than a year before his death, to the reception of a pamphlet on the Greenwich affair: 'As a matter of fact I never knew anything of what was called, if I remember rightly, the "Greenwich Bomb Outrage". I was out of England when it happened, and thus I never read what was printed in the newspapers at the time. All I was aware of was the mere fact—my novel being, in intention, the history of Winnie Verloc' (Jean-Aubry, ed., *Joseph Conrad: Life and Letters*, II, p. 322).[3] Then followed the now statutory disclaimer: 'I hope you have seen that the purpose of the book was *not* to attack any doctrine, or even the men holding that doctrine'.

The unvarnished facts are, however, that at the time of the 'Greenwich Bomb Outrage' Conrad was at work on *Almayer's Folly* in Pimlico, and that eleven years later when his thoughts returned to the incident as a topic for fiction, the novel he wrote reproduced the version of events advocated by the very pamphlet he was so peremptorily to dismiss a further fourteen years on (Oliver, *The International Anarchist Movement*, p. 107). Indeed, in preparing *The Secret Agent*, he undertook a full-scale programme of documentary research, which included conversations with his friend and collaborator, Ford Madox Ford, who had had anarchist connections in his youth, visits to Ford's cousin, Helen Rossetti, who as an adolescent had edited an influential anarchist journal, the tracking down of the press coverage of the incident, the study of contemporary anarchist literature, including American pamphlets such as *The Alarm* from which he derived his conception of the Professor, and the perusal of memoirs by participants in the affair, such as Robert Anderson, the CID Assistant Commissioner in charge of the original investigation.[4] Thus we are faced with an elaborate structure of evasiveness in which the refusal to take responsibility for the novel's political content takes the form of a refusal to acknowledge the degree to which the novel is grounded on documentation and observation. We are told repeatedly, and it would seem reductively, that the novel is 'but a tale', and that we are foolish to make any further demands on it.

II

How are we to account for what seems to add up to a deliberate trivialization of a work by its author? The question of Conrad's apparent disinheriting of his novel cannot be ignored, for it has either determined or confirmed the view that *The Secret Agent*, for all its stylistic and narrative brilliance, remains short in intellectual substance and coherence. By seeking to control the responses of his friends, then of his readers, Conrad succeeded only it seems in impoverishing the verdict of posterity. For if there is one point on which critics agree, it is that the novel does not offer a serious intellectual challenge. Jocelyn Baines, Conrad's first modern biographer, thinks that 'the book lacks, unlike most of Conrad's work, a unifying theme, and when it is carefully examined falls apart into a succession of only superficially related scenes' (*Joseph Conrad: A Critical Biography*). Albert J. Guerard, one of Conrad's first modern critics, holds the related view that *The Secret Agent* 'is not (so far as ideas are concerned) a work of exploration and discovery' (*Conrad the Novelist*, p. 244). Alternatively, those who, like the phenomenological J. Hillis Miller, insist on finding a unifying concept, are driven into such vacuities as: 'The theme of *The Secret Agent* seems to be the disjunction between matter and spirit' (*Poets of Reality*, p. 57). Others, like Fleishman, Daleski, and Schwarz, perceptive as their work is, deal with the problem by turning into formalists with the assumption that in this novel 'the vehicle of the metaphor replaces the tenor as the essential quality of the imagined world' (Schwarz, *Conrad*, p. 162), or again, like Howe and Lothe, by turning into rhetoricians, emphasizing a narrative irony that leaves human affairs the sport of accident, fragmentation, and entropy. During the last two decades commentary on the novel – whether politicized, deconstructive, post-colonial, feminist, historical, Freudian, or even plain appreciative – has continued to take for granted that *The Secret Agent* remains a conceptually low-powered work.[5] Thus Conrad's debilitating legacy, which has lasted nearly one hundred years, is still intact. He insists that he is doing no more than telling a story; yet if we are to believe him how are we to account for the socio-historical freight that that story is made to bear? For modern exegesis to demonstrate that this 'story' is no run-of-the-mill narrative, but a super-sophisticated construct, only makes matters worse, for how can a work of literary fiction be simultaneously a technical tour-de-force and an intellectual void? Thomas Mann is reputed to have asked how so gifted a novelist as Georges Simenon could have been so 'brainless'. Whether or not this is fair to the progenitor of Maigret, Mann's difficulty is in principle a real one.

Whenever one finds oneself shunted to and fro between a pair of apparently incompatible alternatives such as 'form' and 'content' or, in this case, 'narration' and 'politics', one should pause to interrogate the oppositional terms. To begin with the first: it has not been sufficiently noticed that the 'mere tale' used in the correspondence to secure the novel's political innocence, is promoted to the 'Simple Tale' of the book's subtitle. In other words, purchasers of the novel are informed from the outset that what they have in their hands is a literary work of art, and not a political pamphlet or philosophical essay. Those who have noticed this subtitle have usually taken it to be a joke at the reader's expense – an overspill of the novel's endemic irony: this 'simple' tale will turn out to be a very complicated one. But it is equally likely that it is the word 'tale' that receives the emphasis: this is a story to be followed for its own sake, not an allegory or an *exemplum* to be decoded for its message. The latter view receives confirmation from the fact that the word is put under pressure. The reader has only to turn the page to encounter the dedication to H. G. Wells: To 'THE CHRONICLER OF MR LEWISHAM'S LOVE/THE BIOGRAPHER OF KIPPS AND/THE HISTORIAN OF THE AGES TO COME/THIS SIMPLE TALE OF THE XIX CENTURY IS AFFECTIONATELY OFFERED'. This formulation has engendered a number of fancy readings, but its point, elucidated by Conrad himself when asking Wells whether he could dedicate the novel to him, is surely clear enough: 'pray observe that in this definition I have stated what the perfect Novelist should be – Chronicler[,] Biographer and Historian' (*Letters*, III, p. 461). In this definition, to write no more than a novel is more than enough: a literary narrative able to take 'THE XIX CENTURY' into itself does not need to apologize for its deficiencies. Conrad seems to be playing a double game, deceptive in his correspondence, indicative in his fiction. As far as the latter is concerned, the question ceases to be whether ideas enter into a fictional world; it becomes how they do so.

As for the other pole of the antithesis – the political as opposed to the narrative: Conrad claims that his novel cannot be called 'political' because it does not engage with politics in the discourse of politics. Here it is not fiction that resists politics, but politics that repudiates fiction. Yet elsewhere Conrad defends a much less restrictive idea of the political. In 'Autocracy and War', a major article on the 1905 Russo-Japanese war written during the run-up to *The Secret Agent*, he notes that the 'colourless print of books and newspapers' reporting the distant conflict has failed to make 'its terrible and monotonous phases of pain, death, sickness' real to us; nor has 'the din of humanitarian talk' or even 'the real progress of humanitarian ideas' (*NLL*, pp. 83–4). Neither information nor statistics (which have 'all the futility of precision without force') are able to rouse us. Only 'Direct vision of the fact, or the stimulus of great art' are able – and that only intermittently – to break through the 'saving callousness which reconciles us to the conditions of our existence', and to awaken 'our sympathetic imagination, *to which alone we can look for the ultimate triumph of concord and justice*' (*NLL*, p. 84; emphasis added). At the outset of a political essay, Conrad argues that automatic or ready-made emotions, encouraged by the perfected practices of civilization – reportage, information, statistics, humanitarian commentary – are inimical to true compassion which, being less passive and reactive than proactive and positive, demands an effort of imaginative attention if the object of feeling, and hence the feeling itself, are to acquire any reality. Such a feeling will not, of course, engender a political programme; but, without it, politics will remain merely theoretical, or ambitious, or vacuously managerial. In this view, the novel can play a decisive role in the justification of politics; but by the same token politics can and perhaps should impart seriousness and weight to the work of fiction.

To deploy the resources of narrative art, then, in order to make an imagined world real, is to create the conditions for the eventual achievement of 'concord and justice'. But for the novelist this affirmation entails a demystification. What political fiction dismantles or decodes is the unreality of a politics that lacks the justification defined above. Conrad is right to insist that in *The Secret Agent* he is not concerned with refuting anarchism; he performs a more radical operation, which is to relocate it within the discourse of narrative realism. To be more precise, he seeks to challenge – in the name of concord and justice – not so much anarchism as such as the shallow or unimaginative liberal-progressive response to anarchism. In short, the novel's true subject is the mind-set – the catechism of commonplace ideas, attitudes, and emotions – that the *lecteur moyen intellectuel* brings to it.

In this light, Conrad's obsessive defensiveness when writing to his friends about the novel becomes more intelligible, if not more excusable. The main recipients of his letters were variously members of the intellectual left. John

Galsworthy, who published the anti-bourgeois *The Man of Property* in 1906, the year during which Conrad was writing *The Secret Agent*, foresaw and welcomed the social revolution which he thought inevitable (Dupré, *John Galsworthy*, p. 155). In the same year Cunninghame Graham, who had participated in the 1889 congress of the Second International and advocated revolution, campaigned as a socialist well to the left of Parliamentary Labour (Watts and Davies, *Cunninghame Graham*, p. 226). As for Conrad's literary patron, Edward Garnett, he too was, in Zdzisław Najder's unsympathetic phrase, a 'leftist liberal' who, with his wife Constance, the greatest English translator of the Russian classics, had long cultivated distinguished anarchist émigrés like Volkhovsky, Kropotkin, and the former assassin Stepniak (Jefferson, *Edward Garnett*, pp. 19–22). There can be no doubt that Conrad held his English friends in the highest regard; but there is also no doubt that he retained his political independence in his relations with them. How confrontational he could be a single example will show. In 1911, he responded to Garnett's review of *Under Western Eyes*, which had asserted that there was 'something almost vitriolic in Mr Conrad's scathing rejection of the shibboleths of the humanitarian lovers of their kind', by railing against Garnett's posture as 'Russian Embassador [*sic*] to the Republic of Letters': 'You are so russianised my dear', he went on to say, 'that you don't know the truth when you see it – unless it smells of cabbage-soup when it at once secures your profoundest respect' (*Letters*, IV, p. 488). Yet such an outburst is much less radical an attack on Edwardian liberal ideology than a novel like *The Secret Agent*. It is one thing to quarrel with an opinion or a judgement, quite another to call into question the whole value system that supports such individual verdicts. The central issue in the novel is not how anarchism should be judged, but what anarchism reveals about the England of the time. Perhaps Conrad is right to insist that *The Secret Agent* is not an attack on anarchism as such; what it does, rather, is to drop anarchism into London life, and show that life suddenly losing its transparency and precipitating its murkier essences. In so doing it foregrounds the whole question of the genuineness of the English left's commitment to social change. If this is so, then Conrad's evasiveness in his letters to his friends is understandable, for the novel threatens friendship much more seriously than this or that difference of opinion.

III

Once Conrad's special understanding of the ideas of narrative and politics has been established, it becomes clear that he was never in any doubt about what he was trying to do in his novel. When only six weeks into its composition, he told his agent J. B. Pinker that it had 'to be *kept up as a story* with an ironic intention but a dramatic development' (*Letters*, III, p. 326). Later that year he wrote to Methuen that the new novel was 'a fairly successful and sincere piece of ironic treatment applied to a special subject – a sensational subject' (*Letters*, III, p. 371). Eleven months later, just as the novel was about to come out, he repeated this formulation to Cunninghame Graham, as he did again five years later, responding to his aunt's praise of the novel's French translation (Rapin, ed., *Lettres de Joseph Conrad*, p. 199). Now the principal function of irony is to destabilize the settled, and thus predictable, notions of its victims, for it is a use of language that appeals to two audiences within one person, the first seeing only the surface meaning, the second the covert, contradictory meaning. So that when Conrad describes *The Secret Agent* as an exercise in the ironic treatment of melodrama he is engaged in more than 'a new departure in *genre*' (his phrase to Cunninghame Graham); the experiment entails a deconstructive project.

The inadequacy of univocal or un-ironic discourses is a motif that pervades the whole of *The Secret Agent*. Such discourses would include the conventions of late-Victorian terrorist fiction,[6] the language of the daily press, which achieved unprecedented growth between 1890 and 1910, and the various modes of the detective thriller, which developed in response to the establishment of the CID in 1878, and which was brought to some sort of sublimity by Conan Doyle. This last will serve as an entrée into the novel's characteristic procedures. The mode requires the presentation of a criminal mystery that is in principle solvable by the application of disinterested intelligence on the part of a legitimate investigator. From the point of view of Scotland Yard, the Greenwich explosion is initially incomprehensible. But Heat, the Chief Inspector, finds evidence that links the outrage with his own private informer, the anarchist Verloc, and decides to suppress it and find a scapegoat in its place. His superior officer, the Assistant Commissioner, astutely discovers this, and moreover that Verloc is in the pay of the Russian embassy, deducing correctly that Verloc has acted as an *agent provocateur*. Deciding to take the inquiry into his own hands, he obtains from the Home Secretary the authority to offer Verloc protection in exchange for testimony against the reactionary foreign power, and he undertakes to report to the Minister later that evening. He is able to do so triumphantly: his suspicions have been confirmed and Verloc has agreed to turn state witness. To be sure, the Assistant Commissioner has not been wholly 'disinterested': his suspicion of his Chief Inspector was prompted by personal reasons for protecting the paroled anarchist Michaelis, whom the Inspector planned to incriminate as the perpetrator of the explosion; but the novel does not suggest that the Commissioner would have exculpated a guilty Michaelis. So, in terms of police logic the outcome is conclusive: the guilty man has been found, the innocent man has been saved, and the inquiry has touched 'the bottom of this affair' (*SA*, p. 110). But in terms of Conradian irony nothing could be less conclusive. At exactly the moment when the self-possessed Assistant Commissioner is telling the Secretary of State that Verloc has accepted the 'assurances of personal safety' offered to him, he is being knifed to death by his wife (p. 110). Indeed, Conrad has so ordered his narrative as to give us Verloc's murder (chapter XI) after the Assistant Commissioner's final report (chapter X), so that we are able to savour to the full the incomprehension implicit in the self-satisfied little joke with which the Commissioner takes his leave of the Minister: 'From a certain point of view we are here in the presence of a domestic drama' (p. 168). To be sure, Conrad is not denigrating the police; they have indeed succeeded in touching the bottom of the affair, and with a celerity that appalls the foreign diplomat to be found down there, when later that evening he is warned off by the Commissioner. But Conrad's novel undercuts their achievement so decisively that it becomes quite impossible to read *The Secret Agent* as celebrating the power of intelligence or the values of law and order or even the virtues of the English tradition.

Nor is his engagement with another discourse – that of the anarchist novel as it flourished at the end of the nineteenth century – any more conservative. Barbara Melchiori has demonstrated that much of this fiction confirmed the political status quo by presenting all forms of social protest as essentially terroristic (*Terrorism in the Late Victorian Novel*, p. 248). By the use of such figures as the dynamiter-chemist and the *agent provocateur*, and tropes like the secret society and the international conspiracy, these novels sought to spread alarm and provoke reaction. All these elements are present in *The Secret Agent*. The utopian socialist Michaelis, the bloodthirsty nihilist Yundt, and the genetic engineer Ossipon, though distinguished from one another, form a semi-clandestine association that meets regularly in Verloc's Soho shop. Verloc coordinates anarchist movement to and from the Continent, and sets up an *acte provocateur* on behalf of a foreign power. The so-called Professor, clearly a chemist of sorts, runs an *ad-hoc* laboratory in Islington from which he distributes nitroglycerine. A menacingly undefined central society, 'The Future of the Proletariat', nurtures 'all shades of revolutionary opinion' (p. 26), and the 'more or less mysterious ... International Red Committee' runs cells of agents and propagandists. Yet whereas in normal terrorist fiction these elements threaten the very fabric of society, in Conrad's novel they are exposed as harmless and impotent shams. Apart from the

Professor, all the revolutionaries are psychological conformists who lack all energy and power of initiative. They are wholly dependent on women whom they exploit when they can: the decaying Yundt owes his survival to a faithful crone, the helpless Michaelis his freedom to his lady-patroness, the conceited Ossipon his living expenses to the nursemaids he seduces, and the secret agent Verloc his well-being to the unanarchic institution of matrimony – a source of 'astonishment' to the socially-privileged Vladimir in Belgravia (p. 32) and of the even loftier Sir Ethelred in Westminster (p. 167), who take anarchism at its face-value.

In terrorist fiction anarchism is thought of as hyperactive; the agitator and the crowd or 'mob' form an explosive combination. Barbara Melchiori cites a passage from a novel of the 1880s, W. H. Mallock's *The Old Order Changes*, in which the populace is shown to be as volatile as the nitro-glycerine that might be used to ignite it. We are informed that when 'masses of men' suffer a sudden decline in their standard of life, they 'become dangerous by the laws of social chemistry as surely as, under chemical treatment, do the harmless materials of dynamite'.[7] *The Secret Agent* will have none of this. Turning the convention on its head, the novel insists that the London multitudes are, through their sheer scale, as inert, indifferent, and unconscious as an organic phenomenon. The Professor despairs of moving them, whenever he allows himself to be aware of them as they stream past him in the street. The only revolutionary act that Conrad permits in his narrative is an enforced and premature explosion caused by an a-political simpleton who blows up nothing except himself. In short, anarchism in Conrad poses no political threat whatsoever. In this he seems to have historical reality on his side. In late-Victorian England most anarchists were refugees and exiles desperate to preserve the tolerance that harboured them. Indeed, until the end of the century, when anti-immigration laws were put in place, the threat to the state came not from anarchism but from its own permissiveness, which was very provocative to those European powers that had reason to fear anarchism's campaigns of assassination and random terror. It would seem, therefore, that the question raised for *The Secret Agent* by the conventions of terrorist fiction – How dangerous is the Greenwich explosion? – has been answered as decisively as the question raised by the conventions of the police novel – Who is behind the explosion? But like the latter, the former is also subject to Conradian irony. In reality, the harmless explosion that reinforces the security of a complacent Toryism wipes out an entire family – first Stevie, then Verloc, then Winnie, and finally, in effect if not in fact, Winnie's mother. For all its apparently placid routines, *The Secret Agent* shows that ordinary life is terrifyingly insecure, and that London, far from being a haven of tranquillity envied by European capitals shaken by detonations, is the site of stress, fear, effort, anxiety, pain, and defeat for the enormous majority of its inhabitants.

IV

Whenever *The Secret Agent* alludes to the poor or the helpless, its irony takes on a double edge. In the opening chapter Stevie is introduced to us in a surrealistic-comic episode. At the age of fourteen he lets off a succession of fireworks in the staircase of the offices where he has a menial job and causes general panic. 'His motives for this stroke of originality', writes Conrad, 'were difficult to discover'. Later, Stevie's sister learns that he had been worked up by two office-boys with 'tales of injustice and oppression till they had wrought his compassion to the pitch of that frenzy' (p. 13). And Conrad adds: 'After that altruistic exploit Stevie was put to help wash the dishes in the basement kitchen' (p. 14).

What is the target of such phrases as 'stroke of originality' and 'that altruistic exploit'? Evidently, the simple-mindedness of the victim of the insensitive prank from the perspective not of his tormentors, who are plainly cynical bullies, but of a tolerantly patronizing man-of-the-world. Yet already here, long before we discover how fully this episode prefigures Stevie's ultimate fate, we recognize that the irony involves more than amused superiority. This is because of the way in which it has been prepared. We are informed that Stevie frequently fails to find his way home because he is easily distracted – for example, by 'the dramas of fallen horses, whose pathos and violence induced him sometimes to shriek piercingly in a crowd, which disliked to be disturbed by sounds of distress in its quiet enjoyment of the national spectacle' (p. 13). Here, the irony is very much against the crowd and in favour of Stevie. According to 'Autocracy and War', real-life incidents like an 'overworked horse falling in front of our windows' may 'awaken more genuine emotion' than any amount of war reporting in the press (*NLL*, p. 84). Given this context, then, the phrase 'that altruistic exploit' cannot be dismissed as mere mockery. The reader, having registered momentary amusement, will instantly recognize that *that* response is also inadequate. Irony evokes tolerant detachment in order to overturn it, for such detachment, like the crowd's enjoyment of the 'national spectacle', is much further away from true fellow-feeling than Stevie's piercing shriek or his 'angry catherine wheels'. Here Conrad's irony serves a richer realism, in which the recognition of weakness and absurdity does not rule out the acknowledgement of genuine feeling. In the environment which London offers, Stevie's reaction may indeed constitute an 'altruistic exploit'. He may be a simpleton, but he has the heart of the matter in him.

Conrad was always explicit about the doubleness of the irony in *The Secret Agent*. As late as the 'Author's Note' of 1920, he recalled his 'earnest belief that ironic treatment alone would enable me to say all I felt I would have to say *in scorn as well as in pity*'; he insisted that the novel's 'inspiring indignation and underlying *pity and contempt*' had to be registered if it were not to be construed as 'a gratuitous outrage on the feelings of mankind' (pp. 7, 4, 8; emphasis added). Failure to respond to this ambivalence not only hardens the tone of the narrative into an implacable pessimism, but also renders its central concern – the place of compassion, or more accurately 'our sympathetic imagination', in reformist politics – very difficult to perceive. Another reference to 'Autocracy and War' will make this clearer. Illustrating the difficulty of imagining suffering at a distance, Conrad evokes the response of a privileged philanthropist to the sight of the passing population of London: 'An early Victorian, or perhaps a pre-Victorian, sentimentalist, looking out of an upstairs window, I believe, at a street – perhaps Fleet Street itself – full of people, is reported, by an admiring friend, to have wept for joy at seeing so much life' (*NLL*, p. 84). The view from the upstairs window and the 'arcadian tears' it evokes, are a world away from Stevie's piercing shriek at pavement level. Conrad's point is that superiority to the object of feeling, whether physical or social, invites 'facile emotion', that is to say, emotion conditioned by fashion rather than governed by perception. Conrad remarks, *à propos* of this incident, that 'the psychology of individuals, even in the most extreme instances, reflects the general effect of the fears and hopes of its time' (*NLL*, p. 85). In other words, our intimate self is less ours than we like to think; hence it is that we offer much less resistance than we believe to those ready-made sentiments that nurse our indolence or flatter our self-esteem. It follows that the fact of adherence to a liberal cause or support of a radical movement is not yet a guarantee of solidarity with the victims of injustice.

It is one of the functions of Conradian irony to build this insight into the text of the novel. Consider the following example from the magnificent eighth chapter describing Winnie's mother's last cab-ride. The journey is over; while Winnie is helping her mother settle her few belongings inside the alms-house, the one-armed cabman explains to an agitated Stevie why he is obliged to use a horse long past service:

> His jovial purple cheeks bristled with white hairs; and like Virgil's Silenus, who, his face smeared with the juice of berries, discoursed of Olympian Gods to the innocent shepherds of Sicily, he talked to Stevie of domestic matters and the affairs of men whose sufferings are great and immortality by no means assured.
>
> 'I am a night cabby, I am', he whispered, with a sort of boastful exasperation.

'I've got to take out what they will blooming well give me at the yard. I've got my missus and four kids at 'ome'.   (p. 128)

What is the force of the Virgilian analogy? According to Irving Howe, it would typify the novel's ironic excesses, in which the irony, turning on itself and 'becoming facile through its pervasiveness and lack of grading' deprives the characters of every claim to 'dignity and redemption' (*Politics and the Novel*, p. 108). But it is this reaction that is facile. Despite the juxtaposition of Virgilian loftiness and demotic speech, the analogy is not in the mock-heroic mode, which deflates what it describes. It starts by defamiliarizing, and therefore making vivid, the physical effects of old age, relentless hardship, and the abuse of intoxicants. In this novel, even corpulence is not straightforward, for it can signify a variety of states, from the florid plumpness of plenty to the bloated fatness of dearth; the sleekness of Vladimir or the fleshiness of Verloc are very different from the pathological obesity of Michaelis and the glandular infirmity of Winnie's mother. Thus to render the cabman's condition in terms of Silenus's is to bring out the degree to which it is a product of social deprivation: the irony supports the anti-sentimental bias of realism. Yet it also retains an anti-patronizing effect, now served by resemblance rather than contrast. As in Virgil's Sixth Eclogue, the self-indulgent old man has something to say, and the 'innocent' pupil who receives his wisdom something to learn: it is that 'This ain't an easy world'. The cabman cannot alleviate the misery of the old horse because he depends on it to alleviate the misery both of himself and of his 'missus and four kids'. Virgil's Silenus discourses on the origin of the world; Conrad's cabman discloses the inextricable sufferings that attend our earthly journey and its uncertain destination. Thus Conrad's irony presents both the cabman and Stevie as 'one of us'. It checks the sense of superiority that refrigerates our most altruistic impulses, by disclosing the humanity that survives in even the most stricken of lives.

In 'A Familiar Preface' to *A Personal Record*, Conrad remarks that 'it is the capacity for suffering which makes man august in the eyes of men' (p. xvi). The truth of this remark, which implies that the inability to feel trivializes both 'men' and 'man', is evident enough when we think of King Lear. Perhaps the greatest achievement of Conrad's ironic style is that it permits us to carry this insight into the lower ranks of society. The two women who secretly sacrifice personal fulfilment for the protection of their son and brother, one by consigning herself to the ministrations of a man who repels her, the other by removing herself to what we are invited to regard as an anteroom to the grave, and who both thereby ensure his obliteration and their own disappearance, yield little to Shakespeare's royal octogenarian in their capacity to inspire a sense of sublimity. Conrad once told the novelist Arnold Bennett: 'You stop just short of being absolutely real because you are faithful to your dogmas of realism' (*Letters*, II, p. 390). The latter sort of 'realism' strips off ethical, optimistic, and idealistic verbiage in order to call a spade a spade; but that is all it can do. Repudiating most of the resources of art it cannot do justice to the meaning of the facts it exposes. But for Conrad, for whom no human life is without significance, if only by virtue of the fact that it is *inhabited*, such artistic renunciations are impossible. Consider the following description:

> The cab rattled, jingled, jolted; in fact, the last was quite extraordinary. By its disproportionate violence and magnitude it obliterated every sensation of onward movement; and the effect was of being shaken in a stationary apparatus like a mediaeval device for the punishment of crime, or some very newfangled invention for the cure of a sluggish liver. It was extremely distressing; and the raising of Mrs Verloc's mother's voice sounded like a wail of pain.
> (p. 126)

Little could be more 'realistic' than this account, which spares us nothing of the discomforts and dislocations of the physical experience. But how much more it is than that! For all its grim humour, the invocation of an Inquisitorial or medical torture-machine connects the mother's suffering to the greater world; her 'wail of pain', which denotes the difficulty of being heard, betrays an anguish audible only to those who have learnt to know her. Far from being confined to recording the impact of basic sensation, the details of this passage look before and after, not only within the narrative to which they belong, but within the culture of which they are part. Thus Conrad's writing acquires a kind of epic power in which one episode – an uncomfortable cab-ride – is made to express the life-experience of the passengers: the relentlessness of poverty, the laboriousness of communication, the inevitability of defeat. It is not that the cab-ride is converted into a symbolic voyage of life; it is rather that its multi-dimensional 'reality' is more and more fully disclosed as the sentences unfold. Like James Joyce, though to entirely different ends, Conrad places all the resources of high art to the service of humble lives.

V

In a story called 'The Informer' written in January 1906 and published in December of that year, and thus framing the composition of the first draft of *The Secret Agent*, Conrad exposes the political illusions of the *haute bourgeoisie*. The wealthy 'inner' narrator is a connoisseur of Chinese art, of fine cuisine, and of secret political societies; he is also a savagely iconoclastic propagandist of the extreme left, whose support of anarchism is gradually revealed to be yet another form of connoisseurship. His story concerns an upper-society girl who has joined a London anarchist cell in the spirit of a 'high-minded amateur', and who ends by theatrically rejecting a young comrade whose love for her drives him to confess that he is a police spy. The narrator comments that she behaves as a member of a social class whose life, 'being all a matter of pose and gesture ... is unable to realize the power and danger of a real movement and of words that have no sham meaning' (*SS*, p. 78). He is more right than he knows, for everything he says shows that his diagnosis applies first and foremost to himself. This irony shows that the subject of the tale is less anarchism than the character of its patrons, apologists, and fellow-travellers.

No such high-ranking friends can be found within the pages of *The Secret Agent*. (Michaelis's lady-patroness supports him only because she sees him as a harmless victim.) However, my claim remains that they exist, as it were, in front of these pages. An ironic novel – in the sense of a novel that interrogates the presuppositions that it assumes its readers bring to it – constructs, or at least positions, its audience. I have argued that its presentation of suffering is incompatible with a generalized or distant view of it, and in effect constitutes a rebuttal of the sentimentalism and patronage that characterizes well-bred sympathy. I now wish to argue that its presentation of anarchism, a creed that derives whatever dignity it possesses from its resistance to social injustice, is not confined to the actual revolutionists but implicates a mentality diffused throughout modern life.

As we have seen, the anarchism of *The Secret Agent* appears to be politically impotent. The Greenwich bombing, which is the novel's central incident, turns out to be an anti-anarchist gesture; its effects, dreadful as they are, are confined to the domestic sphere. The anarchists we meet, though not uniformly lampooned, are made vacuous by their dependence on the props and comforts they theoretically despise; indeed, they are as institutionalized as policemen like Chief Inspector Heat, who has no real existence outside his department and the name and rank it confers. We have noted, however, that there is one exception. The Professor, who makes a brief but striking appearance in 'The Informer', repudiates all social institutions in earnest, and is prepared to pay the price of self-extraction from organized life. He understands that if an attack on the social system is to remain uncompromised by that system, it cannot be justified, since justification can only exist in terms of the established norms: any rationalized policy of destruction has already surrendered to what it is trying to destroy. In the first of his two conversations with Ossipon, the latter refers to the Greenwich bombing, the news of which has just broken, as follows: 'Under the present circumstances' (the vulnerability of anarchism in England) 'it's nothing short of criminal'. The Professor instantly spots the lapse: 'Criminal! What is that? What *is* crime? What can be the meaning of such an assertion?' (p. 49). The Professor is explicit about what distinguishes him from revolutionists like Ossipon: 'They depend on life, which, in this connection, is a historical fact surrounded by all sorts of restraints and considerations, a complex, organised fact open to attack at every point; whereas I depend on death, which knows no restraint and cannot be attacked' (p. 57). This exalted utterance is intelligible. If your life matters to you, you become vulnerable, for life is something received from the past and from others, and it is therefore beyond control and vigilance. If, however, you decide that your life is of no importance, you cease to be at risk, for you no longer have anything to lose: from being, as it were, dispersed into the historical and the social, you contract into the ideal point of your will-to-renunciation. In this view – which accounts, incidentally, for the Professor's dislike of crowds – life is multiplicity and contingency, death individualism and abstraction.

The distinction is illustrated by the Professor's disclosure that he carries a primed bomb in his pocket in order to deter the police, who know that he is quite capable of detonating it. In this sense death is indeed more powerful than life. Were he to blow himself up in the restaurant where he and Ossipon are having a drink, the deed, being the product of an act of choice, would constitute for him a paradoxical affirmation of selfhood. But for the restaurant's unconscious clientèle: 'Nobody in this room could hope to escape ... Nor yet this couple going up the stairs now' (p. 56). Life, unlike what he calls death, is everywhere outspread and vulnerable to the will of the terrorist. The Professor's distinction is made yet more graphic with Ossipon's discovery that there would be a twenty-second gap between the activating and the detonating of the Professor's bomb – an interim filled with terror for the life-loving Ossipon, but with 'Force of personality' for the death-fixated Professor (p. 56). That 'force' is measured by the capacity to resist the perpetually recuperating embrace of the social, the cultural, the moral, the linguistic. Thus the only political policy the Professor can countenance is the development of a perfect detonator, which is at least 'something conclusive' (p. 57) – though, to judge from Stevie's fate, something yet to be concluded – and the distribution of dynamite wholesale. This is of course the Professor's version of the notorious 'propaganda by deed' originally mooted by an early Italian internationalist, Piscane, who argued that the 'propaganda of the idea' was no better than 'a chimera', because 'ideas result from deeds, not the latter from the former' (Woodcock, *Anarchism*, p. 308).

The Professor's existence shows the price that has to be paid for the philosophy of the clean break. Cancel out the social on the grounds that, as the product of history rather than logic, it remains the realm of the arbitrary, the contingent, the irrational, and the unjust, and you end up with the most abstract individualism. In principle, you sever all links with what is not the self; you cease to be a son, student, comrade, instructor, a proper name, or even an anarchist (all of which the Professor seems to be to an outside perception), and you end up by existing only as an unending effort of renunciation: 'I've the grit to work alone, quite alone, absolutely alone', the Professor declares (p. 58). And what is the outcome? The belief that 'What happens to us as individuals is not of the least consequence' (p. 60). This is the credo of a man who has absconded out of his own life. Unlike even the kamikaze warrior, who after all incinerates himself for his country, the Professor can only sacrifice himself for a future that he cannot allow himself even to imagine lest he soil it with the reality of the hated present.

Like Stevie in his extremism, which is also a form of abnormality, the Professor is an exemplary figure. Stevie's response to the object of his compassion is so intense that it destroys his capacity to relate it to the other demands of life; his ability to make connections loses its purchase on the sensory world, and can only function by multiplying interlocking circles on bits of paper. But he does show us what it means to make others real to us. The Professor's reaction against the historical world is so intense that he recoils into an absolute individualism whose logical purity blinds it to its roots in the puritanical sectarianism of nineteenth-century Britain and America. Yet his too is a representative case, disclosing the contradictions inherent in post-Enlightenment rationality that, according to Conrad, actually undoes the reformist goals it pursues.

VI

In *A Personal Record* Conrad attacks Rousseau on the grounds that 'Inspiration comes from the earth, which has a past, a history, a future, not from the cold and immutable heaven' (p. 95). In this he declares himself an opponent of the Enlightenment, which favoured the authority of reason over that of tradition, and of the natural heart over the social role. More particularly, he was hostile to one of the Enlightenment's more extreme legacies, anarchism, which despite his disclaimers he understood quite well enough to know that it warred against cultural institutions in the name of a naturalistic view of society, that is to say, the view that 'man naturally contains within him all the attributes which make him capable of living in freedom and social concord' (Woodcock, *Anarchism*, p. 19). Far from holding that liberated 'man' will spontaneously bond himself into unforced associations, Conrad asserts that 'L'homme est un animal méchant … Le crime est une condition nécéssaire de l'existence organisée' [Man is a vicious animal … Crime is a necessary condition of organized existence] (*Letters*, II, p. 159). But his target in *The Secret Agent* is more general than anarchism: it is the dogma of rationality that characterizes the modern world. This dogma enters the novel explicitly in the form of 'scientism' or the belief in the autonomy of science. Vladimir's fantastic justification of an attack on the Greenwich Observatory is correct at least in its assumption that 'the middle classes' worship science above religion, and even above art: 'Any imbecile that has got an income believes in that. He does not know why, but he believes it matters somehow. It is the sacro–sanct fetish' (p. 30). The dogma is developed through the figure of Ossipon, ex-medical student and adherent of Lombroso's theory of the genetic origins of criminality, who exhibits that 'insufferable, hopelessly dense sufficiency which nothing but the frequentation of science' can impart (p. 41). The fierceness of these denunciations, undiluted by even a hint of irony, reflects the depth of Conrad's resistance to the claim that scientific rationality constitutes its own foundation of certainty, in Conrad's terms short-circuiting the 'earth' to receive from 'heaven' its self-defining principle of legitimation. In fact we know that the activity we call scientific is not self-generated, but depends on what has been called a context of pre-understanding external to science and consisting of such factors as an original familiarity with ordinary reality, the practical dealing with things and tools, the ability to acquire techniques, the adaptability to collaboration, and so on (Bubner, *Modern German Philosophy*, p. 130).[8] In science as in politics, rationality can only annul the 'earth' by deceiving, and hence denaturing, itself. As one might expect, *The Secret Agent* develops this point by way of rationality's dealings with individual suffering. Ossipon's verdict on Stevie's drawings, 'Very good', turns out to be a diagnosis, not an appreciation: 'Typical of this form of degeneracy', he replies, when Verloc asks him what he means (p. 40). Like the Professor with his anarchism, Ossipon rules out everything that his scientism cannot account for, that is, everything that makes Stevie precious to his mother and his sister, and, indeed, to us. In short, Ossipon regards Stevie as an identity without content.

It is precisely this which is at issue between Verloc and his wife in the stupendous eleventh chapter devoted to his murder. Verloc too is a rationalist, albeit at the much more pragmatic level of working his way out of the consequences of his brother-in-law's death. What makes pragmatism possible at this moment is that he has been accustomed to extending 'as much recognition to Stevie as a man not particularly fond of animals may give to his wife's beloved cat' (p. 35), and has had therefore no scruples about making use of Stevie's sensitivity to suffering in order to meet Vladimir's demands. His first serious words to his wife after she has discovered what has happened to Stevie decide his fate: 'Can't be helped ... Come, Winnie, we've got to think of to-morrow. You'll want all your wits about you after I am taken away' (p. 176). This is said to a woman who has dedicated her entire future, as well as her present and past, to cherishing an adored handicapped younger brother, and who is currently experiencing the effects of a moral shock worse than the worst earthquake (p. 192). What the rational Verloc is in effect telling her is that her brother's death is his business, not hers – that it is not she but he who has been stricken. He invites her to subtract what she is from her attachments, to think of herself as situated elsewhere than in her home, her family, her district – for example in 'Spain' or in 'South America', or whatever location the practicalities of survival dictate (p. 189). But that this is, strictly, an impossible demand is demonstrated by the fact of her terrible grief, sign and measure of the truth of her identity. Her brother's death indeed diminishes her because what she is and what she loves cannot be divided. As the Professor has made clear, an invulnerable subject is, in theory, one that can consign everything that can be attacked to the realm of the non-ego.[9]

Conrad tells us that Verloc's failure to gauge the depth of Winnie's 'affection' for her brother is 'excusable, since it was impossible for him to understand it without ceasing to be himself' (pp. 176–7). To be sure, Winnie is equally excusable for her failure to perceive that Verloc believes himself to be loved for himself, and not as a party in a marital contract she has drawn up by herself for Stevie's benefit. Like all Conrad's major novels, the narrative of *The Secret Agent* is composed of a system of cross purposes. But what is perhaps special about this narrative is its diagnostic intention. It offers its truly virtuoso elaboration of 'purposes mistook fall'n on th' inventors' heads' as symptomatic of a modernity that concentrates enormous masses of people into environments that keep their individual lives anonymous, isolated, and impersonal.[10] The most obvious reason is that modern cities are the product of what Conrad calls 'the true anarchist – which is the millionaire' (*Letters*, III, p. 491). But behind *him* is the rationalist ideology that defines the individual in opposition to the social. In this perspective, the figure of Verloc, which gives the novel its title, becomes paradigmatic, for it suggests that in metropolitan life every citizen is in effect a secret agent – in the sense that his or her social roles become mere masks, external to the self, and thus incapable of nourishing the self. Many, like Winnie and her mother, are forced into hiding their intentions, or into feigning indifference and incuriosity, until the dissimulation becomes a habit. Others embrace imposture in order to prey on 'the vices, the follies, or the baser fears of mankind' (p. 16). Verloc himself lives off envy and rancour as an anarchist, departmental ambitions as a police informer, reactionary conceit as an embassy spy, and prurience as a shopkeeper; but as a result his identity dissolves into a 'moral nihilism' that becomes utterly unable to imagine why to use Stevie as he does is a crime, or why to suffer his loss as Winnie does is more than an inconvenience.

We are now in a position to understand why Conrad found it necessary to add the last two chapters to the serialized version of his novel. The association of Ossipon, practised exploiter of female gullibility and distress, and Winnie, in her naïveté and anguish his easiest as well as his biggest catch, represents a confrontation between the alternative principles operating in this text: autonomous reason and dependent suffering. The reader may be tempted to suppose that Winnie's destruction at the hands of Ossipon, who strips her of her savings and packs her off on a trip by train and boat whose only destination is suicide, marks the defeat of the claims of suffering. But dark as the narrative of *The Secret Agent* may be, it is not as dark as that. For Winnie's defeat is also, paradoxically, a victory – over the 'insufferable, hopelessly dense sufficiency' that has defined Ossipon's life. The process of his final collapse is complex; but it is safe to state that at its climax it crowns the novel's central insight. Seven days after Winnie's disappearance, Ossipon has become obsessed by a piece of journalistic prose alluding to that event: '*An impenetrable mystery seems destined to hang for ever over this act of madness or despair*' (p. 228). Newspaper reporting, a motif that recurs at significant moments in the narrative, has always been for Conrad a discourse without content. 'The printed page of the Press', he writes in 'Autocracy and War', 'makes a sort of still uproar, taking from men both the power to reflect and the faculty of genuine feeling' (*NLL*, p. 90). But now, and here, it has the opposite effect. The phrase that offers a million ignorant readers the illusion of understanding reveals to Ossipon, and perforce to him alone, all the appalling inwardness of the original event. Conrad is not, of course, inviting his readers, who include some of the most distinguished liberal intellectuals of his day, to recognize themselves in the fate of a failed medical student. But he is certainly asking them to consider that more is required for the amelioration of the human world than abstract principle and generalized feeling.

NOTES

1 See Najder, *Joseph Conrad: A Chronicle*, pp. 329–30, and Baines's chapter on *The Secret Agent* in *Joseph Conrad: A Critical Biography*. Harkness and Reid

painstakingly reconstruct the history of composition and revision in the Cambridge Edition of the novel, pp. 235–59.

2 See Howe, *Politics and the Novel*, pp. 76–113. A large part of the relevant chapter is reprinted in Watt, ed., *The Secret Agent: A Casebook*, which contains a useful selection of influential reviews and articles.

3 Nicol's pamphlet on the Greenwich bombing is discussed in Oliver, *The International Anarchist Movement in Late Victorian London*, pp. 105–9, and Sherry, *Conrad's Western World*, pp. 239–44. Both are indispensable studies of the novel's sources.

4 Avrich's 'Conrad's anarchist professor', which deserves to be better known, deals with sources for this character. Sherry's *Conrad's Western World* and Oliver's *The International Anarchist Movement* discuss Anderson's memoirs.

5 See Baines, *Joseph Conrad: A Critical Biography*; Daleski, *Joseph Conrad: The Way of Dispossession*; Fleishman, *Conrad's Politics*; Guerard, *Conrad the Novelist*; Lothe, *Conrad's Narrative Method*; Miller, *Poets of Reality*; and Schwarz, *Conrad: 'Almayer's Folly' to 'Under Western Eyes'*.

6 See Melchiori's *Terrorism in the Late Victorian Novel* for a discussion of this topic.

7 Cited in Melchiori, *Terrorism in the Late Victorian Novel*, p. 190. The quotation is from Mallock's *The Old Order Changes* (III, p. 47).

8 See Bubner's discussion of the 'Philosophy of language and theory of science', *Modern German Philosophy*, pp. 69–130.

9 See Descombes, *The Barometer of Modern Reason*, pp. 142–6. The last two chapters offer an outstanding critique of the legacy of the Enlightenment.

10 See Moore, ed., *Conrad's Cities*, for four essays focusing on London in the novel.

WORKS CITED

Anderson, Sir Robert. *Sidelights on the Home Rule Movement*. London: Murray, 1906

Avrich, Paul. 'Conrad's anarchist professor: an undiscovered source'. *Labour History* 18.3 (1977), 297–302

Baines, Jocelyn. *Joseph Conrad: A Critical Biography*. London: Weidenfeld & Nicolson; New York: McGraw-Hill, 1960. Reprinted Penguin Books, 1971

Berthoud, Jacques. *Joseph Conrad: The Major Phase*. Cambridge: Cambridge University Press, 1978

Bubner, Rüdiger. *Modern German Philosophy*. Cambridge: Cambridge University Press, 1981

Conrad, Joseph. 'Autocracy and War'. 1905. In *Notes on Life and Letters*. 1921. London: Dent, 1970, pp. 83–114

'The Mirror of the Sea' and 'A Personal Record'. 1906 and 1912. Ed. Zdzisław Najder. Oxford: Oxford University Press, 1988

'The Informer'. 1906. In *A Set of Six*. London: Dent, 1954, pp. 73–102

The Secret Agent. 1907. Ed. Bruce Harkness and S. W. Reid. Cambridge: Cambridge University Press, 1990

Daleski, H. M. *Joseph Conrad: The Way of Dispossession*. London: Faber & Faber; New York: Holmes & Meier, 1977

Descombes, Vincent. *Philosophie par gros temps.* 1989. As *The Barometer of Modern Reason: On the Philosophies of Current Events.* Tr. Stephen A. Schwartz. Oxford: Oxford University Press, 1993

Dupré, Catherine. *John Galsworthy: A Biography.* London: Collins, 1976

Fleishman, Avrom. *Conrad's Politics: Community and Anarchy in the Fiction of Joseph Conrad.* Baltimore: Johns Hopkins Press, 1967

Guerard, Albert J. *Conrad the Novelist.* Cambridge, MA: Harvard University Press, 1958

Howe, Irving. *Politics and the Novel.* New York: Meridian, 1957

Jean-Aubry, G., ed. *Joseph Conrad: Life and Letters.* 2 vols. London: Heinemann; Garden City, NY: Doubleday, Page, 1927

Jefferson, George. *Edward Garnett, A Life in Literature.* London: Cape, 1982

Lothe, Jakob. *Conrad's Narrative Method.* Oxford: Clarendon Press, 1989

Mallock, W. H. *The Old Order Changes.* 3 vols. London: Bentley, 1886

Melchiori, Barbara Arnett. *Terrorism in the Late Victorian Novel.* London: Croom Helm, 1985

Miller, J. Hillis. *Poets of Reality: Six Twentieth-Century Writers.* Cambridge, MA: Harvard University Press, 1966

Moore, Gene M., ed. *Conrad's Cities: Essays for Hans van Marle.* Amsterdam: Rodopi, 1992

Najder, Zdzisław. *Joseph Conrad: A Chronicle.* Tr. Halina Carroll-Najder. New Brunswick, NJ: Rutgers University Press; Cambridge: Cambridge University Press, 1983

Nicol, David. *The Greenwich Mystery.* Sheffield, 1897

Oliver, Hermia. *The International Anarchist Movement in Late Victorian London.* London: Croom Helm, 1983

Rapin, René, ed. *Lettres de Joseph Conrad à Marguerite Poradowska.* Geneva: Droz, 1966

Schwarz, Daniel R. *Conrad: 'Almayer's Folly' to 'Under Western Eyes'.* London: Macmillan, 1980

Sherry, Norman. *Conrad's Western World.* Cambridge: Cambridge University Press, 1971

Watt, Ian, ed. *'The Secret Agent': A Casebook.* London: Macmillan, 1973

Watts, Cedric and Laurence Davies. *Cunninghame Graham: A Critical Biography.* Cambridge: Cambridge University Press, 1979

Woodcock, George. *Anarchism.* Harmondsworth: Penguin Books, 1962

7

KEITH CARABINE

Under Western Eyes

Conrad's most succinct and compelling statement about the interdependence of the artist's and of humanity's concerns is contained in a letter to *The New York Times* of 2 August 1901: 'The only legitimate basis of creative work lies in the courageous recognition of all the irreconcilable antagonisms that make our life so enigmatic, so burdensome, so fascinating, so dangerous – so full of hope' (*Letters*, II, pp. 348–9). All his major fictions present, explore, and are constructed out of antagonisms that are never finally resolved. These famously include: egoism and altruism, emotion and reason, solidarity and isolation, moral corruption and redemption, heroism and contingency, loyalty and betrayal, idealism and scepticism, piety and scorn, and fidelity to a code composed of 'a few very simple ideas' and 'truth to one's own sensations' (*PR*, p. xix). Conrad's recognition, in the same letter, of a ceaseless 'struggle of contradictions' springs from an inclusive vision of man's fate, and because for him, as for Flaubert, 'the *whole* of the truth lies in the presentation', his vision sponsors a restless search for a correlative form (*Letters*, II, p. 200).

Issues of form in *Under Western Eyes* will be explored later in this essay. For the moment it is necessary to sketch briefly the factors in Conrad's 'peculiar experience of race and family' (*UWE*, p. xxx) that ensure that the clash of irreconcilable antagonisms has a special acuteness in the only novel set in the land of his birth. Conrad and Razumov are both orphans who share 'an hereditary and personal knowledge of the means by which a historical autocracy represses ideas ... and defends its existence', and they both have 'immense' national parentages that suffer from 'internal dissensions' (*UWE*, pp. 25, 11). Razumov incarnates the clash between autocrats and revolutionists. Conrad inherited two opposed Polish nationalist ideologies. His parents Apollo and Ewa Korzeniowski were Messianic, romantic nationalists who sacrificed their lives in a vain effort to liberate their country from Muscovite oppression. His maternal uncle and guardian, Tadeusz Bobrowski, was a conciliator who sought 'the attainment of a fairly tolerable *modus vivendi*' with the feared Russian autocracy and scorned the impractical political aims and the 'inflammable temperament' of his insurrectionist kin (Najder, ed., *Conrad under Familial Eyes*, p. 36).[1]

Conrad's decision to begin 'Razumov' in December 1907 marked his return to the original source of his vision of irreconcilable antagonisms and involved an engagement with the shadows of his inner life. Not surprisingly, he began with a deeply divided sense of his subject, which is reflected in the novel's double narration. He claimed in a letter of 6 January 1908: 'I am trying to capture the very soul of things Russian' (*Letters*, IV, p. 8). Hence, in order to screen his Polish 'passions, prejudices and even ... personal memories' (*UWE*, p. xxxi), the tri-lingual Conrad, an established English novelist, invented a narrator and editor who is his reverse image – an elderly Anglo-Russian teacher of languages, who disclaims the possession of art, imagination, and a knowledge of Russia but who none the less excoriates 'the Russian soul'. In the same letter, however, Conrad's outline of what he called 'the real subject of the story' – the 'psychological developments' leading to Razumov's betrayal, guilt, and confession (*Letters*, IV, p. 9) – rehearses 'the very soul' of themes Conradian – already explored, for example, in the careers of such divided men as Jim and Nostromo. This version, refracted through the diary of a young Russian, had 'long haunted' Conrad and 'Now it must come out' (*Letters*, IV, p. 14). It is the basic story of the *homo duplex* in Conrad's fiction.[2]

I

Two early reviewers of *Under Western Eyes* anticipated the main lines of its subsequent critical reception. Conrad's friend Edward Garnett remarked that 'its last page leaves us almost as much in the dark as the first. We can only feel sure that certain actual facts have been presented, and that there is probably an explanation of them if we could only hit upon it'. An anonymous reader observed, 'In more than one way ... Mr Conrad's book belies its title, so deeply tinged is its perceptiveness with Russian habits of thought'.[3] Generations of interpreters have felt they were in the dark and have been baffled by and striven to make sense of two striking features of the narrative. One critic calls the novel 'a chronicle of interpretive failures' wherein all the characters talk at cross purposes and often either do not finish their sentences or, simultaneously, deceive and struggle to interpret each other (Szittya, 'Metafiction', p. 830). Consequently, the reader struggles to understand speakers who impede and even defy construction. Our predicament is exacerbated by the complex interplay between the English narrator's conflicting editorial opinions and multiple narrative functions and Razumov's Russian diary.

The astonishingly diverse critical responses to the narrator of *Under Western Eyes* are inseparable from Conrad's own radically split sense of and attitude towards his subject, but they also express the reader's 'increasing bewilderment at the almost unmanageable inclusiveness of what we are being left to piece together' (Watt, *Conrad in the Nineteenth Century*, p. 210). Thus for Jacques Berthoud, the narrator joins Razumov in standing for rationality, and as a generally reliable and trustworthy figure fails to understand the Russians because 'they are not understandable' (*Joseph Conrad: The Major Phase*, p. 163). Most critics, however, take the old teacher at his word and view him as 'a dense Occidental' (*UWE*, p. 112). To Hay he is a 'nonentity' (*The Political Novels of Joseph Conrad*, p. 296); to Rosenfield he is only an 'obtuse observer' (*Paradise of Snakes*, p. 163); to Palmer his 'pompous abstractions often hide the book's subject, instead of bringing it closer' (*Joseph Conrad's Fiction*, p. 131); to Secor he 'seems throughout ludicrously incapable of joining in or comprehending the swirl of motion around him' ('The narrator in *Under Western Eyes*', p. 34); and to Kermode, in a hyper-subtle analysis, he is 'a father of lies', as 'diabolic' as Razumov claims him to be ('Secrets and narrative sequence', p. 153).

The reviewer who noted the novel's perceptiveness about Russian 'habits of thought' anticipated two sets of critical response. First, some critics concentrate on the novel's double focus or double authority and arrive at widely different evaluations of its success. Zabel detects 'a quality of intense personal commitment combined with a severe discipline in moral and humanistic objectivity' (Introduction, p. xxxiv), while for Tanner, Razumov's nightmare is filtered through a complacent narrator whose 'whole nexus of western common sense' is finally rejected ('Nightmare and complacency', p. 200). Secondly, this early reviewer anticipated interpreters who seek to explain the novel's troubled engagement with 'things Russian' through its complex dialogue with Dostoevsky, and in the life and opinions of Conrad, the Pole, who deeply distrusted revolutionaries and inherited a fear and loathing of 'the Russian spirit' from his race and kin.

I have argued that what Conrad calls in the manuscripts of *Under Western Eyes* 'the very secret' behind Razumov's 'record's existence' resides as he knew in his own 'double life one of them peopled only by shadows' (*Letters*, III, p. 491) – those of his dissenting, inescapable Polish shades. Moreover, as the long and troubled composition of the novel and the manuscripts show, and as Conrad confessed in his 'Author's Note', he only grasped the story's 'tragic character' after he had finished Part I (p. xxx).[4] His radically divided sense of and attitude towards his subject profoundly affects the form and presentation of *Under Western Eyes*. This essay canvasses the competing interpretive models the narrator offers to his baffled readers and attempts to show that they all, finally, yield a tragic reading.

II

The disjunction evident between Conrad's intention and his sense of his real subject is immediately apparent in the prefatory remarks of the story's elderly English narrator. He disconcertingly offers two differing sets of reasons for his inability to understand Razumov's diary. The first is that words are 'the great foes of reality', a thought he elaborates when he reflects on the motives behind Razumov's decision to keep a diary: 'There must be a wonderful soothing power in mere words since so many men have used them for self-communion' (p. 5). The narrator's initial, weary remark re-works Conrad's customary, penetrating awareness of the treacherous nature of humankind's gift of expression. Thus both 'soothing words' and 'formula' indicate that 'self-communion', as ever in Conrad, is not to be confused with self-knowledge. Given the inherently unstable and duplicitous nature of words and expression, which impede communication between the self and others, tellers and listeners, and authors and readers, Razumov's reality is always likely to escape both his own comprehension in his diary as well as the narrator's in his transcription and evaluation of it.

This familiar Conradian explanation rests alongside the old teacher's further claim that Russians, anyway, are 'under' his eyes, in that they are 'below' or 'on the inside of' and are therefore incomprehensible to him because of their remote racial and historical traditions and 'the different conditions of Western thought' (p. 25). Despite his professed ignorance the old teacher as commentator immediately attempts to '*capture* the very soul of things Russian' (emphasis added), that is to 'govern, control or bind' them '*under*' his dominating gaze. The narrator's desire for clarity, control, and mastery of a professedly inaccessible subject is itself, however, riven by his opposed attitudes of contempt and compassion towards it. He expresses his contempt in what he oddly calls a 'digression', contending that Russians are characterized by 'the illogicality of their attitude' and 'the arbitrariness of their conclusions'. They possess 'some special human trait', indissolubly connected to their 'extraordinary love of words' (p. 4).

The narrator's pejorative attempt to shape the reader's responses and to distance us from the otherness of the Russian spirit are countermanded by his equally strong and sympathetic assessment of the representative nature of the events recorded in Razumov's journal and of the diarist himself. Thus in chapter 1 he notes the origins of Razumov's diary and magisterially captures the 'the moral corruption' of Tsarism upon 'the noblest aspirations of humanity' such as 'the desire of freedom, an ardent patriotism, the love of justice, the sense of pity, and even the fidelity of simple minds' (p. 7).

This terrible catalogue of wasted aspirations is reinforced by the central model for understanding the tragic nature of Razumov's fate: he incarnates the dissensions that are tearing his nation apart. Razumov is the supreme version of the long line of protagonists – Kurtz, Jim, Captain Whalley, Nostromo – who are split apart by the different kinds of antagonisms Conrad's austere vision of humankind's fate obliges them to recognize and negotiate in order to ensure that their humanity is tested to the full. And, as the narrator's broad and compassionate formulations and the model of the divided man suggest, the protagonist's and his nation's fate can also be interpreted tragically.

Generations of readers have found themselves puzzled and exasperated by the riddle of the narrator's point of view. And no wonder, for the narrator in his roles of translator and editor of Razumov's Russian diary, and as a mediator between East and West, is puzzled by his subject and is himself presented as a puzzle to the reader. He professes his unskillfulness as a writer yet shapes the narrative and assesses the representative and symbolic nature of Razumov's divisions with authorial aplomb. The first Conradian teller to parade his separation from and lack of comprehension of his subject by race, age, and historical and political experience, he none the less offers his readers contradictory models to bring both his subject and them under control. On the one hand, he modestly claims to digress and then vigorously disparages the Russian character, regarding Russians as a race apart and inferior to his Western eyes. On the other, he confidently assesses the tragic impact of an autocratic regime upon a society with a force, range, and a passionate address new to the English novel. Conrad, therefore, makes extraordinary demands upon his readers. He invites us early in his novel to construe Russia and Razumov's journal through the competing models offered by a commentator who seems oblivious to his own deeply divided understanding of his subject. Moreover, to our be-wilderment, all these models remain in play and continue to jostle each other throughout the text.

III

It is entirely characteristic of Conrad's narrative procedures that at the beginning of Part I, chapter 3 (after Razumov has betrayed Haldin) the old teacher in a second digression offers a new and puzzling model for construing Russia's spirit. He re-slants his earlier editorial remarks about the Russification of words and Russia's 'moral corruption' and, surprisingly, announces a new artistic purpose. After strenuously pondering Razumov's strange diary, he now realizes that his task is to render 'the moral conditions ruling over a large part of this earth's surface'. He claims these conditions remain elusive 'till some key-word is found' that 'may perchance hold truth enough to help the moral discovery which should be the object of every tale'. He offers cynicism:

> the mark of Russian autocracy and of Russian revolt...in its strange pretensions of sanctity...the spirit of Russia is the spirit of cynicism. It informs the declarations of statesmen, the theories of her revolutionists, and the mystic vaticinations of prophets...making freedom look like a form of debauch, and the Christian virtues appear actually indecent. (p. 67)

Given his distrust of words and particularly of formulae, how can the narrator think that any keyword suffices? Cynicism, moreover, is immediately problematic because it raises the issue of motive. To be cynical the characters have to possess, as the dictionary indicates, 'a doubt of good motives'. They must sneer and fault-find. But if 'the spirit of cynicism' informs in the sense of 'imbues with feeling, principle, quality', surely, Russians think paralogically and are therefore unaware that they are less users of words than used by them. Are his polemical, excoriating formulations, then, mere off-the-cuff prejudices rather than sustainable interpretations? Given that all his digressions dwindle into *aposiopeses* (a sudden breaking off of speech), do those black dots slyly invite the reader to collude with the author behind the narrator's back, suggesting that his formulae are as arbitrary as those of the Russians he impugns? Furthermore, he himself at this moment fits the popular definition of a cynic as a sneering fault-finder, and he clearly views the Russians, in yet another play on 'under', as inferior to his Western gaze. Is cynicism, then, a digression or the key to moral discovery?

Characteristically, the teacher's second digression invites the reader to reconstrue the narrative up to this point and to notice that cynicism is frequently invoked as the novel's keyword. It is fitting, therefore, to concentrate initially on Part I and to take the narrator at his word, testing this model against its competitors.

The Tsarists' utterances confirm the usual meanings of cynicism. The extract from de P—'s 'famous State paper' which mystically asserts that 'the thought of liberty has never existed in the mind of the Creator' (p. 8) and Mikulin's unfinished thought 'Religious belief, of course, is a great...' (p. 90) possess a doubt of good motives. Moreover, their view of liberty is inseparable from thinking correctly, and they therefore deny the very possibility of political freedoms. Tsarists insist Russia is 'our Christ-loving land' (p. 93), but religious belief is great because it can be cynically exploited for purposes of control, surveillance, repression, and terror.

Haldin's fanatical claim that in assassinating de P— God's will had been done makes, like the Tsarists' formulae, 'the Christian virtues themselves appear actually indecent' (p. 67). In common with all the revolutionaries his 'vaticinations' are mystic and make 'freedom look like a form of debauch' because their 'mission' and commitment to 'a new revelation' (p. 22) seem to begin and end with revolt. This enthusiastic misinterpreter of the saintly qualities of the sot Ziemianitch is surely, however, the antithesis of a cynic as are Tekla 'the Samaritan' (p. 379) and Sophia Antonovna the convinced and generous-hearted revolutionary. As the narrator subsequently reminds us, Haldin's life had been 'sincere, and perhaps its thoughts might have been lofty, its moral sufferings profound, its last act a true sacrifice'. His assessment is couched conditionally, but he immediately appeals directly to the reader, sounding the tragic note of wasted lives: 'It is not for us, the staid lovers calmed by the possession of a conquered liberty, to condemn without appeal the fierceness of thwarted desire' (p. 164). His, Tekla's, and Sophia's loathing of autocracy may be inspired by a blind faith in the efficacy of revolution, but the novel is flooded with sympathy for the terrible thwarting of their deluded and heroic commitment to freedom and their love of justice.

If we assess these utterances from the viewpoint of the narrator's adages about humanity's relationship to and use of words, a more sympathetic judgement emerges. Thus they all vainly seek to bind reality with the force of words and are all incapable of living peacefully within 'the multitude of men's counsel' (p. 8). Like Razumov they cannot endure 'the babble of many voices' (p. 33) that is our common lot on an earth defined, in Natalia's words, by 'antagonistic ideas' (p. 105). They may seek some 'form' but settle instead for 'only some formula of peace', for univocal, mythic utterances such as de P—'s 'God was the Autocrat of the Universe' (p. 8), Razumov's 'great autocrat of the future' (p. 35), Natalia's 'concord' (p. 104), Peter Ivanovich's 'way of salvation' (p. 128) or Sophia's 'Crush the Infamy!' (p. 263). These only ensure or evade the continuation of the antagonisms they yearn to obliterate or reconcile. According to this model, all the speakers manifest a Russian variation of one of Conrad's great concerns, mournfully and comprehensively recorded by the old teacher when he notes that all men are 'everlastingly betrayed by a short-sighted wisdom' (p. 305). Of this Razumov is the supreme instance in the novel.

Cynicism in any of its received meanings and in relation to personal motivation only fits the Tsarists, and even they are not quite as contemptible as the narrator would have the reader believe. Moreover, though the revolutionists, in an apt pun, inform against themselves as and how they speak (Conrad's sly manipulation of black dots on white paper is nigglingly satirical at their expense) they cannot be cynical, if they are unconscious.[5] Nevertheless they do, of course, disturb us precisely because their thought processes are faulty, and their 'terribly corroding simplicity' (p. 104) earns the narrator's scorn.

The second meaning of informs – 'imbues with feeling, principle, quality' – directs us to look for the spirit informing all their utterances. From this viewpoint they speak, to borrow Peter Ivanovich's word, 'figuratively' (p. 128), and their figurations mystically yoke the discourses of Christianity, nationalism, and politics. As their utterances show, Russia's internal dissensions are manifest in the battle between Tsarists and revolutionaries to commandeer the great types of Christian discourse in order to justify their lawless causes. Thus for de P— 'God' is an 'Autocrat', revolution for Haldin a 'new revelation', 'Providence' (p. 44) for Prince K— a Tsarist secret agent, revolutionary activity for Peter Ivanovich 'the way of salvation', and politics for Madame de S— a branch of supernaturalism (p. 222). These utterances deny that Christianity is a transcendent set of beliefs or even a form of personal, spiritual consolation, and disallow the very possibility of rational political discourse. They are, as the narrator says in a third digression, unable to understand, and, indeed, 'scorn all the practical forms of political liberty known to the western world' (p. 104). For the theocratic Tsarists, political issues and praxis are already divinely inscribed and must be defended. For the utopian revolutionaries, with their visions of concord and of justice flowering out of 'blood and violence' (p. 105), such issues are to be settled in an indeterminate future. They are all cynical because their figurative thinking confuses the spiritual and the secular and thereby invites destruction. Judged by this interpretive model the Russians are a race apart, marked to reason falsely and arbitrarily. But this model does not fit the idealistic revolutionists because they are also a Russian version of one of Conrad's great tragic themes – that the devoted pursuit of our noblest aspirations can bring about the opposite of what we intend and destroy ourselves and others.

As we have seen, the reader is obliged to shuttle between two different editorial models: that insisting on the uniqueness of the Russians, and that showing that they are variations of the common human predicament. The former usually subserve the narrator's scorn and the latter his compassion. This indecisiveness riddles the entire narrative and helps explain the large variety of critical responses to it. It is clear, however, that the kinds of moral discovery prompted by cynicism are unsatisfactory for three different sets of reasons.[6] First, and of less consequence here, the narrator's digressions alert us to the author. The old teacher's discoveries rehearse Conrad's Polish prejudices in his polemical attack upon the Russian spirit in his 1905 essay 'Autocracy and War', and to put it simply, as Conrad knew, the case does not hold. After all, his own father Apollo Korzeniowski was in thrall to the 'mystic phrases' that enshrined the myth of his nation's Messianic role among the nations of the world, and Conrad rejected both his father's Messianism and his Catholicism.[7] Secondly, in a novel that explores the ways characters resort to univocal formulae to escape 'the babble' and 'the multitude of men's counsel' and to surmount the antagonisms that constitute our earthly inheritance, the narrator's search for a keyword is inherently suspect and serves to deny the complexity and the universal dimensions of the Russian predicament. Lastly, and most importantly, cynicism fails to convince because the narrator's contempt for the Russian spirit fails, unlike the other more sympathetic assessments, to engage and comprehend Razumov, the supreme example in Conrad's fiction of the *homo duplex*. The belated discovery of the 'tragic character' of his tale is manifest in the ways all the models canvassed here are replayed, and others are introduced that illustrate both its Russian aspects and its more universal, Conradian dimensions. Moreover, as will be argued, Razumov offers Natalia, to whom his journal is addressed, the opportunity for another and very different moral discovery than that of digressive cynicism.

IV

At the beginning of Part IV the narrator abruptly switches back to St Petersburg and again picks up Razumov's agonized conversations with Mikulin that brought Part I to an end. Once again the narrator reverts to being the editor and interpreter of the protagonist's journal, offering us a new fact and another way of understanding his narrative. Determined to be punctilious, he 'takes his stand on the ground of common humanity' when he reveals 'the naked truth' of Razumov's double agency. This was his eventual response to Mikulin's simple 'Where to?' on which 'we left Mr Razumov in St Petersburg' and which 'throws a light on the general meaning of this individual case' (p. 293).

Only now does the reader learn for certain that the old teacher's appeals for sympathy coincide with and are inseparable from the revelation that he has been duped by Conrad the cunning artificer, who by withholding the crucial fact that Razumov is a spy, deliberately manipulates our sensibilities along with his teller's. Only at this point does the reader realize that the teacher's anodyne remarks at the beginning of Part II about the narrative 'proprieties to be observed for clearness and effect' were a hoax and that Mikulin's 'Where to?' occasioned a joke at our expense.

Clearly the old teacher's need for fairness and his appeal for sympathy for Razumov are at odds with his scornful insistence in his digressions that Russians are a race apart. Indeed, from this point on, the narrator's commentary is flooded with his author's burgeoning recognition of the tragic character of the Russians' terrible predicament. Though their tragedy has national lineaments, it also concerns 'other beings very much like ourselves and living under the same sky' who are born to discover that 'the mere liberalism of outlook which for us is a matter of words, of ambitions, of votes (and if of feeling at all, then of the sort ... which leaves our deepest affections untouched') is for them 'a heavy trial of fortitude, a matter of tears and anguish and blood' (p. 318). Taking his stand on the ground of common humanity, the old teacher shows that his Western readers are no longer outsiders, and the Russians are no longer set apart with an unreadable character. Seen in this light, the narrator's inconsistencies stem from Conrad's competing uses of him. He is the vehicle for and the victim of his author's evolving recognition of the novel's tragic dimensions.[8]

Once again, Conrad makes large demands upon his readers because he deliberately accentuates the old teacher's competing interpretations, subverts narrative courtesy, and invites what he called a 'debauch of the imagination' (*Letters*, IV, p. 490). This hoax demands, however, that we reconsider Razumov's career up to this point and our own performances as readers in light of the protagonist's double agency. To discover the meaning of Razumov's case the old teacher suggests that we begin with the ramifications of Mikulin's 'Where to?' which 'was the answer in the form of a gentle question to what we may call Mr Razumov's declaration of independence' (p. 293).

V

Razumov's desire 'To retire' in one form or another motivates a wide range of Conrad's characters and is never fulfilled. Rather they are obliged to recognize and endure 'the irreconcilable antagonisms that make our life'. Thus Razumov's confrontation with the Revolution is obligatory in Conrad's austere moral universe, if his common humanity and many passions are to be fully tested and the frailty and stubbornness of his 'short-sighted wisdom' explored. From this perspective, Razumov's story, in common with all of Conrad's great fiction, is a tale of unrest of a man at the end of his tether.

Razumov's wish 'To retire' is irretrievably connected to the narrator's mournful judgement that we are all 'lost in a wilderness of words', subject to the betrayals lurking in the duplicities of language and blinded by our ingenious facility for figurations. Razumov himself is a deeply divided and troubled interpreter of his own and others' participation in the Russian events he describes. Hence, as with all troubled reflectors, the reader is constantly invited to see simultaneously through his eyes and to see through the inconsistencies and self-deceptions of his self-communion.[9] Consequently, whenever Razumov thinks patriotically to justify his betrayal of Haldin his thoughts either break off – 'A murder is a murder. Though, of course, some sort of liberal institutions...' (p. 26) – or are fractured by ellipses: 'Everything was not for the best. Despotic bureaucracy...abuses... corruption...and so on' (p. 35).

Razumov's broken, hesitant thoughts irresistibly remind us of Lord Jim as he struggles to describe his infamous jump and of Haldin who stammers 'in the middle of all these innocent people – scattering death – I! I!...I wouldn't hurt a fly!' (p. 22). Not surprisingly, Marlow's puzzled musings over Jim's use of and relationship to words covers all three cases and also expresses the reader's predicament: 'I didn't know how much of it he believed himself ... and I suspect he did not know either; for it is my belief no man ever understands quite his own artful dodges to escape from the grim shadow of self-knowledge' (*LJ*, p. 80). All human beings, not just Russians, are prone to faulty thinking and possess, especially when threatened, a 'miserable ingenuity in error'.

In *Under Western Eyes* the shadow of autocracy lies on the Russians and on Razumov, 'darkening his figure to' the narrator's understanding (p. 184). Its destructive reach is inescapable, 'tingeing' Russian thoughts, views, and feelings, and, terribly, 'haunting the secret of their silences' (p. 107). Razumov, especially, is tinged. After Haldin's disruption, his case is tragic because he has to identify himself as a Russian because otherwise, as a friendless orphan, he had nothing. With nowhere to go to he is obliged to make a choice between the warring forces of autocracy and revolution. He chooses the former because as he angrily tells Mikulin, punning on his name (*razum* is the Russian root for reason), 'I am reasonable' (p. 89). He therefore prizes 'the secular logic of human development' that Haldin, like all 'Visionaries', holds in contempt (p. 95).

Shocked by his contact with Haldin, Razumov writes his 'declaration of independence' (p. 293), espousing the five principles of 'History', 'Patriotism', 'Evolution', 'Direction', and 'Unity' (p. 66). As Mikulin later observes these principles constitute 'a sort of political confession of faith' (p. 99). Razumov's faith is reasonable because he does not scorn, like all the other

Russians in the novel, the West's basic political values, and his formulations do not mystically blend the spiritual and secular. Rather he celebrates the distinctly English, secular values of tradition, compromise, slow change, and progress, which find their practical forms in parliamentary institutions, local government, and praxis.

Desperate to stop the revolving cycle of violence that is tearing his nation and himself apart, Razumov, the reasonable man, strives to graft melioristic, liberal values on to the stock of autocracy. It naturally rejects and systematically opposes the fusion. With her Tartar origins Russia has known 'Destruction' and 'Disruption' (p. 67) and lacks any historical experience of the long, slow processes informing evolving traditions. The 'Middle-march' taken for granted in the West is absent in Russia and in the nations she oppresses (such as the Poles) throughout her vast empire. Thus, neither Razumov nor the warring factions in his nation can find 'a form of peace' or a practical form of liberty. His tragedy is that of the reasonable man caught between irreconcilable antagonisms that are impossible to negotiate. Tragically, the middle way of 'the secular logic of human development' and of 'Evolution' (which the West takes for granted) is as great a delusion as the alternatives of either 'Destruction' as the means to a new revelation or of autocracy as God's authority on earth. In Russia, even the Man of Reason is divided from birth, and for the *homo duplex* in such oppressed societies even the politest declaration of independence, 'To retire', is unattainable.

Razumov's eventual answer to Mikulin's 'Where to?' is to accept an offer to infiltrate the revolutionary circle in Geneva. The latter suavely assures him that this decision is the consequence of his liberalism because he will subsequently subvert the very forces that threaten his political faith and that have robbed him of a future in Russia. He discovers, of course, that his moral solitude is exacerbated and that he is doubly ensnared by his mock career of revolutionist and his haunting secret sharer, Haldin. This discovery ensures that he perform the role of *homo duplex* in a very black 'comedy of errors' (p. 284), composed of 'subtly mendacious' dialogues that he solicits, prompts, and loathes. Falsehood will only be purged from him if he confesses to Natalia whom he loves and to the revolutionists whom he despises.

The tragic character of Razumov's intolerable position is most succinctly expressed during a 'mendacious dialogue' with Peter Ivanovich, who accidentally confirms the awful truth that the illegitimate Razumov can only be a successful spy if he is accepts that he is now 'one of us'. In relation to his function in the novel Razumov's famous reply – 'Russia *can't* disown me … I am *it!*' (p. 209) – re-works the definitive model for interpreting his fate. He is tragic not only because he incarnates the larger tragedy of his nation, but because Russia has disowned him in denying him from birth 'the free use of his intelligence' (p. 83). As the deep puns suggest, his career manifests the awful truth that intelligence, in a cynical and 'uneasy despotism' can only be used (Fogel, *Coercion to Speak*, pp. 192–4). Construed through all these models Razumov commands compassion.

VI

Poised to confess to Natalia, Razumov scornfully entertains 'the superstition of an active Providence' and rejects the alternative of 'the personal Devil of our simple ancestors' (p. 350). He canvasses, here, the opposing models he has used to interpret his miserable fate and that unbeknownst to him are rehearsed in order to offer the reader another way of understanding the tragic dimensions of the narrative that contains him. Razumov is bitter because he remembers his father Prince K— and Mikulin who both assure him after his betrayal of Haldin that he is 'the instrument of Providence' (p. 296). Razumov desperately tries to attach himself to Prince K—'s and Mikulin's providential plot when, despite his desolating sense of his abandonment by Providence, he accepts the logic of this design and becomes a spy.

When he tells Natalia that she is 'a predestined victim', Razumov acknowledges that he possesses a satanic power because he can corrupt her soul by either marrying her or by allowing the revolutionary denizens of the Château Borel 'to get hold of' her (pp. 349–50). His acknowledgement, however, also prefigures his enthusiastic embrace in his written confession of an alternative providential model of his own enthusiastic construction – a private theatre of temptation and confession. In this pattern Natalia began as his helpless prey (with the narrator, who has functioned as her hapless intermediary, hysterically granted the bit part of pander-devil) and then is assigned in his written confession the role of a Madonna who saves him and who, according to his schema, thereby saves herself.

Razumov's liberating providential plot manifests his desire to escape 'the comedy of errors' that he feels is orchestrated by the devil. He is, of course, unaware that his editor also invokes the devil-game model to describe Mikulin's 'subtly mendacious' dialogue with him, where he is compassionately construed as a 'tempted soul' (p. 305). More importantly, he cannot realize that the supreme Providence in his fictional life is his creator, who constructs these dialogues. They ironically testify to man's prolific 'ingenuity in error', and they are precisely crafted to cut Razumov to the quick and to stimulate his need for 'air' (p. 334), truth, and freedom. In an elegant and redemptive reversal these needs spur his confessions.

All of Razumov's mendacious dialogues in Parts II and III, composed of dazzling misprisions, half-truths, lies, and silences, in which all the characters, as in Shakespeare, always say and communicate more than they mean, alert us to the author as 'Providence', deceiving while 'talking over' his 'case' (p. 306). Unlike Mikulin and General T—, Conrad uses his secret 'unbounded power' to effect the emancipation of his protagonist from the rack of his suffering and his prison of lies, Natalia from the toils of innocence, and the reader from his hoaxing novel.

Razumov ends his written confession to Natalia on a defiant note: 'I am independent – and therefore perdition is my lot' (p. 362). Thanks to a merciful authorial Providence who demonstrates the tragic paradoxes at the heart of his terrible fate his final self-fashioning turns out to be mistaken. At the close, tended by Tekla and broken to be healed, he finally finds in Russia the 'material' and 'moral refuge' denied him since birth (p. 32). Deafened and placed beyond 'the multitude of men's counsel', Razumov earns his independence and finds his voice. The revolutionaries now visit his remote, humble dwelling not to disrupt but to seek his counsel, for 'He has ideas' and 'He talks well, too' (p. 379). Sophia Antonovna expands neither on his ideas nor on the value of his talk. They are, however, attested to in a remarkable sequence when we learn finally the exact nature of the transmission of Razumov's journal. The old teacher pays a last visit to his beloved Natalia who is set to return to Russia. She hands him 'something living still' – Razumov's diary – sent to her 'wrapped up in my veil'. She instructs the narrator, while he reads it, to remember 'In justice to the man' that she '*was* defenseless' (pp. 375–6).

Despite the narrator's scornful digressions, occasional obtusenesses, and sense of remoteness this 'flat parcel' lives because it claims the power to liberate, as it has transformed Natalia's vision of herself and of her world. Natalia does not finish her thought 'I *was* defenseless. And that he...'. This time, however, the broken speech is not disconnected. Rather it invites us to recognize, as the old teacher divined, that he loved her and therefore desired to free her from the toils of innocence. She is now enabled to return to Russia determined not to 'spare herself in good service' (p. 378), even though she knows that her devotion to freedom and justice are entangled in the net of terrible political conditions, that her brother was an enthusiastic misconstruer, and that all ideals are subject to the duplicities inherent in speech and language.

This passage devoted to transmission echoes and re-works the narrator's disclaimers in the novel's opening paragraphs, which began with a frank despair of words as 'the great foes of reality'. But the book we hold in our hands – unlike either 'the mere litter of blackened paper' (p. 68) of

Razumov's prize essay or his scribbled spy report and unlike Laspara's revolutionary journal *The Living Word*, Peter Ivanovich's autobiographies, and 'other books written with the declared purpose of elevating humanity' (p. 125) – is indeed, 'living still', because our collaboration has re-activated it.[10] Delivered, wrapped in Natalia's veil, symbolic of her suffering, purity, defenselessness, and redemptive power, this book demonstrates the 'high gifts of imagination and expression' that the narrator disclaimed in the novel's opening sentence, and that enabled Conrad to create for the reader a 'living form' that attests his desire 'to render the highest form of justice to the visible universe', and to evoke 'the latent feeling of fellowship with all creation' (*NN*, pp. xxxix, xl). Especially, we might add, in moments of 'great distress' (p. 376). Conrad struggles against all odds to remove the veil that separates words from reality in order to achieve 'a direct grasp upon humanity' (*SA*, p. 67). The reader's bewilderment before the terrible cycle of misinterpretations and the competing interpretive models that constituted his or her experience of this book yields, in the end, a tragic reading that is more generous and enabling than that offered by the old teacher's cynicism. Despite the irreconcilable antagonisms that man is heir to and that manifest themselves so terribly in their Russian aspects, this 'moral discovery' works for release, action, and enlightenment.

NOTES

1 Readers interested in the controversial subject of Conrad's Polish heritage should begin with the documents in Najder's *Conrad under Familial Eyes* and *Conrad's Polish Background*. See also Busza, Carabine in Smith, ed., *Joseph Conrad's 'Under Western Eyes'*, Hodges, Milosz, Morf, and Knowles in ch. 1 of this volume.

2 Conrad wrote 'A Familiar Preface' to *A Personal Record* to explain how he came to write *Under Western Eyes* (see *Letters*, IV, p. 477). In it he confesses that the book's private origin must be sought in the life of the novelist 'who is the only reality in an invented world, among imaginary happenings and people. Writing about them he is only writing about himself.' See Carabine in Smith, ed., *Joseph Conrad's 'Under Western Eyes'*, pp. 1–37.

3 Unsigned review, *Nation*, 21 October 1911, reprinted Sherry, ed., *Conrad: The Critical Heritage*, 237–9, and anonymous review, *Saturday Review*, 14 October 1911, reprinted Carabine, ed., *Joseph Conrad: Critical Assessments*, I, p. 339.

4 See Smith, ed., on Conrad's troubled composition of the novel and on the manuscripts.

5 *Under Western Eyes* is full of references to the act of writing and to the problems of composition, authorship, and interpretation. For a discussion of this topic, see Fleishman, Hawthorn, Kermode, Schliefer, and Szittya. For Carabine's reply to Kermode, see Carabine, ed., *Joseph Conrad: Critical Assessments*, pp. 187–210.

6 Saveson relates Conrad's use of cynicism to Nietzsche's, and concludes that the

novel does contain a 'moral discovery': 'of those moral phenomena indigenous to a master-slave society, surviving in modern Russia' (p. 48). For Schliefer, the narrator's attitude to Russian 'mysticism' is itself cynical. See also, Berthoud, *Joseph Conrad: The Major Phase*, pp. 160–85.

7 See Conrad's letter of 22 December 1902 (*Letters*, II, p. 468). Carabine in Smith, ed., argues that Conrad's breakdown in January 1910, after completing the first draft of the novel which engaged his Polish shades, confirmed his presentiment that coming to terms with his Polish past and context would undo him. See also Miłosz and also Korzeniowski's 'To my son', in Najder, ed., *Conrad under Familial Eyes*, pp. 32–3.

8 Most critics have failed to realize that the narrator bewilders because during Conrad's long and troubled composition of the novel he accumulated a host of roles, functions, characteristics, voices, and opinions that compete against each other. These include: naïve and divided editor of, and commentator upon, Razumov's journal; screen for Conrad's Polish prejudices; spokesman for Western values. Then, from Part II on, he is a character in both his own narrative, and subsequently in Razumov's journal, and the vehicle for Conrad's changing sense of his subject. Szittya is an honorable exception.

9 For an account of the value of reflectors, see Henry James's 'Prefaces' to *What Maisie Knew. The Pupil. In the Cage* (1908), Vol. XI of the New York Edition. Reprinted in *Henry James: Literary Criticism*, pp. 1156–72. Wayne C. Booth's *The Rhetoric of Fiction* is the classic work on the subject.

10 As Conrad's correspondence and prefaces plainly show, he anticipated the central tenets of reader-response criticism. He knew that his 'manner of telling', which was aimed at stimulating vision in my reader', meant 'the reader collaborates with the author' (*Letters*, I, p. 381; II, p. 394).

WORKS CITED

Berthoud, Jacques. *Joseph Conrad: The Major Phase*. Cambridge: Cambridge University Press, 1978

Booth, Wayne C. *The Rhetoric of Fiction*. 2nd edn. Chicago: University of Chicago Press, 1983

Busza, Andrzej. 'Conrad's Polish literary background and some illustrations of Polish literature on his work'. *Antemurale* 10 (1966), 109–255

Carabine, Keith. 'Construing "secrets" and "diabolism" in *Under Western Eyes*: a response to Frank Kermode'. In *Conrad's Literary Career*. Ed. Keith Carabine, Owen Knowles, and Wiesław Krajka. Boulder: East European Monographs, 1992, pp. 187–210

'"The figure behind the veil": Conrad and Razumov in *Under Western Eyes*'. *Joseph Conrad's 'Under Western Eyes': Beginnings, Revisions, Final Forms – Five Essays*. Ed. David R. Smith. Hamden, CT: Archon Books, 1991, pp. 1–37

Carabine, Keith, ed. *Joseph Conrad: Critical Assessments*. Robertsbridge: Helm Information, 1992

Conrad, Joseph. *The Nigger of the 'Narcissus'*. 1897. Ed. Jacques Berthoud. Oxford: Oxford University Press, 1984

Lord Jim, A Tale. 1900. Ed. John Batchelor. Oxford: Oxford University Press, 1983

'The Mirror of the Sea' and 'A Personal Record'. 1906 and 1912. Ed. Zdzisław Najder. Oxford: Oxford University Press, 1988

The Secret Agent. 1907. Ed. Bruce Harkness and S. W. Reid. Cambridge: Cambridge University Press, 1990

Under Western Eyes. 1911. Ed. Jeremy Hawthorn. Oxford: Oxford University Press, 1983

Fleishman, Avrom. 'Speech and writing in Conrad's *Under Western Eyes.* In *Joseph Conrad: A Commemoration.* Ed. Norman Sherry. London: Macmillan; New York: Barnes and Noble, 1976, pp. 119–28

Fogel, Aaron. *Coercion to Speak: Conrad's Poetics of Dialogue.* Cambridge, MA: Harvard University Press, 1985

Hawthorn, Jeremy. *Joseph Conrad: Language and Fictional Self-Consciousness.* London: Arnold; Lincoln: University of Nebraska Press, 1979

Hay, Eloise Knapp. *The Political Novels of Joseph Conrad: A Critical Study.* Chicago: University of Chicago Press, 1963; rev. edn. 1981

Hodges, Robert F. *The Dual Heritage of Joseph Conrad.* The Hague: Mouton, 1967

James, Henry. *French Writers. Other European Writers. The Prefaces to the New York Edition.* New York: Library of America, 1984

Kermode, Frank. 'Secrets and narrative sequence'. *Essays on Fiction: 1971–82.* London: Routledge & Kegan Paul, 1982, pp. 133–55

Miłosz, Czesław. *Kultura,* February 1956, 60–80. Reprinted *Mosaic* 6.4 (1973), 121–40

Najder, Zdzisław, ed. *Conrad's Polish Background: Letters to and from Polish Friends.* Tr. Halina Carroll. London: Oxford University Press, 1964

Conrad under Familial Eyes. Tr. Halina Carroll-Najder. Cambridge: Cambridge University Press, 1983

Palmer, John A. *Joseph Conrad's Fiction: A Study in Literary Growth.* Ithaca: Cornell University Press, 1968

Rosenfield, Claire. *Paradise of Snakes: An Archetypal Analysis of Conrad's Political Novels.* Chicago: Chicago University Press, 1967

Saveson, John E. 'The moral discovery of *Under Western Eyes'. Criticism* 14 (1972), 32–48

Schliefer, Ronald. 'Public and private narrative in *Under Western Eyes'. Conradiana* 9.3 (1977), 237–54

Secor, Robert. 'The function of the narrator in *Under Western Eyes'. Conradiana* 3.1 (1971), 27–38

Sherry, Norman, ed. *Conrad: The Critical Heritage.* London: Routledge & Kegan Paul, 1973

Smith, David R., ed. *Joseph Conrad's 'Under Western Eyes': Beginnings, Revisions, Final Forms – Five Essays.* Hamden, CT: Archon Books, 1991

Stine, Peter. 'Joseph Conrad's confession in *Under Western Eyes'. Cambridge Quarterly* 9.2 (1980), 95–113

Szittya, Penn R. 'Metafiction: the double narration in *Under Western Eyes'. ELH* 48 (1981), 817–40. Reprinted *Critical Essays on Joseph Conrad.* Ed. Ted Billy. Boston: Hall, 1987, pp. 142–62

Tanner, Tony. 'Nightmare and complacency: Razumov and the western eye'. *Critical Quarterly* 4.3 (1982), 197–214

Watt, Ian. *Conrad in the Nineteenth Century.* Berkeley: University of California Press, 1979; London: Chatto & Windus, 1980

Zabel, Morton Dauwen. Introduction. *Under Western Eyes.* New York: Doubleday, 1963, pp. ix–lviii

8

ROBERT HAMPSON

The late novels

Until comparatively recently, Conrad's late novels have suffered from critical neglect and undervaluation. In the 1950s, Douglas Hewitt, Thomas C. Moser, and Albert J. Guerard argued that Conrad's late novels represented a decline after the achievement of the novels of his 'major' period – *Lord Jim*, *Nostromo*, and *The Secret Agent*. These critics established the paradigm within which most subsequent Conrad criticism has operated.[1] There were some dissenting voices: M. C. Bradbrook, Paul Wiley, and Walter F. Wright, for example, argued that there was no decline, and that Conrad's later novels were to be praised as novels of moral affirmation. Over the last twenty years, a third approach has gradually emerged: this bases its positive evaluation of the late fiction not on its supposed moral affirmation but rather on increased attentiveness to its new modes and techniques. This was first adumbrated in an essay by Morton Dauwen Zabel and developed further by John Palmer, Robert Secor, and Gary Geddes. Geddes, for example, argued that the critics of the 1950s misunderstood Conrad's fictional aims through their 'predilection for fictional modes and techniques that were no longer of paramount importance to Conrad' (*Conrad's Later Novels*, p. 1). Their critical approach was biased towards 'fiction that presents the drama of self' and could not cope with 'the wider, more social manifestations of Conrad's moral imperatives' in his late novels (*Ibid.*, p. 5). Recent criticism would suggest that an emphasis on 'moral imperatives' is also inappropriate for the open-ended exploration characteristic of Conrad's late novels. Certainly, Conrad, in his late fiction, was interested in developing modes and techniques other than those of his earlier work. The late novels were not an exhausted return to old subjects, as Moser argued (*Joseph Conrad: Achievement and Decline*, p. 180), but a continuing experimentation with the novel form for subjects that continued to engage him and, it must be added, for new subjects as well. Indeed, Conrad's particular interest in women and sexuality in his late fiction has proved remarkably congenial for recent critical interest in the issue of gender.[2]

I

One of the late works that has not followed the pattern of neglect and undervaluation is *The Shadow-Line*. F. R. Leavis, in 1958, for example, described it as 'central to Conrad's genius'. This is perhaps the same as saying that, although it was written in 1915, it is, in many ways, a return to 'old subjects' and old methods.[3] Conrad described it to his agent, J. B. Pinker, as 'an old subject something in the style of Youth'.[4] As in 'Youth', the story is based directly on Conrad's own experience: in this case, his command of the *Otago* in 1888. But, unlike, 'Youth', its narration is not staged as a tale-within-a-tale; instead, like 'The Secret Sharer', it presents a narrator's first-person reminiscence. Like that story, too, it is concerned with the loneliness of first command, and the account of a journey is used to describe an earlier self's progress 'from innocence to experience and from youth to maturity' (Schwarz, *Conrad: The Later Fiction*, pp. 82–3).

The Shadow-Line begins with the narrator's younger self going through a period of crisis, which is presented as characteristic of 'that twilight region between youth and maturity' (*SL*, p. 26). He gives up his job as mate and moves into the Officers' Sailors' Home, while waiting for a ship to take him back to England. There, he is unexpectedly offered the chance of commanding a ship whose captain has died, and jumps at the opportunity as the 'ultimate test of my profession' (p. 48). The story is then constructed in terms of the young captain's expectations and their frustration by experience. His new role, which he at first sees as the 'magical solution of all his life-problems', proves to involve 'an intricate network of moral imperatives, psychological discoveries, and social responsibilities' (Watt, 'Story and idea', pp. 138–9). Instead of the 'more intense life' that he had expected, he finds himself 'bound hand and foot' (p. 107); instead of feeling supported by the continuity of captaincy through the 'succession of men' (p. 52) who have been his predecessors, he experiences intense 'moral isolation' (p. 106). Subsequently, in the various crises the ship faces he feels himself judged and found wanting. In the end, however, through confronting his feelings of guilt and self-doubt, he achieves his professional identity. Like *The Nigger of the 'Narcissus'* and *Lord Jim*, *The Shadow-Line* addresses the relationship between the personal and the professional: the young captain, like the French Lieutenant of *Lord Jim*, 'may be as fearful as the next man', but his conduct must accord with the maritime values of duty, service, and responsibility (Schwarz, *Conrad: The Later Fiction*, pp. 82, 85–6).

The Shadow-Line recounts a rite of passage into mature identity within the male world of the Merchant Navy. This, however, is not the only border with which the story is concerned. There are also the 'shadow-lines' between sanity and madness, the natural and the supernatural, and life and death. Ransome, for example, is not just the epitome of fidelity to duty, but, with his bad heart, is a constant reminder of the imminence of death. Arguably, what the captain learns is what Ransome physically embodies: the performance of duty in the full consciousness of one's own weakness, the pursuit of 'a difficult vocation upon an ocean of incertitude'. Liminal states and moments of transition, to which the title *The Shadow-Line* draws attention, are a recurrent feature of Conrad's late fiction. Death, in particular, increasingly becomes a focus of attention. However, in the other late works, incertitude has formal as well as thematic implications. Conrad brings to the fore the metaphysical and epistemological scepticism that had always been present in his work to produce fictions that are variously conscious of their own fictionality.

II

Chance, published in January 1914, might, at first glance, look like a return to an 'old subject'. Like 'Youth', 'Heart of Darkness', and *Lord Jim*, it uses Marlow as narrator and tells a tale involving a ship's captain, ships, and the sea. However, its thematic concerns are quite different from those of the earlier fiction, and Marlow is used in quite a different way. Indeed, some of the early critical dissatisfaction with this novel obviously sprang from a sense of disappointment with this new version of Marlow.[5] This reflected changes in the characterization of Marlow but can also be traced to a misreading of Conrad's authorial strategy. These critics desired the subtle, questioning Marlow of 'Heart of Darkness' and *Lord Jim*, a Marlow who could be read as an apparently authoritative commentator and interpreter, whereas this Marlow seemed obtuse, irresponsible, and unreliable. Recent criticism has accepted this irresponsible Marlow not as a mistake but as a deliberate narrative strategy.[6] For a long time also, *Chance* has suffered from being read as a flawed attempt at a Jamesian novel. The stage for such a reading was set by Henry James's own review of the novel, with its puzzled tribute to Marlow's narrative as 'a prolonged hovering flight of the subjective over the outstretched ground of the case exposed' ('The new novel'). Graham Hough, for example, repeated James's criticism of the succession of narrators: he praised the 'immense technical assurance', but noted 'a slightly disturbing sense of being kept at a remove, or rather several removes from the actuality' ('*Chance* and Joseph Conrad', p. 217). However, it is precisely the problematic status of 'actuality' that is the ground for this narrative. Where Marlow told his own story in 'Youth' and explored the interaction between himself and others in both 'Heart of Darkness' and *Lord Jim* he spends the first half of *Chance* discussing Flora de Barral, whom he has met only twice, and the second half discussing Captain Anthony, whom he has never met.

As in *Lord Jim*, Marlow constructs his narrative by induction from details presented to him by a series of witnesses, but, in *Chance*, Marlow emphasizes both the speculative nature of his commentary and the necessarily fictional nature of his narrative. In part, this is because the model for the narrative method is not, in fact, the Jamesian novel but the detective fiction of Edgar Allan Poe or Arthur Conan Doyle. The narrative is explicitly constructed as a series of mysteries: 'the affair of the purloined brother' (*Ch*, p. 148), 'the mystery of the vanishing Powell' (p. 258), and the 'psychological cabin mystery of discomfort' (p. 325) on board Anthony's ship the *Ferndale*. The novel self-consciously uses a genre that is itself famously self-conscious. Todorov noted that the detective novel 'contains not one but two stories: the story of the crime and the story of the investigation' (*The Poetics of Prose*, p. 44), and this second story is an explorative, interpretive narration that is also explicitly aware of itself as narrative.

This use of the detective story has a counterpart in other features of the novel – in particular, the self-conscious use of chivalric romance. Conrad had already made similar use of adventure romance in *Lord Jim*: the first half takes off from and inverts the motifs of the sea novels that had constituted Jim's 'course of light holiday literature' (*LJ*, p. 5), while in Patusan Jim is allowed to become an adventure-romance hero in an adventure-romance world only for that world and its conventions, which are implicated in Jim's self-conception, to be opened to question. In the same way, *Chance*'s affiliation with chivalric romance is flaunted: its two parts, 'The Damsel' and 'The Knight', can be read as a series of rescues. Marlow rescues Flora from suicide; Captain Anthony does the same by running off with her; the Fynes rescue her from the desertion of her scheming governess and, later, from mistreatment at the hands of her relatives. Like the use of the detective novel, the affiliation with chivalric romance is a distancing device, but this distancing is also part of the critique of the self-conception Marlow assigns to Captain Anthony and, more importantly, of the chivalric construction of masculinity that is central to it.

Marlow's interpretation of events aboard the *Ferndale* posits a self-denying decision on Captain Anthony's part derived from this chivalric code. Like Jim, Antony is represented as capable of sacrificing himself for an ideal conception of himself. Like *Nostromo*'s Charles Gould and *Victory*'s Axel Heyst, Anthony is represented as shaped (indeed, damaged) by paternal inheritance, and this is where his self-conception is related to a particular construction of masculinity. His self-denying decision is traced back to the idealization of 'the domestic and social amenities of our age' (*Ch*, p. 38) in his father's poetry. At the same time, Marlow insists on the gap between the 'supra-refined standard' (p. 328) of the poetry and the 'traces of the primitive cave-dwellers' temperament' (p. 38) displayed in the poet's domestic life. Through Carleon Anthony and his son, Conrad offers a critique of chivalric masculinity and of male idealizations of women. Carleon Anthony with his poetic idealization of women has actually worn out two wives, while his son's chivalry causes suffering both to himself and Flora. Captain Anthony's conception of masculinity underestimates the power of his own sexual desire and misreads Flora's needs and desires. Conrad also hints at the idea that Ford was to develop in *The Good Soldier* (1915) that chivalric psychology actually finds erotic stimulation in the distress of the woman it presents itself as rescuing. The woman is thus ambiguously positioned as victim in the script of chivalric desire.

Victory, written between October 1912 and July 1914, continues to explore these ideas and combines its explorations with more obvious technical experimentation. One key to the novel is what Secor calls a 'rhetoric of shifting perspectives': the changes in point of view objectify different states of consciousness, systems of values, and ways of knowing. There is 'a quality in events which is apprehended differently by different minds or even by the same mind at different times' (*Vi*, p. 248), and the narrative method shows how characters live in their own fictional worlds, each with its own particular, limited perspective.

The novel begins with an unnamed narrator who is identified only as one of us 'out there' (p. 3). He claims no direct knowledge of Heyst, but pieces together his narrative about him from the gossip of Europeans in the Malay Archipelago and, in particular, by following Davidson's investigations into Heyst's disappearance. Only in Part II is there a shift to Heyst's perspective and a revelation of his inner world. The unnamed narrator had drawn attention to Heyst's reserve, courtesy, and gentlemanliness, but Part II reveals the programme of drift, the 'system of restless wandering' that Heyst has adopted as a way of 'passing through life without suffering' (p. 90). It exposes the conflict between his rationalist scepticism and his sympathetic temperament, between his elected detachment and repressed aspects of himself. Subsequently, the narrative turns to Lena's perspective and shows her attempts to make sense of Heyst. It shows how, from her different class position, she misreads and overvalues what in Heyst are merely marks of courtesy and how her low self-valuation shapes both her interpretation of Heyst's lack of emotional display and her response to it. Most interesting of all, the narrative shows how, under the influence of her Sunday school lessons and Victorian constructions of femininity, she writes a script for herself in which erotic feelings are displaced into idealistic self-sacrifice. The intrusion of Jones and company onto the island to which Heyst and Lena have withdrawn gives her the opportunity to cast herself in a drama of redemption, but the terms and structure of feeling of this drama derive from sentimental romance.[7]

From the start, Conrad draws attention to the processes of perception and cognition, and to the limitations of interpretation. As the novel proceeds, misinterpretation comes to play a vital role in the development of the narrative. The plot hinges on Schomberg's malicious misinterpretation of Heyst. This leads, in turn, to the misinterpretation of Heyst by Jones and Ricardo, and the complex mutual misinterpretations of Heyst and Lena become the focus of sustained attention in the final chapters.

Victory also makes demands on the reader as interpreter through its use of dramatic presentation and 'doubling'. Conrad had first tried his hand at drama in 1904, when he adapted his short story 'To-morrow' into a one-act play, *One Day More*. During the spring of 1913, while working on *Victory*, he had explored the possibility of collaborating on a play with his friend Perceval Gibbon, and, in March 1914, before completing that novel, had read A. C. Bradley's *Shakespearean Tragedy* (1904). One effect of Conrad's renewed interest in drama is evident in the handling of dialogue: in *Victory* and in his subsequent novels, he often makes use of objectively presented dialogue and actions, with the reader left to deduce motives and implications.[8]

Doubling is a device Conrad had used since his earliest fiction. In *Victory*, there are certain obvious narrative parallels between Schomberg and Heyst: both have an interest in Lena, and both must find a way to deal with Jones and his associates. These situational parallels generate other, subtler parallels between the two men – or the teasing suggestion of possible parallels. For example, Schomberg's dealings with Jones and Ricardo reveal the difference between his inner feelings and the identity he asserts: 'The consciousness of his inwardly abject attitude towards these men caused him always to throw his chest out and assume a severe expression' (pp. 122–3). Schomberg's martial appearance clearly compensates for (and is a sign of) feelings of fear and inadequacy, and this reflects on Heyst who, despite his 'broad, martial presence', is, nevertheless, not 'a fighting man' (p. 9). Doubling, then is a means to explore masculinity. Through Heyst and Schomberg the military construction of masculinity is opened to question, and, through Jones and Heyst, who are linked as 'gentlemen' and wanderers, 'gentlemanly' lack of emotional display, male detachment, homosexuality, and fear and hatred of women are explored. In both cases, the set of relations established between the characters raises questions but does not supply answers. Instead, by hinting at analogies between them, Conrad creates for his readers an open-ended exploration of masculinity, male sexuality, and sexual politics.

III

While *Victory* opens new territory, it is *Chance*, however, that most clearly presents what was to be a major concern in Conrad's late works. At its centre is the figure of Flora de Barral. Marlow's narrative tracks back from her appearance on the edge of the cliff to the events that brought her there: her father's financial success and failure; her traumatic rejection by her governess; the subsequent ontological insecurity that the various episodes of her life reinforce. Marlow then speculates on the interaction between Flora's ontological insecurity and Anthony's chivalric masculinity in his narrative interpretation of the 'cabin mystery' that is their marriage. Flora is the first of the damaged women of the late novels: she anticipates Lena in *Victory*, Rita in *The Arrow of Gold*, Arlette in *The Rover*, and perhaps even Adele in *Suspense*.

The narrative complexity also anticipates a common characteristic of the late novels: *Chance* 'in its very structure' exemplifies 'the struggle of women to make their voices heard over, under and around a male discourse determined to give its own shape and meaning to the lives of women subjects' (Nadelhaft, *Joseph Conrad*, p. 110). It presents 'a variety of men' who 'seem to conspire to aid Flora while in reality they seek to muffle her voice' (*Ibid.*). Roberts has taken this further and argued that the circulation of discourse about women between the men of the novel, 'a secret sharing of male ignorance, a covert fellowship of fear and desire' ('Secret agents and secret objects', p. 97), also takes place outside the narrative between Marlow and the male reader. Both features reappear in *The Arrow of Gold*.

The Arrow of Gold was written during 1917 and 1918, but neither the idea nor material was new. There are obvious points of resemblance to Conrad's early unfinished novel, *The Sisters*, as well as connections between *The Arrow of Gold* and Conrad's autobiographical writings, *The Mirror of the Sea* and *A Personal Record*. A preoccupation with the autobiographical accuracy of *The Arrow of Gold* among early commentators has contributed to its critical neglect, because an approach through Conrad's biography misreads both its mode and M. George's narrative function.[9] Critics have tended to read the novel as an uneven romance (with the implication that Conrad was too close to his material and indulging in the memories of his youth), but ironic and subversive elements should have prevented such a reading.[10] Wiley's sympathetic and insightful early account drew attention to Conrad's technique of 'transcribing objectively the illusions of sense', and argued that 'in no other book does Conrad work quite so steadily as a painter in prose' (*Conrad's Measure of Man*, pp. 158, 163). He instanced the portrait of Rita (*AG*, p. 66); the chiaroscuro portrait of Therese (pp. 138–9); and the *grisaille* presentation of Mrs Blunt (p. 180). In fact, Conrad produces similar vignettes for almost all the characters, and, in each case, produces not just a painterly effect in prose (as Ford had done, for example, in his 1906 novel *The Fifth Queen*), but an effect that explicitly refers to the visual arts. The narrative is characterized not, as Wiley suggested, by the objective transcription of sense-impressions but rather by the organization and evaluation of descriptions in self-consciously aesthetic terms.[11] As in *Victory*, the narrative technique is based on different perspectives, which embody different modes of interpreting what is seen, and the use of self-consciously aesthetic ways of seeing draws attention to this.

M. George is the most important of the various ways of seeing since his interpretation provides the narrative. Yet he is not a privileged interpreter, but like the Marlow of *Chance*, an unreliable, even obtuse, narrator. Where the young male hero of *The Sisters* was provided with a complicated personality, M. George is a much simpler young man: he is, in his own Jamesian phrase, 'beautifully unthinking – infinitely receptive' (p. 8). As he suggests, if he represents anything, 'it was a perfect freshness of sensations and a refreshing ignorance' (p. 31). And the use of 'Two Notes' as a framing device for his narrative (as well as the device of an 'editor' who has shaped and selected from M. George's written text) further deprives him of narrative authority.

The narrative begins in a Marseilles café towards the end of the carnival, seen by the narrator as 'the last evening of that part of my life in which I did not know that woman' (p. 13). Like the young captain in *The Shadow-Line*, M. George will cross the line that separates youth from maturity, and that journey will take him 'to the point of insanity and past it' (Toliver, 'Conrad's *Arrow of Gold*', p. 149). The narrator recounts his initiation into passion, but the focus falls on Rita, the object of his desire, since the narrative circulates her image between the characters and between the narrator and the reader.

Most of Part I is taken up with a discussion between Mills and Blunt, to which M. George listens, which presents a series of images and impressions of Rita.[12] Rita's reification is signalled by the role of the painter and collector Allegre in her life. Through his patronage and through the dialogue between Mills and Blunt about its consequences Rita is presented as an object for consumption and/or exchange – as the aesthetic object of the male gaze, as the sexual object of male desire, and as an image in a discourse between males. Her objectification is confirmed by her 'double', the dummy that stood in for her during Allegre's painting sessions, which continues to act as a surrogate for her for both M. George and the reader. In addition, this 'mutilated dummy' (p. 122) suggests both the implicit sadism of the male gaze and Rita's role as the body upon which male spectators project various roles and identities.

When M. George at last meets Rita in Part II, his immediate identification with her – and his conclusion that 'there was nothing more for us to know about each other' (p. 70) – means that he feels that he does not need to listen to what she says about herself, as Roberts has argued ('The gaze and the dummy'). Her words are not allowed to intrude on his narcissistic involvement and narrative, even while they actively question and subvert it. Instead, he loses himself in the idea of love as an identification with the beloved. But this offers merely another version of male objectification and appropriation since it clearly leaves out of account Rita's subjectivity. While M. George ignores Rita's words, the reader should not. For example, the difference between the two accounts of her first encounter with Allegre is revealing. Blunt's account presents a picture of idyllic innocence: 'She was sitting on a stone, a fragment of some old balustrade, with her feet in the damp grass, and reading a tattered book of some kind' (p. 34). A sentimental Victorian genre painting, this picture of Rita in terms of childhood innocence derives directly from Blunt's problems with her sexuality. Rita's own account of this first meeting offers a significant reinterpretation. Where Blunt's pictorial version fixes her as the passive object of the male gaze— Allegre's gaze, Blunt's, his audience's, and the complicitous male reader's – Rita's version emphasizes that her stasis was actively chosen. Where Blunt is unable to come to terms with Rita's sexuality, her clear understanding of him is evident from her comments about him and dialogues with him. In a similar way, she repeatedly challenges M. George's readings of her. He aestheticizes her; indulges in regressive fantasies about their being like children; seeks communion with silence or dissolution into the absolute; and sees her as an enigma embodying 'that something secret and obscure which is in all women' (p. 146). But he refuses to meet her as a concrete, particular individual.

Rita thus struggles to make her voice heard 'over, under and around' male discourse (Nadelhaft, *Joseph Conrad*, p. 110). In M. George's narrative, the males are active, controlling, desiring, and Rita is positioned as the object of desire, caught up in male discourse, but not accorded a place as a desiring sexual subject, as M. George's repeated references to her 'seduction' establish. This is neither an active part she plays nor expressive of any desire for men on her part. Instead, her 'seduction' reduces her to a signifier of male desire, while depriving her of both desire and subjectivity. So coercive is M. George's rhetoric that it is almost possible to miss the submerged narrative of Rita's relations with women and her reported interest in 'common humanity' (p. 91), which challenges the narrative's emphasis on 'perfection' and male attempts to idealize, aestheticize, universalize, or essentialize her.

Rita's account of her childhood relations with Ortega in Part III offers an explanation of the fear that Blunt reported as the only emotion about which she had no doubt, but, as later events make clear, this is an incomplete account of the trauma that has shaped her. Her first version omits (or minimizes) her sexual desire for Ortega, while it is precisely this desire she needs to acknowledge. Her account of being trapped in a shelter by Ortega is re-enacted in the narrative climax when she and M. George are trapped by him in a locked room. Ortega represents the extreme case of male projections onto women. His tormented desire for and hatred of Rita reflects on and subverts the novel's male discourse, just as the moments when Blunt and Ortega appear as doubles of M. George problematize M. George's 'love' for Rita and prevent it from emerging as a norm or ideal. Rita's account of her childhood 'play' with Ortega similarly subverts the idyllic childhood images that M. George projects onto his relationship with her.

One could argue that in the locked room re-enactment of her traumatic childhood experiences with Ortega, Rita frees herself from these memories. M. George could be seen as occupying the role of analyst, and his witnessing of the scene might then be considered in terms of a male legitimation of her sexual desire. However, after the crisis, M. George finds himself yelling 'in a sort of frenzy as though I had been a second Ortega' (p. 328), and, next morning, when Rita recoils from him, he describes how a 'grown man's bitterness, informed, suspicious, resembling hatred, welled out of my heart' (p. 334). The particular 'grown man' he has in mind is suggested when he goes on to say that he 'won't throw stones' as Ortega used to do (p. 334). Rather than freeing Rita from her traumatic memories, the episode seems to have released in M. George emotions similar to Ortega's, and if M. George's experiences represent a process of maturation, it has to be said that at this stage Ortega seems to be his model.

The Second Note similarly opens the end of the novel onto a range of questions. While it presents a picture of idyllic 'precarious bliss', it leaves open the possibility that this 'bliss' is merely a projection of M. George's, and that he is, unknown to himself, merely another appropriating male rather than the ideal lover that he sees himself as in his narrative. Whatever the answer, in this Second Note, the figure of Rita disappears behind successive veils until we are left with a final exchange between M. George and Mills. According to Mills, Rita has 'sacrificed' her chance of love to the 'integrity' of M. George's life. There is, however, always the possibility, as Roberts has argued, that Mills is telling M. George what he feels M. George needs to hear or, even, that Mills has failed to understand that Rita has acted to protect her own integrity.

Interestingly, the editor of the Second Note is not assigned a gender. The address to 'those who know women' (presumably a different group from those who *are* women) suggests, however, that, as in *Chance*, the circulation of discourse about women within the narrative is replicated outside it between male editor and male readers. In other words, where the original text (according to the First Note) was addressed to a female reader, the editor has suppressed the female addressee and appropriated the revised text for a male audience. The final dialogue between Mills and M. George about the absent Rita has its counterpart in the editor's address to the (male) reader over the head of the excluded female addressee, and the disappearance of Rita from the discourse of males might again be seen not so much as their exclusion of her but as her actively slipping away from and eluding their narratives to save her own integrity.

IV

Where *The Arrow of Gold* features 'young Ulysses', *The Rover*, begun in October 1921 and finished in July 1922, represents a sailor's homecoming. The narrative begins with the return to France of Jean Peyrol after a lifetime spent at sea. Like Rita de Lastaola and Flora de Barral, he has passed through an experience in childhood that has decisively shaped his character. In his case, the early traumatic experience, the death of his mother, has led to emotional self-concealment as a way of accepting 'the new and inexplicable conditions of life' (*Ro*, p. 25). In the opening chapters, Peyrol's lack of emotional display is mirrored by his sense of alienation from his native land. However, just as his lack of display covers a profound emotional responsiveness, his sense of alienation also proves equivocal: the narrative exposes his simultaneous sense of strangeness and belonging and displays his continuous probing of the loss and gain of his forty-year absence from France. At the same time, his lawless past, during the French Revolution and post-revolutionary changes, contributes to a general sense of flux and instability – indeed, of 'precariousness' – as the context for the novel's action.

Peyrol's traumatized personality also anticipates the two other central characters, Arlette and Réal, both traumatized by the Revolution. Arlette's derangement is the result of her parents' violent deaths and her own involvement in the Toulon massacre. Réal, like Arlette, lost his parents to the Revolution and, like Peyrol, has responded to their death by running off to sea. Like Peyrol again, he has adopted a 'schooled reserve which the precariousness of all things' forces on this 'orphan of the Revolution' (p. 71). The relationships between these three characters are central to the narrative, while the parallels between them point to a structure of analogues and repetitions.

Conrad's description of *The Rover* as 'a feat of artistic brevity' is most obviously witnessed in the economic handling of narrative.[13] The 'intensity and concreteness' of the images, the narrative 'tautness', and the way in which the novel's final pages are 'the culmination of a movement that builds from the earliest descriptions of character and place in the novel' have been rightly praised (Geddes, *Conrad's Later Novels*, pp. 179, 174–5). The narrative is propelled through a series of overlapping mysteries: the mystery of Peyrol's motives and purposes; of Arlette's behaviour; of the English ship's mission; of Symons's disappearance; and of Réal's personal and professional motives. These are produced by a further development of the technique of *Victory*. For various reasons, the main characters are isolated from each other: Arlette and Scevola are, in different ways, deranged, and Réal and Peyrol are both the self-contained possessors of secrets. The narrative proceeds through the careful control of point of view and the skilful shifting of narrative perspective.

Peyrol's waistcoat packed with gold, the 'secret of his heavy movements' (p. 11) revealed when he first undresses, is only the first of the novel's many secrets. These secrets have a concrete embodiment in the pervasive motif of locked rooms. In chapter 3, for example, Scevola mentions a tartane in his brief account of the deaths of Arlette's parents. In chapter 7, Peyrol discovers that the tartane he wants to buy, with the 'enormous padlock' on its cabin-door 'as if there had been secrets or treasures inside', is the same boat (p. 84). The first secret released from the tartane is a bloody memory of its part in the Toulon massacre. Accordingly, the boat acts as a memory-symbol for the determinants of Arlette's mental state, and Peyrol's transformation of the tartane parallels his effect on Arlette and Réal. The tartane is later linked with another 'secret' (p. 101) – Symons's capture and imprisonment – which has various implications for the plot. It explains the sailor's mysterious disappearance, reveals retrospectively what had been on Peyrol's mind during his 'forenoon talk' with Réal (p. 126), and anticipates the tartane's use against the English. But Symons's imprisonment in the tartane also leads to the release of some of Peyrol's memories of his time with the Brotherhood of the Coast. This economically concretizes Peyrol's process of ageing and also associates his skilful handling of the tartane with his years at sea. The use of the cabin to imprison Symons also anticipates its later use as a prison for Scevola and its final use as a burial chamber. The replacement of Symons by Scevola as the prisoner in the locked cabin is one of a series of substitutions that occurs at the end in a ritualistic cleansing of the blood-guilt of the Revolution.[14]

Counterpointed against the motif of the padlocked cabin of the tartane is a motif of locked and unlocked rooms used in relation to Arlette. Where the first motif is part of a narrative oriented towards death, the second is involved in a narrative engaged with love. To begin with, immediately after she was brought back to Escampobar from Toulon, Catherine kept Arlette locked in a room to protect her from Scevola's sexual interest. Later, Arlette locks herself in Réal's room to think about him, and the locked door betrays her love for Réal to Scevola. Later still, Arlette locks Réal in his room with her in order to reveal to him both her regained reason and her love, and the locked room now provides space for their first real communication. By contrast, the crisis that has produced this resolution takes place in an unlocked room, the *salle*, while the rest of the household are next door in the kitchen. Arlette and Réal give separate accounts of the incident, and, in both cases, events in locked and unlocked rooms are juxtaposed

The Rover is very much a novel of watching, interpreting, and problem-solving. Peyrol and Réal spend much of their time at the 'lookout' watching the English ship, the *Amelia*, which is itself watching the French coast. This, in turn, can be seen as an analogue for the domestic system of surveillance: Réal watches Arlette and Peyrol; Peyrol watches Réal and Arlette; Catherine watches over Arlette; Arlette watches over Réal; and Scevola maintains his paranoid revolutionary vigilance. The watching of Arlette, in which the reader is encouraged to collude, has in it something of the nature of medical observation: her restless eyes and her fingers 'clawing the dress over her chest' (p. 42) are clearly neurotic symptoms.

Watching and reading signs, however, is an uncertain business for as *Victory* shows, it produces readings and misreadings, interpretations and misinterpretations. In *The Rover*, as the narrative perspective and focalization change, the reader's privileged position grants insights into secrets, mysteries, and misinterpretations. Bolt's picture of Escampobar as 'the sort of spot that nothing could change' (p. 56), for example, is wide of the mark. Ironically, Escampobar has changed, in part, precisely because of the earlier visits that he now so fondly recalls. Indeed, Bolt's memory of these visits to Arlette's parents provides the reader with confirmation that they were in

contact with the English enemy. Elsewhere, as in his conviction of a conspiracy between Peyrol and Réal against him, Scevola's paranoid narrative,
with its forging of false connections, operates as a parody and subversion of
interpretation. Conversely, in the final chapter, the French have to deduce
Peyrol's fate from two seemingly unconnected incidents: the observed pursuit
of his tartane by the *Amelia* and the reported story of a tartane being fired
upon by a man-of-war the following day. Again the reader has been given,
from the English perspective, a narrative linking the two events.

The Rover also continues Conrad's exploration of the nature of the gaze.
Peyrol's first sight of Arlette, for example, produces her as an object of
desire, just as later, Réal's relationship with her is largely ocular. In both
cases, Arlette's awakening is marked by a reversal of the power-situation.
Arlette forces information from Peyrol by capturing 'his desperately
dodging eyes with her black and compelling glance' (p. 175), while, later,
she takes Réal to the window to look at him and 'her black eyes, immensely
profound, looked into his ... with a searching and appropriating expression' (pp. 215–6). In both instances, she takes on the 'masculine' role of
bearer of the gaze. The entire relationship of Arlette and Réal, in fact, is
charted ocularly, and the crisis in their relationship arises when he allows
himself 'to be caught looking at her' (p. 212). Arlette's 'terrestrial revelation'
(p. 160) is produced by this incident, and her account of it involves a
choreography of the gaze. The alternation of gazing and being gazed at
bring her to self-awareness and empowers her to meet the gaze of others
'without embarrassment' (p. 161).

VI

Conrad's last novel, *Suspense*, was published posthumously in 1925. In his
Introduction to the first edition, Richard Curle described it as Conrad's
'long-pondered novel of Napoleonic times', and noted that *The Rover* was
'but an interlude suggested by the longer story' (*Su*, p. vi). Where *The
Arrow of Gold* is framed by two 'Notes', *Suspense* is effectively framed by
two meetings between Cosmo Latham and Attilio. The meeting that begins
the novel takes place on a tower overlooking Genoa harbour; the second
meeting, which ends the novel, begins at the foot of the same tower. The
first meeting, in various ways, anticipates the second. At the first encounter,
Attilio expresses concern that Cosmo's friends or the servants at the inn
'may become uneasy' at his 'long absence' (p. 7). Their second encounter
supplies the solution to Cosmo's mysterious disappearance, which has,
indeed, alarmed his friends and the servants at the inn. In both encounters,
Cosmo willingly joins in with Attilio's 'mysterious proceedings' (p. 13).

Perhaps more important, after their first encounter, Cosmo expresses his wish to meet Attilio again. Subsequently, awareness of this wish is maintained by Cosmo's instructions to his servant to watch out for Attilio, and, in the novel's final section, this wish is fulfilled. This narrative strand might be described as boy meets boy, boy loses boy, boy meets boy again. Certainly, while heterosexual romances are presented as enigmas (whether it is Cosmo's father's love for the Marquise d'Armand or Cosmo's own love for the Marquise's daughter, Adele), relations between men figure prominently in the foreground.

The final chapter, however, not only brings Cosmo and Attilio together again, but ends with a lengthy account of a boat-journey out of the guarded harbour of Genoa. ('The Rescuer' manuscript ends with a similarly lengthy account of Lingard and Mrs Travers in a small boat journeying towards a boundary, the reef that marks the entrance to the Shallows around Darat-es-Salam. In undertaking this journey, Lingard has surrendered his old identity and committed himself to another existence, the life of impulse, desire, and passion. *Suspense* ends with the crossing of similar borders.) Cosmo commits himself to act with Attilio, and this is also a commitment to the unknown: 'to go off secretly ... at the mere bidding of a man bound on some secret work, God knows where and for what object' (p. 270). At the same time, the old man who had been roused to row Cosmo across the harbour has crossed his own border. Attilio's last words offer an epitaph to the old man whose 'last bit of work', to steer a boat, was, perhaps, 'done for Italy' (p. 274). Like *The Rover*, *Suspense* ends with the death of an old man in the service of a political cause – though, in both cases, the perspective of history suggests that the sacrifice was wasted.

As with Ford's later novels, *Suspense* recounts the events of two or three days (here the three days that Cosmo spends in Genoa) but sets those events in a deeper temporal perspective.[15] Part I, for example, after introducing Cosmo and Attilio, takes the reader back to Cosmo's father's youthful adventures in pre-revolutionary France and in Italy, his friendship with the Marquis and Marquise d'Armand, and his subsequent marriage to Molly Aston. Part II, which is occupied with Cosmo's meetings with Adele and her husband the Count de Montevesso and with Cosmo's introduction into the political world of Genoa, includes a flashback to the start of Adele's marriage in London and to her life in Paris during the First Empire, in which both her marriage and the Empire are represented as masquerades. Cosmo plays M. George to Adele's Rita: the naïve young man and the young woman aged and hardened by her experiences. Part III describes the events leading up to Cosmo's disappearance. Like Ford's later novels again, *Suspense* also makes considerable play with 'mystery'. Part IV resolves the mystery of Cosmo's disappearance, but the end of the novel leaves many other mysteries unsolved. The political intrigues of both Attilio and the Count de Montevesso remain shadowy; Cosmo's apparent love for Adele remains undeveloped; and the possibility that Adele might actually be his half-sister remains only a strong hint. Clelia's identity, her relationship to the Count de Montevesso, and her desire for Cosmo also remain to be explored. The greatest mystery, however, is the traumatic moment that prompts Cosmo's flight:

> She must have been foretold to him in some picture he had seen in Latham Hall, where one came on pictures (mostly of the Italian school) in unexpected places, on landings, at the end of dark corridors, in spare bed-rooms. A luminous oval face on the dark background – the noble full-length woman, stepping out of the narrow frame with long draperies held by jewelled clasps and girdle, with pearls on head and bosom, carrying a book and a pen (or was it a palm?) and – yes! he saw it plainly with terror – with her left breast pierced by a dagger. (p. 195)

The detailed description invites interpretation: in Christian iconography the palm denotes a martyr; the book and pen (if it is a pen) suggest a saint – a St Catherine of Alexandria or a St Barbara, but the iconography is not exactly right for either of these and the dress inappropriate.[16] It is unclear whether the woman has been murdered or has committed suicide. More important, it is not clear why this is such a traumatic experience for Cosmo, nor is it clear what it means to him or how to interpret it in relation to him. The explanation for his disappearance, in other words, merely raises other unanswered questions.

Nevertheless, against this indeterminate background of unresolved enigmas and unanswered questions, certain features of the narrative stand out clearly, particularly the emphasis on male-bonding and heroic males, and the striking image of violence directed against the female body. In a novel that has repeated recourse to the pictorial for its representation of women, the fact that the trauma the hero experiences involves such an image not only suggests, perhaps, Cosmo's horrified recognition of Adele's self-sacrifice in marriage or even, possibly, a precognition of her fate in this marriage, but also, inescapably, the sadism of the male gaze.

Laura Mulvey has suggested that, where the female is the object of the gaze, 'the woman as icon, displayed for the gaze and enjoyment of men ... always threatens to evoke the anxiety it originally signified' (*Visual and Other Pleasures*, p. 21). She suggests two avenues of escape for the male unconscious: the re-enactment of the original trauma (which involves investigating the woman and demystifying her mystery) or fetishistic scopophilia, a Freudian term that denotes the combining of pleasure in looking with the disavowal of castration. In *The Arrow of Gold* and *Chance*, the re-enactment of this trauma is attempted both within the narrative by the male characters and outside the narrative by the editor/narrator and male reader. In *The Arrow of Gold*, there are also repeated attempts to present Rita as the object of fetishistic scopophilia. However, where the male is the object of the male gaze, Mulvey suggests that his characteristics are 'not those of the erotic object of his gaze, but those of the more perfect, more complete, more powerful ideal ego' (*Ibid.*, p. 20). Instead of sexual instincts, focus shifts to the role of identification processes in the symbolic order that articulates desire. It is perhaps significant that Mills and Cervoni act as tutors to M. George in his process of maturation, much as Peyrol acts as sponsor to Réal or Captain Giles to the narrator of *The Shadow-Line*. Given the focalization of the narrative, M. George's attitude towards Mills and Cervoni can also be read as a narcissistic identification with them. In the same way, it might be argued that Peyrol's sacrifice and triumph in *The Rover* involve a narcissistic identification with Nelson, while, in *Suspense*, Cosmo's narrative contains as latent content a narcissistic identification with Napoleon. In these last two novels, Nelson and Napoleon could be seen as determining absences in a narrative of narcissistic identification. At the same time, in both novels, any possibility of eroticism in the act of looking at the male body is firmly repressed by playing out the sadism inherent in voyeurism through scenes of conflict, displacing display from the male body to ritualized scenes of combat.

If then, Conrad's last novels return to old subjects, it is to the concern with women and sexuality that featured in his earliest works, *Almayer's Folly* and *An Outcast of the Islands*. These topics are now approached and represented, however, in radically different ways. Where he had earlier entangled discourses of race and gender in narratives of European and Malay cross-cultural encounters, the Mediterranean settings of his last three novels combine with a sharper focus on issues of gender. Recent criticism has revealed that what was once called Conrad's 'uncongenial subject' is, in fact, an area of subtle and complex analysis, and the historical and political material of his last fictions provides the basis for the thoroughgoing examination of masculinity that *Chance* and *Victory* began.

NOTES

1 The continuing influence of this view is evidenced in a number of more recent works. See, for example, Berthoud, *Joseph Conrad: The Major Phase*; Fogel,

Coercion to Speak; Gekoski, *Conrad: The Moral World of the Novelist*; Lothe, *Conrad's Narrative Method*; and Raval, *The Art of Failure*.

2 See, for instance, the essays by Jones, Davies, and Roberts in Roberts, ed., *Conrad and Gender*.

3 In *Joseph Conrad: Achievement and Decline*, Moser dates Conrad's decline to after *The Shadow-Line*. Hewitt singles it out as 'free from all the flaws of lush rhetoric and moralizing' that disfigure the other late works (*Conrad: A Reassessment*, p. 112), a position that Lothe repeats (*Conrad's Narrative Method*, p. 129).

4 Conrad to Pinker, 3 February 1915, Berg Collection, New York Public Library.

5 See, for example, Hewitt, *Conrad: A Reassessment*, and Moser, *Joseph Conrad: Achievement and Decline*.

6 See, for example, Erdinast-Vulcan, 'Textuality and surrogacy in Conrad's *Chance*'; Hampson, '*Chance* and the secret life'; and Nadelhaft, *Joseph Conrad*.

7 Compare Conrad's presentation of Lena through her idiom with Joyce's treatment of Gerty McDowell in the 'Nausicaa' section of *Ulysses*.

8 During 1916 Basil Macdonald Hastings and Henry Irving approached Conrad with proposals to adapt *Victory* for the stage, and, over the next three years, he was highly interested in its dramatization.

9 For a discussion of the autobiographical aspects of the novel, see Baines, *Joseph Conrad*, pp. 51–80; Karl, *Joseph Conrad*, pp. 156–78; van Marle, 'Young Ulysses ashore'; and Visiak, *The Mirror of Conrad*, pp. 99–103.

10 Erdinast-Vulcan, 'Textuality and surrrogacy in Conrad's *Chance*', and Roberts, 'Secret agents and secret objects', draw attention to these elements to argue that the novel involves a transvaluation of romance.

11 See also Bickley and Hampson, ' "Lips that have been kissed" ', and Geddes, *Conrad's Later Novels*, pp. 9, 121.

12 This discussion of *The Arrow of Gold* is indebted to Andrew Michael Roberts.

13 Conrad to Garnett, 4 December 1923, Jean-Aubry, ed., *Joseph Conrad: Life and Letters*, II, p. 327. As Geddes says, '*The Rover* is the work of a writer very much at one with his art', *Conrad's Later Novels*, p. 186.

14 For an anthropological reading of this substitution, see Hampson, 'Frazer, Conrad, and the "truth of primitive passion" '.

15 Ford's *A Little Less than Gods* (1928) was his version of this Napoleonic story.

16 On the iconography of this painting and on pictorial representation in *Suspense* in general, see Jones, 'The representation of women in the works of Joseph Conrad'.

WORKS CITED

Baines, Jocelyn. *Joseph Conrad: A Critical Biography*. London: Weidenfeld & Nicolson; New York: McGraw-Hill, 1960. Reprinted Penguin Books, 1971

Berthoud, Jacques. *Joseph Conrad: The Major Phase*. Cambridge: Cambridge University Press, 1978

Bickley, Pamela and Robert Hampson. ' "Lips that have been kissed": Boccacio,

Verdi, Rossetti and *The Arrow of Gold*. *L'Epoque Conradienne* 14 (1988), 77–91

Bradbrook, M. C. *Joseph Conrad: England's Polish Genius*. Cambridge: Cambridge University Press; New York: Macmillan, 1941. Reprinted New York: Russell & Russell, 1965

Conrad, Joseph. *The Arrow of Gold*. 1919. London: Dent, 1924

  Chance. 1914. Ed. Martin Ray. Oxford: Oxford University Press, 1988

  Lord Jim, A Tale. 1900. Ed. John Batchelor. Oxford: Oxford University Press, 1983

  The Rover. 1923. Ed. Andrzej Busza and J. H. Stape. Oxford: Oxford University Press, 1992

  The Shadow-Line. 1917. Ed. Jeremy Hawthorn. Oxford: Oxford University Press, 1988

  Suspense. Ed. Richard Curle. London: Dent, 1925

  Victory. 1915. Ed. John Batchelor. Oxford: Oxford University Press, 1986

Erdinast-Vulcan, Daphna. 'Textuality and surrogacy in Conrad's *Chance*'. *L'Epoque Conradienne* 15 (1989), 51–65

Fogel, Aaron. *Coercion to Speak: Conrad's Poetics of Dialogue*. Cambridge, MA: Harvard University Press, 1985

Geddes, Gary. *Conrad's Later Novels*. Montreal: McGill-Queen's University Press, 1980

Gekoski, R. A. *Conrad: The Moral World of the Novelist*. London: Elek, 1978

Guerard, Albert J. *Conrad the Novelist*. Cambridge, MA: Harvard University Press, 1958

Hampson, Robert. '*Chance* and the secret life: Conrad, Thackeray, Stevenson'. In *Conrad and Gender*. Ed. Andrew Michael Roberts. Amsterdam: Rodopi, 1993, pp. 105–22

  'Frazer, Conrad and the "truth of primitive passion"'. In *Sir James Frazer and the Literary Imagination*. Ed. Robert Frazer. London: Macmillan, 1990, pp. 172–91

  Joseph Conrad: Betrayal and Identity. London: Macmillan, 1992

Hewitt, Douglas. *Conrad: A Reassessment*. Cambridge: Bowes & Bowes, 1952

Hough, Graham. '*Chance* and Joseph Conrad'. In *Image and Experience: Studies in a Literary Revolution*. London: Duckworth, 1960; Lincoln: University of Nebraska Press, 1964, pp. 211–22

James, Henry. 'The new novel'. In *Notes on Novelists*. London: Dent, 1914, pp. 273–8

Jean-Aubry, G., ed. *Joseph Conrad: Life and Letters*. 2 vols. London: Heinemann; Garden City, NY: Doubleday, Page, 1927

Jones, Susan. 'The representation of women in the works of Joseph Conrad', DPhil thesis, Oxford University. In progress

Karl, Frederick R. *Joseph Conrad: The Three Lives – A Biography*. New York: Farrar, Straus, and Giroux; London: Faber & Faber, 1979

Leavis, F. R. 'Joseph Conrad'. *Sewanee Review* 66.2 (1958), 179–200. Reprinted as 'The Shadow-Line' in *Anna Karenina and Other Essays*. London: Chatto & Windus, 1967, pp. 92–110

Lothe, Jakob. *Conrad's Narrative Method*. Oxford: Clarendon Press, 1989

Marle, Hans van. 'Young Ulysses ashore: young Korzeniowski's adventures in the Caribbean'. *L'Epoque Conradienne* 2 (1976), 22–35

Moser, Thomas C. *Joseph Conrad: Achievement and Decline*. Cambridge, MA: Harvard University Press, 1957. Reprinted Hamden, CT: Archon Books, 1966

Mulvey, Laura. *Visual and Other Pleasures*. London: Macmillan, 1989

Nadelhaft, Ruth L. *Joseph Conrad*. Atlantic Highlands, NJ: Humanities Press; Hemel Hempstead: Harvester Wheatsheaf, 1991

Palmer, John A. *Joseph Conrad's Fiction: A Study in Literary Growth*. Ithaca: Cornell University Press, 1968

Raval, Suresh. *The Art of Failure: Conrad's Fiction*. Boston: Allen & Unwin, 1986

Roberts, Andrew Michael. 'The gaze and the dummy: sexual politics in *The Arrow of Gold*'. Third International Symposium of the Scandinavian Joseph Conrad Society, Lund and Copenhagen, September 1990

'Secret agents and secret objects: action, passivity, and gender in *Chance*'. In *Conrad and Gender*. Ed. Andrew Michael Roberts. Amsterdam: Rodopi, 1993, pp. 89–104

Roberts, Andrew Michael, ed. *Conrad and Gender*. Amsterdam: Rodopi, 1993

Schwarz, Daniel R. *Conrad: The Later Fiction*. London: Macmillan, 1982

Secor, Robert. *The Rhetoric of Shifting Perspectives: Conrad's 'Victory'*. University Park: Pennsylvania University Press, 1971

Todorov, Tzvetan. *The Poetics of Prose*. Tr. Richard Howard Oxford: Blackwell, 1977

Toliver, Harold E. 'Conrad's *Arrow of Gold* and pastoral tradition'. *Modern Fiction Studies* 8.2 (1962), 148–58

Visiak, E. H. *The Mirror of Conrad*. London: Laurie, 1955

Wiley, Paul. *Conrad's Measure of Man*. Madison: University of Wisconsin Press, 1954

Wright, Walter F. *Romance and Tragedy in Joseph Conrad*. Lincoln: University of Nebraska Press, 1949

Watt, Ian. 'Story and idea in Conrad's *The Shadow-Line*'. *Critical Quarterly* 2.2 (1960), 133–48

Zabel, Morton Dauwen. 'Joseph Conrad: chance and recognition'. *Sewanee Review* 53 (1945), 1–22. Reprinted as 'Conrad' in *Craft and Character in Modern Fiction*. New York: Viking, 1957, pp. 147–227

9

JAKOB LOTHE

Conradian narrative

I

Conradian narrative is not only exceptionally sophisticated and varied but also remarkably productive thematically. In common with all major writers, Conrad's fictional content is inextricable from narrative presentation. To make this point is not to regard the concept of content as unimportant. It is to stress that the rhetorical persuasiveness, ideological tension, dramatic intensity, and continuing interest and relevance of Conrad's fictional vision depend upon and are indeed generated and shaped by diverse and original narrative techniques. It follows that a discussion of Conradian narrative is a substantial critical venture.[1] This treatment will focus on a selection of particularly important constituent aspects of Conrad's narrative strategies. Progressing chronologically, it ranges over most of Conrad's major works and concludes with a consideration of the thematic significance of Conradian narrative.

Even though the dramatic intensity and thematic suggestiveness of Conradian narrative can vary considerably from work to work, there is no direct or obvious correlation between narrative success and date of composition in Conrad's fiction. Although the artistic quality of the fiction subsequent to *Under Western Eyes* generally deteriorates, texts such as *Victory*, 'The Tale', and *The Shadow-Line* are notable exceptions. More importantly, Conradian narrative matured very rapidly. In *Almayer's Folly*, Conrad's first novel, the narrative presents not just the main action revealing Almayer's inglorious situation and futile dreams, but also a covert plot centred on Abdullah's schemes to eliminate Almayer as a trading rival. While supporting the main plot's characterization of Almayer, this covert plot also, as we are more likely to discover on a second rather than a first reading, precipitates its outcome (Watts, *A Preface to Conrad*, p. 119). Considering that it is Conrad's first novel, the presentation of verbal thought is also sophisticated in *Almayer's Folly*. This applies in particular to the author's use of free indirect discourse, a technique that provides Conrad with great 'narrative flexibility and mobility' (Hawthorn, *Joseph Conrad: Narrative Technique*, p. 1).[2]

Two years after *Almayer's Folly* Conrad published *The Nigger of the 'Narcissus'*, a significant text in the evolution of his narrative method. This novella has a compelling narrative rhetoric that goes far to override its flaws and inconsistencies, where various technical problems are conspicuous. Before we briefly consider this text, some theoretical observations need to be made to provide a basis for the introduction of supplementary concepts in the later discussion of individual texts.

The concept of narrative is understood inclusively: it both designates and incorporates the various constituent aspects of Conrad's literary world. This world, which the narrative serves to present and shape, is a fictional one: rather than recording what has happened, it dramatizes – on a more generalized and less explicit level – what *could* happen. As the historical author, Conrad is a *writer* – a designer of a fictional universe. While Conrad remains outside this universe, 'traces' of his views, doubts, fears, hopes, and so forth are observable in the fiction he produced. Such traces can be subsumed under the abstract concept of the implied author, the author's second self constructed from the text's narrative discourse. Interestingly, when we refer to 'Conrad' we often think of Conrad as the implied author, that is, as represented by, or emerging through, his fiction. However, since for Conrad there is no objective representation of reality, 'the dialogic dynamism of the novels operate ... on more than one level: the form of the novel, the mode of representation, is just as ideologically charged as the explicit or implicit discourse of the protagonists' (Erdinast-Vulcan, *Joseph Conrad and the Modern Temper*, p. 8). Furthermore, the concept of author, whether historical or implied, needs to be related to that of the narrator. As an integral part of the fictional creation, the narrator, or the combination of narrators, is the author's primary means of shaping a text, which consists of the activities and functions the narrator is made to perform. In Conrad's fiction these functions are, in most cases, crucially important for presenting the fictional content. That the narrator's functions are also closely related to other textual aspects is illustrated by, for instance, the light/dark imagery that permeates *Lord Jim*. Although this metaphorical contrast is not, strictly speaking, part of the novel's narrative progression, it is inseparable from Marlow's functions as narrator.

While narrators can be variously grouped and re-grouped, depending on one's criteria, the most essential distinction to draw – generally as well as in Conrad – is that between third- and first-person narrators. Although this distinction is not unproblematic, much is to be gained by applying it to

Conradian narrative. Moreover, a crucial point is involved here concerning the narrator's ontological status. The contrast

> between an embodied narrator and a narrator without such bodily determina-
> tion, that is to say, between a first-person narrator and third-person narrator,
> accounts for the most important difference in the motivation of the narrator to
> narrate. For an embodied narrator, this motivation is existential; it is directly
> connected with his practical experiences ... For the third-person narrator, on
> the other hand, there is no existential compulsion to narrate.
>
> (Stanzel, *A Theory of Narrative*, p. 93)

Conrad's fiction confirms the validity of this critical distinction. Conradian narrative can be consistently and intensely first-person – as in *The Shadow-Line* – wide-rangingly third-person – as in *Nostromo* – or can attempt to combine the two main variants – as in *Lord Jim*. Although the gains of such a combination are potentially considerable, it also presents the author with narrative problems, complicating the presentation of the text as the narrative incoherences of *The Nigger of the 'Narcissus'* illustrate.

While Conrad's first two novels, *Almayer's Folly* and *An Outcast of the Islands*, employ third-person narrative in order to portray extremes of isolation, *The Nigger of the 'Narcissus'* focuses on the ship's crew and their relationship with James Wait, the sick Barbadan who eventually dies and is buried at sea. This crew is presented as a threatened variant of *Gemeinschaft*, that is, a hierarchically structured community in which all are members of a family or a village or a ship. The term is Ferdinand Tönnies's, and its complement forms the second half of his classic study *Gemeinschaft und Gesellschaft* (1887). For Tönnies, *Gesellschaft* (society) is the modern equivalent of *Gemeinschaft* (community). It is a horizontal rather than hierarchical social formation, and its members are free to make their own choices between different trade unions or political parties.[3]

This distinction has a twofold relevance for the narrative of *The Nigger of the 'Narcissus'*. First, it highlights an important stage in the historical process towards modernity; this transition is, on a high level of abstraction, an integral part of the metanarrative underlying the novella's narrative discourse. To make this point is to agree with a basic tenet in Ian Watt's discussion of early Conrad: innovative as it is, Conradian narrative is anchored in the historical and cultural upheavals of the nineteenth century. Conrad's Polish background made him particularly responsive to contemporary historical events and trends such as, for example, 'the new imperialism which emerged and gained strength during the 1890s' (Trotter, *The English Novel in History*, p. 143). He also responded – indirectly but powerfully, through his fiction – to the theories of Darwin, Schopenhauer, and others, and formally as well as thematically he received significant impulses from writers such as Flaubert, Maupassant, and Dickens.

Secondly, Tönnies's two social formations are effectively contrasted in the narrative of *The Nigger of the 'Narcissus'*. Individualism and special interests assert themselves when, for instance, Belfast steals from the officers' table. Such interests are associated with the 'they' narrator, who contrasts his own identity with that of the group: 'But older, communal claims assert themselves when the cook braves the storm to make coffee, when the crew fights the gale and forgets about Wait, and when Singleton stays at the wheel alone for thirty hours. The "we" voice suggests such community' (Henricksen, *Nomadic Voices*, p. 30). This central thematic conflict in *The Nigger of the 'Narcissus'* is closely connected with its narrative presentation. Technically, the narrative problem is related to 'they' and 'we' as pronominal references to what appears to be the same narrator. This is problematic in the novella's narrative: although the story seems to be told by an unnamed, third-person narrator, it also increasingly displays characteristics of first-person narrative.

The narrative variations at the beginning include descriptive passages that rank among the most suggestive and visually striking in Conrad's fiction. Thus in the opening of chapter 2, for instance, the third-person narrative establishes three different, yet closely related, focuses. First, there is the *Narcissus* herself. Then there is nature, especially the sea – with the implied suggestion of harmony and peace at sea, and the ship as an integral part of nature, separated from and contrasted with life ashore. And finally there is the crew, including Captain Allistoun, 'the ruler of that minute world' (*NN*, p. 31). The first paragraph in particular demonstrates how these three focuses are fused through technical devices more commonly associated with poetry than with narrative fiction:

> Next morning, at daylight, the *Narcissus* went to sea.
> A slight haze blurred the horizon. Outside the harbour the measureless expanse of smooth water lay sparkling like a floor of jewels, and as empty as the sky ... The loose upper canvas blew out in the breeze with soft round contours, resembling small white clouds snared in the maze of ropes. Then the sheets were hauled home, the yards hoisted, and the ship became a high and lonely pyramid, gliding, all shining and white, through the sunlit mist. (p. 27)

Reflecting dissimilar modes of perception, the passage illustrates how they are given narrative form. The suggestive simile of the water 'sparkling like a floor of jewels, and as empty as the sky' is followed by a powerful identification metaphor: 'the ship became a high and lonely pyramid'. Visual observation blends into reflection, while the third mode – the clusters of metaphors that may suggest a mythical voyage – becomes a constituent of both.

This kind of elevated, descriptive third-person narrative differs greatly from the other variant, which, later in the novella, seems related to the personal recollection of a seaman who 'was there', involved in the action. One reason why this gradual slanting into first-person narrative becomes problematic is that it makes the reader wonder about the kind of authority the narrator possesses. Thus, if we say that *The Nigger of the 'Narcissus'* has two narrative voices, one unnamed (third-person) and one identified (first-person), we must add that it is often unclear *which* voice is speaking. In part Conrad succeeds, because of the kind of rhetoric illustrated above, in diverting the reader's attention from the points at which technical problems become obvious. Instead our interest is focused on the novella's elaborate interplay of changes in perspective and distance.[4]

These perspectival variations make the narrative more fragmented and multi-faceted and can be related to one of the central notions about the novel as a genre: its flowering 'is always connected with a disintegration of stable verbal-ideological systems and with an intensification ... of speech diversity' (Bakhtin, *The Dialogic Imagination*, pp. 370–1). On the textual level, they can also be related to what has been called the novella's 'microviewpoints' – constituting, within the narrative discourse, 'evaluative accents that are structural responses to the competing voices in the world the narrative describes' (Henricksen, *Nomadic Voices*, p. 31). Still it would seem that, overall, the narrative of *The Nigger of the 'Narcissus'*, including its various 'evaluative accents', is characterized by an undertone of nostalgia and collective loss – of a *Gemeinschaft* that can now only be found aboard a ship and that is threatened even there. That the kind of life led aboard the *Narcissus* is, as the ending of the novella indicates, temporally limited, not only augments its value but also enhances 'the nostalgic seductiveness of an achievement seen in retrospect' (Berthoud, 'Conrad and the sea', p. vii).

II

The fiction Conrad wrote from 1897 to 1900 was crucially important for the development of his narrative method: following *The Nigger of the 'Narcissus'* he published, in rapid succession, such major works as 'An Outpost of Progress', 'Heart of Darkness', and *Lord Jim*. 'An Outpost of Progress', whose third-person narrative anticipates *Nostromo* rather than 'Heart of Darkness', is an impressive feat of narrative concentration. Its portrayal of Kayerts and Carlier is terse, panoramic, and omniscient, and its narrative discourse is infused with irony, as in this example: 'For days the two pioneers of trade and progress would look on their empty courtyard in the vibrating brilliance of vertical sunshine' (*HD*, p. 10). The irony here arises from a difference between how Kayerts and Carlier regard themselves and what they actually are in the third-person narrator's judgement (with the implication that this judgement be accepted). Beyond this obvious irony, however, is the play on the word 'progress', with the suggestion of an ironic contrast between its common meaning (an 'advance to better and better conditions, continuous improvement' as the *Oxford English Dictionary* defines it) and the action referred to as 'progress' throughout the story. This irony forms part of the scepticism inherent in the narrator's generalizations.

If a distinctive feature of 'An Outpost of Progress' is the focus on a particular situation, closely related to a rendering of monotony, futility, and absurdity, the short story is also characterized by an accumulative thematic suggestiveness – of questions Conrad was to explore further in 'Heart of Darkness', in which an oblique narrative technique proves strikingly congenial with the novella's thematics. The discussion here will focus on a few particularly characteristic features of Conradian narrative at this stage of the writer's career.[5]

Conradian narrative requires not only close reading, but frequently re-reading as well. To focus on textual structure does not, however, imply that a literary text exists in a historical and cultural vacuum; nor does it follow that the connections between the historical author and the text's various narrative constituents are unimportant. In a sense, the opposition between locutions such as 'narrative', on the one hand, and 'history', on the other, is factitious, possibly even theoretically untenable: 'it is only on the level of structures that we can describe literary development' (Todorov, *Introduction to Poetics*, p. 61). Any discussion of Conrad's fictional achievement needs then to include some consideration of its narrative form.

Writing of 'Heart of Darkness', Peter Madsen notes that

> Language is more than a dictionary and a grammar, but this 'more' is not, as the formalist-structuralist poetics would have it, like a specifically literary grammar which is neutral in relation to experience. Literary forms are formulations of experience – they are, as Adorno puts it, sedimentation of experience ... The narrative forms are of this kind. Any new story is related to earlier stories to the extent that these have interfered with the author's formulation of experience ... But the word 'narrative' is ambiguous. Pointing beyond the text itself, it refers not only to the chain of events (the 'story'), but also to the act of narration. ('Modernity and melancholy', p. 100)

This is a nuanced view of the complicated relationship between personal experience and literary text. The observation can, for instance, be related to the numerous intertextual echoes in 'Heart of Darkness' – from Virgil via Dante to more recent travel literature. It can also be related to Conrad's use of Marlow as the main narrator.

The introduction of Marlow marks a turning-point in Conradian narrative. This shift is not merely technical, but intimately connected with Conrad's uncertainty and experimentation as a writer of fiction. Zdzisław Najder helpfully comments on Marlow's importance for Conrad's writing:

> Marlow, a model English gentleman, ex-officer of the merchant marine, was the embodiment of all that Conrad would wish to be if he were to become completely anglicized. And since that was not the case, and since he did not quite share his hero's point of view, there was no need to identify himself with Marlow, either emotionally or intellectually. Thanks to Marlow's duality, Conrad could feel solidarity with, and a sense of belonging to, England by proxy, at the same time maintaining a distance such as one has toward a creation of one's imagination. Thus, Conrad, although he did not permanently resolve his search for a consistent consciousness of self-identity, found an integrating point of view that enabled him, at last, to break out of the worst crisis of his writing career. (*Joseph Conrad: A Chronicle*, p. 231)

This comment is persuasive partly because of its implied suggestion that, for Conrad, Marlow is not only a main narrator and an important character, but a distancing device that helps the author control and shape his fictional material. In a classic essay published as early as 1912, Edward Bullough regarded 'distance' as the quality that gives an expression aesthetic validity: 'Distancing means the separation of personal affections, whether idea or complex experience, from the concrete personality of the experience' ('Psychical distance', p. 127). Thus understood, the concept serves to identify one of the most distinctive aspects of Conradian narrative. As far as Conrad is concerned, Bullough's general observation blends into the author's *need for distance* both from his fiction and, in a complex way, from his audience, in order to write at all.

The concept of distance needs, however, to be diversified to be helpful critically. The most important variants are temporal, spatial, and attitudinal distance. In 'Heart of Darkness', there is a significant temporal distance between Conrad's personal experience in the Congo in 1890, on which the fiction is based, and the time of the novella's writing approximately eight years later. There is also a very considerable spatial distance between London, the setting of the narrative act, and the Congo, the place of the main action. Finally, the temporal and spatial distances are related to the 'attitudinal' distance, the ideological perspectives of the narrator(s) and the implied author. This last variant is the most complex because it is more closely connected with the varying levels of insight of the implied author, the narrator, and character, and because it is, as a critical metaphor, related to the reader's interpretive activity.

A good illustration of modulations of distance is provided by the opening of 'Heart of Darkness'. The novella begins by introducing us to a narrative setting that establishes a peculiarly static frame around the main action. A group of five men are aboard a cruising yawl, waiting for the turn of the tide:

> The sea-reach of the Thames stretched before us like the beginning of an interminable waterway. In the offing the sea and the sky were welded together without a joint, and in the luminous space the tanned sails of the barges drifting up with the tide seemed to stand still in red clusters of canvas sharply peaked, with gleams of varnished sprits. (p. 135)

The visual qualities of this introductory description resemble those often referred to in discussions of Conrad's literary impressionism. Suggesting a first-person narrative, the pronoun 'us' refers to the five characters aboard the *Nellie*. One of them is Marlow; however, not Marlow but an anonymous first-person narrator is speaking here. This frame narrator introduces us to the setting of the novella as well as to Marlow as the main narrator. When Marlow is duly introduced and embarks on his tale, the function of the frame narrator becomes more complex, since he also becomes a *narratee* in the group Marlow addresses.[6] To put this another way: in accordance with the narrative convention employed, the frame narrator functions first as a narratee, and then as a first-person narrator relaying Marlow's story to the reader. The phrase 'narrative convention' is necessary because the time of traditional, simple narratives is over in 'Heart of Darkness'. At first sight, the novella's narrative situation seems to resemble what Wolfgang's Kayser calls *epische Ursituation* (*Das sprachliche Kunstwerke*, p. 349), that is, the 'original' narrative situation in which a narrator is telling his audience something that has happened. (If related to the historical metanarrative, this is the narrative situation of *Gemeinschaft*.) However interesting, the resemblance is none the less superficial – not only because Kayser's concept of original narrative situation excludes the device of the frame narrator, but also because in 'Heart of Darkness' both the narrative act and its motivations are much more problematic.

In the classic frame narrative the frame narrator is often the most authoritative and knowledgeable of the narrators. This is not so in 'Heart of Darkness'. For although the frame narrator passes on Marlow's story and appears to be reliable, his insights are distinctly inferior to Marlow's. A second example will illustrate this point. Having finished his introductory description, the narrator exclaims: 'What greatness had not floated on the ebb of that river into the mystery of an unknown earth!...The dreams of men, the seed of commonwealths, the germs of empires' (p. 137). Isolated from its context, the exclamation sounds like a piece of imperialistic rhetoric. This impression increases the impact and suggestiveness of Marlow's first words: 'And this also ... has been one of the dark places of the earth' (p. 138).

This narrative variation is one of the most effective in all of Conrad's fiction. Marlow's remark exposes the relative naïveté and limited insight of the frame narrator and prefigures the complex, sombre implications of the tale he is about to tell. The comment anticipates his later reflections on the arrival of the Romans in Britain, 'nineteen hundred years ago – the other day' (p. 139). For the Romans, Marlow plausibly goes on to suggest, Britain must have seemed an inhospitable wilderness at 'the very end of the world'. Additionally, it is indicative of the extraordinary narrative economy of 'Heart of Darkness' that Marlow's opening words also function as a prolepsis of 'darkness', the text's central metaphor.[7] Although the Romans 'were men enough to face the darkness ... They were conquerors, and for that you want only brute force – nothing to boast of, when you have it, since your strength is just an accident arising from the weakness of others' (pp. 139–40). This generalizing statement obviously refers to the Romans, but also includes a proleptic reference to the narrative Marlow is just starting.

Suggesting that Marlow's level of insight is superior to that of the frame narrator, these brief observations also indicate some key characteristics of Marlow's first-person narrative: a reflective rhetoric designed to impress and persuade, a peculiar blend of personal and intellectual curiosity, and a tendency to generalize on the basis of individual experience. Conrad thus uses two first-person narrators in 'Heart of Darkness', and the effect of Marlow's narrative is inseparable from the function of the frame narrator.

The use of a narrator is a distancing device, and 'Heart of Darkness' accentuates the distancing process by the use of two narrators rather than one. At the same time, the novella is also a good example of a text where distancing narrative devices paradoxically increase the reader's attention and interest. Conrad effectively exploits the conventional or common character of the frame narrator to make Marlow's story more plausible. The frame narrative manipulates the reader into a position resembling that of the frame narrator *as narratee*, a position distinguished by a meditative but broadly accepting response to the disillusioned insights of Marlow's story. This effect is particularly evident in the novella's last paragraph, which is spoken by the frame narrator. Echoing the numerous references to 'darkness', its concluding words – 'immense darkness' (p. 252) – repeat Marlow's last words in the paragraph above.

In 'Heart of Darkness', there is a productive correlation of Marlow's first-person narration, which takes the form of an ordering and existentially motivated re-experience, and that of the frame narrator, which proceeds from an unexpected involvement and a surprising understanding. The frame narrator's involvement increases as a result of the impressionist narrative he himself transmits. Ian Watt has coined the term delayed decoding to describe this aspect of Conrad's impressionist narrative: through delayed decoding the author attempts 'to present a sense impression and to withhold naming it or explaining its meaning until later ... This takes us directly into the observer's consciousness at the very moment of the perception, before it has been translated into its cause' (Conrad in the Nineteenth Century, p. 175). Conrad used this device prior to 'Heart of Darkness', but one of its notable manifestations is Marlow's confusion when his boat is attacked just below Kurtz's station. Only later does he discover the cause of the various odd changes he observes: 'Arrows, by Jove! We were being shot at!' (p. 200).

The concept of delayed decoding is probably most helpful in describing relatively simple instances of temporarily inexplicable impressions and occurrences. A larger problem – Marlow's impression of Kurtz, for example – is not decoded, but it does not, however, follow that Marlow's encounter with the novella's other protagonist may not be meaningful.

This point also applies to Lord Jim: although the novel has several examples of delayed decoding, its central problem – the possible reasons for and consequences of Jim's jump from the Patna – is persistently explored rather than satisfactorily or unambiguously 'resolved'. If this 'negative' conclusion is a strength rather than a weakness, the reason is to be sought in the narrative presentation of Jim's problem as intrinsically difficult and possibly even insoluble. If 'Heart of Darkness' is a fictional exploration of the human condition and the human psyche provoked by an exposure to imperialism and its consequences, Lord Jim, similarly developing its narrative from a crucially decisive test to which the protagonist is exposed, combines the investigation of Jim's life with the more general question of 'how to be' (LJ, p. 213).

Much of Lord Jim revolves around the relationship between Jim and Marlow. Problematic and distressing, this relationship contributes to the novel's pervasive scepticism; yet at the same time it develops into a strange kind of friendship. Ostensibly first-person, the function of Marlow's narrative is often interestingly editorial and explanatory. Lord Jim displays Conradian narrative at its most varied and sophisticated, involving an intricate interplay of perspective, voice, and various forms of narrative distance. The novel's narrative intensity is partly due to the seriousness of Jim's moral problem, but it is even more strongly related to the tension observable in Marlow's attitude to Jim: the tension between a fundamental, existential doubt and an unplanned, growing friendship. This tension, and Marlow's change of character associated with it, are intimately connected with Marlow's crucial narrative function. As Marlow comes to doubt his belief in the 'sovereign power' (p. 50), the thematic association of this doubt with the threat of loss of ground, direction, and coherence increases the complexity of Jim as a character; at the same time it also makes the relationship between main narrator and main character less predictable and more interesting. This thematic association depends on the characteristics and modulations of Marlow's activity as a narrator as well as on the way in which his narrative is related to his pensive narratees and reinforced by the surrounding third-person narrative: 'And later on, many times, in distant parts of the world, Marlow showed himself willing to remember Jim, to remember him at length, in detail and audibly' (p. 33).

As the final transitional stage from the novel's opening, third-person narrative to Marlow's first-person one, this sentence presents highly relevant information informing the discourse of *Lord Jim* and characterizing Conradian narrative in general. The words 'later on ... in distant parts of the world' suggest something the rest of the novel affirms: that spatial and temporal distance are key elements of Conradian narrative. While they enable Conrad to establish, and retain, a strong narrative focus on Jim, they also serve to highlight more general (essentially epistemological and moral) problems extractable from Jim's experience. Temporal distance as observable here strengthens the novel's characteristic combination of two interrelated concerns: it presents a dramatic – and in one sense increasingly melodramatic – life story, and combines it with reflections on how and why it all came to happen as it did. Spatial distance is also emphasized several times later and is connected with both Marlow and Jim. In the case of Marlow, spatial or geographical mobility seems to operate mainly as a technical device: it enables him to track Jim down in his continual retreat eastwards. But narrative issues blend into thematic ones as we notice that, for Marlow, Jim is 'one of us'. The tale's relevance and significance are enhanced by Marlow's insistence that Jim's problem is general and present everywhere.

Furthermore, informing us that Marlow is willing to remember Jim 'at length' and 'many times', this sentence accentuates the problem of repetition in the novel and warns us that Marlow's account will be long in the telling. Considering why *Lord Jim*, originally planned as a short story, expanded into a long novel, Ian Watt finds that 'Conrad's scepticism ... leads him to present and explore with exceptional thoroughness whatever pieces of evidence are available, however fragmentary or ambiguous, which may provide clues to understanding what the characters do and are' (*Conrad in the Nineteenth Century*, p. 269). This carefully phrased point bears an obvious relation to the narrative technique of *Lord Jim*: the enumeration of narrative voices, which are more easily included once the device of Marlow as first-person narrator is adopted, tends to increase textual quantity.

But if the structure of *Lord Jim* is in this sense repetitive, the problem of repetition also looms large thematically. In *Lord Jim*, as in *Nostromo* and *Under Western Eyes*, the critical potential of repetition is particularly rich, if only for the way in which it blends aspects of narrative (such as Marlow's repetitive telling of a story to whose formation other narrators also contribute) with a thematic exploration of complex questions of personal origin, identity, integrity, responsibility, and fear. In *Lord Jim*, repetition is related to the 'design of recurrent images' (Miller, *Fiction and Repetition*, p. 31). This point can also be made about Conradian narrative in general – especially the way in which repetition is used to transform images or physical objects into symbols. (Two of the best-known examples are 'darkness' in 'Heart of Darkness' and 'silver' in *Nostromo*.)

Although Marlow's narrative is not the only one in *Lord Jim*, the manner in which his telling is supplemented and 'framed' differs from 'Heart of Darkness'. In that novella, the frame narrator is relatively naïve compared to Marlow (and, as a narratee, learning from the tale Marlow tells). By contrast, the omniscient third-person narrative at the beginning of *Lord Jim* introduces us to the novel's protagonist, analeptically outlining his background and proleptically indicating some of his major weaknesses. Thus the mention of Jim's *Conway* training informs the reader of Jim's élitist education and emphasizes the gravity of his mistake. More broadly, Jim's background is so described as to make his subsequent jump especially unexpected and disquieting. Seen in this light, the training-ship episode takes on additional significance because of its *twofold* prolepsis: it adumbrates Jim's jump from the *Patna* as a form of repetitive action, and provides the reader with a crucial piece of background information that makes him or her more sceptical about Jim's defensive explanation of his jump. Since Marlow does not share this information, it also makes the reader more critical of Marlow's sympathies and of the motivation for his narrative undertaking. Having said this, it needs to be added that once Marlow is introduced as the main narrator, the third-person narrator largely refrains from imposing evaluative judgements on him. This is yet another indication of the narrative and thematic centrality of Marlow as a first-person narrator with an original and productive function.

III

Ian Watt has suggested that 'thematic apposition' is 'perhaps the most characteristic feature of Conrad's mature narrative technique' (*Conrad in the Nineteenth Century*, p. 285). In *Lord Jim* this kind of apposition, that is to say the juxtaposition of thematically related scenes, is intimately connected with Marlow's associative narrative. The diversity of thematic apposition in *Nostromo* is similarly inseparable from the elasticity of Conradian narrative as it operates in this novel. In *Nostromo*, thematic apposition frequently depends on a combination of narrative omniscience and narrative mobility. Both contribute essentially to the novel's characteristic narrative flexibility, dynamism, and thematic range. The best indication of this range is probably provided by the narrative device of irony as it functions as an integral part of the third-person narrative: irony serves both to diversify characterization and to provide an attitudinal distance necessitated by the novel's thematic concerns and disillusioned insights. With regard to characterization, the third-person narrator employs different forms of ironic modulation in order to introduce and develop essential aspects of textual content, including moral issues such as personal integrity and depravity as well as socio-economic questions such as the relationship between power and influence.

The third-person narrator's attitude is most directly related to the variations of narrative perspective and distance. It is as though the narrator (and Conrad behind him) needs a very substantial, and frequently ironic, distance from the novel's action and characters in order to retain a lasting narrative focus on his tale's sombre subject matter. Even if distance decreases and irony temporarily disappears, as in the description of Decoud on the Great Isabel, both devices recur before long and are further modulated. This form of ironic attitude and the novel's pervasive scepticism are importantly related. Furthermore, the need for distance associated with this variant of irony reinforces the more technical motivation for *Nostromo*'s third-person narrative: as the novel's narrative flexibility and thematic range depend upon narrative omniscience and panoramic overview, so the distance related to such omniscience is paradoxically motivated by the narrator's serious, even threatening, involvement in the story he tells.

Another significant feature of Conradian narrative is chronological distortion. In *Nostromo* this is particularly noticeable in Part One, which, instead of progressing forward in the conventional manner of history, spirals backwards, providing detailed information about past events. One of the gains of this technique is that it 'gives an unusual plausibility to the fictional historical events' which thereby acquire 'a stereoscopic quality' (Watts, *A Preface to Conrad*, p. 158). The novel's long, analeptic detour gives some of its ironies 'a radical and tentacular quality' (*Ibid.*). Reading about Ribiera's inaugural banquet in chapter 5, for instance, we can appreciate the irony arising from the contrast between the President-Dictator's imposing stature here and his humiliating arrival in Sulaco the following year, an event we are already aware of. In a word, an early prolepsis enables the reader to estimate rightly the irony embedded in an extended analepsis.

A related aspect of Conradian narrative is defamiliarization, a technique that in combining linguistic and narrative devices makes something familiar appear unfamiliar and strange. The following example is illustrative:

> On this memorable day of the riot his arms were not folded on his chest. His hand grasped the barrel of the gun grounded on the threshold; he did not look up once at the white dome of Higuerota, whose cool purity seemed to hold itself aloof from a hot earth. His eyes examined the plain curiously ... Single figures on foot raced desperately. Horsemen galloped towards each other, wheeled round together, separated at speed. Giorgio saw one fall, rider and horse disappearing as if they had galloped into a chasm, and the movements of the animated scene were like the passages of a violent game played upon the plain by dwarfs mounted and on foot, yelling with tiny throats, under the mountain that seemed a colossal embodiment of silence. (*No*, pp. 26–7)

Although related to a minor character – Giorgio Viola, who witnesses a battle during the riot – the third-person narrative's voice and panoramic perspective are noticeable in this generalized description of war. This is not to consider the personal colouring as unimportant; on the contrary, it augments both the visual intensity and thematic suggestiveness of the description. For Giorgio, like most of the inhabitants of Costaguana, war is all too familiar. However, at this moment his spatial distance from the fighting, combined with the large plain and the enormous mountain rising above it, make the battle look like 'a violent game played ... by dwarfs'. This metaphoric substitution accentuates the absurdity of the killing, for Giorgio and, by implication, for the reader. The contrast between the activity on the plain and the silent mountain contributes decisively to the defamiliarizing effect.

Nostromo and *The Secret Agent* represent the peak of Conrad's achievement with third-person narrative. Both novels rely upon a third-person narrative that is flexible, wide-ranging, and frequently ironic, but in contrast to the characteristically collective focus of *Nostromo*, the narrative of *The*

Secret Agent explores more selectively (though in great depth) a number of tensions and unresolved contradictions between the public and private spheres. This impression of unresolved contradictions and bewildering fragmentation is nowhere stronger than in the narrator's portrayal of Stevie. As Stevie is destroyed as a result of the ideological forces and personal weaknesses the novel depicts, the tragic fate of this simple character, whom the narrator treats with sympathy and little or no irony, reinforces the sceptical disillusionment of both the third-person narrative and the thematics it informs.

If both *Nostromo* and *The Secret Agent* are characterized by a highly flexible third-person narrative, the narrative complexity of *Under Western Eyes* is essentially paradoxical: it revolves around and develops from a covert contrast between the pronounced views of the first-person narrator, the teacher of languages, and the thematic implications of the narrative as a whole. The originality of this novel resides not least in the manner in which the language teacher's first-person narrative is modulated and ironically undermined.

The plot of *Under Western Eyes* would seem to suggest that it is a spy story, 'generically a story of anomy' (Cave, *Recognitions*, p. 466). Yet this story's narrative presentation greatly complicates its meaning. The first-person narrator's 'discourse – the novel as it stands – is written in retrospect, from a position of full knowledge and saturated interpretation ... However, the story is not presented in the order of the narrator's progression from ignorance to knowledge' (*Ibid.*, p. 469). *Under Western Eyes* dramatizes a thematic concern with the possibilities and problems of narrative as a form of linguistic meditation and human communication. In this sense the novel is one of Conrad's most acutely personal. Furthermore, in its exploration of issues such as self-referentiality, intertextuality, and narrative authority it is one of his most distinctly Modernist texts. The problems of writing and communication in *Under Western Eyes* are closely related to the narrative presentation of a fragmented fictional universe. This fragmentation is primarily established through the contrast we have noted: that between the language teacher's narrative – a large portion of which is his paraphrase of what others have written or said – and the novel's 'complete' text. The latter includes the *title* of the novel; this title, which can be related to the views of the implied author, draws attention to the language teacher's limited understanding of his tale's subject matter.

Exploring human communication as a problem and challenge, *Under Western Eyes* also investigates its various forms (verbal, visual, and gestural). The issue of communication informs Razumov's relationship with all the other characters of the novel, and is further elaborated through the problematic relationship between the teacher of languages and the sources on which his narration is based. As in most of Conrad's major works, the presentation of what the characters say and think forms an integral part of his narrative technique. This paragraph, from Razumov's interview with Councillor Mikulin towards the end of Part I, is characteristic:

> 'Could it be a wig?' Razumov detected himself wondering with an unexpected detachment. His self-confidence was much shaken. He resolved to chatter no more. Reserve! Reserve! All he had to do was to keep the Ziemianitch episode secret with absolute determination, when the questions came. Keep Ziemianitch strictly out of all the answers. (*UWE*, p. 90)

Starting with direct speech, the writing continues as a narrative statement, and then quickly slants into free indirect discourse. Technically sophisticated, the presentation of Razumov's thought is also thematically rich in establishing an interesting contrast: Razumov attempts to restrict his output of spoken words, but enjoins himself in verbal imperatives (Hawthorn, *Joseph Conrad: Narrative Technique*, p. 49). Moreover, the use of free indirect discourse (represented thought) has the effect 'of increasing the distance between the narrator and Razumov' (*Ibid.*, p. 49).

Reducing the reader's ability to form a coherent picture of the Russian characters in the novel, the narrator's peculiar combination of reservations, paraphrase, inconsistencies, and simplifying generalizations also makes us doubt his intellectual integrity and perhaps even the coherence and superiority of his Western culture. Yet *Under Western Eyes* demonstrates that even in Modernist fiction narrative consistency and thematic effect have no direct relation. Large sections of the novel are distinguished by a strikingly effective psychological realism that seems to defy, or run counter to, the problematic position and function of the teacher of languages. That this psychological realism can be presented and persuasively explored through a first-person narrative that is repeatedly subjected to ironic comment is a measure of the achievement of Conradian narrative in the novel.

While the functions of the first-person narrator are, then, complex and paradoxical in *Under Western Eyes*, the first-person narrative of *The Shadow-Line* exploits the narrative and thematic potential associated with temporal distance, which is closely linked to the protagonist's process of learning. The narrative of this late novella resembles a sustained act of intensified memory. Focused on the first-person narrator's instructive experience, this act of memory dramatizes his initiation into a society that gives him the independence and responsibility of a captain.

The form of narrative diversification and sophistication observable in Conrad varies from work to work and demands close reading, and thus generalized statements about his narrative do scant justice to its exceptional diversity. Rather than attempt to summarize the author's various narrative techniques, it is more helpful to conclude by stressing three of its key characteristics.

First, although Conradian narrative may usefully be grouped into third- and first-person narratives, several of his most important texts contain elements of both. These two main variants of Conradian narrative are remarkably flexible. The best examples can probably be found in the intricate combination of third- and first-person narrative in *Lord Jim*, and in the extraordinary range and elasticity of the third-person narrative of *Nostromo*.

Secondly, Conrad's fictional work is distinguished by a tendency towards paradox, one of which is that: 'A declared fear of the corrosive and faith-destroying intellect – [is] doubled by a profound and ironic skepticism' (Guerard, *Conrad the Novelist*, p. 57). Although such paradoxes identify tensions in the literary *content* of Conrad's fiction, these tensions or conflicts are shaped, dramatized, and intensified through his narrative. In 'Heart of Darkness' and *Lord Jim*, for example, the pressure towards paradox is inseparable from Conrad's oblique narrative method – including the compli-cated, unstable relations between the different narrators and characters. 'Conrad's tragic awareness of the reciprocal but conflicting demands of the individual and of society' (Watt, *Conrad in the Nineteenth Century*, pp. 358–9) is also in a sense paradoxical; and it suggests interesting affinities with, as well as significant differences from, major Modernist writers such as Hamsun, Proust, Kafka, and Joyce.

This observation blends into a concluding comment. For Conrad, narra-tive experimentation is not an aim in itself, but strengthens the dialectical relationship between narrative technique and thematics in his work. Thus we have seen, for example, that Jim is 'under a cloud' (*LJ*, p. 416) because his problem is *intrinsically* difficult: therefore it is convincing that neither Marlow as narrator nor we as readers can see him clearly. The relationship between Conrad and his narrators is complicated, but it surely does not follow that it is unimportant. In Conrad's fiction, the narrator's relationship with the story told cannot be separated from the author's relationship with his work – and, by implication, with the world that the work portrays.

NOTES

1 For an extended discussion of Conradian narrative, see my *Conrad's Narrative Method* and the following studies: Ambrosini, *Conrad's Fiction as Critical Discourse*; Berthoud, *Joseph Conrad: The Major Phase*; Guerard, *Conrad the Novelist*; Hawthorn, *Joseph Conrad: Narrative Technique*; Henricksen,

Nomadic Voices; Watt, *Conrad and the Nineteenth Century*; and Watts, *A Preface to Conrad*.

2 Dorrit Cohn defines free indirect discourse as 'the technique for rendering a character's thought in his own idiom while maintaining the third-person reference and the basic time of narration' (*Transparent Minds*, p. 100). See the example in the discussion of *Under Western Eyes* below.

3 For a presentation and discussion of Tönnies's work, see Watt, *Conrad in the Nineteenth Century*, pp. 112–15. See also Erdinast-Vulcan, *Joseph Conrad and the Modern Temper*, pp. 1–34.

4 See Henricksen, *Nomadic Voices*, p. 31. Following Genette, 'perspective' refers to the instance that 'sees' (i.e., orients the narrative perspective) in the narrative text, whereas 'voice' indicates the narrating instance (i.e., the speaker). See *Narrative Discourse*, p. 186. 'Distance' is explained in the discussion of 'Heart of Darkness' below.

5 This critical procedure is also adopted in the treatment of the major novels.

6 The narratee is the agent who is at least implicitly, and in Conrad often also explicitly, addressed by the narrator.

7 Genette defines prolepsis as 'any narrative manoeuvre that consists of narrating or evoking in advance an event that will take place later' (*Narrative Discourse*, p. 40). More frequent than prolepsis, analepsis designates 'an evocation after the fact of an event that took place earlier than the point in the story where we are at any given moment' (*Ibid.*).

WORKS CITED

Ambrosini, Richard. *Conrad's Fiction as Critical Discourse*. Cambridge: Cambridge University Press, 1991

Bakhtin, M. M. *The Dialogic Imagination: Four Essays*. Ed. Michael Holquist. Tr. Caryl Emerson and Michael Holquist. Austin: University of Texas Press, 1982

Berthoud, Jacques. *Joseph Conrad: The Major Phase*. Cambridge: Cambridge University Press, 1978

'Conrad and the sea'. Introduction. *The Nigger of the 'Narcissus'*. Ed. Jacques Berthoud. Oxford: Oxford University Press, 1984, pp. vii–xxvi

Bullough, Edward. 'Psychical distance'. 1912. In *Aesthetics: Lectures and Essays*. Ed. Elizabeth M. Wilkinson. Stanford: Stanford University Press, 1957, pp. 124–45

Cave, Terence. *Recognitions: A Study in Poetics*. Oxford: Clarendon Press, 1988

Cohn, Dorrit. *Transparent Minds: Narrative Modes for Presenting Consciousness in Fiction*. Princeton: Princeton University Press, 1978

Conrad, Joseph. *The Nigger of the 'Narcissus'*. 1897. Ed. Jacques Berthoud. Oxford: Oxford University Press, 1984

'Heart of Darkness' and Other Tales*. Ed. Cedric Watts. Oxford: Oxford University Press, 1990

Lord Jim, A Tale. 1900. Ed. John Batchelor. Oxford: Oxford University Press, 1983

Nostromo. 1904. Ed. Keith Carabine. Oxford: Oxford University Press, 1984

Under Western Eyes. 1911. Ed. Jeremy Hawthorn. Oxford: Oxford University Press, 1983

Erdinast-Vulcan, Daphna. *Joseph Conrad and the Modern Temper*. Oxford: Clarendon Press, 1991

Genette, Gérard. *Narrative Discourse*. Oxford: Blackwell, 1980

Guerard, Albert J. *Conrad the Novelist*. Cambridge, MA: Harvard University Press, 1958

Hawthorn, Jeremy. *Joseph Conrad: Narrative Technique and Ideological Commitment*. London: Arnold, 1990

Henricksen, Bruce. *Nomadic Voices: Conrad and the Subject of Narrative*. Urbana: University of Illinois Press, 1992

Kayser, Wolfgang. *Das sprachliche Kunstwerk*. 1948. Berne: Francke Verlag, 1971

Lothe, Jakob. *Conrad's Narrative Method*. Oxford: Clarendon Press, 1989

Madsen, Peter. 'Modernitet og melankoli: Fortælling, diskurs og identitet i Joseph Conrads *Mörkets hjerte*' ['Modernity and melancholy: narration, discourse, and identity in "Heart of Darkness"']. In *Fortaelling og erfaring*. Ed. O. B. Andersen *et al.* Aarhus: Aarhus University Press, 1988, pp. 97–118 (English version: *Conrad in Scandinavia*. Ed. Jakob Lothe. New York: Columbia University Press, 1995, pp. 127–54)

Miller, J. Hillis. *Fiction and Repetition: Seven English Novels*. Oxford: Blackwell, 1982

Najder, Zdzisław. *Joseph Conrad: A Chronicle*. Tr. Halina Carroll-Najder. New Brunswick, NJ: Rutgers University Press; Cambridge: Cambridge University Press, 1983

Stanzel, Franz K. *A Theory of Narrative*. Cambridge: Cambridge University Press, 1986

Todorov, Tzvetan. *Introduction to Poetics*. Tr. Richard Howard. Brighton: Harvester, 1981

Trotter, David. *The English Novel in History: 1895–1920*. London: Routledge, 1993

Watt, Ian. *Conrad in the Nineteenth Century*. Berkeley: University of California Press, 1979; London: Chatto & Windus, 1980

Watts, Cedric. *A Preface to Conrad*. 2nd edn. London: Longman, 1993

10

ANDREA WHITE

Conrad and imperialism

'It must not be supposed that Mr. Conrad makes attack upon colonisation, expansion, even upon Imperialism', *The Manchester Guardian*'s reviewer assured contemporary readers of 'Heart of Darkness' (Sherry, ed., *Conrad: The Critical Heritage*, p. 135). In December 1902, in *Academy and Literature*, Edward Garnett noted the novella's subversiveness, as 'a page torn from the life of the Dark Continent – a page which has been hitherto carefully blurred and kept away from European eyes' (*Ibid.*, p. 133). Conrad's fiction continues to excite such antithetical responses. Within the past thirty years in particular, the political aspects of his work have been a central focus of Conrad studies, and while Garnett's views have generally prevailed, these two early opinions frame an on-going discussion that continues to be shaped by multiple points of view.

The arguments range widely, in fact, from those who view Conrad as committed to a conservative, 'English view' of imperialism to those who see him as sceptical of the whole enterprise and a champion of anti-colonial revolts (Eagleton, *Criticism and Ideology*, p. 135, and Hawkins, 'The psychology of colonialism', p. 86). The Nigerian novelist Chinua Achebe's accusation that Conrad was 'a bloody racist' is countered by the contention of Ezekiel Mphahlele, a South African writer, that Conrad was one of the few 'outstanding white novelists who portray competently characters belonging to cultural groups outside their own' (*The African Image*, p. 125). D. C. R. A. Goonetilleke, writing from Sri Lanka, places Conrad with ' a distinguished minority of radical contemporary critics of imperialism such as Mark Twain, Roger Casement and E. D. Morel' (*Developing Countries*, p. 1).[1] For some readers, then, Conrad's works re-present his time's dominant congratulatory imperial discourse; for others they subvert it. While many have agreed that in any case, the psychology of the colonialist most engages Conrad's attention, others contend that that very backgrounding of native peoples and landscapes is objectionable.

If, as Salman Rushdie asserts, 'we are all irradiated by history' (*Imaginary*

Homelands, p. 100), then indeed there are no neutral places from which to act or observe, to write or read. Thus these diverse and conflicting readings – and our own – necessarily reflect the events and currents of thought from the 1960s to the 1990s. We enter Conrad's texts, inevitably, as marked subjects. None the less, while his works reflect this complexity, and even instability, they constitute profound studies of the imperial situation in late nineteenth- and early twentieth-century Europe and reveal that imperialism was never the stable monolith that it might appear to be from a distance. His works trace distinctive moments of that development, from the loosely administered, *ad hoc* arrangement in Malaya, to the intensified scramble for land in Africa, to the financial dependencies established in South America.

I

'When I grow up I shall go *there*', the eleven-year-old Józef Teodor Konrad Korzeniowski promised himself, '*there* being the region of Stanley Falls which in '68 was the blankest of blank spaces on the earth's figured surface' (*PR*, p. 13). Although he would complain that geography was an under-valued subject in Polish schools, such map-gazing must not have been an uncommon pursuit for mid-century Europeans stirred by the myriad reports of adventure and exploration filtering back to metropolitan centres from the colonial outposts of Africa, Asia, and the Pacific. If we are to believe the older author, he had been profoundly excited by the journals of Captain James Cook, Sir Leopold McClintock, and David Livingstone; the young Pole had admired these 'search[ers] for truth' (*LE*, p. 10). But between the time of his early admiration and his youthful vow to travel to Africa himself, and his actual arrival in the Congo in 1890, those early dreams of adventure had become what Martin Green calls 'deeds of empire'. That 'blank' space on the map of Africa had already been darkened by European imperialism.

By the time Conrad began working in the British Merchant Service in 1878, ten years after his childish boast, European imperial rule over the non-European world extended to nearly two-thirds of the Earth's land surface, and Britain's empire accounted for much of those holdings. From possessions in Oceania, New Zealand, and Australia, to the Straits Settlements and the Federated Malay States, to India, Canada, Africa, the Caribbean, China, and a more informal empire of trade in South America, the British empire Conrad served was extensive. By the end of the century, it would comprise nearly a quarter of the land surface and more than a quarter of the world's population.

It was with some wonder and pride, then, that the recently naturalized

British subject spoke of himself at this time as a 'Polish nobleman, cased in British tar' (*Letters*, I, p. 52). For Conrad, 'home' by this time was the 'hospitable shores of Great Britain' (*Letters*, I, p. 12), and the empire he served was doing, as far as he could see, good work. His sympathies were clearly conservative. A few years before, he had written to a friend of his disappointment at the Liberal victory in the 1885 General Election and had despaired that 'all that is respectable, venerable and holy', the 'great British Empire' had gone 'over the edge' (*Letters*, I, p. 16). In 1890, then, when Conrad first steamed up the Congo, he carried these attitudes with him, along with the 'Africa' already currently available, an 'imaginative geography', in Edward Said's words (*Orientalism*, p. 49), that equipped the European traveller to Africa as inevitably as map, mosquito boots, or solar topi. As Said has characterized the mythical production of 'Orientalism', so 'Africa' too already existed in the minds of first-time travellers to it. The adventurous accounts Conrad had read by such explorers as Mungo Park and David Livingstone had already powerfully created 'Africa' for him. By the time he found himself aboard a Congo steamer, he was at least partially a victim of 'the Victorian myth of the Dark Continent' (Brantlinger, *Rule of Darkness*, p. 173). Not surprisingly his early diary entries recorded on that first trip up the Congo depict a young sahib, complaining that things were not exactly pukka.[2] And yet, the fictional accounts of this trip, written in 1898 and 1899, would reveal, as well as the fictions that preceded and followed, a more hostile attitude towards imperialistic Europe's 'civilizing mission'. What Peter Nazareth notices about Marlow is also true of Conrad: while he went to Africa expecting to find the darkness there, and in Africans, he had to admit, in spite of himself, that the darkness is in 'us' ('Out of darkness', p. 175).

What accounts for this shift from the young seaman's apparently insensitive view to his own intrusive role in colonial adventurism to the fledgling novelist's desire to expose imperialism's fraudulent pretensions of benevolence? The answer lies partly in the complex ways in which Conrad's attitudes towards imperialism were initially shaped. Certainly he saw his own family as victims of Russian imperialism. As *szlachta* or Polish landed gentry, both the paternal Korzeniowskis and the maternal Bobrowskis were patriots who opposed autocracy. In the year of the 'ill-omened rising of 1863' (*PR*, p. 24), one uncle was killed and another exiled to Siberia where he died ten years later. Conrad's father had been deported in 1862 for his patriotic efforts to achieve Polish independence, and the five-year-old Conrad accompanied his parents into an exile that was so harsh that his mother died a few years later while his father suffered poor health for a few years and died in 1869.

Conrad's view of these events came to be filtered through the more conservative outlook of Tadeusz Bobrowski, his maternal uncle and guardian, and throughout his life the Korzeniowski impulse for patriotic action against oppression was always to some extent qualified, in Conrad's mind, by Bobrowski's rational, sceptical conservatism. The inheritance was both a sensitivity to oppressive autocracy and a profound scepticism about the idealism of social, and particularly nationalistic, movements. One critic goes so far as to claim that 'every aspect' of Conrad's youth and later development was affected by Russian rule and by Russia's occupation of Poland (Szczypien, 'Conrad's *A Personal Record*', p. 12). Certainly his own self-willed exile at age seventeen was in great part a desire to escape the consequences of being a Russian subject in Poland, particularly military service.

Another answer lies in the shifting nature of European imperialism itself between 1880 and 1914, a period during which colonial conquests accelerated greatly and worldwide. This 'new imperialism', a complex response to the industrialized countries' growing needs and desires for food, raw materials, markets, and investment opportunities, was pursued by such newcomers as Germany, Belgium, Italy, the United States, and Japan, while Britain – which had been accumulating colonies for over two hundred years – and France redoubled their efforts. This multiplication of colonial powers seeking claims on ever-dwindling space, especially in the tropics, intensified rivalry. In Africa alone, European holdings climbed from eleven percent in 1875 to ninety percent by 1902. This jump was made possible, in large part, by the Berlin-Congo Conference of 1884–5 which effectively partitioned Africa among England and thirteen other Western nations and created King Leopold's infamous and improperly designated 'Congo Free State'. By 1914 all of Africa except for Ethiopia, Liberia, and parts of Morocco had been carved out and claimed by Western Powers, and the Pacific totally distributed. During this period, then, access to and control of the tropics, particularly, became a compelling issue of public discussion and European rivalry. European nations found that their technology – the very technological superiority that enabled conquest and annexation – increasingly depended on such tropical products as rubber and that their 'civilization' also required tropical foodstuffs including cocoa, tea, coffee, cane sugar, and vegetable oils. And while global free trade had been the rule until the Great Depression of the 1880s, protectionism characterized much of the international economic scene. The scramble for colonial possessions was not only a political and economic rivalry but also led to an intensification of military might to extend imperial holdings and defend existing empires.[3]

When Mary Kingsley, whose *West African Studies* (1899) Conrad read and enjoyed, spoke of her disaffection for modern imperialism as opposed to the old-fashioned imperialism of her ancestors she was noting a shift that her contemporaries felt to be a novel and historically central development. To contemporary analyses of what was soon called imperialism – Hobsbawm argues that the word was not in general currency until the 1890s – this almost total partition of the world into territories under the formal rule or informal political domination of a few countries seemed a new phase in the general pattern of national and international development, 'notably different from the free-trading and freely competing liberal world of the mid-century' (Hobsbawm, *The Age of Empire*, p. 59). Perhaps it was the old empire Conrad regretted going off the edge in 1885, a fact to be regretted in the face of its successor. Ian Watt understands Marlow's admission that 'real work was being done in the red' as Conrad's nod to his late-Victorian audience, but perhaps Conrad also thought there had been such a time before the devastation of the new imperialism's ruinous consequences to both the colonized and the colonizer had become evident.

By 1900 the major powers had claimed most of the world and competition between them was keen; metropolitan centres, especially London, had become powerful hubs of world finance while the merchant navy Conrad served had become one of the leading carriers of raw materials and finished products. By 1886, when the twenty-nine-year-old *szlachta* son of a Polish patriot became a British subject and a master in the British Merchant Service, he had been about the empire's business for eight years, in ships carrying cargoes of wool to Australia, coal to Bangkok, manufactured goods from Singapore to the Bornean interior and returning with gutta percha, rattan, pearl shells, and beeswax from up-river Dyaks. Conrad's initial thinking about 'trade' and 'exchange' probably resembled Thomas Raffles's elaboration of Adam Smith's idea that trade was an exchange of wealth that mutually benefitted both parties (Bennett, *The Concept of Empire*, p. 67). Less available to Conrad was the view held by such recent writers as Mary Louise Pratt that 'trade' and 'exchange' were never the innocent, mutually beneficial arrangements they were represented as being. 'Reciprocity has always been capitalism's ideology of itself', Pratt argued (*Imperial Eyes*, p. 84). By the time he started writing, however, Conrad too has begun to doubt the 'natural' straightforwardness of 'trade'. While it might have been more difficult for empire's agents to understand the totality, cloaked as it was in ideology, it was possible for someone in Conrad's unique position to see beyond the burgeoning rhetoric of the empire's civilizing mission that accompanied and legitimated the endeavour and to notice, as he soon did, the disparity between that discourse and the actuality of grabbing 'for the sake of what could be got' (*HD*, p. 140). He understood that under all the 'civilizing talk', the business of extending and annexing colonial possessions resulted from economic needs. The company was indeed run for profit, as Marlow reminds his sentimental aunt.

This period chronicles an external shift in the nature of imperialism itself and marks crucial developments in Conrad's experience and outlook. He started to see colonialism closer up. Engaged in trade between the various colonial outposts, he had always been the privileged European ship's mate or captain. No lover of the 'primitive', like Marlow he was in no danger of 'going native' or even 'ashore for a howl and a dance' in the exotic lands he travelled to. He even kept his distance from other ship's officers in the various ports his voyages took him to. But in the *Vidar* – where he spent his thirtieth birthday – steaming up and down the coasts of the Malay Archipelago, Conrad was afforded another glimpse behind the apparently smooth workings of imperial trade. As the *Vidar* churned up-river in Borneo, penetrating its jungles and leaving behind the facades of the colonized world, the institutions, port buildings, and all-white hotels that had comprised his actual experience of a far-flung empire, to the flimsy trading stations of European encampments, he saw the actual conditions of colonized and colonizer. They struck him as neither grand nor progressive but as absurd. The image of 'the white man in the tropics', described in official pronouncements and in the day's abundant travel writing and adventure fiction was not to be found. Instead of the efficient, benevolent bearers of civilization's torch, he saw men cut off from and nostalgic for Europe, and drunk on power, their presumed racial superiority, and alcohol (Najder, *Joseph Conrad: A Chronicle*, p. 99). The disjunction between the routine business of imperial trade – of benefit, purportedly, to all concerned – and its actual conditions engaged him profoundly.

And as he saw empire more closely and the brutalities that accompanied expansion, his scepticism about the claims to moral improvement of the 'civilizing' endeavour deepened. Similarly, the power struggles he witnessed between competing colonial powers and conflicting cultures spoke to his own youthful memories of political struggle and stirred his imagination, as well as his regret, connected as they were for him with the compelling accounts of heroic adventure he had read about in his youth. He had followed in the tracks of the searchers of 'truth' he had so admired only to find ignoble evidence of the exploitation that had followed the courageous exploration. Out of this experience, he would begin writing, two years later, his first novel, *Almayer's Folly*, a work that seriously questions the imperial subject as constructed by the dominant discourse of the day. After signing off the *Vidar* in 1888, and eager for another berth, Conrad steamed up the Congo. His seven months there transformed him, forcing on him an even more reflective view, critical of European imperial endeavours. This under-standing profoundly shaped all the fiction to come, including *Almayer's Folly*, the beginnings of which he took to Africa.

From 1891, when he spent months in a London hospital recovering from his experience in the Congo, to 1895 and the publication of *Almayer's Folly*, Conrad was in England as much as he was at sea. A great reader of newspapers by then, he must have been well informed about the various arguments on the subject of continued imperial expansion. Most partici-pants in the discussion distinguished between India – an imperial fact more or less – 'white settler' colonies, and tropical possessions. Whether the 'white settler' colonies should be part of an Imperial Federation or not was a separate but not unrelated aspect of the discussion. But arguments for and against continued expansion in the tropics, particularly Africa, were thorn-ier and more agitated. Even though the Berlin Conference had effectively carved up Africa, arguments continued in England as to methods of control and the status of new territories: Should Uganda be made a protectorate? Should the Sudan be annexed? In 1881, John Seeley, professor of Modern History at Cambridge, saw the debate over empire divided into two camps, the 'bombastic', which argued for continued expansion and annexation, and the 'pessimistic', which viewed empire as useless and burdensome and favoured abandoning it at the earliest possible opportunity. While 'bom-bastic' spokesmen argued that Englishmen would be shirking their duty in abandoning the empire, others countered that further expansion would lead to bankruptcy. But these 'pessimists' or 'Little Englanders' were generally shouted down and condemned as unpatriotic roadblocks to progress. The new imperialism was forcefully and often expressed by Robert Cecil, Marquess of Salisbury, Prime Minister in 1885, 1886 to 1892, and again from 1895 to 1902, and by his Colonial Secretary, Joseph Chamberlain. Salisbury argued for continued expansion and annexation as the Govern-ment's 'moral duty' to 'make smooth the paths for British commerce, British enterprise, the application of British capital' (Bennett, *The Concept of Empire*, p. 312). They both collapsed the economic into the moral with rhetorical effectiveness.

Europeans generally based their claims to rule 'primitive' people on the basis of their own superiority, both technological and moral, and the English were no exception. 'The white man must rule', Lord Milner told the Municipal Congress in Johannesburg in 1903 'because he is elevated by many, many steps above the black man' (*Ibid.*, p. 343). This view is a major tenet of evolutionary thought intrinsic to the understanding of late nine-teenth-century Europeans. The model Darwin suggested and anthropolo-gists and sociologists such as Edward Tylor, Herbert Spencer, and Benjamin

Kidd had greatly elaborated – the central model then available – was evolutionary: humanity developed from 'barbarism' to 'civilization', and progress was inevitable and universal. Civilizations progress much as children develop into adults, more or less homogeneously, from lower child-like stages marked by impulsiveness, concrete thinking, and a belief in magic to higher stages characterized by adult-like qualities such as reflective-ness, abstract thinking, and a receptiveness to 'true' religion. In fact, Kidd's *Control of the Tropics* (1898) advised against European colonization in order to protect the more highly evolved races from contamination. It was clear, Kidd argued, 'going bush', 'fantee', or 'troppo' would be the unfortunate result of such an experiment. While the 'lower' races should be allowed to evolve more or less naturally, he argued, their 'low efficiency' would dangerously influence resident white populations. Firm administrative control was necessary – natives could not be expected to develop their resources themselves – but establishing permanent colonies was not to be considered. Kidd was so intent on warning against the disastrous conse-quences of white settlement in the tropics that he noticed no possible contradiction between this retrogressive potential and the evolutionary model's claim for the survival of the fittest. Rather, he saw the highly evolved European's need to stay connected to the forces that had civilized him, 'the moral, ethical, political, and physical conditions' that had pro-duced him (*Control of the Tropics*, p. 50), as somehow a credit to his complexity and further justification for his continued authority. That native peoples were at a less evolved stage of human development was rarely contested, and that it was the 'duty' of a more developed people to help their 'younger' brothers and sisters along was also generally agreed upon and conveniently served arguments for expansion.

Such arguments depicted continued expansion and control as not only moral and practical but somehow natural. Conrad's fictions, on the other hand, show the European intrusion as 'fantastic'. The 'mythological propor-tions' of the civilizing mission and 'the blinding brightness of its light' served to eclipse these other, less palatable stories of an East-West encounter (Sharp, 'Figures of colonial resistance', p. 143), ones that Conrad's fictions exposed. In 1897, he wrote of 'the languid imbecility' of Salisbury's Govern-ment (*Letters*, I, p. 339); Salisbury's and the other expansionists' pro-fessions of moral superiority, enlightenment, and progress must have struck Conrad as disingenuous and destructive fine words. His fictional depictions of imperial intrusions – Dutch, Belgian, French, English, or American – are seen not as outposts of progress but as unnatural and fatal disruptions. Constitutionally sceptical, his experience had been that ideals and high-mindedness generally vanish when translated into action, and from his vantage point in and out of various colonial ports he could see nothing resembling the much touted 'progress'.

The increasingly organized, controlled, and administered global connectedness of the new imperialism was the great historical fact at the end of the nineteenth and beginning of the twentieth centuries. The economy that generated this new imperialism was, of necessity, global and 'became steadily more so during the nineteenth century as it extended its operations to ever more remote parts of the planet, and transformed all areas ever more profoundly' (Hobsbawm, *The Age of Empire*, p. 41). This transformation was not marked in Conrad's fiction as progressive but rather as a regrettable diminishment from the adventures and achievements of such figures as Rajah James Brooke of Sarawak, for whom Conrad expressed 'a boyish admiration', or Captain James Cook.[4] In his fiction he depicts this 'new' imperial world of expanding total administration with some nostalgia for a time when there still were some 'empty' spaces. No wonder, then, that Borneo initially stirred Conrad's imagination, for it offered a final moment in the world's history when an individual like Captain Tom Lingard could still enjoy a maverick trading monopoly up a solitary reach of a muddy river, when the relatively unorganized and lawless world of quasi-governmental charter companies in the Malay States was giving way to the global world of commercial trade and competing empires. And events were moving so quickly that by the time he started to write *Almayer's Folly*, he had to set it ten years in the past in order to depict the lone trader working within the shifting trading realities that operated in that part of the world (Tennant, *Joseph Conrad*, p. 77). Because the first fifteen years of Conrad's writing life spanned this turn-of-the-century preoccupation with the new global imperialism, his major writings of this period reflect this concern.

II

Almayer's Folly and *An Outcast of the Islands*

Conrad's first two novels – *Almayer's Folly* and *An Outcast of the Islands* – *The Rescue*, many of his early stories, *Lord Jim*, and *Victory*, depict the complex and competing racial and cultural relationships of native Dyaks, immigrant Chinese, Malay sultans, Arab rajahs, and Dutch and English traders. No one group is idealized; rather our sense is of a succession of displacements and power struggles, internally and externally fuelled by a common human greed. It is a world of multiple viewpoints, rich and historic, not the homogeneous, self-congratulatory story of unenlightened, backward 'them' and heroic, progressive 'us', a Manichean opposition central, as Abdul JanMohamed has shown, to most of the day's colonial fictions. The imperial world as represented in the popular press, in the contemporary adventure fiction of heroic white men in the tropics, in the public pronouncements of England's political leaders of the white man's moral – and economic – duty to civilize the dark places of the earth is nowhere to be found.

What Robert Louis Stevenson had also described in his South Seas fictions and J. A. Hobson later observed in his critique of Empire, *Imperialism* (1902), Conrad had seen for himself: that 'Greater Britain ... furnishes a convenient limbo for damaged characters and careers' (Hobson, p. 52), rather than emissaries of light going forth on the civilizing mission. Goonetilleke notes the correspondence between Conrad's and Hobson's thinking in this respect in *Victory* (*Developing Countries*, pp. 68–9), but the observation holds true for Conrad's other fictions of imperial outposts as well. *Almayer's Folly* reflects Conrad's scepticism about the imperial venture generally and about the accompanying 'fine words' in particular, in its refusal to depict the Europeans in Sambir heroically. Almayer himself is a bitter, failed Dutchman whose dreams of gold and glory in this backwater outpost have come to nothing. Lingard, an English trader who 'invaded the Malay Archipelago in search of money and adventure' (*AF*, p. 7), becomes increasingly insubstantial and shadowy, and his flimsy hopes fail. It is hard to see here among the 'damaged characters and careers' the superior white men Kidd and others would speak of.

Conrad's fictions not only fail to privilege the Europeans appropriately, but represent the native point of view towards them generally, a view that does not distinguish one hated white man from another. While the natives call Lingard 'Rajah Laut' (King of the Sea), we are also given their less admiring view – that white men are duplicitous and destructive opportunists who have arrived 'with prayers on their lips and loaded guns in their hands' (*AF*, p. 115). Mrs Almayer's and Nina's views as well as those of Babalatchi, chief counsellor to the native ruler in both *Almayer's Folly* and *An Outcast*, fail to reflect proper admiration for the European or his endeavours. Babalatchi hates the 'Orang Blanda' and longs for the days before the arrival of the now ubiquitous white man whose coming brought 'sudden ruin and destruction of all that he deemed indispensable to a happy and glorious existence' (*OI*, p. 52). He conspires with Mrs Almayer, made bitter by receiving the white man's 'advantages', 'rescued' from her pirate clan, sent to a European school, and married to the Dutchman, Kaspar Almayer. Similarly, after ten years of European education in Singapore, Nina carries only the scars of the white man's racial prejudice and is struck moreover by the emptiness of European culture when contrasted with her mother's and Dain's stories of native courage and adventure. Almayer's final defeat is his much loved daughter's rejection of him; 'feeble and traditionless', he has nothing to pass on to her. Rather than the native's reputed moral inferiority, it is European civilization that Nina condemns for its narrowness, moral emptiness, racial exclusivity, and lack of vigour. In *An Outcast*, Aïssa will think similarly of Willems's people: 'nothing but misfortune comes to those who are not white ... [from] that people that steals every land, masters every sea, that knows no mercy and no truth – knows nothing but its own strength' (p. 153). Here the native, usually silenced by the colonial discourse of the day, disturbs the monologic telling of 'them' and 'us'. Peter Willems is an even less sympathetic figure than Almayer, and we attribute his fall to his own hollowness as well as to the hollowness of the 'civilizing' endeavour itself. There is no ennobling work of empire going on here, only 'the quiet deal in opium; the illegal traffic in gunpowder; the great affair of smuggled firearms' (p. 8).

Both novels also indict Captain Lingard's benevolent paternalism that presumes that only he and his trade can bring happiness and prosperity to that corner of the world he thought of as his own. And a sense of loss is measured in the contrast between Lingard and the actual Rajah James Brooke of Sarawak. Lingard vanquished the local pirates and brought order to Sambir as Brooke had to Sarawak, but Lingard is depicted as a failed Brooke, and his dreams of benevolent despotism are only momentarily realized. Thus Conrad's first two novels question one of the central professions of imperialism, that European civilization was superior and could illuminate the earth's dark places. Rather than bringing progress, trade has only increased various rivalries and introduced opium, that dream-inducing drug that finally and ironically kills Almayer.

While Conrad's depictions of the white man in the tropics is subversively unheroic, his representations of the native also work to destabilize the hegemonic versions of the imperial endeavour. Babalatchi, for example, is indefatigable; we do not recognize him as belonging to a race of 'low efficiency'. Hunt Hawkins argues that Conrad's fiction challenges one of the dominant theories of the day that worked to justify imperial intrusions, that natives thought of the European as a god, a super-being upon whom they became dependent. Hawkins remarks that while Frantz Fanon would investigate colonial psychology in his *Black Skin, White Masks* (1952), Conrad similarly questioned the theory of native dependency ('Psychology of colonialism', pp. 86–7). While Conrad's natives are often in dependent positions, Hawkins argues, they finally 'transcend whatever dependency they may have on Europeans and enter into active revolt ... and most have as their primary goal in life the expulsion of the colonialists from their lands' (*Ibid.*, p. 87). Discussing the early story 'Karain' and its depiction of a Mindanao chief as a displaced victim, Hawkins speaks of Conrad as a champion of 'anti-colonial revolts', his own personal history making him particularly sympathetic to other victims of imperial intrusion. In this story, Conrad again stresses the unnaturalness and madness of the European invasion – in this case that of the Spanish in the Philippines – and the inevitability of native resistance. And as Benita Parry argues, this very disruption of the accepted idea of the passive, submissive native, the decentring of the native 'as a fixed, unified object of colonialist knowledge', is fundamental to the project of deconstructing imperialist discourse ('Problems in current theories', p. 29).

The African fictions

After its serial publication, 'Karain' was republished in *Tales of Unrest* (1898) along with 'An Outpost of Progress', Conrad's first African fiction. In the 'Author's Note' to that volume, Conrad speaks of 'An Outpost' as 'the lightest part of the loot I carried off from Central Africa, the main portion being of course "The Heart of Darkness"' (*TU*, p. ix). Although he justifies his own plunder as 'very small' and not 'of much use to anybody else', his irony works here to unmask the purported benevolence of European incursions into Africa and reveal their actual self-serving nature as commonplace. 'An Outpost' as well as 'Heart of Darkness' also refute then current attitudes about race that naturalized native inferiority and justified European domination. Kayerts and Carlier, the two resident white men at this outpost of 'progress', are such 'damaged characters' that they must depend on the native bookkeeper, Makola, to run the company's business of ivory collecting and on the neighbouring chief Gobila for their daily sustenance. Kidd's attribution of the 'unquestionable ascendency of Western Civilization' to the 'energetic races' is thus effectively refuted. And, of course, the 'progress' that was to justify their intrusion is utterly absent: in 'Heart of Darkness' there are only the aborted railroad, native chain gangs, and the grove of death. Kayerts and Carlier's outpost is so bereft of imperial light that ivory-trading degenerates into slave-trading, and Gobila's people are killed and their villages burned. Conrad's irony intensifies his criticism of the civilizing work of empire underway in Africa. He juxtaposes the story of Kayerts and Carlier's utter uselessness with their self-congratulatory reading of fictional and newspaper accounts that proclaim 'the sacredness of the civilizing work, and extolled the merits of those who went about bringing light, and faith and commerce to the dark places of the earth' (*HD*, p. 11)

Again, it is the unnaturalness of 'the fantastic invasion' that both African stories dramatize, particularly the displacement of native people. The ten station men in 'An Outpost' come from a distant tribe, and though engaged only for six months, somehow 'had been serving the cause of progress for upwards of two years' (*HD*, p. 17). They are described as generally miserable and unhealthy, far from friends, family, familiar food, and comforting beliefs. Kayerts and Carlier, uncomprehending, notice only the Africans' inefficiency and apparent laziness. In 'Heart of Darkness', Marlow tries to dramatize this aspect of colonial brutality, that his listeners in the *Nellie* might not have thought about, by suggesting an analogy meant to disturb. Describing to them his overland tramp to the company's Central Station on the Congo, Marlow reports 'a solitude, nobody, not a hut':

> The population had cleared out a long time ago. Well, if a lot of mysterious niggers armed with all kinds of fearful weapons suddenly took to travelling on the road between Deal and Gravesend, catching the yokels right and left to carry heavy loads for them, I fancy every farm and cottage thereabouts would get empty very soon. (*HD*, p. 160)

Although Marlow uses the racist language of his day, he is more alive than his listeners – or readers, presumably – to such an invasion's absurd outrageousness, one 'naturalized' by the engravings in daily illustrated newspapers of the inevitable string of black carriers accompanying white 'civilizers' through swamps and along jungle paths in 'darkest Africa'.

In both African stories we see another part of the unblurring that Edward Garnett originally noticed, an aspect of imperialism not yet exposed in the period's colonial discourse – the necessity for 'pretty fictions' to conceal imperialism's actual business. As Jeremy Hawthorn observes, Makola anticipates the Accountant of 'Heart of Darkness': both put their neat handwriting and accurate record-keeping at the service of the bureaucratic obfuscation necessary to legitimizing burglary. Makola, in particular, understands the necessity of covering up the truth, and that imperialism, in fact, depends upon concealment (Hawthorn, *Narrative Technique*, pp. 160–3). But Kayerts and Carlier – those two 'pioneers of trade and progress' as they think of themselves – more Conradian protagonists who cannot or will not distinguish fact from fiction – prefer the fiction Makola provides to the truth, that they are, in fact, slave dealers and that imperialism necessitates such barbarism. That the ends so brutally justify the means had not been part of this discourse before and constitutes a serious critique of empire and its propagandizing rhetoric.

The anti-imperialism of 'Heart of Darkness' was heard by E. D. Morel, among others. His Congo Reform Movement was dedicated to abolishing slavery in King Leopold's 'Free' State, and he felt inspired by 'Heart of Darkness' in his endeavour. The introduction to his pamphlet *The Congo Slave State* (1903) reads: 'We turned again to the African world, to the 'heart of darkness' as Joseph Conrad described it in his memorable story' (*History of the Congo Reform Movement*, p. 616). No doubt the current press reports of atrocities in the Congo made Conrad's words more resonant to his English audience. But if 'An Outpost' seemed to some a critique of specifically Belgian imperialism, then 'Heart of Darkness' clearly aimed its scepticism at a much wider, more international target: no imperial power escapes blame. Marlow, the English sea-captain, comes to Africa in a French steamer and once there encounters a French man-of-war anchored off the West African coast, firing upon 'enemies' in the bush. He is taken aboard an up-river steamer whose captain is Swedish and will meet, at the company's stations, many Belgians and a Russian. Kurtz himself had been educated partly in England and his parents were of mixed English and French ancestry: 'All Europe contributed to the making of Kurtz' (p. 207). Marlow, aboard the *Nellie* in the Thames – another of 'the dark places of the earth' – tells his story to an Accountant, a Lawyer, and a Company Director, English stockholders all, the investors that made empire possible. By this point, Conrad's awareness is clearly J. A. Hobson's. Whether or not he had read Hobson's *Evolution of Modern Capitalism* (1894) or *The War in South Africa* (1900), his fiction evinces agreement with Hobson's basic tenet, more fully developed in *Imperialism: A Study* (1902), that imperialism benefitted the few at the expense of the many.[5]

Lord Jim

Conrad had already written three novels and five stories set in the Eastern seas, when in 1898 he first sketched a beginning to *Lord Jim*. A more antithetical tale to the discourse of European supremacy could not have been told. The story of the actual *Jeddah*, a ship that carried Muslim pilgrims from Singapore to Jeddah was abandoned in stormy seas by her European officers in August 1880, must have deeply troubled those whose ideas of empire had been shaped by such public pronouncements as Chamberlain's and Salisbury's, that native people were backward brutes needing the more enlightened help of European civilizers. When the *Jeddah* was towed into Aden, the event caused a great stir, and the London papers carried on heated discussions about it.[6] Concern was with the loss of European – and as more facts came in, specifically British – honour. Most saw it as breaking a code at the very heart of Europe's domination of native peoples. The court felt similarly, for the captain's certificate was cancelled – as is Jim's. And the story of the 'white men who left their ship' must have been told and retold on colonial verandahs and in the offices of Australian and Eastern ports for years afterwards, casting a shadow on professions of European moral supremacy. Brierly's suicide probably seemed a likely response to such an egregious betrayal of a code intrinsic to the myth whereby a governing class justifies its rule.

At first, Jim seems familiar to readers of adventure fiction, a protagonist clad in white – 'one of us' – whose desires have been shaped by fiction that served to construct the imperial dream. But Jim is no Rajah James Brooke or fictional adventure hero, and unlike them he brings tragic disorder to Patusan. While even Marlow remarks on the initial improvements Jim's presence there has brought about, his final acts bring disaster to the people and tragedy to Dain Waris's parents. To his own great misfortune and that of Doramin's family and community, Jim mistakes the imperial facts for the imperial fictions he has consumed.[7]

As Jim is no Brooke, similarly the 1880s were not the 1840s. That Conrad has by now 'abandoned heroes as well as heroism' (Darras, *Joseph Conrad and the West*, p. 142) is a function, in large part, of the new set of circumstances occasioned by the new global economy. Gentleman Brown's disastrous appearance is not a novelist's use of wild coincidence. By the 1880s, civilization's nets were so extensive and imperialistic civilization's arms so long that, as Heyst would discover in *Victory*, no place was outside history. Some such meeting was inevitable. 'A blind accomplice of the Dark Powers' (*LJ*, p. 354), Brown is the unforeseen but inevitable consequence of modern imperialistic ideology in its commercial ruthlessness. On imperial business also, this Western Pacific trading skipper was financed, it is rumoured, 'on the quiet by a most respectable firm of copra merchants' (p. 353). Brown exemplifies the brutalizing effects of an imperial policy 'whose workings are pervasive and whose concerns are only financial profit' (Zelnick, 'Conrad's *Lord Jim*', p. 77). Here, as elsewhere, Conrad is intent on exposing what ideology seeks to obscure.

The Inheritors

Contemporary events as well as Conrad's fiction demonstrated that imperialism's consequences were pervasive and pernicious. Towards the end of 1899, the Boer War broke out, a brutal colonial war that revealed to many who might not have noticed before the costs of an imperial policy in lives, money, and energy of spirit. Although Conrad's ideas about this conflict were complex, he knew that it had not been undertaken for democracy (as Kipling and others claimed) and that its price was too high: 'The whole business is inexpressibly stupid – even on general principles; for evidently a war should be a conclusive proceeding while this noble enterprise ... must be the beginning of an endless contest' (*Letters*, II, p. 207). For him the Boer War epitomized the tendency of modern democracies to abandon moral traditions for 'material interests' whose purported supremacy justified imperial incursions, and he may well have suspected that whatever claims the 'fine words' of Chamberlain, Salisbury, and others made for British hegemony in South Africa, the real motive was gold.

In the month that war broke out in South Africa, Conrad and Ford Madox Ford began work on *The Inheritors*, at the same time that *Lord Jim* was beginning to be serialized in *Blackwood's* and Conrad was completing it. While neither Conrad nor his later readers have considered the collaboration a major effort, *The Inheritors* was topical, indeed, and illuminates Conrad's understanding at this point, that imperialism was enabled not by fine words but by investors and that the new imperialism was international. The novel concerns European capitalists investing in colonial schemes and the coming to power of a ruthless new imperialism depicted by the Joseph Chamberlain-like aggressive Gurnard and by the international financier the Duc de Mersch. This barely disguised Leopold II heads the Congo-like colonial territory of 'Greenland' and founds the 'Society for the Regeneration of the Arctic Regions' (*In*, p. 92). While the perceptive few claim that his 'great Society' is 'neither more nor less than a corporate exploitation of unhappy Esquimaux' (p. 80), the share-holders upon whom that exploitation depends would rather see him as 'a true philanthropist'.[8]

Nostromo

In *Nostromo*, which Conrad first thought of in 1898 as a prospective story, he turns to a different kind of imperialism. While Costaguana is an independent country, it is an economic colony, and its leadership made up of Blanco families, the remaining Spanish élite, who, in turn, depend on foreign investment. The intervention of English and American money enables the silver from Charles Gould's San Tomé mine to flow out, enriching foreign investors and Costaguana's Blanco families. Today's readers recognize this situation as 'economic imperialism', a term unavailable to Conrad (Goonetilleke, *Developing Countries*, p. 120).

South America was a relatively new subject, particularly American imperialism in South America, and Conrad was prescient in understanding the shift that was underway. In 1898, while working on *Lord Jim* and 'Heart of Darkness' and starting to think about *Nostromo*, Conrad was reading Cunninghame Graham's articles in *The Saturday Review* about the on-going Spanish-American War. In contrast to Kipling, who would urge America to 'take up the White Man's Burden' and annex the Philippines,

Graham spoke only of the dangers of European and American intervention in the internal affairs of South America. Conrad agreed with Graham's opinions on this matter: he accuses the United States of 'ruffianism' and refers to both it and Germany – another aggressive newcomer to imperialism – as 'thieves' (*Letters*, II, pp. 60, 81). As he began *Nostromo*, America was making its destiny manifest, much to Conrad and Graham's shared consternation.

Conrad knew that American intervention was as mischievous, as imperialistically motivated, and as destructive as any of Europe's various incursions, partitionings, and annexations in Africa and Asia, or as Russia's in Poland. In *Nostromo*, then, Decoud's idea to encourage and aid Sulaco's secession from Costaguana in order to benefit investors abroad and the Blancos at home serves material interests as effectively as the Yankee incursion in Panama. While Conrad's novel again illustrates Hobson's central tenet that imperial ventures benefit the few at the expense of the many, it also dramatizes a more familiar Conradian truth. Like Almayer's gold and Kurtz's ivory, Gould's silver corrupts, exercising its influence over 'private individuals, colonial companies and imperial powers', in a manner Goonetilleke finds representative of developing nations (*Developing Countries*, p. 120). Economic imperialism, then, corrupts even the few it seems to advantage.

Our regard for Jim's improvements in Patusan is generally sympathetic, if also critical. But in *Nostromo*, the criticism deepens; the destructive power of 'material interests' touches everyone's life. As surely as the rumours of 'heaps of shining gold' cast their 'fatal spell' on the gringos in the cautionary tale that prefaces the novel so the silver of the San Tomé mine enchants and possesses both the incorruptible Nostromo himself and Charles Gould. From the age of twenty, Charles had fallen 'under the spell' of the mine (*No*, p. 59) and was soon 'mine-ridden' (p. 55). Here Conrad transforms the tale of King Midas into a modern warning against 'pinning' one's 'faith to material interests' (p. 84), as Gould so mistakenly does, for the resulting evil spreads. As Emilia Gould realizes soon enough, the price to pay for the 'progress' used to justify the re-opening of the mine is high indeed. Early on, even though she is still in the grip of her husband's vision of progress, she admits misgivings. While she shares her husband's conviction that the railway will bring much needed improvements to the country, she also regrets the wholesale change this future will necessarily entail: 'there are simple and picturesque things that one would like to preserve' (p. 120). But 'material interests' prevail, and as she has feared, the price will be the one she has foreseen, as well as her own private sorrow at losing to the silver both her husband and her hopes for personal happiness.

Progress is the novel's watchword. Sir John certainly believes in it and promotes his railway as essential 'for the progressive and patriotic undertaking' (p. 34). And while it is clear that the mine has brought prosperity – the new cable cars run along improved streets, and there are a developed harbour and quayside and miles of railway – it is also clear that it has benefitted the few at the expense of the many. The modern villas of the Ricos contrast tellingly with 'three lumpy knots of banana patches, palm-leaf roots, and shady trees mark[ing] the Village One, Village Two, Village Three, housing the miners of the Gould Concession' (p. 101). And progress has required repression. Accounting for the enforced recruitment into the army, by lasso, Don Pépé, 'with a helpless shrug', confesses to Mrs Gould: 'What would you! Poor people! Pobrecitos! Pobrecitos! But the State must have its soldiers' (p. 97). Any social change visible is clearly the result of exploitation, and at the novel's conclusion instability and prospects of new revolutions threaten the apparent new order. The destructiveness of this particular 'fantastic invasion' seems to have no end. The future, in fact, looks as turbulent as the past. And even the ever-hopeful Emilia Gould must admit finally in the full force of her own personal anguish that she can no longer deny that the mine and its silver are oppressors, not the liberators that she and her husband had idealistically believed them to be. That Captain Mitchell's optimism for the future is ill-founded is suggested by the form of the novel. Chronology is so disrupted in *Nostromo* that, as Jocelyn Baines has noticed, 'nothing is ever achieved. By the end of the book we are virtually back where we started; it looks as if the future of Costaguana will be very similar to her past' (*Joseph Conrad: A Critical Biography*, p. 301).

III

While a few perceptive contemporary readers like Garnett saw the subversiveness of Conrad's fictions, some present-day readers criticize those same fictions for their ideological ambivalence and even conservatism. But the world that has 'irradiated us' did not, of course, inform Conrad. James Clifford discusses the new light shed by such post-colonial writers as Aimé Césaire who speaks of culture as 'something complex and hybrid, salvaged from a lost origin, constructed out of a squalid present, articulated within and against a colonial tongue' (*The Predicament of Culture*, p. 50).

But until late in the nineteenth century ' "culture" referred to a single evolutionary process ... the basic, progressive movement of humanity' (*Ibid.*, p. 93), and while contemporary anthropological and sociological thinking had spread knowledge about non-European peoples, it had done little more than codify difference in order to explain 'their barbarism' and 'our civilization'. 'By the turn of the century, however', Clifford continues, 'evolutionist confidence began to falter, and a new ethnographic conception of culture became possible. The word began to be used in the plural, suggesting a world of separate, distinctive, and equally meaningful ways of life' (*Ibid.*).

This was neither Conrad's understanding nor that of most of his peers. As an early modern, he sensed the current of a world-wide disruption of peoples and ideas, of exiles and rootlessness, but while his writing acknowledges and even participates in the dencentring of monolithic unities and traditional hierarchies, it also expresses his sense of loss and anxiety in response to the perceived disorder. Although his fiction was certainly more complex than the responses of most of his contemporaries, little of Césaire's acceptance of heterogeneity and hybridity can be discerned in it. On the other hand, this 'unsettling anxiety' distinguishes Conrad's fiction from the 'optimism, affirmation, and serene confidence' of contemporary novels, based as they were 'on the exhilaration and interest of adventure in the colonial world [which] far from casting doubt on the imperial undertaking, serves to confirm and celebrate its success' (Said, *Culture and Imperialism*, p. 187). More than anyone else Conrad's response is complex; he alone 'tackled the subtle cultural reinforcements and manifestations of empire' (*Ibid.*). And Conrad's fiction destabilized the authority of that exclusive European telling of the world's story, even before it was challenged by the independence movements of the 1950s and 1960s, before the colonized themselves started 'writing back'. Conrad, at the turn of the century, knew little of the 'independent histories and cultures' of native people. Nor could he have known the extent of the destruction wrought by European expansionism in Asia, Africa, and South America or of the devastating and still resounding after-effects of neo-colonialism.

That he contested to the extent he did the 'optimism, affirmation, and serene confidence' of much contemporary writing about empire can perhaps be attributed in part to this own culturally complex experience with culture-crossing, to his status as a 'hyphenated white man' (Pratt, *Imperial Eyes*, p. 213). And as another member of a disrupted culture, Peter Nazareth, a Goan-Ugandan writer, speaks of the profound influence Conrad's work exercised on his own 'writing back' as well as on that of Kenyan writer, Ngugi Wa Thiong'o. Nazareth contends that Conrad was the first to provide some criticism of imperialism. In the colonial world, Nazareth maintains, censors had banished Marx and Lenin:

But there was Conrad, sneaking through as a member of Leavis's Great Tradition, actually undermining that tradition. Jane Austen's characters in *Mansfield Park* could live a luxurious life which the patriarch left for the colonies; Conrad actually takes us to the colonies to show us what happened there when the patriarch or his agents arrived and how his wealth at home came from brutal colonial action. Conrad was therefore a mental liberator.

('Out of darkness', p. 178).

His fiction was instructive to colonized peoples, making them conscious in a new way of what it meant, exactly, to be colonized and to live in the 'glass cage' of an imposed world-view, the first task in any project that undertakes the decolonization of the mind. The Guyanese novelist Wilson Harris also speaks of the liberating effects of Conrad's fiction on his own writing which is also apparent in other 'post-Conradian legacies' such as Jean Toomer's novel *Cane* (1923) and Wole Soyinka's play *The Road* (1973). Harris argues that for these writers 'Heart of Darkness' was 'a frontier novel', occupying 'a threshold of capacity to which Conrad pointed though he never attained that capacity himself' ('The frontier', p. 87). These post-colonial writers have found that Conrad anticipated them in 'writing back' at 'fine words' and claim him as 'one of us'.

Even those critics who are inclined to emphasize Conrad's ambivalence and hear in his fiction, as does Benita Parry, only a 'muffled' political protest, find his early contribution to demythologizing imperial pretensions highly significant:

> If Conrad did not see imperialism steadily, he did, in fictions that dramatise the war of the hemispheres within a structurally joined and spiritually divided universe, see it whole, thereby inviting readers to scrutinise the ethical founda-tions to the civilisation of expansionist capitalism and engaging them in a critical view of imperialism's urge to conquer the earth.
>
> (*Conrad and Imperialism*, p. 8)

While Conrad's fictions inevitably bear traces of pervasive contemporary attitudes towards empire, and reveal his own anxiety, they contribute in a crucial way to a revaluation of imperialism. As Garnett had first noticed about 'Heart of Darkness', the work exposed the machinery behind the apparent naturalness and inevitability of the imperial endeavour and made visible the conqueror's face hidden behind the mask of a civilizing mission's protestations of benevolence.[9]

NOTES

1   E. D. Morel, a journalist and reformer, founded the Congo Reform Association in 1904, with Roger Casement, British Consul in the Congo Free State, reformer

and later Irish Nationalist. In his *History of the Congo Reform Movement*, Morel declared that 'Heart of Darkness' was 'the most powerful thing ever written on the subject' of Belgian atrocities in the Congo (p. 205, n. 1). For his part, Conrad wrote Casement, whom he had met in the Congo, to thank him for Morel's pamphlet *The Congo Slave State*, confirming Morel's grim facts about Leopold's colonial brutality (*Letters* III, p. 96).

2 For example, see *Congo Diary*, pp. 9–10.

3 See Weber, *A Modern History of Europe*, p. 738, and Hobsbawm, *The Age of Empire*, pp. 58–61, in particular, for a more detailed discussion of this historical background.

4 The Englishman James Brooke served as a model for various characters in Conrad's fictions set in the Eastern Seas. When he first came to Sarawak in 1839, Brooke – like Jim – was confronted with rebellion underway. He helped the country's ruler, Muda Hassim, uncle of the Sultan of Borneo, put down a local rebellion. He saved inland Dyaks from Malay pirates, thereby making the area safer for English trade, and was made Rajah of Sarawak in recompense. Like Jim, he dispensed justice and was loved and trusted by his people. For Brooke's influence on Conrad's fiction, see Gordan, *Joseph Conrad*; Fleishman, *Conrad's Politics*; Saveson, *Joseph Conrad: The Making of a Moralist*; and Watts, ed., *Joseph Conrad's Letters to R. B. Cunninghame Graham*.

5 According to Zelnick, Conrad echoes Hobson's assertion that imperialism is a 'play of forces that does not openly appear'. Hobson's awareness was Conrad's that the obscurity of modern politics results from a system in operation for which general public support is orchestrated at particular moments (such as the 1897 Jubilee) working to arouse overwhelming sentiment for 'empire' when that empire actually served the few at the expense of the many.

6 See Sherry, *Conrad's Eastern World*, pp. 61ff. for an extended discussion of the actual event and contemporary responses to it.

7 See Zelnick on *Lord Jim*'s subversion of colonialist discourse, particularly of the heroic, imperial sort so popular in the late nineteenth century, by its very telling. The original omniscient narrator is superceded by Marlow's voice, which weaves together multiple points of view, with no overarching authority. The principle of progression is not a straightforward chronology of heroic deeds, but the disjointed, interpretive acts of an involved but flawed narrator. *Lord Jim*'s structure subverts by upsetting expected conventions that had always served imperialism, for neither imperial hero, order, nor closure are available.

8 See Fleishman's *Conrad's Politics* for readings of both *The Inheritors* and *Romance* as protests against the Boer War and as indictments of imperialism generally.

9 For further reading on the subject of Conrad and imperialism, see Brantlinger, *Rule of Darkness*; Darras, *Joseph Conrad and the West*; Fleishman, *Conrad's Politics*; Goonetilleke, *Developing Countries in British Fiction*; Hawkins, 'Conrad's critique of imperialism' and 'Conrad and the psychology of colonialism'; Hay, *The Political Novels of Joseph Conrad*; Krenn, *Conrad's Lingard Trilogy*; Mahood, *The Colonial Encounter*; Parry, *Conrad and Imperialism*; Watt, *Conrad in the Nineteenth Century*; and White, *Joseph Conrad and the Adventure Tradition*.

ANDREA WHITE

WORKS CITED

Achebe, Chinua. 'An image of Africa: racism in Conrad's "Heart of Darkness"'. *Massachusetts Review* 17.4 (1977), 782–94

Baines, Jocelyn. *Joseph Conrad: A Critical Biography*. London: Weidenfeld & Nicolson; New York: McGraw-Hill, 1960. Reprinted Penguin Books, 1971

Bennett, George. *The Concept of Empire: Burke to Attlee, 1774–1947*. Vol. 6 of *The British Political Tradition*. Ed. Alan Bullock and F. W. Deakin. London: Black, 1953

Brantlinger, Patrick. *Rule of Darkness: British Literature and Imperialism, 1830–1914*. Ithaca: Cornell University Press, 1988

Clifford. James. *The Predicament of Culture*. Cambridge, MA: Harvard University Press, 1988

Conrad, Joseph. *Almayer's Folly*. 1895. Ed. Floyd Eugene Eddleman and David Leon Higdon. Cambridge: Cambridge University Press, 1994

'Congo Diary' and Other Uncollected Pieces. Ed. Zdzisław Najder. Garden City, NY: Doubleday, 1978

'Heart of Darkness' and Other Tales. Ed. Cedric Watts. Oxford: Oxford University Press, 1990

The Inheritors. 1901. Garden City, NY: Doubleday, 1924

Last Essays. Ed. Richard Curle. London: Dent, 1926

Lord Jim, A Tale. 1900. Ed. John Batchelor. Oxford: Oxford University Press, 1983

'The Mirror of the Sea' and 'A Personal Record'. 1906 and 1912. Ed. Zdzisław Najder. Oxford: Oxford University Press, 1988

Nostromo. 1904. Ed. Keith Carabine. Oxford: Oxford University Press, 1984

An Outcast of the Islands. 1896. Ed. J. H. Stape and Hans van Marle. Oxford: Oxford University Press, 1992

Tales of Unrest. 1898. New York: Doubleday & Doran, 1928

Darras, Jacques. *Joseph Conrad and the West: Signs of Empire*. London: Macmillan, 1982

Eagleton, Terry. *Criticism and Ideology: A Study in Marxist Literary Theory*. London: Verso, 1976

Fanon, Frantz. *Black Skin, White Masks*. 1952. New York: Grove, 1967

The Wretched of the Earth. New York: Grove, 1963

Fleishman, Avrom. *Conrad's Politics: Community and Anarchy in the Fiction of Joseph Conrad*. Baltimore: Johns Hopkins University Press, 1967

Frank, Katherine. *A Voyager Out*. New York: Ballantine Books, 1986

Goonetilleke, D. C. R. A. *Developing Countries in British Fiction*. London: Macmillan; Totowa, NJ: Rowman & Littlefield, 1977

Gordan, John Dozier. *Joseph Conrad*. 1940. New York: Russell & Russell, 1963

Green, Martin. *Dreams of Adventure, Deeds of Empire*. New York: Basic Books, 1979

Harris, Wilson. 'The frontier on which "Heart of Darkness" stands'. *Research on African Literature* 12 (1981), 86–92

Hawkins, Hunt. 'Conrad's critique of imperialism in "Heart of Darkness"'. *PMLA* 94 (1979), 286–99

'Conrad and the psychology of colonialism'. In *Conrad Revisited: Essays for the*

Eighties. Ed. Ross C. Murfin. University: University of Alabama Press, 1985, pp. 71–88

Hawthorn, Jeremy. *Joseph Conrad: Narrative Technique and Ideological Commitment.* London: Arnold, 1990

Hay, Eloise Knapp. *The Political Novels of Joseph Conrad.* Chicago: Chicago University Press, 1963; rev. edn. 1981

Hobsbawm, Eric. *The Age of Empire.* New York: Vintage, 1989

Humphries, Reynold. 'The discourse of colonialism: its meaning and relevance for Conrad's fiction'. *Conradiana* 21.2 (1989), 107–33

Hunter, Allan. *Joseph Conrad and the Ethics of Darwinism: The Challenges of Science.* London: Croom Helm, 1983

Jameson, Fredric. *The Political Unconscious.* Ithaca: Cornell University Press, 1981

JanMohamed, Abdul. *Manichean Aesthetics.* Amherst: University of Massachusetts Press, 1983

Kidd, Benjamin. *The Control of the Tropics.* New York: Macmillan, 1898

Krenn, Heliéna. *Conrad's Lingard Trilogy: Empire, Race, and Women in the Malay Novels.* New York: Garland Publishing, 1990

Mahood, Molly. *The Colonial Encounter.* London: Collins, 1977

Morel, E. D. *History of the Congo Reform Movement.* 1924. Ed. Roger Louis and Jean Stengers. Oxford: Clarendon Press, 1968

Mphahlele, Ezekiel. *The African Image.* New York: Praeger, 1974

Najder, Zdzisław. *Joseph Conrad: A Chronicle.* Tr. Halina Carroll-Najder. New Brunswick. NJ: Rutgers University Press; Cambridge: Cambridge University Press, 1983

Nazareth, Peter. 'Out of darkness: Conrad and other third world writers'. *Conradiana* 14.3 (1982), 172–87

Parry, Benita. *Conrad and Imperialism: Ideological Boundaries and Visionary Frontiers.* London: Macmillan, 1983; Topsfield, MA: Salem Academy/Merrimack Publishing, 1984

Pratt, Mary Louise. *Imperial Eyes.* London: Routledge & Kegan Paul, 1992

Rushdie, Salman. *Imaginary Homelands.* London: Granta, 1992

Said, Edward. *Culture and Imperialism.* New York: Knopf, 1993

Orientalism. New York: Random House, 1978

Saveson, John E. *Joseph Conrad: The Making of a Moralist.* Amsterdam: Rodopi, 1972

Sharp, Jenny. 'Figures of colonial resistance'. *Modern Fiction Studies* 35 (1989), 137–55

Sherry, Norman. *Conrad's Eastern World.* Cambridge: Cambridge University Press, 1966

Sherry, Norman, ed. *Conrad: The Critical Heritage.* London: Routledge & Kegan Paul, 1973

Szczypien, Jean M. 'Conrad's *A Personal Record*'. *The Conradian* 15.2 (1991), 12–32

Tennant, Roger. *Joseph Conrad: A Biography.* London: Sheldon Press; New York: Atheneum, 1981

Thornton, A. P. *The Imperial Idea and its Enemies.* London: Macmillan, 1985

Watt, Ian. *Conrad in the Nineteenth Century.* Berkeley: University of California Press, 1979; London: Chatto & Windus, 1980

Watts, C. T., ed. *Joseph Conrad's Letters to R. B. Cunninghame Graham.* Cambridge: Cambridge University Press, 1969

Weber, Eugen. *A Modern History of Europe.* New York: Norton, 1971

White, Andrea. *Joseph Conrad and the Adventure Tradition: Constructing and Deconstructing the Imperial Subject.* Cambridge: Cambridge University Press, 1993

Zelnick, Stephen. 'Conrad's *Lord Jim*: meditations on the other hemisphere'. *Minnesota Review* 11 (1978), 73–89

11

KENNETH GRAHAM

Conrad and Modernism

I

If we take 'Modernism' to mean certain fundamental and more or less shared characteristics of those writers, thinkers, and artists of the period 1900–30, in Britain, Europe, America, and elsewhere, who are now (subjectively and from our own stance in history) seen as the most 'new' or responsive or influential of that time, it seems inevitable that Conrad should figure in that grouping.[1]

In terms of dating there is little doubt about this. The period of his major creativity is from 'Heart of Darkness' (1899) to at least *Under Western Eyes* (1911) and possibly beyond, to *Victory* (1915) and *The Shadow-Line* (1917). During that period there also appeared Freud's *Interpretation of Dreams* (1900), Einstein's theory of relativity (1905), William James's *Pragmatism* (1907), and Jung's *Psychology of the Unconscious* (1912). In 1907, the year of *The Secret Agent*, Picasso's *Les Demoiselles d'Avignon* revolutionized modern painting, and saw the birth of Cubism (hailed by Apollinaire in 1913). In 1908, Schönberg composed his first complex atonal pieces, and changed the course of modern music; Proust, in 1913, published the first volumes of *A la recherche du temps perdu*, which in its own way changed the tonality of modern fiction (and was at once read and admired by Conrad). In 1912, the year of Conrad's dream-like narrative of the double self, 'The Secret Sharer', Mann published *Death in Venice*, perhaps the most resonant, and certainly the most Nietzschean, of Modernism's characteristic studies of self-division. In 1914, Conrad's *Chance* came out at the same time as Gide's *Les Caves du Vatican* (an author whom Conrad knew and, with reservations, admired). Rilke's *New Poems*, in 1907–8, and his prose work, *Malte Laurids Brigge*, in 1910, were milestones in the development of Symbolism and in the exploration of the growing alienation of the creative sensibility from the contemporary world. Kafka's 'Metamorphosis' appeared in 1915, which was something of an *annus mirabilis*, being the year of Conrad's *Victory*, of Woolf's first novel, *The Voyage Out*, Dorothy Richardson's *Pointed Roofs*, Ford's *The Good Soldier*, Lawrence's *The Rainbow*, the last volume of Frazer's *The Golden Bough*, Eliot's 'The Love Song of J. Alfred Prufrock', and the serial version of Joyce's *A Portrait of the Artist as a Young Man*. In 1917, the year of *The Shadow-Line*, Pound's first three *Cantos*, Valéry's *La Jeune Parque*, and Yeats's *The Wild Swans at Coole* were published. And in the years before Conrad's death in 1924, Eliot's *The Waste Land* (1922), Joyce's *Ulysses* (1922), and Forster's *A Passage to India* (1924) set the seal on the achievements of literary Modernism in English.

Nevertheless, much of Conrad's writing might be seen, initially at least, to continue the nineteenth-century realist tradition: for example, the opening description of Verloc's walk across London in *The Secret Agent*, or the graphic narrative of Jim's adventures on Patusan in *Lord Jim*, or the St Petersburg section of *Under Western Eyes*. The presence of a pragmatic, observing, realist's eye always persists in Conrad, even when so much of his tendency, as in 'Heart of Darkness' and *Victory*, is to convey the underlying dream-effect that erodes the normal solidity of the world. Conrad may be a Modernist in his capacity to tear away the surface of things and to show certain of his characters hypnotized and fatally becalmed by the falling-away of physical appearances. But his partial attachment to a nineteenth-century tradition – confirmed by his admiration for Balzac, Flaubert, and Maupassant – is what allowed him to demonstrate how resistant the world is, for good as well as for bad, to the dangerous play of consciousness, and to express with intensity the tension between the two.[2] And it is noteworthy, and entirely typical, that in a statement of his credo as a novelist made in 1902 to Blackwood, his then publisher, he claimed that, unlike George Eliot, he was 'modern', but went on to describe his modernity in terms that George Eliot or even Balzac might well have subscribed to: 'in its essence [my work] is action ... action observed, felt and interpreted with an absolute truth to my sensations (which are the basis of art in literature) – action of human beings that will bleed to a prick, and are moving in a visible world' (*Letters*, II, p. 418).

That letter interestingly associates surface realism of technique with the subject-matter, and therefore the theme, of 'action'. And this, too, is one of the most important pre-modern elements of Conrad's mind, which, as in the case of his 'realism', made his Modernism, his distrust of action, paradoxically the more forcible. He highlighted the horror and omnipresence of loss of will – which is at least a part of Kurtz's perception of 'horror', and therefore also of T. S. Eliot's 'The Hollow Men' (1925), which took the death of Kurtz for its epigraph – by the very stubbornness with which a part of his mind clung to a nineteenth-century image of the hero, the man of action. (His earliest reading included James Fenimore Cooper and Captain Marryat.) At various levels, Conrad's novels and tales can be seen to contain vestigial images or even parodies of their nineteenth-century forerunners. *Lord Jim* and *Nostromo*, for example, are tales of heroic self-justification and initiation through physical action. *Victory* is the tale of a high-souled solitary fighting the forces of evil on his tropical island for the sake of a woman in distress. And parody, comic or uncomic, as in Eliot, Pound, Joyce, or Kafka, becomes one of Modernism's favoured genres. Only a writer, like Conrad, whose mind could still entertain nineteenth-century images of heroism and meaningful action – including Polish Romantic images of the same – could offer a fully dramatic and involved critique of those same images and values.[3]

Another important nineteenth-century 'presence' within the shaping of Conrad's fiction is the Victorian formula, almost obsessive in the Victorian novel, of individual moral choice. Conrad resembles George Eliot in few things, but certainly in this: both novelists construct their plots around crises of moral testing and are always concerned to analyze the underlying causes and widespread effects of a crucial act of decision on the part of an individual. In the characteristic words of George Eliot's own motto to chapter 30 of *Middlemarch* (1881): 'Our deeds still travel with us from afar, / And what we have been makes us what we are'. With the same interest in the complex pathology of choice, Conrad sees the individual life as forever shaped by a moment of loss of nerve, in the case of Jim and Razumov, or by a moment of willed commitment, as in the case of Decoud and Nostromo, or by a casual, lazy act of egotism, such as Verloc's decision to make fatal use of Stevie. Far more than is common with other Modernist writers, with perhaps the exception of Lawrence, Conrad lays enormous stress on personal responsibility and critical moments of moral testing; and this one aspect of his view of life seems to emerge directly from the nineteenth-century liberal tradition: the anguished liberal tradition that runs from John Stuart Mill (and even earlier, from Wordsworth) through the fiction of Trollope and George Eliot to Henry James.

Even if we acknowledge the strong sense of an impersonal destiny and doom in Conrad's novels that clearly detracts from the idea of personal free will – '*An impenetrable mystery seems destined to hang for ever over this act of madness or despair*' (SA, p. 228) – we would have to remember that this sense of doom, too, is as much a late-Victorian as a Modernist characteristic. Through the 1880s and 1890s Hardy and Gissing had fully expressed the late nineteenth-century pessimistic idea of the universe as a hostile and irresistible force that makes a mockery of the idea of independent responsibility – and Hardy's conclusion to *Tess of the D'Urbervilles*, 'The President of the Immortals … had ended his sport with Tess' had in 1891 a resonance that exactly anticipates the 'all-conquering jaws of darkness' at the end of 'Heart of Darkness' or the 'impenetrable mystery' of Winnie's suicide in *The Secret Agent*. Not for the last time in this account of Conrad, are we left with the sense of a defining contradictoriness in his writing: in this case, that he seemed to have combined George Eliot's insistence on the individual's responsibility for his or her fate with Hardy's blanketing determinism. To have taken up two such opposed strains, both set deep in pre-Modernist sensibility, and transmitted them, in uneasy juxtaposition and with a new anxious edge and language of his own, to the new century's intellectual arena was not the least of Conrad's paradoxical contributions to Modernism.

II

To see Conrad in a nineteenth-century context (and it is easy to forget that he was born as early as 1857, when Dickens and Thackeray were still writing) is not just to detect traces of an older mentality or technique still operative within his twentieth-century fictions, but to query the whole idea that a clear border-line divides the two centuries. When we think of Conrad's pessimism in a context of Hardy and Gissing, for example, we think of the well-documented influence of Schopenhauer's philosophy of universal pessimism – and his *The World as Will and Idea* was published almost at the beginning of the century, in 1819. Yet such scepticism, based on a denial of free will and immortality, and on the chilling notion that the world itself is a malignant illusion, passes straight into the twentieth-century scepticism that is traditionally seen as one of Modernism's dominating features. So that Conrad's own philosophic scepticism looks both backwards and forward. It looks back to Schopenhauer (whom he had read); and it also looks back to Nietzsche (whom he disliked and may possibly have read), whose assertion of the relativity of all values and privileging of the darker urges of human nature dates from the 1880s.[4] Yet simultaneously, his searing scepticism, the most dominant of his mental traits, looks forward to the world-picture of fragmentation, contingency, and provisionality that underlies the main Modernist writings of the 1920s. A famous letter compares the universe to an impersonal machine: 'It knits us in and it knits us out. It has knitted time space, pain, death, corruption, despair and all the illusions – and nothing matters' (*Letters*, I, p. 425). And in another letter: 'Faith is a myth and beliefs shift like mists on the shore; thoughts vanish; words, once pronounced, die; and the memory of yesterday is as shadowy as the hope of to-morrow' (*Letters*, II, p. 17). Such reductiveness may echo Hardy; but it is as bleakly powerful and as annunciatory for the age to come as Mrs Moore's encounter with the emptiness of the Absolute in Forster's Marabar Caves in *A Passage to India*, or Quentin Compson's final vision of sawdust-filled figures trapped in the ticking of a watch in Faulkner's *The Sound and the Fury* (1929).

Similarly, Conrad's debt to Flaubert and Maupassant as literary realists seems to point backwards.[5] But the mental attitude, and above all the fictional technique, of impersonality that connects Conrad to the French realists points forward to another of Modernism's main facets: its tendency to aim at detachment, at the perfectly encapsulating and 'objective' image (as in Pound and the Imagists), and at deploying personae and narrative intricacy to provide a multiplicity of viewpoints that will conceal the artist yet express his view – his sceptical view – of the world's lack of fixed meaning. The omnipresence, indeed the omnivorousness, of irony in Conrad's fiction bespeaks a Flaubertian (and nineteenth-century) detachment. But equally, along with his use of Marlow and others as internal narrators, and other devices of narrative obliquity and distancing, the technique of impersonality leads straight into Ford's *The Good Soldier*, Fitzgerald's *The Great Gatsby* (1925), Hemingway's *In Our Time* (1925), Eliot's use of the Tiresias persona and the other voices of *The Waste Land*, and to what Joyce consciously elaborated, out of Flaubert, and via his artist-hero Stephen Dedalus, as the keynote of his own art: 'The artist, like the God of the creation, remains within or behind or beyond or above his handiwork, invisible, refined out of existence, indifferent, paring his fingernails' (*A Portrait of the Artist as a Young Man*, p. 233).

As well as being a writer steeped in Fenimore Cooper, Balzac, Hugo, Dickens, and Turgenev, and under the influence of Flaubert and later realists, Conrad was also a writer who began in the Nineties, a period that more and more appears as the forerunner, and even as the first stage, of Modernism. Much of early Pound and Eliot, a great deal of Yeats and Stevens, much of Joyce's *A Portrait of the Artist* (and certainly his poems), early Lawrence and much of Faulkner, and certain central aspects of Woolf's sensibility and language, come straight from the so-called Decadent Movement: above all, from its use of image and symbol, from its conscious blurring of the outlines of things in order to release more spiritual suggestions from within, its view of the artist as having replaced the priest, its sardonic dismissal of the world of action and of morality, its stylization and even denial of 'character', its love of form, and its basic urge to replace the natural and contemporary world by another, art-generated reality. Conrad had overtly nothing good to say for the Symbolistes as a whole (and some derision for Maeterlinck in particular), though he knew the writings of poets like Baudelaire and Rimbaud, close to the Symbolistes, and may well have been influenced by Villiers de l'Isle-Adam in his conception of Axel Heyst in *Victory*, as well as by the Symboliste-influenced rhetoric of Pierre Loti. The main similarity to the sensibility and ideas of the Nineties lies in Conrad's frequent rhetorical invocation of 'mystery' and the 'unutterable', his glorification of the lonely artist (as in the Preface to *The Nigger of the 'Narcissus'*), and perhaps above all in his insertion of episodes of dream-like experience, of hallucination, the effects of sudden loss of practical will, the sense of the world's reality falling away, into almost all his narratives of practical action and search – the disorienting effects of the river's fog on Marlow in 'Heart of Darkness', the evocation of a paralyzing darkness in the Isabels episode of *Nostromo* and throughout *The Shadow-Line*, Razumov's long entrapment amid the phantasmagoria and unreal voices of the Château Borel, and Heyst's doomed brooding and inertia on Samburan.

To place Conrad in a context of the Nineties only confirms the continuity between that decade and the thirty years that followed, and this is further confirmed – both for Conrad and for the Nineties – by considering the historically transitional figure with whom Conrad was far more closely associated than with any writer of the Decadence: that is, Henry James.[6]

His 1905 essay, 'Henry James: An Appreciation', reprinted in *Notes on Life and Letters*, is the only considerable piece of criticism Conrad wrote on any of his contemporaries, apart from two slight pieces on Stephen Crane and one on Galsworthy. The things that Conrad singles out are that James is a hero of art by his 'volume and force', and his characters are heroes – presumably also heroines – by their ability to renounce for the sake of virtue; that 'imperishable consciousness' is somewhere at the centre of James's achievement, and that he is a 'historian of fine consciences' (Conrad seems to equate 'consciousness' and 'conscience') and therefore of 'essentials'. This is a pretty thin account of James, for all the essay's honorific rhetoric. But it does at least clarify two of the most important features that link the two writers: the exalted view of the responsibility and potentiality of the novel as a form, and the overriding importance in art of inwardness ('consciousness' and 'conscience') and of 'essentials'. Conrad's heroizing of the artist here anticipates Stephen Dedalus's evocation of the mythic father of art, Daedalus, the 'old artificer', and 'the uncreated conscience of my race' as the goal of his own creativity, at the end of *A Portrait of the Artist*. It anticipates Virginia Woolf's artist-figure, Bernard, at the end of *The Waves* (1931), celebrating the 'perpetual warfare' and effort of his consciousness against 'formlessness' and the falling of time's waves; the dying triumph-and-loss of Mann's artist-hero and artist-victim, Aschenbach, on the beach at Venice, in *Death in Venice*; Wallace Stevens's lyrical apotheosis of the poet as the spiritual fount and formal shaper of all values; and even, beyond the strict historic limits of such Modernist triumphalism, Faulkner's 1950 Nobel Prize acceptance speech, with its perfectly Conradian eulogy of the artist's toil and 'endurance', the 'dying evening' of the awaiting apocalypse, and 'the agony and sweat of the human spirit'. For all that 'Modernism' so often evokes an image of irony, non-commitment, pessimism, and ellipsis, it also has running right through it, from Conrad's Preface to *The Nigger of the 'Narcissus'* and his essay on James to the very end of the half-century, a strain that directly celebrates the artist's high craft and spirituality, his priestly transmission of 'all the truth of life', and is as exalted as any Renaissance or Romantic paean on behalf of poetry.

James, in whom the early twentieth-century religion of art found one of its most illustrious examples – yet at the same time one of its most subtly deprecating critics – took his concern with consciousness, mediated through an extreme eccentricity of language, into areas of experience untouched by Conrad. And, on the other hand, Conrad pushed the language of rhetorical suggestion and his fictional images of nightmare, existential betrayal, and personal disintegration beyond the reaches of even James's haunted imagination. The four lovers and plotters of *The Golden Bowl* (1904), yoked together in a system of lying and evasion, take one another into the outskirts of hell, but in the end the broken bowl, figuratively, is patched together again – if at a cost. And in that same year, 1904, Conrad, more unsparingly than James, ended *Nostromo*, as he began it, on the all-devouring image of the 'dark gulf' ironically named Placido. The conscious pursuit of structural coherence and elegance, of indirect modes of narration, the underlying sceptical anxiety about human nature and culture, the fascination with acts of betrayal and lying, and with the downfall of idealists, the overall meditative presence, more felt than revealed, of the author, all these and more connect James and Conrad in ways far more profound than either of them recognized in their mutually inadequate critical accounts of the other's writing. (Conrad was very hurt by James's disparaging account of *Chance* in his review-article, 'The Younger Generation', in 1914.) In the exemplary shaping and analytic intensity of their fiction, they transmitted to their contemporaries the experience of being between two worlds: the American and the Polish expatriot, both brought up in their respective traditions of idealism and commitment to values-in-action, and now confronting with comparable intelligence and feeling and formal experimentation, in their new modern age, its broken bowl and its heart of darkness.

III

Despite the continuity of the nineteenth and twentieth centuries, there is no doubt that for the artists and thinkers themselves, and for their audience, the years around 1910 seemed to be a new dawn of almost fearful volatility. Virginia Woolf, in 1924, put it with only slight facetiousness: 'on or about December 1910 human character changed' ('Character in Fiction', p. 421). And her husband Leonard Woolf, looking back over fifty years later, described 1911 as a year when he 'lived in a kaleidoscopic dream': 'it was exciting to be alive in London ... Profound changes were taking place in every direction ... Freud and Rutherford and Einstein were at work beginning to revolutionize our knowledge of our own minds and of the universe. Equally exciting things were happening in the arts' (*Beginning Again*, p. 37). And Wyndham Lewis's manifesto for the new and (he hoped) epoch-making periodical, *Blast*, in 1914, did no more than harness to its own hectoring style and its own chosen metaphor of the shape of a vortex to express radical renovation, an energy that had clearly already been unleashed on the artistic scene: 'Long live the Vortex! Long live the great art vortex sprung up in the centre of this town! ... We need the unconsciousness of humanity – their stupidity, animalism and dreams. We believe in no perfectibility except our own' ('Long live the vortex', pp. 42–6). And so it went on, Blasting.

Aloof, fastidious, a scion of the Polish gentry transposed to the Kentish countryside, Conrad could hardly have been impressed by the raucousness of *Blast* as the organ of its age, despite the (fragile) common link of Ford Madox Ford between him and Wyndham Lewis. Nevertheless, he had plenty to say on precisely such topics as the unconsciousness of humanity, its stupidity, animalism, dreams, and selfish delusions of perfectibility. The new age – whether of 1910 or 1914 or 1924, and whether its spokesman was Wyndham Lewis or T. S. Eliot or even the maverick D. H. Lawrence – was nothing if it was not sardonic, knowing, exhortatory, and concerned to expose the buried truths of human nature. 'Truth stripped of its cloak of time' is one of the many ringing phrases of 'Heart of Darkness' (*HD*, p. 187) – Conrad's *Blast*, so to speak – that catches something of this Modernist mood of bleak-eyed, undeluded penetration beneath the shams of an older, conventional generation. Kurtz has many facets in Conrad's and in Marlow's shifting presentation of him, but a major one is that of the specifically modern hero: diabolic in the concentration of his deviant will and his intellectual gaze, pursuing forbidden experience with the inverted dedication of a questing knight-at-arms, contemptuous of others and of himself, radical and unsatisfied, without outer convention or inner core, the lonely alien in our midst. He is the subverting *étranger*, the man-without-qualities (in Musil's phrase), who overthrows all the impostures and seeming values of the world around him:

> This is the reason why I affirm that Kurtz was a remarkable man. He had something to say. He said it. Since I had peeped over the edge myself, I understand better the meaning of his stare, that could not see the flame of the candle, but was wide enough to embrace the whole universe, piercing enough to penetrate all the hearts that beat in the darkness. He had summed up – he had judged. 'The horror!' He was a remarkable man. After all, this was the expression of some sort of belief; it had candour, it had conviction, it had a vibrating note of revolt in its whisper, it had the appalling face of a glimpsed truth – the strange commingling of desire and hate.   (*HD*, p. 241)

Here surely, eleven years before 'human character changed' for Virginia Woolf, is a keynote for the new age far more complex and significant than the drum-beating of a Wyndham Lewis. The perception of an underlying and ungraspable 'horror' in experience, of 'truth' being 'appalling', and even the ambiguity of the word 'horror' in its context as a word of moral 'judgement' yet also, cancellingly, a word of 'revolt' and of the amoral passions of 'desire' and 'hate' – all this, together with the posture of one intense and damned individual taking on 'the whole universe', and heroic in having 'something' to say, no matter how damnable the word, is an almost formal manifesto for the epoch of relativism, anxiety, and logocentricity.

'Heart of Darkness' calls for some further consideration as a Modernist manifesto, announcing in 1899 the note of its new era. The tale in its very essence concerns the unspoken, the buried side of human nature, with Kurtz as Marlow's unacknowledged other self – at the very outset of what many have seen as essentially the Freudian age.[7] Freud's writings themselves, from *Studies in Hysteria* (1895) and *The Interpretation of Dreams* (1900) through *Totem and Taboo* (1912–13) and *Civilization and its Discontents* (1920), had a very mixed reaction from writers like Joyce and Woolf, a hostile reaction from Lawrence, and overtly none at all from Conrad. But the development of 'stream of consciousness' by the first two of these writers as an expressive technique in narration could hardly have been possible without the revolutionary impact of Freudian concepts of the unconscious and of the role of free association in the workings of consciousness. Even more basically, the pronounced shift in the basis of characterization in fiction after about 1900, from the outward to the inner, from the mode of action to the mode of concealed motivation, dream, reverie, and atavistic drive, from the traditional area of chronological time and outward space to the radically new dimensions of psychological time and non-logical organization, suggests if not necessarily Freud's direct influence then at the very least a widely shared re-orienting of perception about the individual that deserves to bear his name as its most systematic and articulate theorizer. As W. H. Auden put it in his 'In Memory of Sigmund Freud' (1939): 'To us he is no more a person / Now but a whole climate of opinion / Under whom we conduct our differing lives' (*Selected Poems*, p. 93).

'Heart of Darkness', characteristically, is not simply about Marlow's pursuit of his double, his shadow self, in neo-Freudian or even Jungian terms (a theme repeated intermittently throughout Conrad's work, through 'The Secret Sharer' and *Victory* down to *The Shadow-Line*), but is specifically Modernist in that its technique as a narrative directly reflects its descent into the disorienting world of a new psychology. The dislocating achronological technique of frequent anticipation and flashback, the only half-explained repetition and mirroring of leitmotifs (the knitters in the Brussels office, the incubus-like weight of the dead helmsman and of Kurtz, the disembodied voices, the open mouth), the incongruous encounters (the Harlequin), the extreme variations of tempo, the occasional grotesque humour, the general atmosphere of dream and hallucination can all be seen as formal devices to destabilize creatively the familiar structures of knowledge and the self, and to release the Freudian 'discontents' of a hidden reality, the Kurtzian world of primeval power-seeking and gratification, into the 'civilization' of our everyday consciousness.

'Heart of Darkness' also has some of that quality of myth that, simultaneous with Freudianism and closely allied to it, so formed the literary imagination of the early part of the century.[8] The quest-structure of the narrative, its pattern of the questing hero being initiated through tests, its related pattern of the reluctant acolyte hunting down, 'slaying', and replacing the older figure of authority, so close to the basic myth-pattern of the young priest sacrificing and absorbing the old that Frazer disseminated in *The Golden Bough* (1890–1915), along with the mythic hints of the Parcae in the knitters, of the Congo as universal snake, of the malign and the benign goddesses in the Savage Queen and the Intended: all these, and more, are examples of what Eliot, having himself demonstrated the new usability of myth in *The Waste Land*, was to hail as innovatory in Joyce's *Ulysses*:

> In using the myth, in manipulating a continuous parallel between contemporaneity and antiquity, Mr. Joyce is pursuing a method which others must pursue after him ... It is simply a way of controlling, of ordering, of giving a shape and a significance to the immense panorama of futility and anarchy which is contemporary history ... Instead of narrative method, we may now use the mythical method. It is, I seriously believe, a step towards making the modern world possible for art.   ('*Ulysses*, order and myth', pp. 198–202)

But more innovatory, because more total than its use of myth, and at least as significant as its positing of an unconscious zone in personal experience, was the epistemological ambiguity of 'Heart of Darkness'. Borne out as it was to be by almost all of Conrad's other major writings, this ambiguity was enough in itself to constitute an early manifesto of a Modernism that came to define itself in opposition to the positivistic, mechanical view of the universe that saw meaning as objective and single, and to the idea of the artist as, in George Eliot's phrase, 'natural historian', extracting and presenting a single kernel of meaning, untroubled by the constitutive (and even destructive) role of consciousness and of words in meaning. The whole force of 'Heart of Darkness' seems from beginning to end fixed on challenging the idea of single meaning, and the related idea that the act of communication in words is reliable. Marlow sets a keynote by querying the validity of his own (Conradian) act of verbal tale-telling in such a way as to associate such artistic anxiety with the book's philosophic anxiety concerning truth and personal identity:

> Do you see the story? Do you see anything? It seems to me I am trying to tell you a dream – making a vain attempt, because no relation of a dream can convey the dream-sensation ... that notion of being captured by the incredible which is of the very essence of dreams...
>
> No it is impossible. We live, as we dream – alone...   (*HD*, p. 172)

And there is nothing more radically ambiguous in modern English fiction than the 'dream-sensation', the 'word', of Kurtz's concluding cry, 'The horror! The horror!' (p. 239). This can be either an ethical judgement against himself (thereby sustaining the concept of human values) or a summing-up of the 'truth' about life that destroys the whole basis of ethical judgement and humanist confidence – a doubleness that is then echoed in the concluding ambivalence over whether Marlow's lie to the Intended meaningfully asserts the values of idealism and generosity, or whether it marks his final succumbing to the 'death' – the 'darkness' – he has always identified with lying. Exemplary Modernist ambiguities such as whether Joyce's Stephen Dedalus is ironized or not for his intellectual and aesthetic flights in *A Portrait of the Artist*, and whether the 'forms' achieved by Mrs Ramsay and by Lily Briscoe are vital or illusory set against the chaos of passing time in *To the Lighthouse* (1927), or whether Ursula Brangwyn in *The Rainbow* (1915) is more self-creative than destructive of others in her search for the new, seem almost tame in comparison. The most comparable exercise in ambiguity would perhaps be Forster's *A Passage to India*, which does two opposed things with equal power. On the one hand, it forcefully upholds the life of personal relationships, feeling, and intelligence. And, on the other, its vision of the Marabar Caves demonstrates that the Absolute, though it may accidentally touch on human values, is basically other, alien to all values and to all graspable meaning.

Still taking 'Heart of Darkness' as representing what is strongest and most characteristic in Conrad, another of its features that might have gone to constitute an early Modernist manifesto is its pronounced current in the direction of the apocalypse. Even without the hint from Francis Ford Coppola's film *Apocalypse Now*, we can detect Conrad's tug towards the eschatological: towards the image of a final, universal dissolution. Kurtz, in his last words, 'had made that last stride, he had stepped over the edge ... the threshold of the invisible' (p. 241). And 'darkness' becomes a concluding invocation in which everything – the 'saving illusion' of the Intended's faith in an empty ideal, the listeners, the 'tranquil waterway', and 'the ends of the earth' – are all swallowed up: 'I had a vision of [Kurtz] on the stretcher, opening his mouth voraciously, as if to devour all the earth with all its mankind' (p. 245). It is like the final apocalyptic image of the Professor, planning the 'ruin and destruction' of the world, in the last lines of *The Secret Agent*; or the single concluding word 'Nothing' on which the ironically-named *Victory*, like Heyst, its hero, finally consumes itself. And while concluding disasters are as old as literature itself, Modernism seems to articulate some irresistible tendency towards an image of all-embracing destruction or at least of some terrible final revelation. This is what Frank Kermode, comparing it to the late mediaeval preoccupation with the day of doom, sees as Modernism's one 'persistent world-view' from the Nineties onwards: 'the sense of an ending or the trembling of the veil' ('The Modern', p. 40). And again: 'Apocalypse is a part of the modern Absurd' (*The Sense of an Ending*, p. 123).

Even Lawrence, who fought against the apocalyptic pessimism of his contemporaries – 'why this giving in before you start, that pervades all Conrad and such folks – the Writers among the Ruins. I can't forgive Conrad for being so sad and for giving in'[9] – is as drawn as any of them by the allure of the apocalypse – for example, in his nightmare vision in *St Mawr* (1925) of a world filled with the 'swollen rottenness of our teeming existences', which needs destruction and 'a break' to be made clean again. Yeats's famous figure of the 'rough beast' that 'slouches towards Bethlehem to be born' while 'mere anarchy is loosed upon the world', at the end of 'The Second Coming' (1919), is often seen as having struck the keynote of apocalyptic Modernism. But it was long anticipated in Conrad's equally haunting image of Kurtz's open mouth – a long, long way from Bethlehem – railing, pleading, threatening, and devouring all the earth.

IV

One particular characteristic of Conrad's writing, closely related to the foregoing, helps to focus his relationship with other major novelists in English of the Modernist movement. This is the intellectual tension and narrative obliquity that arise from an explosive contradiction between two things: on the one hand, Conrad's belief in order, duty, solidarity, and, on the other, his intuitive perception, more like an obsession or a dream than a conscious belief, of some primary chaos that negates all order, duty, and solidarity. In one aspect he is a moral ironist, no writer being quicker to pounce on instances of self-delusion, hypocrisy, moral laziness, sentimentalism: on the Donkins, Verlocs, Peter Ivanoviches, Schombergs, Sotillos, and Massys of his fictional world. Yet in another aspect, and simultaneously – and this is why these contradictions so affect the forms of his fiction – his irony goes far beyond the ethical, and erodes equally the characters and attitudes that might have offered alternatives to his bilge-rats and false pilgrims and treacherous self-seekers. It erodes Marlow, who succumbs to the 'death' that is present in his lie to the Intended; it erodes figures like Captains Allistoun, MacWhirr, and Ellis, whose upholding of the seamanly code of duty is undercut by their woodenness and imperceptiveness; it erodes a Winnie Verloc whose sisterly love, the only positive thing in the loveless world of *The Secret Agent*, is undercut by a moral myopia and laziness similar to her husband's; it erodes a Mrs Gould who has connived at the petrification of her husband; it erodes even the self-torturing Razumov by sardonically depriving his final act of confession, for which the whole narrative has been aching, of any real meaningful relief for him or effect on others. Conrad's irony is as unsparing and voracious as Kurtz's open mouth, and he finds himself continually in the intellectually intolerable, but imaginatively exciting, position of subverting by dramatic irony the values, language, and concepts he also upholds by irony. What redeems the self-contradiction in terms of artistic effect is quite simply the passion with which it is lived out, and what makes it 'modern' is its extremism, its only half-disguised totality, and the particular volatility of narrative forms and language that it gives rise to.

For example, when Stein, in the pivotal chapter 20 of *Lord Jim*, oracularly endorses Jim's commitment to the 'destructive element' of his sham-heroic image of himself, this deconstruction by Conrad of Conrad's own moral code of behaviour, the transformation of a moral quandary into an immeasurable mystery, playing myth and symbol against the previous narrative mode of inquest, judgement, and categorization, produces a symptomatically explosive juxtaposition of two utterly irreconcilable images: that of 'a crystalline void' that Stein's candles (and his words) light up ominously in his room, and that of 'absolute Truth' floating, yet approachable, in 'the silent still waters of mystery', apparently also within those same words of Stein about Jim's destiny. The abyss, it seems, is present hollowly within the forms of truth and meaning. Yet truth, carried to its highest authority, as an Absolute, is floating triumphantly but on a void. And the sudden leap in style from the analytic, reflective mode of the *Patna* affair to the heroic-action mode of the Patusan episode is not the flaw, the over-Romantic incongruity it is so often criticized for being, but in fact a striking expression of those inner strains that constitute the book's whole 'case' and interest.[10]

In another succinct example, in 'Heart of Darkness' we find compressed in a stunning throw-away clause a startling conflation of 'evil' and 'truth' that comes close to emptying both of meaning, only a few sentences after the narration has asserted such moral categories by its confident judgement of the 'pilgrims' at the Central Station, 'A taint of imbecile rapacity blew through it all': 'And outside, the silent wilderness . . . struck me as something great and invincible, like evil or truth, waiting patiently for the passing away of this fantastic invasion' (p. 166). When evil can be so easily, so casually identified with truth, there seems little authority left to that act of contemptuous and confident dismissal: 'imbecile rapacity'. Yet Conrad will always remain locked into that paradoxical conflation – 'like evil or truth' – trying to build up his structures of judgement and clarification on 'the redeeming facts of life' (p. 165) as indefatigably as his *other* imagination, his imagination for 'panic and emptiness', in Forsterian phrase, tears them down.[11]

Two further things might be deduced from this proposition about the binary conflict in Conrad's creative temperament. First, it links him significantly with figures like Lawrence, Woolf, Forster, Faulkner, and others, to such an extent that the terms of Conrad's tension might be taken as suggesting a model for Modernism. And, secondly, the doubleness in outlook produces specifically formal characteristics that are in themselves distinctly Modernist.

Even Lawrence, for example, whose didactic mission to reform human nature has for many people placed him outside Modernism's mainstream, invents, like Conrad, an experimental narrative form of juxtaposed opposites, of changing moods and internal crises, of alternating scene and commentary, of transposed rather than consistent symbols, of self-contradiction carried to the degree of implosion – and therefore of revelation. And he does so in response to those fundamental collisions in his thinking and feeling that include at least one polarity as radical as Conrad's: that is, Lawrence's belief in the constructive value of sexual relationships and of 'wholeness of self' set against his transcendental urge towards impersonality and a dehumanizing absolute or elementalism (Ursula's desire to be the moon or a part of the Sussex Downs in *The Rainbow*, Birkin's Pharaonic transfiguration in *Women in Love*, the cult of the leader in *Kangaroo*, the glacier in 'The Captain's Doll'). Lawrence, like Conrad, at a deep level identifies with the very forces of abstraction and disintegration that all his other energies are bent on combatting. And the fact that such inner contradictions are allowed, with hardly any mediation, to be expressed directly, and extremely, in the irregular, vital rhythms and incongruities of a new form is what differentiates between the contradictions common to artists of any era and those specifically of Modernism.

Virginia Woolf, too, sets up as ironic and self-eroding a rhythm as Conrad's, between her vision of form – 'order rules ... some absolute good, some crystal of intensity' – and her darker, more surrealist anarchism – 'gigantic chaos streaked with lightning ... leviathans ... mounted one on top of another' (*To the Lighthouse*, pp. 113, 115). Her play with consciousness and with imagery is far more fluid than anything in Conrad, but the central anxiety is the same, and above all the formal effects of that anxiety being released so extravagantly into Modernist images of grotesque distortion, heightened moments of revelation and turning-point, and a narrative's expressionist enactment of psychological rather than clock time.

Even closer to the Conradian example, Forster's humanist privileging of relationships and sympathetic intelligence, formulated in the motto 'Only connect' in *Howards End* (1910) is characteristically undercut by the virtually Conradian irony of having Margaret Schlegel, in the midst of the concluding scene of plenitude, birth, and harvest, betray herself and her values by the protective lie to her husband that 'Nothing has been done wrong'. Thus the phrase 'again and again fell the word [good-bye], like the ebb of a dying sea' – reminiscent of the 'We have lost the first of the ebb' following Marlow's ultimate lie in 'Heart of Darkness' – startlingly reverses the book's previous current, and like the echoing 'Ou-boum' of the Marabar Caves in *A Passage to India*, creates an irreconcilable heart of darkness in the very centre of Forster's tentative structures of enlightenment and connection.

The forms of Forster's narrative, for all his inheritance from Jane Austen, respond to his own contradictions through devices that are no more, and no less, Modernist than Conrad's: the ironic twists of plot and phrase, the use of anti-climax, the unexpected repetitions and encounters, the sudden only half-controlled moments of violence or melodrama, the switches of tone. Joyce, perhaps, is the most wittily cerebral, and Jesuitical, of them all, and submits his own extremism of psychological investigation and of *outré* technical experiment to a highly controlling and formal suavity of allusiveness, parody, and multi-layered verbal pyrotechnics that makes Conrad in comparison seem almost raw – though therefore all the more suggestive and less systematic. In Faulkner, although Joyce's most obvious disciple in terms of stream-of-consciousness technique, the Conradian model is more dominant, and Faulkner's dynamic equivocations between a dissolving nihilism and an ethical code-building (between the opposed narrative modes of Quentin and of Dilsey in *The Sound and the Fury*) create a fictional texture of violent experiment and dislocation, without the Joycean cool-headed macropaedia to restrain it, and with all the force of Conrad's more open-ended, because more surreptitious, commitment.

The question in the end may come down simply to extremism. Modernism is nothing if not extreme. And perhaps the only way of distinguishing satisfactorily between the contradictions of Modernist writers and of the Romantics are the extreme disjunctions of form that the Modernists' yielding to inner contradiction produced. Romanticism, too, shows much that is paradoxical and unresolved, dynamic rather than fixed, self-centred, self-unmaking, and self-remaking, seeking the 'inward' and the 'essence', in the tradition of a Keats, Novalis, Nietzsche, Baudelaire, or Dostoevsky.[12] But the Conradian self-division is very much of its time in that it expresses its governing antinomy in a particularly fluid and dominating way that is dramatically close to fracture. It does so through such 'discontents' of form as these: varying and unreliable point of view in narration; the 'placing' of overheated, even melodramatic, climaxes; sudden over-compensations or destabilizations by rhetoric and symbol; devastating ironic juxtapositions and repetitions; chronological 'loopings' as perturbing as a maze; violent switches of narrative tempo from claustrophobic slow motion to vivid speed; passages of phantasmagoria or dream set against passages of comparative realism; one authorial voice or tone set against another; and so on. These are some of the strongest marks of Conrad's narrative manner, and in their expressive contradictoriness, their opening up of possibilities that deny narrative closure, their general effect of shape being in a perpetual interplay with fragmentation, desire with fear, self-control with panic, arrogance with self-loss, statement with symbol, lucidity with darkness, they go far beyond the boundaries of his Romantic and nineteenth-century precursors – having, like Kurtz, 'made that last stride ... stepped over the edge'.

All the pressures behind a generation poised 'on the edge' flow into this inner strain and duplicity of Conrad's creative mind. It was an era obsessed, both liberatingly and despairingly, by the sense of its own fragmentation: the break-up of old structures, old conventions of art and thought and politics, with individual personality itself dissolving like a mirror held up to a mirror, or else revealing unconscious strata that could drive, abstract, or transform the self. It was an age of extremism, and it was an age of war, of 'the War to end all Wars'. Possessed by irony, these duplicitous writers of their time turned to extreme forms of experimentation to express their two-edged (and therefore Conradian) view of 'order': they express what Kermode calls in 'the great experimental novels of early Modernism – Kafka, Proust, Joyce, Musil ... a kind of formal desperation' ('The Modern', p. 48). And only some such oxymoron as 'formal desperation', like the virtual oxymoron of 'truth or evil', like the hidden oxymoron of 'heart' and 'darkness', is adequate to suggest the self-vexing dynamism and power of the Conradian enigma: which in its essence was the enigma, and even the driving force, of Modernism itself.

NOTES

1 On Modernism in general, including the many fluctuations in the word's meaning, see Bradbury, *Possibilities*; Bradbury and McFarlane, ed., *Modernism 1890–1930*; Faulkner, *Modernism*; Josipovici, *The Lessons of Modernism*; Kermode, *Modern Essays*; Levin, 'What was Modernism?'; and Spender, *The Struggle of the Modern*.

2 The most comprehensive attempt to set Conrad in this tradition is Watt's *Conrad in the Nineteenth Century*. For an impressively exhaustive account of Conrad and the French tradition, see Hervouet's *The French Face of Joseph Conrad*.

3 For a study of how nineteenth-century adventure fiction shaped Conrad's discourse, see White, ch. 10 of this volume, and her *Joseph Conrad and the Adventure Tradition*. On Conrad's debt to the nineteenth-century Polish tradition, see Najder, *Conrad's Polish Background*, pp. 1–31.

4 On Conrad's debt to Schopenhauer, see Kirschner, *Conrad: The Psychologist as Artist*, pp. 266–75; Knowles, 'Who's afraid of Arthur Schopenhauer?'; and Wollaeger, *Joseph Conrad and the Fictions of Skepticism*, pp. 28–57. On Conrad and Nietzsche, see Johnson, *Conrad's Model of Mind*, and Said, 'Conrad and Nietzsche'.

5 Conrad's admiration for Flaubert and Maupassant, as well as for Anatole France, and the almost alarming extent of his borrowings from all three writers, are very fully documented in Hervouet's *The French Face of Joseph Conrad*.

6 For a discussion of the literary relationship of Conrad and James, see Nettels, *James and Conrad*.

7 Hough's *Image and Experience*, for example, compares the effect of Freud on the arts to that of Plato in the Renaissance. On Freud's impact see, Moore, *The Age of the Modern*, and Nelson, ed., *Freud and the Twentieth Century*.

8 In 'Freud and the future' (1936) Thomas Mann wrote: 'The mythical interest is as native to psychoanalysis as the psychological interest is to all creative writing.

Its penetration into the childhood of the individual soul is at the same time a penetration into the childhood of mankind, into the primitive and mythical ... For the myth is the foundation of life; it is the timeless schema, the pious formula into which life flows when it reproduces its traits out of the unconscious' (p. 317). The whole essay is an important account of Modernism and includes an interesting evaluation of Schopenhauer.

9 Letter to Edward Garnett, 30 October 1912, *The Letters of D. H. Lawrence*, I, p. 465.

10 Batchelor links Marlow, Stein, and Jim, asserting: ' "Romantic" unites these three men reinforcing my sense of them as a triple self-portrait, three aspects of the Conradian identity seeking "solidarity", the reintegration of the suffering and depressed artist' (*The Life of Joseph Conrad*, p. 111).

11 For a detailed analysis of obliquities and tensions in narrative form in 'Heart of Darkness', *Lord Jim*, *Nostromo*, *Under Western Eyes*, and *The Shadow-Line*, see Graham, *Indirections of the Novel*, pp. 93–153.

12 On the intimate links between Modernism and Romanticism, see Bradbury, *The Social Context of Modern English Literature*; Kermode, 'The Modern'; Langbaum, *The Modern Spirit*; and Trilling, 'Art and neurosis' and 'Freud and literature'. See also Thorburn's *Conrad and Romanticism*. Conrad read Baudelaire with appreciation (Hervouet, *The French Face of Joseph Conrad*, pp. 244–6), but his dislike for Dostoevsky was extreme (compared with his admiration for Turgenev.) However, the influence of Dostoevsky – or at least the parallelism between the two writers – has often been commented on. See Guerard, *Conrad the Novelist*, pp. 236–46, and Sandstrom, 'The roots of anguish in Dostoevsky and Conrad'.

WORKS CITED

Auden, W. H. 'In Memory of Sigmund Freud'. *Selected Poems*. Ed. Edward Mendelson. London: Faber & Faber, pp. 91–5

Batchelor, John. *The Life of Joseph Conrad: A Critical Biography*. Oxford: Blackwell, 1994

Bradbury, Malcolm. *Possibilities: Essays on the State of the Novel*. Oxford: Oxford University Press, 1966

The Social Context of Modern English Literature. Oxford: Blackwell, 1971

Bradbury, Malcolm and James MacFarlane, ed. *Modernism 1890–1930*. Harmondsworth: Penguin Books, 1976

Conrad, Joseph. *'Heart of Darkness' and Other Tales*. Ed. Cedric Watts. Oxford: Oxford University Press, 1990

The Secret Agent. 1907. Ed. Bruce Harkness and S. W. Reid. Cambridge: Cambridge University Press, 1990

Eliot, T. S. *'Ulysses*, order and myth'. *Dial* 75 (1923), 480–3.

Faulkner, Peter. *Modernism*. London: Methuen, 1977

Graham, Kenneth. *Indirections of the Novel: James, Conrad, and Forster*. Cambridge: Cambridge University Press, 1988

Guerard, Albert J. *Conrad the Novelist*. Cambridge, MA: Harvard University Press, 1958

Hervouet, Yves. *The French Face of Joseph Conrad*. Cambridge: Cambridge University Press, 1990

Hough, Graham. *Image and Experience: Studies in a Literary Revolution*. London: Duckworth, 1960

Johnson, Bruce. *Conrad's Models of Mind*. Minneapolis: University of Minnesota Press, 1971

Josipovici, Gabriel. 'The Lessons of Modernism' and Other Essays. London: Macmillan, 1977

Joyce, James. *A Portrait of the Artist as a Young Man*. 1915. Ed. Seamus Deane. Harmondsworth: Penguin Books, 1992

Kermode, Frank. 'The Modern'. In *Modern Essays*. London: Collins, 1971, pp. 39–70

'The Modern Apocalypse'. In *The Sense of an Ending*. Oxford: Oxford University Press, 1968, pp. 93–124

Romantic Image. London: Routledge & Kegan Paul, 1957

Kirschner, Paul. *Conrad: The Psychologist as Artist*. Edinburgh: Oliver & Boyd, 1968

Knowles, Owen. ' "Who's afraid of Arthur Schopenhauer?": a new context for Conrad's "Heart of Darkness" '. *Nineteenth Century Literature* 49.1 (1994), 75–106

Langbaum, Robert. *The Modern Spirit: Essays on the Continuity of Nineteenth and Twentieth Century Literature*. New York: Oxford University Press, 1970

Lawrence, D. H. *The Letters of D. H. Lawrence, Volume I*. Ed. James T. Boulton. Cambridge: Cambridge University Press, 1979

Levin, Harry. 'What was Modernism?'. In *Refractions: Essays in Comparative Literature*. New York: Oxford University Press, 1968, pp. 271–95

Lewis, Wyndham. 'Long live the vortex'. *Blast* (1914). Reprinted in *A Modernist Reader: Modernism in England*. Ed. Peter Faulkner. London: Batsford, 1985, pp. 42–6

Mann, Thomas. 'Freud and the future'. In *Essays by Thomas Mann*. New York: Vintage Books, 1958, pp. 303–24

Moore, Harry T. 'The Age of the Modern' and Other Literary Essays. Carbondale: Southern Illinois University Press, 1971

Najder, Zdzisław. Introduction. *Conrad's Polish Background: Letters to and from Polish Friends*. Ed. Zdzisław Najder. Tr. Halina Carroll. London: Oxford University Press, 1964, pp. 1–31

Nelson, Benjamin, ed. *Freud and the Twentieth Century*. London: Allen & Unwin, 1958

Nettels, Elsa. *James and Conrad*. Athens: University of Georgia Press, 1977

Said, Edward. 'Conrad and Nietzsche'. In *Joseph Conrad: An Appreciation*. Ed. Norman Sherry. London: Macmillan, 1976, pp. 65–77

Sandstrom, Glenn. 'The roots of anguish in Dostoevsky and Conrad'. *Polish Review* 20.2–3 (1975), 71–7

Spender, Stephen. *The Struggle of the Modern*. London: Hamish Hamilton, 1963

Thorburn, David. *Conrad's Romanticism*. New Haven: Yale University Press, 1974

Trilling, Lionel. 'Art and neurosis' and 'Freud and literature'. In *The Liberal Imagination*. New York: Doubleday, 1957, pp. 155–75 and 32–54

Watt, Ian. *Conrad in the Nineteenth Century*. Berkeley: University of California Press, 1979; London: Chatto & Windus, 1980

White, Andrea. *Joseph Conrad and the Adventure Tradition: Constructing and Deconstructing the Imperial Subject*. Cambridge: Cambridge University Press, 1993

Wollaeger, Mark A. *Joseph Conrad and the Fictions of Skepticism*. Stanford: Stanford University Press, 1990

Woolf, Leonard. *Beginning Again: An Autobiography of the Years 1911–1918*. London: Hogarth Press, 1964

Woolf, Virginia. 'Character in Fiction'. 1924. *The Essays of Virginia Woolf*. Ed. Andrew McNeillie. London: Hogarth Press, 1988, III, pp. 420–36

To the Lighthouse. 1927. Ed. Susan Dick. Oxford: Blackwell, 1992

12

GENE M. MOORE

Conrad's influence

If it is true, as Conrad once wrote, that 'A man's real life is that accorded to him in the thoughts of other men' (*UWE*, p. 14), then the real life of Joseph Conrad is manifest throughout modern and contemporary literature, and has become a living part of our cultural self-awareness. His works have been translated into more than forty languages, from Albanian and Yiddish to Korean and Swahili. Conrad is one of the defining founders of literary Modernism, and his influence has been acknowledged by writers as different from him, and from each other, as André Gide, Ralph Ellison, Graham Greene, Jorge Luis Borges, V. S. Naipaul, William S. Burroughs, and Italo Calvino, to name only a few. Some of his works have been taken as models for the development of new literary genres. *The Secret Agent* and *Under Western Eyes* were among the first studies of spies who cannot come in from the cold, *Nostromo* is the first panoramic epic of South American colonialism, and 'Heart of Darkness' is frequently invoked as a cultural token signifying the 'horror' at the heart of modern Western civilization. The life and works of Conrad have inspired films, journeys, sculptures, comic books, Conrad societies and journals, and well over one thousand academic books and articles.

Why have Conrad's works had such a profound influence on the way we perceive and define the modern condition? The answer has something to do with the sense in which Conrad is a figure of the crossroads, determined to portray and explore the conflicting loyalties and multiple identities of those who, like him, have been denied their cultural birthright. Conrad writes with the passionate irony of an exile, from the necessarily false position of a cultural colonist who speaks, in a language not quite his own, for both the dispossessed and their dispossessors.

THE PROBLEM OF INFLUENCE

An artist's work influences or 'flows into' the popular imagination in ways that are difficult to trace in detail or describe with precision. Intertextuality has no end or beginning, and Conrad's works can be read as products or signs of the various influences that contributed to the shaping of his own life and literary career. It is possible to cite the comments of writers who have acknowledged their debts to Conrad, and even in the absence of explicit testimonies one can point to parallels and resemblances that seem too striking to be accidental; but in the final analysis we have no terms with which to measure the strength of influence.[1] The nature of influence is not susceptible to proof. Moreover, influence can be negative as well as positive: if an author can serve as a model to emulate, his works can also, as Harold Bloom has shown, provoke an 'anxiety' that engages his followers in an Oedipal struggle to overcome the suffocating dominance of an overwhelmingly eloquent literary patriarch. As a younger writer struggles to absorb and transcend his predecessors, their influence may well manifest itself not only in terms of similarity, but paradoxically also as the very measure of the difference between the younger writer and his or her models. The process of influence is rarely as direct or unitary as this Freudian model implies. As Viktor Shklovsky has suggested, the course of literary history devolves not only from fathers to sons, but also from uncles to nephews, in the form of a 'knight's move' that is not straightforward but oblique. Literary influence travels by many routes, all of them indirect.

The shaping of an author's influence is also conditioned by a variety of factors that have nothing to do with the nature or quality of the works themselves. For critics as well as general readers, Conrad's works tend to be reduced to his 'masterpieces', and these reduced in turn to a few famous catch phrases or mottoes (like Kurtz's 'The horror!' or Marlow's 'one of us'). Shorter texts like 'Heart of Darkness' will often be given precedence over longer ones like *Lord Jim* or *Nostromo* in the selection of representative works for university survey courses. The considerations that determine the formation of canons will also affect the impact of an author's influence. Once it has achieved a certain currency, a given work's canonical standing will be determined by its ability to withstand and remain responsive to the demands of changing critical fashions and popular tastes.

Canons also vary across disciplines and media, and Conrad's influence has extended into film, music, and the visual arts. The 'film canon' of Conrad's works is thus quite different from his literary one. No doubt a great many more people have seen the 'action/adventure' film *Apocalypse Now* (1979) than have read the story on which the script was 'structured', yet this film also disseminates an influence attributable to 'Conrad'. Inspired by 'Heart of Darkness', the American pianist John Powell composed a piece called *Rhapsodie Nègre* and performed it for Conrad in July 1920. In the 1960s and 1970s Conrad's works inspired a number of operas: *Jutro*

('To-morrow') by Tadeusz Baird (Warsaw, 1966), *Under Western Eyes* by John Joubert (London, 1969), *Victory* by Richard Rodney Bennett (London, 1970), and *Lord Jim* by Romuald Twardowski (Warsaw, 1973). As writers go, Conrad was remarkably photogenic, especially in his later years, and his striking personal appearance has been fixed as a memorable image in the public mind. His rugged profile, pointed beard, and heavy eyelids have been portrayed in drawings, paintings, and photographs, and sculptured heads or busts of him were fashioned by Jacob Epstein, Jo Davidson, Bruce Rogers, and Dora Clarke.[2]

As an author's works achieve significance as tokens of cultural literacy, they inevitably become caricatured or distorted, and are readily available as points of reference in arguments that go far beyond merely literary issues. For example, the point of Chinua Achebe's famous charge that 'Conrad was a bloody racist' (Hamner, ed., *Joseph Conrad: Third World Perspectives*, p. 124) was not only to challenge traditional opinions about the ethical values of 'Heart of Darkness', but to argue more generally that the problem of racism lies much deeper in Western culture than is normally recognized or admitted. For this purpose, Conrad's reputation as an arbiter of 'Western eyes' and a spokesperson for Third World populations provided Achebe with a particularly effective target.

THE INNER CIRCLE

Conrad was fortunate in his early friendships. From the moment he settled down to the life of a writer, he found himself in an artistic milieu that included such fellow novelists as John Galsworthy, Henry James, Stephen Crane, and H. G. Wells. Conrad made the deepest impression on Ford Madox Ford, who shared three novels with him and otherwise served him as a secretary and editor. Were it not for Ford's constant encouragement and his willingness to take dictation, it is unlikely that Conrad's two volumes of memoirs, *The Mirror of the Sea* and *A Personal Record*, would ever have been published. As Ford declared to Herbert Read in 1920, 'I learned all I know of Literature from Conrad – and England has learned all it knows of Literature from me' (Ludwig, ed., *Letters of Ford Madox Ford*, p. 127). Although their friendship cooled after 1909, Ford never ceased to admire and venerate Conrad. In his own memoirs, and especially in *Joseph Conrad: A Personal Remembrance* (1924), Ford described the principles of literary impressionism that he and Conrad had developed in the early years of their collaboration. Techniques like the 'time-shift' and the *progression d'effet* can be found throughout Ford's own works, and the fact that Ford provided the original ideas and drafts for their collaborations makes it possible to trace the nature of Conrad's contributions in substantial detail.[3] Ford parodied Conrad in a novel entitled *The Simple Life Limited*; and when Conrad died in 1924, leaving his long-promised 'Mediterranean novel' apparently unfinished, Ford took up the same basic elements of plot and setting and produced a curious sequel to *Suspense* entitled *A Little Less Than Gods* (1928).

Conrad encouraged and helped to 'launch' younger writers like Norman Douglas and Stephen Reynolds. Many of the writers who frequented the Tuesday lunches held in London by Edward Garnett at the Mont Blanc Restaurant in Gerrard Street would remember the force of his personality as well as his prose style. One member of this circle was H. M. Tomlinson, whose account of a voyage by steamer to Brazil, *The Sea and the Jungle* (1912), is written with a fine irony and stylistic precision that immediately recall Conrad's example. Writers like R. B. Cunninghame Graham, who shared Conrad's interest in Latin American themes, and Hugh Walpole, who published a book about Conrad in 1916, remained faithful friends and frequent house guests of the Conrads.

Conrad's personal influence was not limited to English writers only, although his public impact elsewhere would ultimately depend on the availability of translations. He met and was admired by a number of French writers and critics, including Paul Valéry, St.-John Perse, and Valery Larbaud. André Gide translated 'Typhoon' into French and supervised the first French collected edition of Conrad's works; he also dedicated an account of his own travels in the Congo (*Voyage au Congo*, 1927) to the memory of Conrad. G. Jean-Aubry's two-volume *Joseph Conrad: Life and Letters* (1927) was the first sustained attempt to write Conrad's biography.

Not all of Conrad's personal influence was purely literary. His wife Jessie and his two sons published memoirs of their lives with him, and several of his fellow seamen were inspired to set down their recollections of sailing with him, including G. F. W. Hope, J. G. Sutherland, and David Bone.[4]

MODERNIST ECHOES

T. S. Eliot contributed immensely to the propagation of Conrad's influence by taking 'Mistah Kurtz – he dead' as the epigraph to 'The Hollow Men'. Eliot had planned to use Kurtz's 'The horror! The horror!' as the epigraph to *The Waste Land*, but was dissuaded by Ezra Pound. Nevertheless, the association of Conrad with the 'horror' of modern existence owes its origin largely to Eliot.

Conrad's works were not yet taught at Princeton when F. Scott Fitzgerald was a student there, but Fitzgerald studied them closely and applied what he learned from Conrad about indirect narration and disrupted chronology to the writing of the *The Great Gatsby* (1925). Fitzgerald acknowledged his debt to Conrad in a letter to H. L. Mencken, in which he listed not only *Gatsby* but also Eugene O'Neill's play *The Emperor Jones* (1920) and W. Somerset Maugham's *The Moon and Sixpence* (1919) as works written in imitation of Conrad (Turnbull, ed., *Letters of F. Scott Fitzgerald*, p. 482). The idea of using Nick Carraway as a participant-observer was suggested by Conrad's experiments with the indirect narratives of Marlow. Arthur Mizener has suggested that Conrad's influence on *The Great Gatsby* can also be seen in phrases like 'the abortive sorrows and short-winded elations of men'.[5] When Conrad visited the United States in May 1923, Fitzgerald and Ring Lardner tried to attract his attention by performing a drunken dance on the lawn of the Doubleday estate in Oyster Bay, where Conrad was staying; but they were merely caught and expelled by a caretaker. Fitzgerald warned Ernest Hemingway against the influence of Conrad in dialogue: 'like me you must beware of Conrad rhythms in direct quotations from characters, especially if you're pointing a single phrase and making a man live by it' (Turnbull, ed., *Ibid.*, p. 300). Later, when reviewers criticized the undramatic ending of *Tender is the Night* (1934), Fitzgerald defended himself by citing both Conrad and Hemingway: 'I believe it was Ernest Hemingway who developed to me, in conversation, that the dying fall was preferable to the dramatic ending under certain conditions, and I think we both got the germ of the idea from Conrad' (Turnbull, ed., *Ibid.*, p. 363).

In a memorial tribute published in Ford's *transatlantic review*, Hemingway described his own special relation to Conrad's works and argued irreverently against the critical wisdom of the day: 'It is agreed by most of the people I know that Conrad is a bad writer, just as it is agreed that T. S. Eliot is a good writer. If I know that by grinding Mr. Eliot into a fine dry powder and sprinkling that powder over Mr. Conrad's grave Mr. Conrad would shortly appear, looking very annoyed at the forced return, and commence writing I would leave for London early tomorrow morning with a sausage grinder'. Hemingway claimed that he could not reread Conrad, but would save up his works for occasions when 'I needed them badly, when the disgust with writing, writers and everything written of and to write would be too much'. Conrad was often Hemingway's choice for travel reading, and once on a trip to Canada he stayed up all night reading the serial version of *The Rover*, only to regret it the morning after: 'I had hoped it would last me the trip, and felt like a young man who has blown his patrimony' (*By-Line: Ernest Hemingway*, pp. 114–15).

In an interview in 1931, William Faulkner claimed that 'The two books I

like best are *Moby Dick* and *The Nigger of the Narcissus*' (Meriwether and
Millgate, ed., *Lion in the Garden*, p. 21). His taste for Conrad had not
diminished by 1955, when he told another interviewer, 'I read in and out of
Dickens some every year, and in and out of Conrad, the same way, some
every year'; and he recommended *Lord Jim* and *Nostromo* as books that
young writers might read with profit (*Ibid.*, pp. 49, 111). Faulkner's 1950
Nobel Prize acceptance speech has been described as a 'blatant appropriation' of Conrad's 1905 essay on Henry James (Meyers, 'Conrad's influence
on modern writers', p. 191).[6]

Among the most obvious inheritors of the legacy of Conrad is Graham
Greene, who, like Conrad, journeyed to many out-of-the-way places and
witnessed the moral desperation of guilt-ridden colonial administrators in
search of a lost religious or political 'idea'. Thus *The End of the Affair*
(1951) echoes 'The End of the Tether' in its title, while the dubious world
of espionage portrayed in novels like *The Confidential Agent* (1939) and
The Human Factor (1978) and 'entertainments' like *The Ministry of Fear*
(1943) follow in the tradition launched by *The Secret Agent*. *The Come-
dians* (1966) can be read as a latter-day reflection of *Nostromo*, and *A
Burnt-Out Case* (1961) merges elements of *Victory* with the setting of
'Heart of Darkness'. Greene was well aware of his susceptibility to the
force of Conrad's example; this relation is explored in detail in Robert
Pendleton's study *Graham Greene's Conradian Masterplot*. Greene felt
that his own early works like *Rumour at Nightfall* (1931) owed too much
to the later style of *The Arrow of Gold* (in which Greene believed that
Conrad had himself come under the influence of Henry James). As a result,
Greene decided to stop reading Conrad; as he put it, 'I abandoned him
about 1932 because his influence on me was too great and too disastrous'
(*In Search of a Character*, p. 31). Greene kept this vow for twenty-five
years, until he finally took up 'Heart of Darkness' when he decided to
travel to the Congo to gather material for the novel that eventually became
A Burnt-Out Case. His journey to leper colonies on the Congo River is
described in a notebook reprinted as the 'Congo Journal' section of *In
Search of a Character* (1961), which repeats the voyage traced in Conrad's
'Congo Diary'. Greene's travel reading also included Romain Gary's
African novel, *The Roots of Heaven* (*Les Racines du ciel*, 1956), which he
called 'an admirable book if only it were not quite so obviously modelled
on the language and method of Conrad'; he described its protagonist,
Morel, as 'a French Marlow' (*In Search of a Character*, p. 48). Gary,
whose Slavic origins were similar to those of Conrad, later commented on
the originality of Conrad's position as a 'foreign body' in English literature,
and claimed that 'The English have not yet forgiven him for being without

doubt their greatest novelist of this century' (*La Nuit sera calme*, p. 258; translation mine).

Malcolm Lowry registered his respect for Conrad's achievement in an eloquent sonnet written in 1940. More recently, the fictions of Paul Theroux also reveal their author's preoccupation with the settings and themes of Conrad's novels: *Jungle Lovers* (1971) can easily be read as a commentary on 'Heart of Darkness'; *Saint Jack* (1973) owes more than its Singapore setting and its title to *Lord Jim*; and, like Greene's *It's a Battlefield* (1934), Theroux's *The Family Arsenal* (1976) explores the domestic and political implications of terrorism in London along lines first traced by Conrad in *The Secret Agent*.

In an essay called 'Cutting up characters' reprinted in *The Adding Machine: Collected Essays* (1986), William S. Burroughs has admitted that the 'interview' between Carl Peterson and Dr Benway in his novel *Naked Lunch* (1959) was taken directly and deliberately from Councillor Mikulin's interrogation of Razumov in *Under Western Eyes*. He documents his conscious re-use of Conrad by juxtaposing his own text with the relevant passages from the original.

Conrad's extensive influence on modern Polish literature is the subject of a book by Stefan Zabierowski. Conrad also had early admirers in Germany, including Thomas Mann, and his postwar influence has extended throughout Europe. Interesting parallels can be drawn between Siegfried Lenz's novella *Das Feuerschiff* (*The Lightship*, 1960) and Conrad's *Victory*. Like Gide and Greene, Alberto Moravia also mentioned Conrad in connection with his own travels in Africa; and Italo Calvino completed his university studies with a thesis on Conrad.

In one instance, Conrad's novels have served not only as an influential example, but even as the actual setting of a work of fiction: the title story of Howard Norman's *'Kiss in the Hotel Joseph Conrad' and Other Stories* (1989) describes a hotel in Halifax whose owner has papered its hallways with pages from Conrad's books, using a different novel on each floor. Norman pokes fun at the fanaticism of Conradians: 'Occasionally, tourists dropped in, wanting to see the room where the author slept or the table he wrote a book on' (p. 23). The narrator also tells how one night he got drunk and read aloud 'maybe a whole chapter' of *Nostromo* off the walls. (Strictly speaking, the proprietor would have had to sacrifice two copies of the novel to make this possible, but Norman is not concerned with such technicalities, which are not likely to have been noticed by the inebriated narrator.)

By no means all those who have been exposed to Conrad's influence have reacted positively. Edmund Wilson described *Under Western Eyes* as 'about the worst-told story I have ever read' and added that 'The whole book from the end of Part Two seems to be a masterpiece of mishandling' (*Letters on Literature and Politics*, p. 367). Vladimir Nabokov, who was chronically annoyed with the comparisons frequently drawn between his own situation and that of Conrad, dismissed his Polish predecessor as a writer of romantic adventure stories for children:

> I used to enjoy tremendously the romantic productions ... of such people as Conan Doyle, Kipling, Joseph Conrad, Chesterton, Oscar Wilde, and other authors who are essentially writers for very young people. But as I have well said somewhere before, I differ from Joseph Conradically. First of all, he had not been writing in his native tongue before he became an English writer, and secondly, I cannot stand today his polished clichés and primitive clashes. He once wrote that he preferred Mrs. Garnett's translation of *Anna Karenin* to the original! This makes one dream – 'ça fait rêver' as Flaubert used to say when faced with some abysmal stupidity.
>
> (*Strong Opinions*, pp. 56–7)

This last remark evidently refers to Conrad's letter to Edward Garnett of 10 June 1902, where he described the translation as 'splendid' and added, 'Of the thing itself I think but little, so that her merit shines with the greater lustre' (*Letters*, II, p. 425). Whether Conrad knew enough Russian to be able to read 'the thing itself' remains an unresolved mystery.

FICTIONAL BIOGRAPHIES

Conrad's early years were as adventurous as his fictions, and at least three fictionalized biographies or *vies romancées* have explored the relations between episodes in his life and their reflections in his work. Two of these works are by Polish authors and not available in English translation, although Adam Gillon has described them and published excerpts in *Conradiana*. Leszek Prorok's *Smuga Blasku* (*The Radiant Line*, 1982) takes up Conrad's voyage to Mauritius in the *Otago* in 1886 and describes his romantic involvement with two young ladies on the island, Eugénie Renouf and Alice Shaw. In the final section of the novel, his hopes defeated, Korzeniowski sails away and returns to work on his first work of fiction, 'The Black Mate'. *Sprawa w Marsylii* (*The Affair in Marseilles*, 1982), by Wacław Biliński, is concerned with an earlier incident in Conrad's life, when he found himself barred from serving in French ships and had squandered the allowance he received from his uncle Tadeusz Bobrowski. Conrad then borrowed money from a German friend, gambled it away at Monte Carlo, and finally shot himself in an apparent suicide attempt. Alerted by telegram, Conrad's uncle immediately traveled from Kiev to Marseilles to take care of his wayward nephew. (Conrad later claimed that he had been wounded in a duel, and produced his own fictional version of this 'affair' in *The Arrow of Gold*; his attempted suicide did not become known until many years after his death.) Gillon's account of the novel is unprepossessing: *Sprawa w Marsylii* 'contains practically no action', and Bobrowski, its 'real protagonist', is presented as a pompous bigot who never misses a chance to vent his anti-Semitism. Korzeniowski's share in the novel is limited to laconic and evasive replies to his uncle's questions.

The most experimental of these fictional biographies is James Lansbury's *Korzeniowski* (1992), cast in the form of an investigation into the case of 'The Secret Sharer'. Based on the clever premise that 'Captain Korzeniow-ski's claim to be a writer of fiction was not a true claim', Lansbury's novel traces the elements of 'The Secret Sharer' through a wide variety of genres, including letters, memoirs, a poem, a mini-play in two acts, a newspaper ad, and even Freud's own analysis of the story as 'a case of male inversion'. In a passage linking the homerotic elements of the story with Conrad's situation as an outsider sympathetic to oppressed peoples, Lansbury's truly fictional Freud asserts that 'It is clear beyond doubt that the oft-used word "stranger" is meant to denote "homosexual" in this story. Such substitution is common to persecuted minorities' (*Korzeniowski*, p. 133). Lansbury's novel not only plays with some of the secret signs latent, in Conrad's story, but also comments ironically on many of the conventional generic and disciplinary approaches to Conrad.

ANXIETIES OF INFLUENCE

Conrad had a greater personal experience of 'Third World' populations than most writers of his time, and the protagonists of his first two novels, Kaspar Almayer and Peter Willems, are memorable examples of the moral degeneracy of colonialism founded on racial prejudice. Almayer is deva-stated when his daughter Nina rejects his Eurocentric ambitions in favour of a native prince, while Aïssa in *An Outcast of the Islands* castigates Willems's homeland as 'A land of lies and of evil from which nothing but misfortune ever comes to us – who are not white' (*OI*, p. 144). It is therefore not surprising that Conrad's influence has been deeply felt by writers who have sought to chronicle the human history of colonies and the struggles of those seeking a *modus vivendi* between the rights and claims of native traditions and the access to a larger world available through Western technologies and means of communication. For some, like Achebe, Conrad remains hope-lessly Anglophile and racist, while others have found in his works a subtle and complex mixture of cultural awareness with imperialist blindness: thus, although writers like V. S. Naipaul and Edward Said greatly admire

Conrad's achievement, Naipaul has characterized *Lord Jim* as an 'imperialist' novel with a 'racial straggler' for a hero, and Said has described a similar imperialist bias in *Nostromo*.

Conrad has had a profound influence on African novelists writing in English. Jacqueline Bardolphe has claimed that in the work of the Kenyan novelist Ngugi Wa Thiong'o, 'Conrad's work is not an "influence" but a fundamental intertext ... in such a determining way that the two major novels [*A Grain of Wheat* (1967) and *Petals of Blood* (1977)] are "parodies" in the full sense that they provide readings of Conrad' ('Ngugi Wa Thiong'o's *A Grain of Wheat* and *Petals of Blood*, p. 37). In *Mawsim al-hedjra ilā al-shimāl* (*Season of Migration to the North*, 1969), by the Sudanese writer Tayyib Sālih, the hero reverses the direction of Marlow's voyage in 'Heart of Darkness'.[7]

V. S. Naipaul has described his encounters with Conrad in an eloquent essay entitled 'Conrad's Darkness', but his major fictional tribute to Conrad's legacy remains *A Bend in the River* (1979), which retells the story of 'Heart of Darkness' from the 'other side', from the perspective of the Islamic and Hindu colonialism of the east coast of Africa. Naipaul's account of a young man who takes up shopkeeping in a village that had been Kurtz's Inner Station only seventy years earlier is filled with commentaries on the difficulty of maintaining a sense of cultural identity between the pressures of Western domination and the weight of a less hegemonic, but no less colonial tradition lacking sophisticated terms for self-justification. Thus, in passages like the following, Naipaul's narrator clarifies what Marlow may have meant when he asserted that the only justification for colonial exploitation lay in the 'idea' behind it:

> If it was Europe that gave us on the coast some idea of our history, it was Europe, I feel, that also introduced us to the lie. Those of us who had been in that part of Africa before the Europeans had never lied about ourselves. Not because we were more moral. We didn't lie because we never assessed ourselves and didn't think there was anything for us to lie about; we were people who simply did what we did. But the Europeans could do one thing and say something quite different; and they could act in this way because they had an idea of what they owed to their civilization. It was their great advantage over us. (*A Bend in the River*, pp. 16–17)

The ambiguities of what we 'owe' to our civilization, and the hypocrisies of what it demands of us in return, are among Conrad's abiding themes. Naipaul has also relived Conrad's struggle for recognition as an English novelist despite his foreign origins, and he has often, like Conrad, been confronted with misunderstanding and disapproval from both sides. Third

World ideologues have criticized him for his dreary portrayals of the garbage and litter of the colonies and for his enigmatic desire to enact the life of an English gentleman, while Western critics find it difficult to accept him other than as a Third World writer whose aspirations to 'arrival' are dismissed as a presumptuous dereliction of his duty to his 'own' people. This situation closely resembles Conrad's struggles to gain acceptance as an English writer and not merely as a curious case of linguistic and cultural assimilation. If, as Romain Gary suggested, the English could never fully accept Conrad as 'one of us', others have been eager to reclaim him for Poland by arguing that the essence of his achievement can best be understood in terms of a guilt-ridden 'betrayal' of his cultural origins.

In terms of this cultural conflict, the writer whose personal situation most directly re-enacted the case of Conrad is Jerzy Kosinski, whose last book, *The Hermit of 69th Street* (1988), is an obsessive compendium of self-conscious witticisms, snippets of Talmudic or philosophical wisdom (complete with footnotes and references), parenthetical correctives to the printer, and recurring allusions to sexual encounters, psychoanalysis, yoga, and the Holocaust.[8] It also includes a great many references to Conrad. Like Conrad, Kosinski survived an oppressive regime to achieve fame as a stylist in an adopted language, and, like Conrad, he paid a heavy price for the transformation: where Conrad's cultural and personal neuroses expressed themselves in chronic gout, hypochondria, and a series of nervous breakdowns, Kosinski's childhood traumas took the more drastic form of paranoia and ultimately suicide. Kosinski's very name shares its initials with Józef Korzeniowski, and the name of his protagonist, Norbert Kosky, is virtually a phonic anagram of Conrad's original surname.

GENERIC INFLUENCE

Every great novel is both unique and exemplary, and at least three of Conrad's masterpieces have come to stand as models for novelistic subgenres. The river voyage of 'Heart of Darkness', which is also a descent into inner darkness, recurs in works including *Los pasos perdidos* (*The Lost Steps*, 1953) by the Cuban novelist Alejo Carpentier, *Palace of the Peacock* (1960) by the Guyanese novelist Wilson Harris, and *Deliverance* (1970) by the American poet James Dickey.[9] It has also inspired two Swedish works, *Färd med Mörkrets hjärta* (*Journey with Heart of Darkness*, 1987) by Olof Lagercrantz, and *Utrota varenda jävel* (*Exterminate All the Devils*, 1992) by Sven Lindqvist. The theme of the river also recurs explicitly in the title of a Dutch novel by Mineke Schipper, *Conrads Rivier* (*Conrad's River*, 1994). 'Heart of Darkness' has also provided inspiration for a number of science fiction novels, most explicitly in Robert Silverberg's *Downward to the Earth* (1970). Silverberg also borrowed a Conradian title for his novella *The Secret Sharer* (1988).[10]

Even though it was written by a non-'native', *Nostromo* is the first epic novel of colonial Latin America, and thus stands at the origin of a tradition that leads to the panoramic chronicles of writers like Carpentier, Gabriel García Márquez (Colombia), Mario Vargas Llosa (Peru), or Augusto Roa Bastos (Paraguay). The historical Conrad even makes a cameo appearance as a gun-runner in García Márquez's novel *Love in the Time of Cholera* (p. 320). Conrad's influence arrived in Latin America through the mediation of Faulkner, whose Yoknapatawpha County served García Márquez direct-ly as a model for his own fictional village of Macondo. Nevertheless, the silver mine in Costaguana is both mythical and material, demonic and economic; and Conrad's portrayal of the conflict between dreams and 'material interests' precedes the development of 'magical realism' as a technique for rendering a sense of history and cultural identity specific to post-colonial Latin American conditions. Jorge Luis Borges considered Conrad a greater novelist than James or Dostoevsky, 'because in Conrad you feel that everything is real and at the same time very poetical, no?' (Burgin, *Conversations with Jorge Luis Borges*, p. 71). Borges deemed Conrad the greatest novelist, although he considered James the better 'story-teller'. Borges's short story 'Guayaquil' (in *Doctor Brodie's Report*) is a historical fantasy based on *Nostromo*, and Borges entitled one of his poems 'Manuscript Found in a Book of Joseph Conrad'.

The clearest case of generic influence is evident in Conrad's two novels of espionage, *The Secret Agent* and *Under Western Eyes*, where the mixture of moral ambiguity, political intrigue, and domestic squalor has found a lasting echo in the spy fictions of W. Somerset Maugham, Graham Greene, and especially John Le Carré. Credit for founding the novel of espionage must be shared to some extent with the creator of Sherlock Holmes, and with other early studies of international intrigue like Dostoevsky's *Besy* (*The Possessed*, 1872) or Erskine Childers's *The Riddle of the Sands* (1903). Nevertheless, the murky moral depths of the world of counter-espionage were first explored by Conrad's half-hearted double agents, who are caught in a double bind between their emotional attachments and their political duties and ultimately do not know where their final allegiance lies. Conrad has provided a durable and useful model for understanding the tensions and petty worries of those on the front line of the Cold War, and his example has been further developed in Le Carré's 'Smiley Trilogy' (1974–80) consisting of *Tinker, Tailor, Soldier, Spy*, then *The Honourable Schoolboy* (whose protagonist Jerry Westerby reads Greene and Conrad in Saigon), and finally *Smiley's People*. Le Carré has paid a discreet tribute to Conrad by using 'Charlie', 'Joseph', and 'Kurtz' as names or code-names for the characters in *The Little Drummer Girl* (1983). Direct echoes of *Lord Jim* have also been noted in Le Carré's 1986 novel *A Perfect Spy* (Daleski, 'A Perfect Spy and a great tradition', p. 62).

FOLLOWERS IN THE FOOTSTEPS

In an essay entitled 'The Conrad of my generation', the Polish author Jan Józef Szczepański has described the extraordinary impact of Conrad's works on young readers in the Polish resistance under the Nazi Occupation. In at least one instance, Conrad's influence proved fatal: in a story called 'Przypadek' ('The Accident'), based on a true incident, Szczepański describes how a young fugitive from the Gestapo was inspired by the ethical imperatives of *Lord Jim* to return home to retrieve a compromising photograph, and was captured and executed.

The first serious and scholarly attempt to study Conrad's works against the historical context of his travels was undertaken by Norman Sherry in two companion volumes, *Conrad's Eastern World* (1966) and *Conrad's Western World* (1971). The journalist and travel writer Gavin Young has retraced Sherry's footsteps with *In Search of Conrad* (1991), which mixes passages from Conrad with accounts of Young's journeys in the Malay Archipelago. An earlier and less touristic account is provided by the German dramatist Horst Laube in *Zwischen des Flüssen: Reisen zu Joseph Conrad* (*Between the Rivers: Journeys to Joseph Conrad*, 1982), which describes the stages of Laube's journey to Conrad's Sambir. Conrad's footsteps have been followed not only by intrepid literary scholars, but also by writer-adventurers who have been less interested in the details of Conrad's works than in their potential as a source of evocative images. His influence is evident in the titles of travel works like Redmond O'Hanlon's *Into the Heart of Borneo* (1984) and Andrew Eames's *Crossing the Shadow Line: Travels in South-East Asia* (1986).

NON-LITERARY FORMS OF INFLUENCE

Since the appearance of Maurice Tourneur's first silent film of *Victory* in 1919, more than seventy film and video versions of Conrad's works have been made by directors including Alfred Hitchcock, Andrzej Wajda, and Francis Ford Coppola. During his own lifetime, Conrad was by no means averse to the propagation of his work in other, more lucrative forms: he adapted *The Secret Agent* and two short stories for the stage, and wrote a 'film-play' based on his own short story 'Gaspar Ruiz'.

These films vary greatly in the degree of their fidelity to the literary texts, but even the most faithful of them introduce distortions that can influence the public perception of Conrad's work. For example, Conrad scholars have frequently described Carol Reed's version of *An Outcast of the Islands* (1951) as one of the 'best' of the films, although all of the native or half-native spouses in the novel have been replaced by white European women in Victorian costume. None of the Malay novels have been filmed in their original locales, and filmmakers have shown little respect for the ethnic or cultural specificity of Conrad's settings. Richard Brooks's adaption of *Lord Jim* (1965) was filmed in Cambodia, and the Islamic world of Patusan was replaced with Buddhist ceremonies and a classic stage villain in the form of a French colonial warlord. Conrad's Malay novels describe complex local situations in which 'natives', Arabs, 'Portuguese', and Chinese are all engaged with Dutch and British interests in a struggle for survival and control; but on the screen such historical and ethnic complexities are either ignored altogether, or at best reduced to the terms of a private conflict between Westerners (like that between Willard/Marlow and Kurtz in Coppola's *Apocalypse Now*). Similar considerations have required that 'happy endings' be added to Hitchcock's *Sabotage* (1936), based on *The Secret Agent*, and to all of the film versions of *Victory*.[11] 'Heart of Darkness' has even been taken as the basis for a low-budget 'reverse-gender' comedy film entitled *Cannibal Women in the Avocado Jungle of Death* (1988).

Conrad's cinematic influence sometimes extends beyond those films devoted directly to the adaptation of his works: many of the experimental techniques that Orson Welles planned to use in a film version of 'Heart of Darkness' appear in *Citizen Kane* (1941), the film he made instead (Sinyard, 'Joseph Conrad and Orson Welles'). The British director Ridley Scott, who filmed 'The Duel' as *The Duellists* (1977), has also paid tribute to Conrad by naming the space-freighters in his *Aliens* series the *Nostromo* and the *Sulaco*. The importance of film as a means of transmitting influence should not be underestimated, since far more people will have seen film versions of Conrad's works than have actually read his books.[12]

Another important form of influence, and one hitherto neglected in Conrad's scholarship, is propagated by the 'classic' comic-books addressed primarily to children. Comic-book versions of *Lord Jim* and *The Secret Agent* have been published in the United States and the United Kingdom. Dan Malan, the author of *The Complete Guide to Classics Illustrated*, notes that the 'Classics Illustrated' edition of *Lord Jim* was reprinted in English at least five times between 1957 and 1975, and foreign-language editions were published in ten other countries, including Brazil, Finland, and Mexico. Although the amount of 'Conrad' surviving in such adaptations is questionable, many younger readers will first have encountered his influence in this form.

THE LEGACY OF JOSEPH CONRAD

Why has Conrad's influence been so extensive and profound? What is it about the example of his life and the record of his works that modern writers and readers have found so appealing? Perhaps an answer lies in the rare combination of the remarkable range of his experience with the fathomless depths of his irony.

Conrad was one of the first Western writers to give voice to the claims and aspirations of non-Western peoples. His own lack of a national homeland led him to speak for a larger constituency, and the essential statelessness of his own condition is reflected in the wide variety of national types that people his fictions. The protagonists of his first two novels are Dutch colonials, Nostromo is a South American immigrant of Italian origin, Razumov is an uprooted Russian, and Heyst is of Swedish descent. Mr Verloc's background is obscurely continental, and 'all Europe' contributed to the making of Kurtz. In *Lord Jim*, the crew of the *Patna* offers a typical example of the many nationalities to be met in Conrad's works: the owner is Chinese, the skipper is 'a sort of renegade New South Wales German' (p. 14), the second engineer is Cockney English, the helmsmen are Malay, and the 'cargo' consists of 800 Muslim pilgrims. Although Conrad remained an ardent Anglophile, his work embodies a lifelong commitment to the recognition voiced in the 'Author's Note' to his first novel, that 'there is a bond between us and that humanity so far away' (*AF*, p. 3). He remained faithful to this bond, and as the world has grown smaller we have come to understand him as an early and powerful advocate of the essential oneness of humankind. Marlow claimed that Jim was 'one of us', but the 'us' in his phrase includes us all.

As an expatriate determined to earn his living as a writer in an acquired language, Conrad was locked in a constant and fundamental struggle with words. He could never achieve the confidence of a native speaker of English, and this want of a linguistic and cultural birthright found expression in the haunting ironies and ambiguities of his style. As T. E. Lawrence observed, 'all things end in a kind of hunger, a suggestion of something he can't say or do or think' (Garnett, ed., *Letters of T. E. Lawrence*, p. 302). Like the language teacher who narrates *Under Western Eyes*, Conrad knew only too well that 'Words ... are the great foes of reality' (*UWE*, p. 3). Modern literature is the creation of linguistic exiles, but unlike Joyce or Nabokov, Conrad was never tempted to celebrate his extraterritoriality by means of puns or neologisms. Instead, the fundamental insecurity of his cultural identity is embedded in the tone of his narrative voice, which speaks towards an idea of home from a condition of radical and multiple otherness. In the opening chapter of Conrad's last novel, *Suspense*, Cosmo Latham encounters a stranger, a 'secret sharer' named Attilio, who tells him how he once abandoned his ship to join a hermit in the wilderness. After hearing the story, Cosmo asks him: 'You deserted from your ship simply because the tone of his voice appealed to your heart. Is that your meaning?' and Attilio replies, 'You have guessed it signorino' (*Su*, p. 7). There is perhaps no better explanation for Conrad's enduring influence.

NOTES

1 These difficulties notwithstanding, Jeffrey Meyers has attempted to quantify the effects of Conrad's influence by stating that 'nearly twenty of his works ... have influenced at least thirty-five American, Latin American, English, German, French, and Polish authors' ('Conrad's influence on modern writers', p. 186). Although prone to overstatement, Meyers provides a useful introduction to the subject of Conrad's literary influence. *Conradiana* 22.2 (Summer 1990) was devoted to 'The Influence of Conrad'.

2 The most famous portrait of Conrad is Walter Tittle's (National Gallery, London). Bruce Rogers and Dora Clarke designed their sculptures of Conrad in the form of a ship's figurehead. A copy of Rogers's work still adorns the sailing ship *Joseph Conrad*, now on permanent exhibit in the Mystic Seaport Museum of Connecticut.

3 In addition to Ford's correspondence with Conrad and memoirs such as his *Return to Yesterday* (1931), see also Morey, 'Joseph Conrad and Ford Madox Ford', and Brebach, *Joseph Conrad, Ford Madox Ford and the Making of 'Romance'*.

4 The memoirs of G. F. W. Hope, one of Conrad's oldest friends, survive in the form of an unpublished typescript entitled 'Friend of Conrad' (Harry Ransom Humanities Research Center, University of Texas at Austin).

5 Mizener, *The Far Side of Paradise: A Biography of F. Scott Fitzgerald*, p. 186. The example is from the end of the fourth paragraph of chapter 1 of *The Great Gatsby*. See also Long, '*The Great Gatsby* and the tradition of Joseph Conrad'.

6 See Ross on Conrad's influence on *Absalom, Absalom!* For a general survey of Conrad's impact on American literature, see Secor and Moddelmog, comp., *Joseph Conrad and American Writers*, and Carabine, 'Conrad and American literature'.

7 For a comparison of *Nostromo* with *Petals of Blood*, see Fincham, 'Orality, literacy, and community'. A brief survey of Conrad's influence on African writers is found in Nazareth, 'Conrad's descendants'. *Joseph Conrad: Third World Perspectives*, Hamner, ed., reprints a number of important essays and

provides an annotated bibliography of materials on Conrad and the colonial world.

8 Kosinski's Kosky evidently found it impossible to read his own proofs, and the printers he so frequently taunted appear to have taken their revenge, since the volume contains a great many errata.

9 See Peters, 'The significance of dream consciousness in *Heart of Darkness* and *Palace of the Peacock*'. For a general survey of Conrad's influence on Caribbean writers, see Huggan, 'Anxieties of influence: Conrad in the Caribbean'.

10 For Conrad's influence on science fiction, see Kleiner, 'Joseph Conrad's forgotten role in the emergence of science fiction'.

11 Hitchcock's film entitled *The Secret Agent* was based not on Conrad's novel but on W. Somerset Maugham's 'Ashenden' stories.

12 In December 1987, a Conrad film festival entitled 'The Art of Darkness' was held at the National Film Theatre, London.

WORKS CITED

Achebe, Chinua. 'An image of Africa: racism in Conrad's "Heart of Darkness"'. *Massachusetts Review* 17.4 (1977), 782–94. Reprinted in Hamner, ed., pp. 119–29

Bardolphe, Jacqueline. 'Ngugi Wa Thiong'o's *A Grain of Wheat* and *Petals of Blood* as readings of Conrad's *Under Western Eyes* and *Victory*'. *The Conradian* 12.1 (1987), 32–49

Bloom, Harold. *The Anxiety of Influence*. Oxford: Oxford University Press, 1973

Borges, Jorge Luis. *Borges: A Reader*. Ed. Emir Rodriguez Monegal and Alastair Reid. New York: Dutton, 1981

  Doctor Brodie's Report. Tr. Norman Thomas di Giovanni. New York: Dutton, 1972

Brebach, Raymond. *Joseph Conrad, Ford Madox Ford, and the Making of 'Romance'*. Ann Arbor: UMI Research Press, 1985

Burgin, Richard. *Conversations with Jorge Luis Borges*. 1969. New York: Avon, 1970

Carabine, Keith. 'Conrad and American literature: a review essay'. *The Conradian* 13.2 (1988), 207–19

Conrad, Joseph. *Almayer's Folly*. 1895. Ed. Floyd Eugene Eddleman and David Leon Higdon. Cambridge: Cambridge University Press, 1994

  Lord Jim. 1900. Ed. John Batchelor. Oxford: Oxford University Press, 1983

  An Outcast of the Islands. 1896. Ed. J. H. Stape and Hans van Marle. Oxford: Oxford University Press, 1992

  Suspense. 1925. Ed. Richard Curle. London: Dent, 1954

  Under Western Eyes. 1911. Ed. Jeremy Hawthorn. Oxford: Oxford University Press, 1983

Daleski, H. M. '*A Perfect Spy* and a great tradition'. *Journal of Narrative Technique* 20.1 (1990), 56–64

Fincham, Gail. 'Orality, literacy, and community: Conrad's *Nostromo* and Ngugi's *Petals of Blood*'. *The Conradian* 17.1 (1992), 45–71

Ford, Ford Madox. *Joseph Conrad: A Personal Remembrance*. London: Duckworth, 1924

García Márquez, Gabriel. *Love in the Time of Cholera*. Tr. Edith Grossman. New York: Knopf, 1988

Garnett, David, ed. *The Letters of T. E. Lawrence*. London: Cape, 1938

Gary, Romain. *La Nuit sera calme*. Paris: Gallimard, 1974

Gillon, Adam. 'The *Radiant Line*: a new Polish novel about Conrad'. *Conradiana* 17.2 (1985), 109–17

   'The *Affair in Marseilles*: another Polish novel about Conrad'. *Conradiana* 25.1 (1993), 53–67

Greene, Graham. *In Search of a Character*. 1961. Harmondsworth: Penguin Books, 1968

Hamner, Robert D., ed. *Joseph Conrad: Third World Perspectives*. Washington, DC: Three Continents Press, 1990

Hemingway, Ernest. 'Conrad, optimist and moralist'. 1924. Reprinted in *By-Line: Ernest Hemingway*. Ed. William White. New York: Bantam, 1968, pp. 114–15

Hervouet, Yves. *The French Face of Joseph Conrad*. Cambridge: Cambridge University Press, 1990

Huggan, Graham. 'Anxieties of influence: Conrad in the Caribbean'. *Commonwealth* 11.1 (1988), 1–12

Kirschner, Paul. *Conrad: The Psychologist as Artist*. Edinburgh: Oliver & Boyd, 1968

Kleiner, Elaine L. 'Joseph Conrad's forgotten role in the emergence of science fiction'. *Extrapolation* 15 (1973), 25–34

Knowles, Owen. 'Conrad, Anatole France, and the early French Romantic tradition: some influences'. *Conradiana* 11.1 (1979), 41–61

Lansbury, James. *Korzeniowski*. London: Serpent's Tail, 1992

Laube, Horst. *Zwischen den Flüssen: Reisen zu Joseph Conrad*. Frankfurt: Syndikat, 1982

Long, Robert Emmet. '*The Great Gatsby* and the tradition of Joseph Conrad'. *Texas Studies in Literature and Language* 8 (1966), 257–76, 407–22

Lowry, Malcolm. 'Joseph Conrad'. *The Collected Poetry of Malcolm Lowry*. Ed. Kathleen Scherf. Vancouver: UBC Press, 1992, pp. 117–18

Ludwig, Richard M., ed. *Letters of Ford Madox Ford*. Princeton: Princeton University Press, 1965

Meriwether, James, B. and Michael Millgate, ed. *Lion in the Garden: Interviews with William Faulkner, 1926–1962*. Lincoln: University of Nebraska Press, 1968

Meyers, Jeffrey. 'Conrad's influence on modern writers'. *Twentieth Century Literature* 36.2 (1990), 186–206

Mizener, Arthur. *The Far Side of Paradise: A Biography of F. Scott Fitzgerald*. New York: Vintage, 1959

Morey, John Hope. 'Joseph Conrad and Ford Madox Ford: a study in collaboration'. Unpublished PhD thesis, Cornell University, 1960

Morf, Gustav. *The Polish Heritage of Joseph Conrad*. London: Sampson Low, Marston, 1930

Nabokov, Vladimir. *Strong Opinions*. London: Weidenfeld & Nicolson, 1973

Naipaul, V. S. *A Bend in the River*. 1979. New York: Vintage, 1980

'Conrad's darkness'. 1974. In *The Return of Eva Perón*. New York: Vintage, 1981, pp. 221–45

Nazareth, Peter. 'Conrad's descendants'. *Conradiana* 22.2 (1990), 101–09

Norman, Howard. *'Kiss in the Hotel Joseph Conrad' and Other Stories*. New York: Summit, 1989

Pendleton, Robert. *Graham Greene's Conradian Masterplot*. London: Macmillan, 1995

Peters, Bradley T. 'The significance of dream consciousness in *Heart of Darkness* and *Palace of the Peacock*'. *Conradiana* 22.2 (1990), 127–41

Ross, Stephen. 'Conrad's influence on *Absalom, Absalom!*'. *Studies in American Fiction* 2 (1974), 199–209

Said, Edward. 'Through gringo eyes: with Conrad in Latin America'. *Harper's Magazine*, April 1988, 70–2

Secor, Robert and Debra Moddelmog, comp. *Joseph Conrad and American Writers: A Bibliographical Study of Affinities, Influences, and Relations*. Greenwood, CT: Westport, 1985

Sherry, Norman. *Conrad's Eastern World*. Cambridge: Cambridge University Press, 1966

Conrad's Western World. Cambridge: Cambridge University Press, 1971

Shklovsky, Viktor. *Theory of Prose*. 1925. Tr. Benjamin Sher. Elmwood Park, IL: Dalkey Archive Press, 1990

Sinyard, Neil. 'Joseph Conrad and Orson Welles'. In *Filming Literature: The Art of Screen Adaptation*. London: Croom Helm, 1986, pp. 111–16

Sutherland, J. G. *At Sea with Joseph Conrad*. 1922. Reprinted Brooklyn: Haskell House, 1971

Szczepański, Jan Józef. 'Przypadek'. *Tygodnik powszechny* 4 (1948). Also as 'In Lord Jim's boots'. Tr. Edward Rothert. *Polish Perspectives* 18.1 (1975), 31–44

Turnbull, Andrew, ed. *The Letters of F. Scott Fitzgerald*. New York: Delta, 1965

Wilson, Edmund. *Letters on Literature and Politics, 1912–1972*. Ed. Elena Wilson. New York: Farrar, Straus, Giroux, 1977

Young, Gavin. *In Search of Conrad*. London: Hutchinson, 1991

Zabierowski, Stefan. *Dziedzictwo Conrada w literaturze polskiej XX wieku* [*The Legacy of Conrad in Twentieth-Century Polish Literature*]. Cracow: Oficyna Literacka, 1992

FURTHER READING

The books, articles, and notes about Conrad's life and work are dauntingly varied in their quality and range. The bibliographies listed below provide reliable and comprehensive information about this continually growing body of writing. In addition to listing basic reference sources, the following offers a selective chronological guide to the major scholarship and criticism published since the 1940s. Although a few key essays are mentioned, emphasis falls on full-length studies in English dealing with Conrad's achievement as a whole or with selected aspects of it. The notes to the chapters of the present volume refer to studies of particular relevance to the works they consider or to the broader topics in their purview.

TEXTS

No reliable edition of Conrad's complete works is available. Textual scholarship began in the 1960s, but only with the advent of computer-generated collations has the extreme complexity of Conrad's textual situations become evident. The Cambridge Edition of the Works of Joseph Conrad, currently in course of publication by Cambridge University Press, will offer critical texts of the canon. Editions of Conrad in French, Italian, and Polish translation have been published.

Dent's Collected Edition of the Works of Joseph Conrad. London: Dent, 1946–55. The most widely accessible complete edition but lacking the dramatizations and *The Nature of a Crime* (written with Ford). A re-issue of the Uniform Edition of 1923–8, this edition's pagination is identical to it and to that of the numerous collected 'editions' (in fact, issues) published in the United States throughout the 1920s.

Opere. Ed. Ugo Mursia. 5 vols. Milan: Mursia, 1967–82. Thematic arrangement of the complete works, with erudite commentaries and useful explanatory notes. In Italian.

Oeuvres. Ed. Sylvère Monod. Pléiade edition. 5 vols. Paris: Gallimard, 1982–92. Monod's general introductions offer valuable critical perspectives. Frequently illuminating 'Notices' on individual works by their translators or other critics. The informative and thorough explanatory notes are authoritative on Conrad's Gallicisms, French borrowings, and French literary connections. In French.

Oxford World's Classics. Oxford: Oxford University Press, 1983–. Photo-offset reprintings, purged of printer's errors, of many of the volumes of Dent's Collected Edition. The texts are augmented by a critical introduction, chronology of Conrad's life, selected bibliography, note on the text, maps, and explanatory notes.

Penguin Twentieth-Century Classics. Harmondsworth: Penguin Books, 1983–. Using various copy-texts, this collection presents most of Conrad's fiction in a format similar to that of Oxford's World's Classics series.

The Cambridge Edition of the Works of Joseph Conrad. Cambridge: Cambridge University Press, 1990–. A critical edition of the canon providing a detailed history of composition, revision, publication, and reception, with textual variants, and explanatory and textual notes. *The Secret Agent*, ed. Bruce Harkness and S. W. Reid (1990), and *Almayer's Folly*, ed. Floyd Eugene Eddleman and David Leon Higdon (1994), have appeared to date.

The standard canon is supplemented by:

'Congo Diary' and Other Uncollected Pieces. Ed. Zdzisław Najder. Garden City, NY: Doubleday, 1978. Includes the Congo notebooks, the unfinished novel *The Sisters, The Nature of a Crime*, and uncollected minor pieces.

Of the many paperback and separate re-issues of Conrad's works a few merit special mention:

The Portable Conrad. Ed. Morton Dauwen Zabel. New York: Viking, 1947; rev. edn. Frederick R. Karl, 1969. A handy compendium for the reader beginning to explore Conrad. Includes selected short fiction with some letters and extracts from the critical prose. Classic introduction by Zabel.

Norton Critical Editions. New York: Norton. *Heart of Darkness*, ed. Robert Kimbrough, 1963; 3rd edn. 1988. *Lord Jim*, ed. Thomas Moser, 1968. *The Nigger of the 'Narcissus'*, ed. Robert Kimbrough, 1979. While boasting 'authoritative texts', the series in fact reprints the corrupt Heinemann Collected Edition texts of 1921. The volumes none the less offer valuable selections of criticism and extensive background materials on Conrad's sources.

Selected Literary Criticism and 'The Shadow-Line'. Ed. Allan Ingram. London: Methuen, 1986. Provides a setting for the novella in extracts from Conrad's letters and 'Author's Notes'.

'Heart of Darkness': A Case Study in Contemporary Criticism. Ed. Ross C. Murfin. New York: Bedford Books of St Martin's Press, 1989. Reprints the Heinemann Edition's defective text without explanatory notes but offers a kaleidoscopic view of current critical trends in five essays covering the psychoanalytic, reader-response, feminist, deconstructive, and new historicist perspectives.

The Complete Short Stories of Joseph Conrad. Ed. Samuel Hynes. 4 vols. London: Pickering; Hopewell, NJ: Ecco Press, 1992–3. Reprints the novellas and short stories from the Kent Edition (essentially Doubleday's 'Sun-Dial' typesetting). Provides a brief chronology of Conrad's life and a few textual emendations. Lacks explanatory notes.

LETTERS

Individual collections of letters were published by Conrad's wife and friends as early as the 1920s, but all are casual in their textual transcriptions and overly protective.

(Sensitive topics such as his finances and allusions to persons then living occasioned editorial deletions.) Collections based on scholarly principles were published beginning in the late 1950s and in the wake of Jocelyn Baines's 1960 biography. The earliest collections have now been or are being superseded by the *Collected Letters* in course of publication by Cambridge University Press. Until that project is completed, the second volume of *Joseph Conrad: Life and Letters*, edited by G. Jean-Aubry (London: Heinemann; Garden City, NY: Doubleday, Page, 1927) remains indispensable.

The Collected Letters of Joseph Conrad. Ed. Frederick R. Karl and Laurence Davies. 8 vols. Cambridge: Cambridge University Press, 1983–. Aims to present reliable texts of the some 4,000 extant letters, including the letters written in French and translations of those in Polish. Each volume includes a detailed chronology, introduction, short biographies of Conrad's correspondents, description of editorial procedures, illustrations, brief annotations, and indices. (Letters discovered after the publication of individual volumes normally appear in the journals listed below or in *Notes and Queries*. These will appear in the final volume.)

Of the separately published volumes of letters three remain essential:

Joseph Conrad: Letters to William Blackwood and David S. Meldrum. Ed. William Blackburn. Durham, NC: Duke University Press, 1958. Supplements Conrad's letters of the period of the *Youth* volume and *Lord Jim* with correspondence from the files of the Blackwood firm.
Conrad's Polish Background: Letters to and from Polish Friends. Ed. Zdzisław Najder. Tr. Halina Carroll. London: Oxford University Press, 1964. Presents translations of the letters Conrad's uncle and guardian Tadeusz Bobrowski addressed to him as well as other correspondence translated from Polish. An invaluable biographical source.
Joseph Conrad's Letters to R. B. Cunninghame Graham. Ed. C. T. Watts. Cambridge: Cambridge University Press, 1969. A solid introduction and highly informative notes situate an important friendship.

Conrad's correspondence is supplemented by:

A Portrait in Letters: Correspondence to and about Conrad. Ed. J. H. Stape and Owen Knowles. Amsterdam: Rodopi, 1996. A selection of letters addressed to or principally about Conrad with a guide to archival sources for letters to him.

BIOGRAPHIES

Conrad's extraordinary life attracted the attention of the biographers as early as the 1920s. His friend Jean-Aubry preserved material that might otherwise have been lost but produced a poor and sometimes unreliable life. A genuinely scholarly approach to Conrad's biography was essayed only some three decades after his death. The unusual shape of his life and career has demanded research into his Polish background, Marseilles years, and maritime experience as well as into his wide circle of friends, acquaintances, and fellow writers in England. Documentary materials are scattered in public archives and private collections in Europe, North America, Asia, and Australia. The biographer must also cope with lacunae caused by the depredations of time, in particular, the destruction of records and crucial collections of letters during the Russian Revolution and the Second World War. Archival work undertaken during the past two decades has now securely established the main outline of Conrad's life, although the challenging conditions mentioned here do not disallow further discoveries.

Baines, Jocelyn. *Joseph Conrad: A Critical Biography*. London: Weidenfeld & Nicolson; New York: McGraw-Hill, 1960. Reprinted Penguin Books, 1971. First significant full-length biography based on scholarly research. Repays reading despite its now outdated discussion of the fiction. Later scholarship has fully pursued Baines's major revelations.

Sherry, Norman. *Conrad's Eastern World*. Cambridge: Cambridge University Press, 1966. Traces models and sources for Conrad's Eastern fiction in his actual experience and wide reading. Influential in showing how Conrad altered his sources and in having stimulated further biographical research.

Conrad's Western World. Cambridge: Cambridge University Press, 1971. Continues the approach of Sherry's first volume, covering 'Heart of Darkness', *Nostromo*, and *The Secret Agent*.

Conrad and His World. London: Thames & Hudson, 1972, reprinted 1988; New York: Scribner's, 1977. Handsomely illustrated and well-informed brief summary of the main events of Conrad's life and literary career. Excellent starting-point for the student new to Conrad.

Karl, Frederick R. *Joseph Conrad: The Three Lives – A Biography*. New York: Farrar, Straus, and Giroux; London: Faber & Faber, 1979. An ungainly organization and factual inaccuracies mar this volume which none the less contains information about Conrad's career and finances that remains otherwise unprinted.

Najder, Zdzisław. *Joseph Conrad: A Chronicle*. Tr. Halina Carroll-Najder. New Brunswick, NJ: Rutgers University Press; Cambridge: Cambridge University Press, 1983. Of the full-length lives, the most reliable and scholarly, based on painstaking archival research. Unlikely to be surpassed on Conrad's Polish context.

Tennant, Roger. *Joseph Conrad: A Biography*. London: Sheldon Press; New York: Atheneum, 1981. Popular account based on secondary sources. Of no interest to the scholar.

Meyers, Jeffrey. *Joseph Conrad: A Biography*. London: Murray; New York: Scribner's, 1991. Aimed mainly at the mass market, suffers from eccentric emphases in its search for new 'angles'. Of little interest to the scholar.

Batchelor, John. *The Life of Joseph Conrad: A Critical Biography*. Oxford: Blackwell, 1994. Traverses familiar biographical territory but sensitively relates Conrad's writings to his life in balanced readings of the major fiction and short stories.

Specialized biographical works concentrate on selected aspects of or particular approaches to Conrad's life:

Allen, Jerry. *The Sea Years of Joseph Conrad*. Garden City, NY: Doubleday, 1965;

London: Methuen, 1967. Pioneering study of Conrad's maritime career but seriously marred by relying on the fiction as a trustworthy biographical source.

Meyer, Bernard C. *Joseph Conrad: A Psychoanalytical Biography*. Princeton, NJ: Princeton University Press, 1967. Discusses Conrad's psychology and writings from a Freudian perspective but frequently eludes the straitjacket of its orientation.

Watts, Cedric. *Joseph Conrad: A Literary Life*. London: Macmillan, 1989. Foreshortened account of the historical and economic circumstances of the writing career, covering such topics as serialization and Conrad's relations with his agent and publishers. Suggests some of the formal consequences of marketplace pressures.

Three works complement the scholarly biographies:

Najder, Zdzisław, ed. *Conrad under Familial Eyes*. Tr. Halina Carroll-Najder. Cambridge: Cambridge University Press, 1983. Presents documents and letters related to Conrad's family and early years as well as reminiscences by Polish relatives and friends.

Knowles, Owen. *A Conrad Chronology*. London: Macmillan; Boston: Hall, 1989. Highly readable annual and sometimes day-by-day account of Conrad's life and writing career in the form of crisply written diary entries.

Ray, Martin, ed. *Joseph Conrad: Interviews and Recollections*. London: Macmillan, 1990. A wide-ranging and generously annotated selection of reminiscences by family, friends, acquaintances, and fellow writers.

BIBLIOGRAPHIES

William R. Cagle's scholarly primary bibliography of Conrad's *oeuvre*, begun in the 1960s, is unpublished. (Photocopies may be obtained at cost from: The Curator, The Lilly Library, Indiana University, Bloomington, IN 47405–3301, USA). A number of descriptions of major collections and more-wide ranging compilations serve advanced researchers.

Wise, T. J., ed. *A Bibliography of Joseph Conrad*. 2nd edn. London: Richard Clay & Sons, 1921. Describes Wise's large personal collection of manuscripts, typescripts, limited-edition pamphlets, and signed first editions, now mostly in the British Library's Ashley Collection.

Keating, George T., ed. *A Conrad Memorial Library: The Collection of George T. Keating*. Garden City, NY: Doubleday, Doran, 1929. Catalogues the largest single collection of original materials and other Conradiana, now in Yale University's Beinecke Rare Book and Manuscript Library.

Ehrsam, Theodore G., comp. *A Bibliography of Joseph Conrad*. Metuchen, NJ: Scarecrow Press, 1969. Comprehensive, if flawed, listing of first editions, contemporary reviews, translations, and miscellanea including obituaries, memoirs, and early auction records.

Lindstrand, Gordon. 'A bibliographical survey of manuscripts of Joseph Conrad'. *Conradiana* 2.1 (1969–70), 23–32; 2.2 (1969–70), 105–14; 2.3 (1969–70), 153–62. Preliminary list of locations of Conrad's holograph and typescript materials. Numerous later discoveries, especially by Donald W. Rude, have usually been noted in the journals listed below.

Fagnani, Flavio, comp. *Catalogo della collezione Conradiana di Ugo Mursia*. Milan: Mursia, 1984. Lists holdings of the Ugo Mursia Memorial Collection at the Università di Pisa (see Study Centres below).

Criticism and scholarship in English and other major languages has been carefully recorded and evaluated in a number of bibliographical surveys:

Higdon, David Leon, *et al.*, comp. 'Conrad bibliography: a continuing checklist'. *Conradiana*. 1968–. Comprehensive update of recent criticism. Originally published annually, now appears every two years.

Teets, Bruce E. and Helmut E. Gerber, comp. *Joseph Conrad: An Annotated Bibliography of Writings about Him*. DeKalb: Northern Illinois University Press, 1971. A guide up to 1966 of reviews, criticism, scholarship, and doctoral theses.

Knowles, Owen. 'The year's work in Conrad studies: a survey of periodical literature'. *The Conradian* 9.1 (1984) to 12.1 (1987). A series of shrewd and engaging evaluative essays surveying criticism published during 1983–6.

Secor, Robert and Debra Moddelmog, comp. *Joseph Conrad and American Writers: A Bibliographical Study of Affinities, Influences, and Relations*. Westport, CT: Greenwood Press, 1985. Useful listing of comparative and influence studies but making somewhat exaggerated claims for affinity.

Teets, Bruce E., comp. *Joseph Conrad: An Annotated Bibliography*. New York and London: Garland Publishing, 1990. An updating of and supplement through 1975 of Teets and Gerber's earlier volume.

Knowles, Owen, comp. *An Annotated Critical Bibliography of Joseph Conrad*. Hemel Hempstead: Harvester Wheatsheaf; New York: St Martin's Press, 1992. Critically sophisticated and judiciously selective guide to criticism from 1914 to 1990. The main emphasis is on books and articles published after 1975.

Perczak, Wanda, comp. *Polska Bibliografia Conradowska 1896–1992*. Toruń: Wydawnictwo Universytetu Mikołaj Kopernika, 1993. Comprehensive listing of translations and of books and articles in Polish. Also lists works in English about Conrad's Polish experience, influence, and reception.

INTRODUCTIONS

Karl, Frederick R. *A Reader's Guide to Joseph Conrad*. London: Thames & Hudson; New York: Noonday Press, 1960. An overview, now dated, stressing Conrad's Modernist and experimental techniques.

Daleski, H. M. *Joseph Conrad: The Way of Dispossession*. London: Faber & Faber; New York: Holmes & Meier, 1977. Discriminating and subtle account of philosophical issues in the major fiction. For the advanced student.

Berthoud, Jacques. *Joseph Conrad: The Major Phase*. Cambridge: Cambridge University Press, 1978. A model of its kind, offering nuanced and informed discussions of the fiction from *The Nigger of the 'Narcissus'* to *Under Western Eyes*.

Gillon, Adam. *Joseph Conrad*. Twayne English Authors No. 333. Boston: Twayne, 1982. Thematic survey for the general reader and beginning undergraduate. Elementary.

Watts, Cedric. *A Preface to Conrad.* London: Longman, 1982; rev. edn. 1993. A brief treatment of Conrad's biographical and cultural circumstances and of Conradian narrative techniques with particular attention to *Nostromo*.

Ray, Martin. *Joseph Conrad.* London: Arnold, 1993. A brief overview focusing on the major fiction. For the beginning undergraduate.

Watts, Cedric. *Joseph Conrad.* Writers and Their Work. Plymouth: Northcote for the British Council, 1994. Pamphlet-length survey of Conrad's life and major works for the reader desiring a very compact overview and guidance to further reading.

REFERENCE

Sherry, Norman, ed. *Conrad: The Critical Heritage.* London: Routledge & Kegan Paul, 1973. Representative selection of contemporary reviews of the novels and most of the short story collections.

Bender, Todd K., comp. *Condordances to the Works of Joseph Conrad.* New York and London: Garland Publishing, 1976–. Multi-volume computer-generated concordance providing a word-by-word listing and an analysis of Conrad's word usages.

Page, Norman. *A Conrad Companion.* London: Macmillan; New York: St Martin's Press, 1986. First attempt to provide a reference guide to Conrad's life and canon.

Tutein, David W. *Joseph Conrad's Reading: An Annotated Bibliography.* West Cornwall, CT: Locust Hill Press, 1990. Alphabetical list of titles. Surveys an important and previously neglected subject but is inadequately documented.

Marle, Hans van. 'A novelist's dukedom: from Conrad's library'. *The Conradian* 16.1 (1991), 55–78. Adds numerous additional titles to Tutein's census and establishes a scholarly approach to researching Conrad's reading.

Carabine, Keith, ed. *Joseph Conrad: Critical Assessments.* 4 vols. Robertsbridge: Helm Information, 1992. Massive compendium of criticism from the beginnings of Conrad's career to the 1990s. Of particular interest to libraries lacking standard journals and monographs.

CRITICISM

Following Conrad's death, his reputation suffered a decline. A revival of interest, which consolidated his reputation as a major writer and roughly coincided with the decline of the impressionistic essay and the rise of academic criticism, set in during the 1940s in both England and America. Conrad's major fiction has now been subjected to intense investigation for some decades, and even some of his minor writings have been extensively, possibly exhaustively, analyzed. Criticism of Conrad's work has invariably reflected prevailing critical fashions. (These are ably surveyed in Knowles's bibliography listed above.) Only essential work can be mentioned here for the earlier decades, while an attempt has been made to suggest the range and diversity of recent criticism.

The 1930s to the 1950s

In England, the recovery of Conrad's reputation began with general surveys by Edward Crankshaw and Muriel Bradbrook, and gained momentum and sophistication under the impetus of F. R. Leavis. At the same time in America, John Dozier Gordan and Morton Dauwen Zaubel were laying the foundations for an increasingly nuanced perception of Conrad's achievement by closely examining its sources. Influenced by post-war preoccupations and urged on by the expansion of post-secondary education, a new professionalism among university teachers, and the then-emergent New Criticism, the serious academic revaluation and interpretation of Conrad's writings was underway during the 1950s.

Crankshaw, Edward. *Joseph Conrad: Some Aspects of the Art of the Novel.* London: John Lane, 1936. Reprinted New York: Russell & Russell, 1963. Appreciative treatment by a friend of Ford Madox Ford. Mainly of historical interest.

Gordan, John Dozier. *Joseph Conrad: The Making of a Novelist.* Cambridge, MA: Harvard University Press, 1940. Pace-setting study of documentary sources and composition history. The foundation for much subsequent scholarly work.

Bradbrook, M. C. *Joseph Conrad: England's Polish Genius.* Cambridge: Cambridge University Press; New York: Macmillan, 1941. Reprinted New York: Russell & Russell, 1965. General overview. Mainly of historical interest.

Leavis, F. R. 'Revaluations: Joseph Conrad'. *Scrutiny* 10.1 (1941), 22–50 and 10.2 (1941), 157–81. Reprinted in *The Great Tradition: George Eliot, Henry James, Joseph Conrad.* London: Chatto & Windus; New York: G. W. Stewart, 1948. Enormously influential revisionist essay placing Conrad in the line of the major English realists.

Hewitt, Douglas. *Conrad: A Reassessment.* Cambridge: Bowes & Bowes, 1952; 3rd edn. Bowes & Bowes and Totowa, NJ: Rowman & Littlefield, 1975. Brief but perceptive discussion consolidating the upward movement of Conrad's reputation.

Moser, Thomas C. *Joseph Conrad: Achievement and Decline.* Cambridge, MA: Harvard University Press, 1957. Reprinted Hamden, CT: Archon Books, 1966. Long influential in its negative assessment of the late fiction and for its thesis that Conrad could not treat sexual psychology convincingly. Considerably challenged by revisionist trends in the 1980s and 1990s.

Guerard, Albert J. *Conrad the Novelist.* Cambridge, MA: Harvard University Press, 1958. Reprinted 1979. Influential psychological and myth-oriented study that despite occasional reductiveness provides acute readings of individual works.

The 1960s and 1970s

The criticism of the 1960s pursued the arguments suggested by Moser and Guerard and was influenced by the archetypal approach generated by Northrop Frye's *Anatomy of Criticism* (1957). Likely the more lasting critical achievements of this period were original discussions of Conrad's philosophical orientations and politics and his relationship to dominant nineteenth-century ideologies. His continental context also became an area of interest. The 1960s, particularly in doctoral theses in the United States, also witnessed a dawning awareness of the deficiencies of Conrad's received texts and the beginnings of textual scholarship. Conferences held in Texas, Miami, Canterbury, and San Diego to observe the fiftieth anniversary of Conrad's death marked a watershed in Conrad studies, confirming Conrad's status as a writer of world stature diversely investigated by a far-flung community of scholar-critics. In addition to refining the insights of the previous two decades of criticism, they announced an interest in rhetoric and narratology.

Hay, Eloise Knapp. *The Political Novels of Joseph Conrad: A Critical Study*. Chicago: University of Chicago Press, 1963; rev. edn. 1981. Detailed treatment of selected fiction with an emphasis on Conrad's emerging political viewpoints.

Watt, Ian. 'Joseph Conrad: alienation and commitment'. *The English Mind: Studies in the English Moralists Presented to Basil Willey*. Ed. Hugh Sykes Davies and George Watson. Cambridge: Cambridge University Press, 1964, pp. 257–78. Seminal essay brilliantly situating Conrad's response to philosophical and political ideas, including conservatism, existentialism, and Marxism.

Busza, Andrzej. 'Conrad's Polish literary background and some illustrations of Polish literature on his work'. *Antemurale* 10 (1966), 109–255. Identifies Conrad's debts to the Polish literary tradition, traces sources, and sensitively treats the inter-cultural dimensions of his aesthetics.

Miller, J. Hillis. *Poets of Reality: Six Twentieth-Century Writers*. Cambridge, MA: Harvard University Press, 1966. Highly influential phenomenological approach to Conrad, highlighting *The Secret Agent*.

Fleishman, Avrom. *Conrad's Politics: Community and Anarchy in the Fiction of Joseph Conrad*. Baltimore: Johns Hopkins Press, 1967. Traces Conrad's political thought in his familial and cultural circumstances and analyses his publicistic writings.

Kirschner, Paul. *Conrad: The Psychologist as Artist*. Edinburgh: Oliver & Boyd, 1968. Pioneers the exploration of Conrad's continental influences in studying his borrowings from Maupassant and Anatole France. Offers suggestive close readings of individual works focusing on the self and society.

Graver, Lawrence. *Conrad's Shorter Fiction*. Berkeley: University of California Press, 1969. First full-length study of the short fiction, presenting some individually illuminating insights and a useful overview of Conrad as a writer of short stories and novellas. Now mostly superseded.

Thorburn, David. *Conrad's Romanticism*. New Haven, CT: Yale University Press, 1974. Intelligently places Conrad in the context of English literary Romanticism.

Sherry, Norman, ed. *Joseph Conrad: A Commemoration*. London: Macmillan; New York: Barnes and Noble, 1976. A richly varied and stimulating selection of papers from the 1974 Canterbury Conference.

Hawthorn, Jeremy. *Joseph Conrad: Language and Fictional Self-Consciousness*. London: Arnold; Lincoln: University of Nebraska Press, 1979. Explores relationships between narrative technique, language, and ideology from a Marxist perspective.

Watt, Ian. *Conrad in the Nineteenth Century*. Berkeley: University of California Press, 1979; London: Chatto & Windus, 1980. Gathers up and considerably extends Watt's substantial work on Conrad's literary and intellectual contexts and offers an original study of his methods. Widely regarded as the most important full-length critical study of the early fiction.

The 1980s and 1990s

In addition to assimilating the work of the previous decade, including major biographies, increasingly refined textual studies, and much original criticism recent students of Conrad have had to take into account newly emergent critical trends, including post-structuralism, new historicism, and feminism, which emphasize extrinsic approaches to the study of literature. While scholarship continues to pursue traditional interests – aesthetics, contextualization, the discovery and preservation of documents – recent criticism has inevitably reflected the crosscurrents of interpretive debates. A number of recent studies often explicitly or implicitly attempt revaluations of a given work or of the canon.

Senn, Werner. *Conrad's Narrative Voice: Stylistic Aspects of his Fiction*. Berne: Francke Verlag, 1980. Detailed study of Conrad's style and its relationship to his aesthetic and philosophical positions.

Hunter, Jefferson. *Edwardian Fiction*. Cambridge, MA: Harvard University Press, 1982. Contains an important chapter situating Conrad in his Edwardian context and dealing with his responses to adventure fiction and imperialism.

Hunter, Allan. *Joseph Conrad and the Ethics of Darwinism: The Challenges of Science*. London: Croom Helm, 1983. Addresses an important subject but unconvincingly asserts specific debts.

Berthoud, Jacques. Introductions to *The Nigger of the 'Narcissus'* and *Almayer's Folly*. Oxford: Oxford University Press, 1984, 1992. Introductions to *The Shadow-Line* and *Chance*. Harmondsworth: Penguin Books. 1986, 1996. Critically ambitious and stimulating essays that, as a group, represent an acute and impressive understanding of Conrad's literary and historical contexts, the discussion of which informs an analysis of the formal aspects of individual works.

O'Hanlon, Redmond. *Joseph Conrad and Charles Darwin: The Influence of Scientific Thought on Conrad's Fiction*. Edinburgh: Salamander Press; Atlantic Highlands, NJ: Humanities Press, 1984. Despite its title, concentrates only on *Lord Jim*, and, like Hunter, over-eagerly assigns specific influences.

Parry, Benita. *Conrad and Imperialism: Ideological Boundaries and Visionary Frontiers*. London: Macmillan; Topsfield, MA: Salem Academy/Merrimack Publishing, 1984. Drawing on modern ideological criticism, eschews historical and contextual perspectives for a critically eclectic and comprehensive reading of the colonial fiction.

Purdy, Dwight H. *Joseph Conrad's Bible*. Norman: University of Oklahoma Press, 1984. Identifies and analyses the rhetorical and ideological consequences of Conrad's extensive use of biblical allusion.

Watts, Cedric. *The Deceptive Text: An Introduction to Covert Plots*. Brighton: Harvester; Totowa, NJ: Barnes & Noble, 1984. Concentrates on Conrad's fiction in investigating narratorial duplicity and ambiguous plotting.

Conroy, Mark. *Modernism and Authority: Strategies of Legitimation in Flaubert and Conrad*. Baltimore: Johns Hopkins University Press, 1985. Informed by Jameson's Marxism and influenced by Foucault, takes on the Modernist writer's legitimation of his work for a bourgeois capitalist audience.

Fogel, Aaron. *Coercion to Speak: Conrad's Poetics of Dialogue*. Cambridge, MA: Harvard University Press, 1985. Draws on Bakhtinian discourse theory to analyse the functions of dialogue.

Murfin, Ross C., ed. *Conrad Revisited: Essays for the Eighties*. University: University of Alabama Press, 1985. Selected conference papers on, among other topics, colonialism and the late fiction, both typical concerns of recent criticism.

Bloom, Harold, ed. *Joseph Conrad: Modern Critical Views*. New York: Chelsea House, 1986. Reprints classic essays and includes feminist and post-structural studies. Seriously fails to represent the range and quality of contemporary criticism in limiting itself to work published in the United States. Similar volumes are available for 'Heart of Darkness', *Lord Jim*, and *Nostromo* (all 1987). *Marlow* (1992), in Chelsea House's Major Literary Characters series, ranges more widely in its choice of critics.

Raval, Suresh. *The Art of Failure: Conrad's Fiction*. London: Allen & Unwin, 1986. Analyses and pursues the implications of the radical scepticism informing Conrad's major fiction.

Billy, Ted, ed. *Critical Essays on Joseph Conrad*. Boston: Hall, 1987. Useful compendium of trends, reprinting articles published during 1971–84.

Hamner, Robert D., ed. *Joseph Conrad: Third World Perspectives*. Washington, DC: Three Continents Press, 1990. Conveniently reprints articles dealing with Conrad's African, Asian, and South American worlds and includes evaluations from non-Western viewpoints.

Hawthorn, Jeremy. *Joseph Conrad: Narrative Technique and Ideological Commitment*. London: Arnold, 1990. Extends the implications of Hawthorn's earlier volume and offers a detailed and nuanced analysis of free indirect style.

Erdinast-Vulcan, Daphna. *Joseph Conrad and the Modern Temper*. Oxford: Oxford University Press, 1991. Informed by Bakhtinian discourse theory, targets fissures and ambiguities, focusing on Conrad's notorious unevenness.

Hervouet, Yves. *The French Face of Joseph Conrad*. Cambridge: Cambridge University Press, 1991. Illuminates Conrad's position in the history of the aesthetics of the novel through abundant evidence of his extensive borrowings from French authors. Discusses the influence of Flaubert, Anatole France, and Maupassant.

Nadelhaft, Ruth L. *Joseph Conrad*. Atlantic Highlands, NJ: Humanities Press; Hemel Hempstead: Harvester Wheatsheaf, 1991. A reductively partisan feminist study unconvincing in its revisionist programme.

Smith, David R., ed. *Joseph Conrad's 'Under Western Eyes': Beginnings, Revisions, Final Forms – Five Essays*. Hamden, CT: Archon Books, 1991. Well-edited cluster of essays focusing on the composition and personal and cultural sources of a novel that has now moved to the centre of the Conrad canon.

Henricksen, Bruce. *Nomadic Voices: Conrad and the Subject of Narrative*. Urbana: University of Illinois Press, 1992. Deconstructionist study of narrative technique in the major works.

Moore, Gene M., ed. *Conrad's Cities: Essays for Hans van Marle*. Amsterdam: Rodopi, 1992. Well-edited and wide-ranging gathering of biographical, historical, and interpretive essays exploring the several influences on and uses of cityscapes in Conrad's fiction.

STUDY CENTRES

The Joseph Conrad Study Centre. Joseph Conrad Society (United Kingdom). The Conrad Room of the Polish Social and Cultural Association, London, holds a non-lending collection of first and later editions and a large selection of journals and monographs. Individuals desiring to consult the collection should contact the Society's Honorary Secretary (address in Journals below).

The Center for Conrad Studies. Institute for Bibliography and Editing, Kent State University. The centre holds a wide variety of primary and secondary materials (in both print and digital form) to support the editing of the Cambridge Edition of the Works of Joseph Conrad. Scholars desiring to consult the collection should contact The Chief Executive Editor, Cambridge Edition of Joseph Conrad, Kent State University, 1118 Library, PO Box 5190, Kent, OH 44242–0001, USA.

The Ugo Mursia Memorial Collection. Università di Pisa, Pisa, Italy. Extensive non-lending collection of first editions and later states of Conrad's texts. Large holdings of standard critical monographs and also of Conrad criticism in Italian. (For the collection's catalogue, see Bibliographies above). Scholars desiring to consult the collection should contact the University's Department of English.

JOURNALS

Articles on Conrad are to be found in a number of academic journals. The four listed below publish scholarship and criticism concerned with all aspects of his life and work and provide information about regular and occasional conferences.

The Conradian: Journal of the Joseph Conrad Society (UK), issued twice yearly, publishes papers from the Society's annual conference, articles, notes, and reviews. Subscriptions are available from: The Honorary Secretary, The Joseph Conrad Society (United Kingdom), c/o The Polish Social and Cultural Association, 238–246 King Street, London W6 0RF, UK.

Conradiana: A Journal of Joseph Conrad Studies, issued thrice yearly, publishes articles, notes, reviews, and a checklist of recent scholarship. Subscriptions are available from: Texas Tech Press, Sales Office, Texas Tech University, Lubbock, TX 79409–1037, USA.

L'Epoque Conradienne, issued annually, publishes articles and conference proceedings. Recent issues have also included reviews. (Mainly in English.) Subscriptions are available from: Société Conradienne Française, Faculté des Lettres et des Sciences Humaines, Campus universitaire de Limoges-Vanteaux, 39E rue Camille-Guérin, 87036 Limoges, France.

Joseph Conrad Today: The Newsletter of the Joseph Conrad Society of America, issued twice yearly, publishes brief notes and reviews, announcements about and reports on the Society's sessions at the annual convention of the Modern Language Association of America. Includes news about other scholarly conferences. Subscriptions are available from: The Joseph Conrad Society of America, c/o Department of Humanities, Drexel University, Philadelphia, PA 19104–2875, USA.

Index

Index